1985

THE TWO YEMENS

Other books by the same author
Affairs of Kuwait (2 vols) Affairs of Arabia (2 vols), 1973
Travellers in Arabia, 1976

The Two Yemens

ROBIN BIDWELL

LONGMAN
WESTVIEW PRESS

Longman Group Ltd.
Longman House
Burnt Mill
Harlow
Essex

Westview Press
5500 Central Avenue
Boulder,
Colorado 80301
U.S.A.

First published 1983

ISBN 0 582 78321 6 (British)
ISBN 0 86531-295-8 (United States of America)

Library of Congress Cataloging in Publication Data
Bidwell, Robin Leonard.
  The two Yemens.

  Bibliography: p.
  Includes index.
  1. Yemen–History.
  2. Yemen (People's Democratic Republic)–History. I. Title.
  DS247.Y45B53   953'.3   82–15352
  ISBN 0 86531-295-8   AACR2

British Library Cataloguing in Publication Data
Bidwell, Robin L.
  The two Yemens
  1. Yemen–History
  I. Title
  953'.32   DS247.Y45

  ISBN 0-582-78321-6

Printed and bound by Singapore National Printers (Pte) Ltd.

Printed and bound in Singapore

*To my Yemeni friends
in the hope that
their future will be as glorious
and as prosperous as much of their past*

Contents

Abbreviations

APL	Aden Protectorate Levies
ATUC	Aden Trade Union Congress
EAP	Eastern Aden Protectorate
FLOSY	Front for the Liberation of Occupied South Yemen
FNG	Federal National Guard
FRA	Federal Regular Army
GG	Government Guards
HBL	Hadhrami Beduin Legion
MCC	Military Command Council
NDF	National Democratic Front
NFLOSY	National Front for the Liberation of Occupied South Yemen
NLA	National Liberation Army
NLF	National Liberation Front
OLOS	Organisation for the Liberation of Occupied South Yemen
PDRY	People's Democratic Republic of Yemen
PDU	People's Democratic Union
PORF	People's Organisation of Revolutionary Forces
PRSY	People's Republic of South Yemen
PSP	People's Socialist Party
SAAF	South Arabian Armed Forces
SAL	South Arabian League
UNF	United National Front
UNFPO	United National Front Political Organisation
WAP	Western Aden Protectorate
YAR	Yemen Arab Republic
YSP	Yemeni Socialist Party

Glossary

Banyan	an Indian trader.
Dola	literally "The State" but used to mean the ruling family and its hangers-on in the Aden Protectorates.
Jihad	literally "striving" but used to mean holy war.
Naib	a Deputy.
Qadi	in most of the Islamic world a judge of religious law but used in Zaydi areas for any member of the hereditary class of scholars or administrators.
qat	(leaves from) a shrub which resembles privet and which is chewed as a stimulant by Yemenis.
Sayyid	a title denoting proven descent from the Prophet Muhammad through his grandson Hussayn ibn Ali.
Shariah	Muslim law based on the Qur'an and the doings and sayings of the Prophet.
Sharif	a title denoting proven descent from the Prophet Muhammad through his grandson Hassan ibn Ali.
Shaykh	in most of Arabia a title of respect or the head of a tribal group. In the Aden Protectorate it has the special meaning of a member of an hereditary religious family not descended from the Prophet. Some may be of pre-Islamic origin while others stem from popular saints.
ulama	men learned in Muslim law and traditions.
waqf	(*pl. awqaf*) property bequeathed to provide income for a pious purpose.

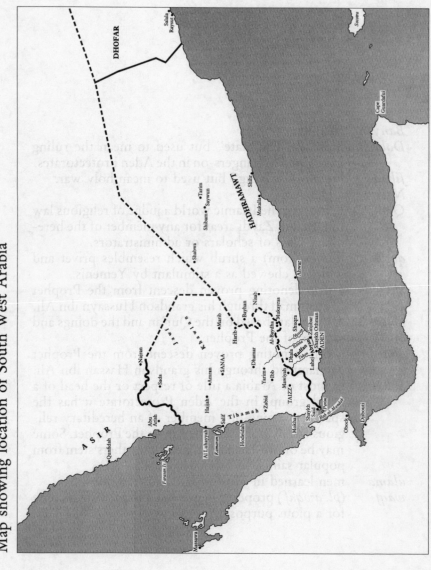

Map showing location of South West Arabia

Introduction

A Classics Don once said to me "what we ordinary chaps want is a history of Arabia without a mass of confusing names and details". This advice I have borne in mind in the hope that this, the first book in over a hundred years to treat North and South Yemen as a single unit, will be of interest to the general reader, although I should be happy if my academic colleagues also found it useful.

Thus I have made it a rule not to introduce too many names and have avoided doing so whenever possible unless a character is mentioned several times. My more pedantic friends will be shocked to find that I have written "Ahmad Muhammad al-Shami" instead of "Aḥmad Muḥammad al-Shāmī" and have used the simplest form of place names ("Sanaa" instead of "Ṣanʿāʾ"), but I think that the general reader would prefer it this way. I have also refrained from an intimidating barrage of notes and references.

South West Arabia is an area of great strategic importance, controlling as it does the entrance to the Red Sea which gives access to the "front doors" of Saudi Arabia, Sudan and Ethiopia, and the "back doors" of Egypt and Israel. There is no doubt that it possesses oil, although it has yet to be found in quantities which would make its exploitation commercially worthwhile. It contains half the population of the Arabian Peninsula, attractive people of much charm, intelligence and commercial skill.

Few parts of the world have more to offer to visitors. Most of it is far removed from the stereotyped image of sandy desert, for few places are greener than the fields around Ibb or provide more beautiful colour, changing with every passing cloud, than the mountains of Audhali and Dathinah. The most experienced traveller still stands amazed at the unique architecture of Sanaa or Shibam.

Traditional Muslim genealogists have held that the ancestor of the Arabs was Shem, the son of Noah, and that subsequently his descendants have divided into two lines – the sons of Adnan in the North of the Peninsula and those of Qahtan in the South. There is indeed a quite noticeable physical difference between the usually small, slightly-built Yemenis and their larger, sturdier brethren of the Hejaz or Najd: in the *suqs* of Riyadh or Jeddah one is rarely mistaken when saying to someone "you must be a Yemeni". There is also a strong emotional feeling that they are a distinct part of the Arab nation, a single people despite the vicissitudes of history. This book aims to tell the story of the Yemeni people, treating them as a single people.

For the first part of this book, historical fact indeed dictates that this should be done. We begin by showing that all over South West Arabia a unique civilisation arose in antiquity and many of its manifestations so conformed to the Yemeni temperament that they have lingered, little changed, until the present day. The coming of Sunni Islam carried the pattern a stage further and gave the people religious links which stretched from Morocco to the East Indies. Two hundred and fifty years after the death of the Prophet, his descendants secured a permanent following amongst the great tribal confederations of the northern mountains who adopted, almost as a badge, their own individual form of Shi'ite religion. With this rise of the Zaydi Imamate, South West Arabia had assembled all the elements that were to last a millennium. The rest of the first chapter shows that despite intermittent strife between groups of its people, life in mediaeval Yemen was as rich and as cultured as anywhere in the contemporary world – another fact which distinguishes it from the rest of the Arabian Peninsula.

Our treatment of the Yemenis as a single people extends indeed over two thousand years, for the second chapter, covering three centuries from 1530 to 1830 shows them also as an entity if not always as a unitary state. This period ends as firstly the British and then the Ottoman Turks came upon the scene. For the first time a formal frontier, artificially created to suit Imperial needs, divided North from South, and although all the Zaydis were within the Turkish sphere, the Shafais were, without being consulted, divided in half. The two areas were subjected to different systems of rule for over a hundred years and they developed in such divergent ways that for this period, and for this period only, we have to study them separately.

A new era began in 1967 with the withdrawal of the British and the almost simultaneous coming to power in North and South of regimes which claimed that a united Yemen was their dearest wish. Although twice since then formal agreements to bring this about have been signed, they have not taken effect: the reasons are discussed in the final two chapters. This book was completed in the spring of 1980 so I have added a brief postscript.

It will be obvious that in my account of the events of the last thirty years, I have had the advantage of much private information from friends, both Arab and British, who participated in events. As some have wished to remain anonymous, I have decided to name none of them: they know, however, that I am most grateful for their help. I can, however, mention my old friend, Dr Rex Smith of Durham University, a mine of information on the country, with whom I could discuss any problem. Naturally neither he, nor anyone else, is responsible for my mistakes.

Robin Bidwell

October 1981   Middle East Centre, Cambridge

Map showing tribes of South West Arabia

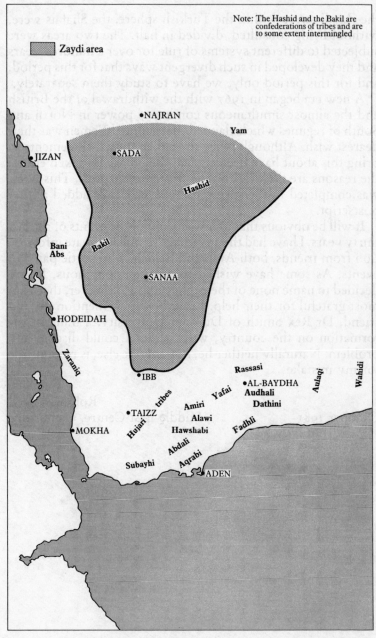

Note: The Hashid and the Bakil are confederations of tribes and are to some extent intermingled

Zaydi area

NAJRAN

Yam

JIZAN

SADA

Hashid

Bani Abs

Bakil

SANAA

HODEIDAH

Zaraniq

IBB

Rassasi

AL-BAYDHA

Yafai

Audhali

Dathini

Aulaqi

Wahidi

TAIZZ

tribes

Amiri

Alawi

Hujari

Hawshabi

Fadhli

MOKHA

Abdali

Subayhi

Aqrabi

ADEN

Chapter One

Pre-Islamic
and Mediaeval Yemen

The Yemen in the Pre-Islamic Era

As late as the 1960s it was the custom of every commentator
on North Yemen to state, with the air of one making a profound and original observation, that the country was still living
in the Middle Ages. There was more than a grain of truth in this
view, and, indeed, some of the customs of the country were
even older; so it is necessary, in a way that it is not for other
Arabian states whose history effectively begins with the discovery of oil, to say something about the early history of the
area. Able scholars have chronicled these years in detail so it is
not the intention of this author to give particulars of the
fortunes of dynasties long since disappeared, but rather to
give an outline which will show their relevance to the present
day.

There is no doubt that man was active in South-West Arabia
from ancient times. We need not accept the legend that Cain
was exiled to Aden (although a tomb reputed to be his was
shown near the Main Pass), but archaeologists say that the area
was used for hunting 75,000 years ago, and flints used 15,000
years ago have been recovered. Tradition identifies Joktan, the
great-great-great-grandson of Noah, with Qahtan, who is regarded as the ancestor of the Southern Arabs and as the man
who brought agriculture to the Yemen. His son, the Jerah of
Genesis, was said to have separated the Arabic and Hebrew
languages. Hud, whose tomb may still be seen in the Hadhramawt, was mentioned in the Holy Qur'an as the first of the
Prophets of Arabia, while Job was also reputed to be a native of
the Yemen.

We come on to firmer ground about 1200 BC, for from then

onwards the early inhabitants of the area enjoyed a very considerable culture. The Minaeans seem to have consisted of autonomous communities engaging in trade, while their neighbours, the Sabeans, who emerged a century later, were so active commercially that some of their wares have been found near Esyon Geber, the port of King Solomon. There must be few readers who do not know of the story of the visit to that monarch by the Queen of Saba (Sheba).

The main item of trade was incense, a commodity that was essential in the religious ritual of Egypt, Israel and Babylon and which can only be obtained from the southern shores of Arabia and from parts of East Africa which were often under Sabean rule. The Red Sea, with its storms and shoals, has always proved difficult for navigators but the domestication of the camel about 1000 BC made possible the development of overland trade routes. One writer of ancient times speaks of a caravan of 3,000 camels, which would have stretched twenty miles, arriving at the Mediterranean from South Arabia, while incense is mentioned in many books of the Bible from Exodus to Jeremiah, and Ezekiel refers specifically to trade with Aden. The collection of this precious aromatic was believed to be fraught with difficulties, for Herodotus heard that the trees were guarded by winged serpents whose venom the gatherers could only avoid by covering themselves with the hides of oxen. This did not, according to him, exhaust the wonders of an area where the sheep had such large tails that they had to be fitted with trailers, where laudanum came from the beards of billy-goats and where cinnamon was used by birds for building their nests on inaccessible peaks.

The states of ancient Arabia started as theocracies and although they later became kingdoms, their rulers retained hieratic functions – a tradition that persisted until 1962. The social stratification, which was almost a caste system, also survived until then, practically intact. In stone houses within walled cities dwelt priests, bureaucrats and leading merchants, while in humbler homes lived craftsmen graded from respectable to less noble trades. Outside the town lived the warriors, divided into tribes, who usually protected the peasants from all predators except themselves.

Like other peoples of that time, the South Arabians believed in an after-life and buried useful objects with their dead. They had numerous deities, one of the most prominent being the god Wadd, whose worship was carried by traders as far as the Greek island of Delos. Coins inscribed with Athena and an owl also show the link with Greece, as did the architecture of the temples, although decorations showing bulls' heads were a purely local characteristic. A feature of Yemeni religion was the making of pilgrimages to sacred sites and it appears that some of the ritual has scarcely changed and may be seen at the tombs of saints today. The holy places were taken over by Islam and merely endowed with a more suitable legend; some scholars believe that the descendants of their old priests still survive and administer the sacred enclaves which fulfil a necessary function in providing a neutral ground between warring tribes.

Islam was also to adopt much of the old law of the Yemen, some of which has in consequence persisted until now. The importance attached to oath-taking by groups in specified places and forms can still be seen in tribal justice while the code of regulations for the market at Timna, dating from the fourth century BC, could still be applied practically unchanged.

The agriculture of Egypt and of Mesopotamia was based upon the exploitation of mighty rivers which were lacking in the Yemen, so a system had to be created to take advantage of brief floods after heavy rains. The ancient Arabians built the terraced fields still in use today and arranged to irrigate them by an intricate pattern of deflectors in the *wadis*. The most famous of these was the great dam at the Sabean capital of Marib which was built about 500 BC and was one of the wonders of the Peninsula. An agricultural expert has calculated that this dam irrigated 4,000 acres, which would have provided food for a population of some 300,000 souls. So important was the area that in a brief stay in 1869 the French archaeologist Halévy was able to record over 600 inscriptions, while it was said to have been so fertile that a man might walk under the fruit trees with a basket on his head which in a few minutes would fill with windfalls.

The Mineans and Sabeans started a tradition of craftsmanship for which the Yemen has remained famous. So great was the local industry that King Karib il-Watar erected an inscription in about 450 BC which boasted that he had captured and resettled 1,000 weavers. Islam, with its prohibition of images, brought an end to the often brilliant portraiture which varied from the realistic to the highly stylised – but work has continued until today in bronze and silver.

South-West Arabia was more than an area of flourishing agriculture and manufacture with great exports in incense, myrrh and alabaster, for it was the point at which the trade routes from the Mediterranean, East Africa and the Far East converged. Maritime activity in this area presented few difficulties once the pattern of the monsoons had been understood. Greeks and Romans believed that the silks and spices which the Arabs brought from India and China were locally produced and so regarded Arabia Felix as a land of fabulous wealth.

About 110 BC the Himyarite dynasty arose and eventually came to rule the whole of what is now the two Yemens. Their tradition lingered on, and in the twentieth century monarchs still dwelt with pride upon their asserted Himyaritic descent. The Imams symbolised this descent by "signing" their missives by dipping a finger in a bowl of red ochre and running it along the text – the Arabic roots for *Himyar* and *red* are the same. The state was so well established that it was able to withstand a determined effort by the Romans to conquer it when in 24 BC the prefect of Egypt, Aelius Gallus, collected an army of 10,000 Romans and 15,000 mercenaries, and marched down through the Hejaz. He was finally checked near Nisab by, tradition has it, the Shaykhs of Ma'an, whose *soi-disant* descendants ruled the area until 1967.

It was not, however, the soldiers but the sailors of Rome who destroyed much of the prosperity of South Arabia by learning themselves how to exploit the monsoons. The area was gradually relegated to a back-water as trade passed it by and the incense trade also declined. The crowning catastrophe was the collapse of the dam at Marib, destroying the irrigation system which had enabled agriculture to flourish. This disaster which echoed around Arabia is mentioned in the Qur'an.

Meanwhile, Christianity came to the Yemen. There is a legend that St Thomas preached there on his way to India, but it was not until the fourth century that there were churches in the Himyar capital of Zafar near Yarim and in Aden. These communities were linked with the ecclesiastical authorities in Byzantium and Abyssinia, so it may have been partially as a gesture of Yemeni nationalism that Dhu Nuwas, who seized the Himyarite throne in 490, proclaimed himself a convert to Judaism. He carried out a fierce persecution of Christians, culminating in a famous massacre at Najran where it was said that 20,000 martyrs perished through being cast into pits filled with flaming oil.

The leaders of Christendom felt compelled to avenge this crime and with the encouragement of the Emperor Justin, the Abyssinian ruler, Caleb, sent an army across the Red Sea in 525. Dhu Nuwas was defeated and the Himyarite state fell as he spurred his horse into the sea to avoid capture. It is likely that the Jews of the Yemen – a group of perhaps 50,000 until 1948 and still surviving in small numbers today – stem not from Palestine but from local Arabs who adopted the faith under Dhu Nuwas.

The Abyssinian occupation was to last for half a century, during which time there was a restoration of Christianity symbolised in the construction of a magnificent church in Sanaa, the ruins of which can still be identified. The Abyssinian commander, who was in effect an independent ruler, tried for both religious and commercial reasons to turn this shrine into a rival to the traditional pagan pilgrimage centre of Mecca. In 570 he led forth an army, supported by elephants, to destroy the Kaaba. His force was wiped out, either by small-pox or, according to the Qur'an, by a huge flock of birds which bombed it with stones. In the same year the Prophet Muhammad was born.

The Abyssinian domination provoked a nationalist reaction which was led by a Himyarite prince who had survived the general massacre of his family. He sought aid from the Persian Emperor Chosroes whom he managed to convince that there was immense mineral wealth in the Yemen. He was given an army, consisting entirely of criminals released from jail, with the idea that if they succeeded, Persia would gain a new province; whereas if they failed their loss would hardly matter. The Abyssinians put up little resistance while the Arabs welcomed the descendant of their old Kings, despite his being installed as ruler under Persian sovereignty. He was, however, murdered by his own guards; and after some years of disorder, a Persian general was appointed as *satrap*. His troops settled down, took local wives and became, so many believe, the ancestors of the *Akhdam*, the class that today performs menial tasks in the Yemen.

Persian rule lasted for half a century and for over one hundred years the country was either split by internal religious strife or under foreign occupation. This period cannot radically have altered the bases of Yemeni society for, looking back to the period ending with Dhu Nuwas, it is not fanciful to see in the polity of the Himyarites many of the elements which were to persist with surprisingly little change until the 1960s: obviously they must have suited the people and the country, but there is little wonder that twentieth-century visitors found them archaic.

The coming of Islam and the Middle Ages

After his flight from Mecca to Medina in 622 the Prophet Muhammad addressed a series of letters to the rulers of the world announcing his mission and calling upon them to accept Islam. With the apparent acquiescence of the majority of the people, the Persian *satrap* of Yemen declared himself a Muslim and was confirmed as Governor by the Prophet. The conversion, however, may not have been total, for it seems that in 631 Muhammad sent his cousin and son-in-law, Ali ibn Abu Talib, on a mission during which, according to legend, he converted all the 14,000 members of the great tribal confederation of Hamdan in a single day. Whether or not this happened, there came to exist a link between his descendants and those of Hamdan (who were later known as the Hashid and Bakil tribes) that was to last almost unbroken until the 1960s.

It would be in accordance with South Arabian customs if the Prophet's cousin Ali had been received less as a missionary than as an arbiter of tribal disputes, and the "conversion" indicated a willingness to accept his judgement. There has never been a readiness amongst South-West Arabian tribesmen to accept the verdict of their peers: they prefer to appoint an outsider as umpire. The most acceptable of all umpires to this day is a man of noble and religious ancestry: no family in Arabia was more venerated than the House which controlled the Kaaba.

For a brief while it appeared that Yemeni particularism might prove too strong to accept a faith from outside its own borders, and a false prophet proclaiming a purely local religion attracted considerable support. He was, however, murdered and a rebellion after the death of Muhammad proved short-lived. Yemen became a distant province of the vast Arab Empire to which it contributed such large numbers of men that parts of the Hadhramawt were almost depopulated: families claiming Yemeni origins may still be found on the Atlantic coast of Morocco.

The Caliphs of Baghdad took little interest in the area and when in 822 their Governor, Muhammad ibn Ziyad, declared himself independent, they made no attempt to coerce him. Ibn Ziyad assumed the trappings of sovereignty; prayers were said in his name in the mosques, and he appeared in public under an umbrella with a golden shaft surmounted by balls of gold and jewels. He reunited practically the whole of the old Himyarite state under his sway from the city of Zabid, taxed shipping in the Red Sea and exacted tribute, which included 500 slave girls from the coast of Africa. Although this ruler's dynasty, the Banu Ziyad, lingered on for two centuries, its great days did not long outlast its founder; but it effectually split Yemen away from the main Arab Empire and reasserted its individuality.

Despite its remoteness, Yemen was to find itself one of the arenas in which, for the next three centuries, issues affecting the whole Muslim world were to be fought out. The Prophet had made no provision for the succession to the leadership of what quickly became the greatest empire that the world had yet seen, and this naturally became a matter for eager contention. One group argued that any Muslim endowed with the requisite qualities, including piety, learning and military skill, might become Caliph; while another party maintained that the choice of leader should be confined within the Quraysh tribe, with its tradition of religious and political pre-eminence. Yet a third section held that it was vital to have an Imam of direct descent from the Prophet through his daughter Fatima and her husband Ali. Fanatical adherents of this latter creed began to organise themselves as a secret international conspiracy, dedicated to the seizure of power – much as the Christians had done centuries before and the Communists were to do a millennium later. Much of their doctrine was extremely esoteric, but their organisation was practical and effective, based on a hierarchy of religio-political agents (*Da'is*) acting in the name of an Imam. Their opponents called them Ismailis, while they regarded themselves as Fatimids. They were active throughout the Islamic world from India and Persia to the Maghreb; in the early years of the tenth century, Fatimid groups assumed control of Eastern Arabia and Tunisia almost simultaneously.

We have seen that there already existed in the Yemen a tradition of support for Ali and his descendants and this had been kept alive by a series of Fatimid missionaries. This tendency was given a new impetus and made into an active movement when two secret envoys arrived in 881. The senior was Ibn Hawshab (later known as Mansur al-Yemen) who started recruiting adherents in the western highlands, where after some years of persistent work he established a small principality owing allegiance to the Fatimid Imam. The junior envoy, Ali ibn al-Fadl, who was to prove himself an exceptionally dynamic missionary-warrior, made his base in the mountains of Yafa where today the two Yemens meet. His ruthlessness became legendary and it was recounted that when he captured Zabid he slaughtered 4,000 virgins so that their charms should not divert his warriors from the *jihad*. His powers spread southwards, over-running Aden and Abyan and then, moving north, he took Sanaa after thirty years of campaigning. A Yemeni chronicler recounts that he had the courtyard of the Great Mosque flooded, and ordered that all the local maidens should be assembled and forced to swim naked while he stood in the minaret taking his choice.

Hostile propagandists recounted many such orgies amongst his followers, whose custom after drink and erotic dancing was to extinguish the lights and have sexual intercourse with the first partner that could be seized: "such practices are most shameful and pernicious" the chronicler, Baha al-Din al-Janadi, said severely. In 913 Ibn al-Fadl renounced his loyalty to the Fatimids, declared himself the Mahdi and attacked and defeated his old colleague Ibn Hawshab. Two years later he was murdered: a doctor whom he had summoned sucked his lancet to show that there was no venom on it, then wiped it on his hair which he had previously smeared with poison before performing the operation. Ibn al-Fadl's state did not long survive him, and the Ismailis went underground again for more than a century.

Some years before the arrival of Ibn al-Fadl, the Yufirids, a noble family of Sanaa, rebelled against the Banu Ziyad and managed to confine their former lords to the Tihamah while they ruled the East and South. The Yufirids, who claimed Himyaritic origins, were the first native Yemeni rulers of the country since Dhu Nuwas. The last years of the ninth century were a period of chaos as these two dynasties fought against the Fatimids and against each other. The powerful north-eastern tribes escaped all control, but felt the need of an outside mediator to settle their own disputes, as their ancestors had done 250 years before. Once again their choice fell upon a member of the House of Hashim, a descendant of Zayd, the great-grandson of Ali. His name was al-Hadi ila'l-Haqq.

Al-Hadi arrived in 893, but his rigid insistence on the Shariah law proved so unpopular that after a short while he returned to the Hejaz. However, the tribes found their quarrels impossible to resolve, so in 897 they invited him back, thus clearly accepting a religious and indeed political "platform" that would differentiate them from their neighbours. He arrived at Sada with fifty followers, and proceeded to create a state that was to endure with numerous changes of fortune for over a thousand years all the while retaining many of the characteristics that he had imposed upon it.

Al-Hadi was clearly a very remarkable man. Like his ancestor Ali and his descendant Ahmad, the Imam of the 1950s, his physical strength was legendary. It was recounted that he could grind corn or rub out the inscription on a coin with his bare fingers, and that once when he seized a galloping camel by the tail, the hump and rear remained in his grasp while the head and front legs managed to make their escape over the horizon. He was a man of genuine learning, the author of forty-nine books, some of which are still used by Zaydi theologians, as well as being a poet of distinction: like Ahmad he used verse as a weapon against his foes, and, as with Ahmad, magical powers were attributed to his blessing and his curse.

Like his twentieth-century descendants his rule was well suited to a harsh country: it was austere and rigid but not unjust. He saw himself less as a monarch than as the chief executive of a theocracy, administering immutable laws revealed by God through His Prophet. He therefore demanded absolute obedience in return for putting the spiritual welfare of his people above all other interests. A drunkard received eighty lashes, the Imam himself threw the first stone at adulterers, a village noted for sexual wrong-doing was destroyed, and the religious taxes, regarded in Islamic theory as a form of ritual purification, were punctiliously collected and used only for the benefit of the poor. Al-Hadi refused to dry himself or shelter from the sun with a piece of cloth belonging to the treasury.

Al-Hadi consolidated his state upon these lines. In an age when the Fatimids and the Abbasids aimed at universal rule, he never looked outside the Yemen. Before his death in 911 at the age of fifty-three he had fought seventy-three battles against the Ismailis, as well as campaigns in the Tihamah and Najran. The tenth century was a period of warlordism and in the general chaos Sanaa changed hands twenty times between 901 and 913. By 1000 there was the Zaydi state in the north and the remnants of the Banu Ziyad and the Yufirids in the south, while the Ismailis worked indefatigably underground, greatly encouraged by the establishment in 969 of a Fatimid Caliphate in control of Egypt.

In 1037 the Fatimids found a locally born leader, who with the blessing of Cairo raised his standard with sixty followers. Ali al-Sulayhi, acting as Viceroy on behalf of the Caliph, reunited the old Himyarite state under his control. He showed great military and diplomatic skill and was driven on by fanaticism. He killed the Imam of the Zaydis, and reduced them to impotence for over a century. He set up an effective and honest administration, and refrained from sectarian persecution. He moved the capital back to Sanaa, where he settled tribal leaders as comfortable hostages for the good behaviour of their peoples. Acting as agent for the Caliph, he sent envoys to the

Ismaili communities in India and captured Mecca from the representatives of the rival Sunni Caliph in Baghdad.

In 1067 Ali was murdered and succeeded by his son who, after a few years decided that he preferred merrymaking to the duties of government. These duties he permitted to be exercised by his wife Arwa (Sayyida bint Ahmad), who proceeded to achieve much of the celebrity of her predecessor the Queen of Sheba. Her gifts of statesmanship, sometimes acting as prime minister and sometimes as a general in the field, enabled her to control one of the most turbulent countries in the world for fifty years. During this time she also proved herself a great patron of writers and of the architects that she summoned to her new capital, Dhu Jiblah. She always appeared unveiled, as a sign that her rank was so exalted that no man would presume to harbour improper thoughts about her. Despite the power that she exercised, she still regarded herself as the servant of the Fatimid Caliphate. However, after her death in 1138, although part of the inheritance did fall to two competing Ismaili groups, the Fatimids were never again to dominate the country. They are now reduced to an occasionally-persecuted minority of some 50,000 souls.

Other contestants for control of the Yemen were the Mahdids, a family claiming Himyaritic descent, who succeeded by 1174 in bringing practically all Yemen except Aden and the Zaydi heartlands under an iron rule. This dynasty carried Sunni beliefs to the point of heresy, regarding all sin as infidelity to religion and thus punishable by death. Drinking wine, singing, adultery and failure to visit the graves of parents attracted the extreme penalty.

However, we can get a vivid, though doubtless overdrawn picture of life in mid-twelfth-century Yemen from the poet Umarah. One prince was so fond of poetry that "the stream of his liberality flowed in torrents" as thirty eulogists often held forth at a time and were all rewarded; another prince was more interested in his 1,000 concubines. A beseiged castle was saved when one hundred slave girls and fifty eunuchs dressed in armour charged out to rout the attackers. A Wazir returned home to find his castle occupied by enemies, and he died of shame when he saw his harem forced to dance on the battlements. A princess disposed of a wicked suitor by sending him clothes impregnated in poison so that his flesh mouldered away. All-in-all, Umarah makes mediaeval Yemen sound as exciting as the Baghdad of Harun al-Rashid.

It is hardly surprising that the Yemen, with its wealth and its political divisions, attracted the covetous attention of a powerful neighbour. The great Saladin (Salah al-Din ibn Ayyub) had made himself Sultan of Egypt, finally extinguishing the Fatimid Caliphate. He wished to secure his rear from possible attacks from Fatimid adherents in the Yemen or from the Crusaders. His assumption of independent power had not been forgiven by his old master, the lord of Syria, who might well be expected to try to conquer Cairo. The possession of a rich remote province seemed most desirable, and control of the Red Sea had evident political and economic advantages.

In 1174, therefore, Saladin sent his brother Turanshah to conquer the Yemen which, apart from the inaccessible Zaydis, he succeeded in doing in the course of a year. It needed more hard fighting in the next decade by another brother to consolidate the Ayyubid state, which was to survive for half a century. During this time it built up a more business-like administration than the country had yet known. The dynasty actively encouraged trade, particularly through Aden, whose first walls date from this period. Marco Polo regarded its Sultan as one of the richest princes in the world through his export of horses, and heard that he had sent 30,000 horsemen and 40,000 infantry to campaign in Syria alongside the Ayyubids. An indication, although doubtless exaggerated, of the prosperity of the Yemen at this time may be found in the list of goods that the last Ayyubid took with him on his promotion to Governor of Syria. The chronicler al-Khazraji recorded that seventy ships were needed to carry away 1,000 eunuchs, 400 slave-girls, 500 cases of gorgeous materials, 300 loads of aloe wood, 70,000 pieces of Chinese brocade wrought with gold, and untold jewels, gold and works of art.

Despite the obvious opportunities for enrichment, no other Ayyubid appeared to claim their fief, and power remained in the hands of one of the Amirs that they had appointed. Nur al-Din Umar ibn al-Rasul thus became the founder of a dynasty which was to preside over the two most brilliant centuries of Yemeni history: in 1232 he assumed the signs of independent sovereignty with his own coinage and prayers in his own name. Nur al-Din took over the Ayyubid bureaucracy, turning it into a most sophisticated machine of government. He started the family policy of building, erecting a mosque in every village of the Tihamah and religious colleges with rich endowments in Taizz, Zabid and Aden. He conducted an active foreign policy, driving the Egyptians from Mecca and establishing relations with the Caliphs of Baghdad.

His activities were continued by his son, al-Muzaffar Yusuf, who reigned from 1249 until 1295, and whose magnificent mosque may be seen in Taizz. Encouraging his subordinates to foster learning, Yusuf was himself a skilled physician and a scholar whose legal knowledge put professional jurists to shame. His foreign policy was so active that al-Khazraji claimed that "the hearts of the Princes of Persia and the lords of India and China were filled with fear when they saw his ambition and power". He fought a series of campaigns with the Zaydis, often preceded by chivalric challenges in verse, but although he captured the Imam (courteously ensuring that he had sufficient concubines in jail), he never succeeded in destroying the obdurate mountaineers although he consolidated Sunnism in the south for all time. To the east he was more successful, over-running the Hadhramawt and collecting tribute from Shihr in ambergris, Indian dancing girls and civet cats. He launched, in 1279, a splendidly co-ordinated campaign against the ruler of Dhofar who had raided Aden: one column marched down through the Hadhramawt, a second was sent by sea and a third, supplied from ships, advanced along the coast. It is striking proof of the efficiency of Rasulid administration that the 500 cavalry and 7,000 infantry involved managed to converge on Raysut and kill the bandit chief.

Rasulid Yemen glittered in the next decades under his descendants, many of whom were flamboyant men of great learning and generosity. One used to picnic in the gardens of Zabid with 300 concubines for company; another sent two ship-loads of gifts to the Sultan of Egypt, which, in addition to Chinese jade, porcelains and brocades, included elephants and giraffes dressed in silk. A palace at Thabat near Taizz was decorated with marble and gold, and the eight gates of Zabid were given gilded pinnacles so that they shone like stars. Learning flourished: a survey showed that there were 230 colleges in Zabid alone. Jurists were honoured by having their works carried to the Sultan on the heads of students to the roll of kettle-drums. Agriculture flourished: special officials supervised irrigation and one of the princes even wrote a scientific treatise on the culture of cereals. The Rasulids were respected abroad and exercised great influence in Mecca. Rulers in Abyssinia and India sent gifts and elephants, and a letter written on pure gold came from the King of Ceylon.

To maintain all this splendour, taxation was heavy, and occasional revolts were repressed with much eye gouging: a rising in Aden was defeated by the use of mighty ballistas which threw 40 tons of rock a day at the walls, and after the storming there was mass drowning of the rebels. Despite such troubles and some family disputes, the Rasulids managed to keep the Sultanate in a direct line for eight generations, although in their second century their territories started to shrink. The Zaydis, although frequently torn apart by disputes over the succession, recouped sufficient strength to capture Sanaa in 1323 and in the 1380s to raid Aden and Zabid. To maintain security the Rasulids were increasingly forced to rely upon Mamluks and mercenaries, and in the middle of the fifteenth century these groups split among themselves, often supporting different contenders to the throne.

Thus the Rasulids disintegrated, but much of their territory passed to their former vassals the Banu Tahir, who built up their power from a base in the Lahej–Abyan area. During their rule Aden probably had a population of 50,000, and several European visitors marvelled at its wealth and beauty. Hieronimo de Santo Stefano said in 1493 that "no other infidel potentate" could compare with its Sultan for justice and benevolence. The customs officers used to remove the masts from visiting ships so that they could not depart without paying their dues, and the rest of the administration seems to have shown the same practical efficiency.

In 1505 the Tahirids captured Sanaa from the Zaydis. Shortly afterwards the Italian traveller Ludovico de Varthema became the first European to describe it. He reported that its walls were so thick that eight horses could walk abreast on them. He saw much of the country, including al-Makranah, where he reported that the Sultan kept more gold than 100 camels could carry. This stronghold, approached only by a seven-mile long track on which only two could walk abreast, had cisterns which held water for 100,000 people: as the Sultan kept 16,000 slaves and had another 16,000 in chains, provisions on this scale were obviously necessary. In the pages of Varthema we see a state which ranked amongst the richest and the best administered in the world. The great days of late mediaeval Yemen were, however, numbered: two years after the Tahirids took Sanaa, the Portuguese occupied Socotra.

Chapter Two

European Intervention, Isolation and Renewed Intervention

The first Europeans

When they had finally expelled the Muslims from the Iberian Peninsula in 1492, the Spaniards and the Portuguese by no means regarded their crusade as finished. They counterattacked in North Africa and when the Portuguese entered the Indian Ocean in 1498, they saw this as opening a new arena for the prosecution of the Holy War. The occupation of Socotra, where the people were reputed to be Christians, albeit of the most heterodox sort, was an obvious first step towards operations in the Red Sea, and as we have seen, this took place in 1507. A church and a fort were built on the island.

In 1509 Alfonso de Albuquerque, one of the greatest strategists of imperialist expansion in history, became Governor of the Portuguese possessions in India. He realised that the northern Indian Ocean could be dominated from great military bases at Diu, Goa, Hormuz and Aden. The wealth of this latter city was a further attraction, for, as the traveller Duarte Barbosa recorded "this place has a greater and richer trade than any other in the world, and also this trade is in the most valuable commodities". In March 1513 de Albuquerque arrived off Aden with 1,700 Portuguese troops in twenty ships. He had a friendly reception from the Governor, who sent fowls, sheep, lemons and oranges and offered to surrender the town, but de Albuquerque preferred his usual policy of obtaining submission by force; he therefore refused to parley.

It is possible that had he been less impetuous or less confident of victory, de Albuquerque might have found a local guide who could have shown him how to attack the city from the rear. As it was, he decided upon a direct assault on the

16

strong sea walls. Specially built scaling ladders up which six men could climb at a time were erected, and some soldiers penetrated the town before the ladders broke under the weight of armoured men. Some of the Portuguese trapped in the town escaped, but others refused to retreat in the face of a foe. A Hadhrami chronicler reported that a hundred of "the accursed" were slain. De Albuquerque was unable to attack again and had to content himself with capturing Sira Island, carrying off its guns and burning some forty ships in the harbour.

Undeterred, de Albuquerque sailed on into the Red Sea, where he hoped to make contact with Prester John. Since early mediaeval times, Europeans had believed that there was a mighty Christian Emperor in East Africa: the Portuguese had old plans for a joint campaign against the Muslims. De Albuquerque planned to enlist the help of this potentate to divert the Nile into the Red Sea (thus literally leaving Cairo high and dry) and to raid Medina to carry off the body of the Prophet, which he expected that the Muslims would surrender Jerusalem to regain. Prester John proved to be a myth, and de Albuquerque's grandiose schemes were far too much for his own unaided forces. He could do little more than establish a base on Kamaran Island where in a few months his forces were seriously weakened by deaths from fever. He did not feel strong enough to attack Aden on his way back to India, and he wrote to the King of Portugal that he would need at least 4,000 men.

Although he had actually achieved little there, de Albuquerque's appearance in the Red Sea caused panic amongst the Mamluks ruling Egypt. At the same time they saw themselves threatened from the north by the expansionist Ottomans under the ambitious Selim the Grim. Therefore, for very much the same motives as Saladin nearly 250 years before, the Mamluks decided to send a force to the Yemen in 1515. The Tahirid Sultan refused to supply their troops so they attacked him, achieving an easy superiority by the first use of firearms seen in the Peninsula. The Mamluk capture of Zabid was followed by plunder, burning and rape. The Zaydis, smarting under their recent loss of Sanaa, made common cause with the invaders against the Sultan who was killed; his state fragmented.

The Mamluks carried off the wealth of al-Makranah, looted Taizz and attacked Aden, where they were repulsed by the townspeople. However, Aden's defences were weakened, so when a fleet appeared under de Albuquerque's successor the Governor agreed to acknowledge Portuguese sovereignty. Lopo Soares accepted the keys of the fortress but neglected to garrison it, preferring to sail on to the Red Sea, where the climate of Kamaran claimed the bulk of his forces. When he returned to Aden, he found the defences restored and the people in no mood to admit him. The Portuguese thus lost the best chance that they ever had of controlling the city. Although in 1524 and again in 1530 the local ruler agreed to become their vassal, he ignored his pledge the moment that they were safely over the horizon.

Meanwhile, the Ottoman Sultan had conquered Egypt in 1517, and the Mamluks in Yemen came to accept his suzerainty. For twenty years there was desultory fighting between the Mamluks, the resurgent Zaydis and the remnants of the Tahirids in Aden. By 1537 Ottoman influence had spread as far east as Shihr, where prayers were said in the name of Suleiman the Magnificent who was generally regarded as a sort of protector against the threatening activities of the Portuguese. Indeed, the Turkish Sultan, who had taken the relics of the Prophet to Constantinople and assumed the Caliphate, had become the strong arm of Islam, and even Muslim rulers in India requested his help against the infidel.

In 1538 Suleiman felt ready to challenge Portuguese naval supremacy in the eastern seas, and a fleet was equipped at Suez under a slave named Suleiman al-Khadim – a creature so ugly and so savage that he was said to resemble a beast rather than a man. When his fleet put into Aden, he invited the Tahirid Sultan on board and hanged him from the yardarm. Simultaneously, Turkish soldiers who had been sent ashore on stretchers, allegedly for medical treatment, rose up and seized the fortifications. Al-Khadim went on to India, where he suffered a heavy defeat at the hands of the Portuguese, and on his return landed at Mokha. In a ruthless and treacherous campaign, with many massacres of prisoners, he conquered the Tihamah. He left it to his successor to take Sanaa and to install a Pasha to govern a province that reunited most of the old

Himyaritic state, with the exception of the Zaydis in their mountains.

In 1580 Portugal and its Empire came under the rule of Spain, and Iberian interest in the Indian Ocean started to decline. The next Europeans to arrive were the English and the Dutch. They came purely in pursuit of trade, with no interest in crusading, so that there was no longer any idea of conquest or of missionary endeavour. They aimed to establish Factories (trading posts), not mighty castles, such as those the Portuguese had built in Muscat and the Gulf.

According to Yemeni legend, the Prophet Muhammad appeared in a vision to the fifteenth-century saint Umar al-Shaduli of Mokha, and revealed that a health-giving drink might be made from the berries of the coffee shrub which grew wild in the countryside. By 1554 coffee was known in Constantinople, and fifty years later the trade was important enough to interest the newly formed East India Company. Partly because of its proximity to this major export and partly because it offered greater security from Portuguese piracy to ships from Egypt and Africa, Mokha came to replace Aden as the great trading centre of the Yemen. By the end of the sixteenth century Aden was receiving only two or three small ships a year, bringing textiles from India and Muscat and returning with gum, incense, madder and myrhh. At the same period a visitor counted forty ships in the roads of Mokha. A busy community of Indian, Armenian, Abyssinian and Jewish merchants flourished there.

In April 1609 the East India Company's ship *Ascension* reached Aden. The Governor, a Greek renegado, made it most welcome, feeling, as it later transpired, that the appearance of a well-laden ship with an unknown flag was a heaven-sent opportunity for extortion. Having taken all he could, he let the ship proceed to Mokha, but insisted on sending two of its officers to his superior in Sanaa to obtain permission to trade. John Jourdain thus became the first Briton to travel in the Yemen. The Pasha, a Hungarian renegado, was courteous towards him, but refused to allow the Company to establish a Factory at Mokha, saying that a foreign outpost so near to Mecca would need the consent of the Ottoman Sultan in person.

The following year another English ship appeared at Mokha, where the Governor gave it a hospitable welcome, then captured its commander and some of its crew by treachery. Sir Henry Middleton was "thrown into a dirty dog-kennel...his bed was no better than the hard ground, and his pillow a stone. His companions were grief of heart and a multitude of rats." He was then sent to Sanaa where he was again imprisoned, but he managed to escape, regain his ship and soothe his feelings with a little piracy. Despite these setbacks the English persevered. Diplomatic activity in Constantinople brought a Sultanic *Firman* in 1611 addressed to "all great viceroys and beglerbegs who are on the way, both by sea and land, from my most happy and imperial throne to the confines of the East Indies", and in particular to those in the Yemen, instructing them to show "such offices of benevolence and humanity as shall be meet and convenient to be yielded unto honest men and strangers undertaking so long and painful a voyage". Despite this the Company was still denied permission to open a Factory but it was able, nonetheless, to do some profitable trade.

Shortly after the English traders came the Dutch. In 1614 their first ships arrived off Aden. But instead of turning westwards like their rivals, they went along the coast to Shihr, where they left a party of three men with "a little cash and some Nuremburg wares of poor quality". The local ruler promised them his personal protection, and they claimed (most improbably) to have been even more hospitably received by the local damsels "who are very lascivious and have prettily shaped figures and limbs. Parents hold it a great honour whenever their daughters have knowledge of strangers."

After eighteen months the Dutch commander Pieter van den Broeck collected the two who had survived. He went on to Mokha where he saw a caravan of 1,000 camels arriving from Syria. He then travelled up to Sanaa, where he received permission to trade on a regular basis: agreement was reached that customs duties should be 3½ per cent. He was still not allowed to leave permanent trading representatives, but after 1618 when this was granted to the East India Company, the Dutch assumed the same right. However, due to disputes with corrupt and extortionate officials, their settlement was short-lived. In 1628 they took their first cargo of coffee, but threatened to bombard Mokha after a particularly outrageous act of official piracy. This was vetoed by Amsterdam which set more store by the Levant trade with Turkey, and after the establishment of coffee in Java the Mokha trade lost some of its importance for Holland.

From the accounts of these travellers, as well as from local sources, we may build a picture of Ottoman rule in the Yemen. The highest officials were, as we have seen, renegadoes from the Balkans rather than ethnic Turks, and it is clear that they kept considerable state. The Governor of Aden was able to welcome the *Ascension* with "tabour and pipe and other heathen musick". Van den Broeck found that the Pasha of Sanaa maintained a suite of 200 richly dressed noblemen and a tame leopard. He received visitors on a high stool draped with crimson velvet and expected them to kiss his vest. Many of the senior officials hoped to loot enough during their period in the Yemen to secure a prosperous retirement. Turkish garrisons kept order and Jourdain guessed that there were 300 soldiers in Aden, fifty in Ibb and perhaps 10,000 in all. However, many of these troops were in fact Egyptians. The traditional method of control – the taking of hostages – was not neglected. Van den Broeck reckoned that there were 1,000 hostages in Sanaa, and Middleton also reported a spacious yard filled with women and children.

However, Middleton realised that in the wilder parts the Turks could not pass without a safe conduct from Arab tribal chieftains. It is clear that the Zaydis were never subdued and it is noteworthy that the Turks made no attempt to conciliate the Ismailis to use as allies against them. As so often in Yemeni history, the weight of the individual ruler's fist determined how far from his capital his writ would run. In 1551 Aden revolted against its Ottoman governor and invited in the Portuguese, but the town was quickly brought to heel. Between 1565 and 1567 widespread tribal uprisings brought the whole government near to collapse. However, in 1590 when two Iberian Jesuits were wrecked off the Hadhrami coast the Pasha of Sanaa was strong enough to insist that they should be sent to him, despite the wishes of the local ruler, who hoped to secure any ransom that might be paid. So urgent was his demand that they had to undergo a four-day non-stop journey on camels, in constant terror of falling off through sleepiness. They were probably the first Europeans to see Marib, and were certainly the only ones to enter Yemen from the east before 1935.

European visitors were impressed by Sanaa with its luxurious gardens, orchards and pleasure-houses. There were splendid mosques and public baths to serve a population of about 12,000, which included Greek, Persian and Indian merchants as well as those from areas subjected to the Ottomans. The East India Company Factor hopefully calculated that the market could absorb great quantities of English goods – iron, tin and lead as well as textiles.

The period of Zaydi rule

Unknown to these European visitors, the Zaydis in the north had found a new leader. In 1598 Qasim ibn Muhammad, a direct descendent of al-Hadi, the first of the family to settle in the Yemen, claimed the Imamate with the title al-Mansur Billah – the Victorious by the Grace of God. He proved himself a great guerrilla leader, and some of his exploits recounted by the chronicler al-Sharafi would not have disgraced Robin Hood. Once he escaped from the Turks by hiding in a tree, and on another occasion by disguising himself as an Indian. In one fight his men had only three muskets and no ammunition, until a bag of bullets, apparently sent by God, was miraculously discovered. In another clash the Turks had 2,400 muskets which made a noise like thunder, while "the Faithful" could only reply with stones, but yet prevailed. In a series of spectacular attacks and ambushes he took much of the country north of Sanaa, and in 1607 the Turks agreed to leave him unmolested in this area. Once secure, he re-established the traditional Zaydi polity that had been practised by his ancestor. Once again the chroniclers recount the miraculous powers, the ostentatious simplicity of life, the rigid enforcement of religious law, with the Imam himself stoning adulterers, and the meticulous collection of taxes for distribution to the poor.

In 1620 Qasim died and was succeeded by his son al-Muayyad Muhammad. He resumed the campaign, which took on the character of a genuine national rising against corrupt and unjust foreign rule. The immorality of the Turks caused particular offence, for boys had to be guarded as closely as girls. The Ottoman Empire was undergoing internal difficulties, as well as waging a prolonged war against Venice, so the Sultan could do nothing to help his representative in the Yemen beyond sending a few unwilling Egyptian conscripts. By 1636 the Pasha controlled little more than the Tihamah. He therefore decided that his task was hopeless, and agreed to evacuate his forces to the Hejaz: many stayed behind and took service with the Imam. Al-Muayyad, who was succeeded by his brother, managed to bring the whole of the old Himyarite state as far east as Dhofar under at least nominal sovereignty.

For the next century contact with the West was so limited that a French writer of 1709 believed that no European had ever seen Sanaa. The only exception was at Mokha where the Imam allowed the English, the Dutch and later the French to establish Factories. There was intense competition to buy the coffee crop and to win the race to Europe with it. The East India Company was also interested in buying aloes and selling in return iron, steel, lead and textiles. It maintained a permanent representative in the port, and visiting merchants often stayed for several months. At times there was quite a large expatriate community, who were treated with complete toleration: Indians practised their rites with cattle with gilded horns while Italian priests looked after the Catholics. Renegadoes, including a Greek priest who became a Muslim and an English sailor who styled himself "Captain-General of the Ordnance of the Kingdom of Senna" acted as a bridge between the two communities. The great years of the coffee trade were from 1720 to 1740, after which the French and Dutch interest declined. The first American ship arrived in 1798 and much of the trade passed into their hands; in the Napoleonic wars they were safe from privateers, did not need to travel in convoys and as neutrals paid less insurance. They were anxious to ingratiate themselves, and their hoisting flags on a Muslim feast day shocked a visiting British aristocrat. "I should not have cared for their degradation," wrote Lord Valentia, "had I not been afraid that the natives might have taken these Americans for Europeans and Christians, in consequence of which we might have shared in the contempt they appeared so anxious to acquire."

Relations were not always easy. Captain Hamilton described how he had difficulties in collecting a debt from the Deputy Governor in 1716: he finally succeeded by inviting him to discuss the matter on a high balcony and threatening to throw him over unless he paid at once. In 1737 the French despaired of obtaining money due to them by normal means, and sent four warships to bombard the town. A force of 20,000 was mustered to resist them, but it scattered when confronted by high explosive shells. The French collected their debts and charged another 100,000 piastres to cover their expenses. In 1770 the British Factory was attacked by an angry mob after a ship's captain had seized and flogged a runaway servant who had sought refuge with the Governor and declared himself a Muslim. Two warships were sent from India to punish the citizens, but the Governor hastily extorted a large sum from the resident Indian merchants and escaped further retaliation by paying a fine.

Like most chieftainships in South Western Arabia, the Zaydi Imamate has never been purely hereditary: the Imam is elected from within a definite hereditary group. Any descendant of the Prophet with the qualifications of piety, theological learning, generosity, proven military, political and administrative skill might claim the Imamate. Any physical blemish was a disqualification: an otherwise suitable candidate who unexpectedly lost his beard in an explosion had to withdraw. Naturally on many occasions a son or brother of the previous incumbent started with the advantage of being already well known. During the seventeenth and eighteenth centuries, the succession was often fiercely contested: sometimes a decisive role might be played by the *ulama* – learned men with knowledge of Muslim law and traditions – as collective keepers of the conscience of the state. At other times, the succession could only be decided by the sword.

There were thus several civil wars in the eighteenth century, during which outlying provinces made their escape from the authority of the central government. In 1728 the Governor of Lahej proclaimed himself an independent Sultan, and so Aden also ceased to be part of the Imam's dominions. In 1730 the Governor of Asir, a Sharif of lineage as exalted as that of the Imam, likewise broke away, and established a state based on

Abu Arish. In 1758 it looked as if the whole of Hujariyyah might also be lost when a particularly formidable chief brought most of the Tihamah (except Mokha) and even Taizz under his rule. Finding himself unable to deal with this chief by military means, the Imam of the time had recourse to treachery. The shaykh was invited to Sanaa as an honoured guest, but once inside the city he was seized, stripped and paraded through the streets on a camel with his face to its tail, and was finally decapitated on a dung hill. The Hadhramawt and the Yafai mountains had long enjoyed virtual independence. However, amongst all this tribal unrest and intrigue there was never a concerted attack on the Imamate as such.

We have accounts of some of these Imams. One son of Qasim was so determined never to touch state funds that he earned his living by making the caps that go under turbans, and lived with a single wife and one female slave. Fifty years later a successor of his was living at Muwayhib near Dhamar with 300 concubines; "his Lust having the Ascendant over his Reason" as Hamilton remarked. Aged 87 and ill with an abscess in the ear, this ruler asked that a Doctor from the French fleet at Mokha might be sent to cure him. He was described as extremely simple in his dress, distinguished from others only by a veil of silk fastened to his turban. He kept no state and fed the Frenchmen from his own table – an honour that they did not greatly appreciate. He was cured in three weeks, and celebrated by marrying an eighteen-year-old girl.

In July 1763 the first and one of the greatest explorers of Arabia, Carsten Niebuhr, was received by the Imam in Sanaa. Seated in a large chamber with fountains in the middle, the Ruler was dressed in robes of green with flowing sleeves and embroidered with gold lace. He wore a large white turban and reposed on a throne covered with silken cushions, while on benches on either side sat his sons and his brothers. The travellers were permitted to kiss the back and front of his hand as well as the hem of his robe while a herald shouted "God preserve the Imam" – a sentiment which was echoed by all the bystanders. He received the Europeans courteously, presented them each with a purse of money and invited them to stay a year if they so wished. He settled them in an elegant country house and when they left sent each a suit of fine clothes.

25

Just over thirty years later a British envoy became the first European permitted to enter the city in western dress. The Imam gave him a private orchestra and a guard to hold back the curious populace (foreigners were so rare indeed that the mere sight of a passing Scottish professor in Hodeidah drew the crowds away from a performing baboon). The envoy had set before him sixty dishes of meat dressed in different ways and his successor, having become the first Christian allowed to enter Sanaa on horseback, described a similar banquet "arranged on the floor by the Imam's female housekeeper".

The French visitor of 1709, Niebuhr and an English envoy of 1836 all describe the performance by the Imam of his duties as spiritual leader of his people. Niebuhr recounted that the Imam rode forth attended by the princes and followed by hundreds of soldiers. A parasol, the emblem of royalty, sheltered him from the sun and on each side was borne a standard "having upon it a small silver box filled with amulets whose efficacy was imagined to render him invincible...The riders paced or galloped at pleasure and all was in confusion. Near a gate were stationed some pairs of camels bearing carriages, in which some of the Imam's wives often ride upon such occasions; but the carriages were at this time empty and served only to fill up the procession. Behind the camels which bore these, were twelve others, bearing nothing but small flags fixed by way of ornament to their saddles."

Cruttenden in 1836 saw the Imam carrying a gold shafted spear, riding with his left hand resting on the shoulder of a confidential eunuch. When he arrived in the great open space in front of the palace, his attendants ranged themselves in a square while, followed by his relations, the Imam repeatedly galloped around, making as if to attack the nearest horseman. He then dismounted and stood while any petitioner could approach, kiss his knee and state his case. Cruttenden says that on other days the Imam held a levee at dawn and for the rest of the day caroused drunkenly with his slave-girls: the visiting Englishmen were shocked and declined to participate.

Niebuhr described the administration as it existed in his day. In every major centre was a *dowlah* (Governor), who normally held office for two or three years at the end of which he might be either promoted or imprisoned. The *dowlah* was often of low birth, sometimes even a former slave, for the example of the Sharif of Abu Arish showed that it could be dangerous to appoint a nobleman. He was responsible for the collection of the religious taxes and customs duties, for which he had to submit the most detailed accounts. Niebuhr calculated that this brought the Imam a monthly income of about 40,000 crowns.

The *dowlah* was assisted by a *bash-katib*. The latter's task was also to spy upon the *dowlah* for the Imam. Municipal affairs were in the hands of the *shaykh al-bilad*, an *amir al-suq* controlled the markets, and where appropriate an *amir al-bahr* managed the harbour. Justice was the responsibility of the *qadi* and, Niebuhr thought, was generally honestly administered. The *qadi* of Sanaa, not the Imam, gave judgement in major cases.

There was a standing army of about 1,000 cavalry and 4,000 infantry, which provided each town with a garrison. In Mokha in 1803, Lord Valentia found eight horsemen and two hundred matchlock men who provided their own weapons. Pay seems to have been reasonable, but there was little discipline. In general Niebuhr was astonished at the security which reigned. His companion Forsskal, who had been stripped to the underpants by Beduins within sight of the Pyramids, found that in the Yemen he had "no longer to study plants and robbers simultaneously". Lord Valentia was less impressed: "as a government, they are extortioners and tyrants; as traders they are fraudulent and corrupt; as individuals, they are sunk in the lowest state of ignorance and debauchery; and, in short, require to be civilised more than the inhabitants of the South Seas".

Niebuhr considered Sanaa a paradise, with its courteous and hospitable inhabitants, its *suq* filled with goods from Europe and India and its magnificent buildings both public and private. Forty years later the German explorer Seetzen, who was travelling as a secret agent on behalf of the Czar, thought the city the finest in the Orient, yielding to Constantinople only in its mosques. Nowhere in Arabia was there finer craftsmanship, and Niebuhr was the first to describe the Yemeni Jews who worked in gold and silver. There were some 2,000 of them protected by the Imam in return for a small annual tribute and they were treated contemptuously rather than harshly. They lived in a separate village and were not allowed to spend the night in Sanaa. A French visitor even praised their wine, which, he said, resembled chablis, while their distillation compared not too unfavourably with Marc du Bourgogne.

The re-appearance of the West

Just before the end of the eighteenth century the Red Sea became for the first time an object of interest to the Chancellories of Western Europe. Both the British and the French had possessions in India with which speedy communication was a matter of the utmost concern. For example, in the event of war, the country whose representative first received the news gained an immense advantage. Improved technology made navigation safer and the development of a route across Egypt became attractive. In 1785 the French reached an agreement with the authorities in Cairo which enabled them to transport goods in bond from Alexandria to Suez: ten years later the British brought out the first chart of the Red Sea.

In 1798 Bonaparte invaded Egypt, and it was not inconceivable that he would re-embark at Suez and sail unopposed to India. Indeed, intelligence sources intercepted letters from him to the Imam of Muscat and to various Indian princes announcing that he was on his way. In May 1799, therefore, the British reacted by sending troops to the island of Perim, and thus blocked the Straits of Bab al-Mandab. There was no fresh water there, so in September, at the invitation of the Sultan of Lahej, the force moved to Aden, where it remained until March 1800 when the danger of a French invasion of India had passed. The Governor General, Lord Wellesley, thought that there was no point in prolonging the occupation, although the Sultan was quite agreeable. Aden was described at this time as "a wretched heap of ruins and miserable huts".

The following year, 1801, saw the first use of the Red Sea for strategic purposes since the days of the Portuguese. The British sent an army to land on the Egyptian coast and take the remnants of the French army from the rear. In the same year, the British also made a determined effort to revive their flagging trade with the Yemen and to close the country to the

French: Commodore Sir Home Popham was appointed Ambassador to the States of Arabia and authorised to conclude commercial treaties. For the first time an official Resident, representing the British Government and not the East India Company, was appointed to Mokha and in May 1801 this Dr Pringle was received by the Imam. Negotiations were successful and the Imam agreed to instruct his officials to assist British ships, to deny supplies to the French and to encourage trade. He also permitted the building of a hospital at Mokha. The following year Popham himself decided to visit Sanaa but his tactlessness and arrogance led to a series of incidents which necessitated an undignified retreat when he had got as far as Taizz. Pringle remained on for some years at Mokha until "an unfortunate attachment to spirituous liquors" caused him to threaten to bombard the town: perhaps the impossibility of sleeping at night because of the proximity of the Residency to the stables of the *Dowlah* which were full of amorous and noisy donkeys contributed to his downfall.

The Egyptians in the Yemen

Just over fifty years earlier a religious reformer Shaykh Muhammad ibn Abd al-Wahhab in alliance with a tribal chieftain Muhammad ibn Saud had started to conquer Eastern Arabia in the name of an Islam purified of all accretions since the days of the Prophet. Firstly the townsfolk and then the Beduins of Najd were fanaticised and taught that all who differed from the Wahhabis[1] were heretics who deserved to be despoiled while all who fell in this noble task were assured of instant paradise. An object of their particular abhorrence was the veneration of the descendants of Ali and this was manifested by ruthless destruction and looting of the tombs of the family. The Wahhabis raided into Iraq, menaced Damascus and nearly reached Muscat and Aleppo. In 1803 they occupied

---

[1] The followers of this movement refer to themselves as "Muwahhidun" (Unitarians) and regard the word "Wahhabi" as pejorative. It is, however, so convenient and in such general use that I hope that my employment of the term will be forgiven: certainly no slight is intended, and I have seen it increasingly used by Saudi writers.

Mecca and then later took Medina banning all but themselves from performing the Pilgrimage. The same year they appeared on the borders of the Yemen and the Sharif of Abu Arish deemed it advisable to proclaim himself their adherent. Helped by the fact that the Imam was in his dotage and his sons quarrelling over the inheritance, the Wahhabis raided deep into the Tihamah, and Mokha itself was threatened.

The Ottoman Sultan, who bore the title of Protector of the Holy Places, felt compelled to intervene, so that Mecca and Medina would again be open to the majority of the Faithful. He requested his vassal, Muhammad Ali Pasha of Egypt, to send a force, which expelled the Wahhabis from Mecca and Medina in 1812. The Egyptians then attempted to liquidate the Wahhabi presence in Asir and the Tihamah, but they were routed at Qunfidah, and had to re-embark with the loss of all their animals, weapons and stores. For some years Muhammad Ali abandoned his hopes of gaining the wealth of the Yemen. However, the capture of Diriyah the Saudi capital in 1818 meant that troops were now available for the task. The main ports of the Tihamah were captured, but shortly afterwards the Pasha made an arrangement with the Imam: for an annual tribute of 100,000 dollars the Imam received all the Yemeni territory occupied by the Egyptians.

Relations with the British and the need for a coal depot

The previous year there had occurred a fracas in Mokha, in the course of which the British Residency had been occupied by a mob and some Englishmen beaten. The British authorities in India were slow to react but in December 1820 warships arrived to exact reparations. Over 4,000 shells were fired, drilling neat holes in the mud walls but doing no damage, so that finally troops had to be landed. The incident concluded with the signing of the first formal treaty between the Imam and a European power: the status of the Resident and that of other Britons was regulated and the export tariff on goods shipped was reduced from 3 to 2½ per cent. Muhammad Ali expressed to the Consul General in Cairo his fear of British designs on the Arabian Peninsula, but he was assured that London harboured no ambitions. The mutual suspicion of the two governments was becoming evident: in 1822 the Sultan of Lahej offered to accept a British Resident in Aden in return for help against rebellious tribes and a guarantee against Muhammad Ali. This was a development of the friendly relations which had begun in 1799 and had been consolidated, at least on paper, by a "Treaty of Amity and Commerce" concluded with the Sultan in 1802.

The importance of the Red Sea was greatly increased by the advent of steam navigation. In 1823 a Committee was established in India to study the use of this new technology and this interest was echoed in Whitehall. When in 1828 Lord Ellenborough was put in charge of Indian affairs he found that his Department was dealing with events that had occurred two years earlier. He considered that one year should be enough to write a letter and receive a reply, and he wished that "every public servant in India (should) feel that he was at all times under the eye and within the reach of the British government". The Mediterranean and Red Sea route, using steam, would reduce the five-month journey round the Cape to two months. This was, of course, only practicable provided that a steamer could refuel at some point between Bombay and Suez.

In 1828 arrangements were made to dump coal at Mokha and in 1829 in Aden on Sira Island. However, when the steamer *Hugh Lindsay* made her first voyage she was greatly delayed in Aden because of a shortage of men to do the actual loading. Furthermore, it was obviously desirable that the coal should be stored somewhere under the British flag where it would not be subject to the whims of a foreign potentate. In 1832, therefore, Commander Haines of the Bombay Marine was ordered to survey the southern shore of Arabia to find a suitable place. At first the island of Socotra looked attractive, and Haines was authorised to buy it from the Mahri Sultan for 10,000 dollars. He found the Ruler old, blind, deformed and attired in rags but adamant that he would not sell an inch of land, saying that it was "a gift of the Almighty and has descended from our forefathers to their children". Haines admired his integrity, but nonetheless in 1835 a British force landed on the island. A few months later it withdrew, decimated by fever.

Haines was left in no doubt that the only possible base was Aden.

Although Muhammad Ali had arrived as the Ottoman Sultan's vassal, his forces continued to occupy western Arabia after his denunciation of Ottoman sovereignty in 1831. The following year Turkish intrigue inspired one of Muhammad Ali's Albanian officers stationed in Jeddah, Turkce Bilmez (literally "He who knows no Turkish") to revolt, by dangling before him the prospect of an independent pashalik. Egyptian forces quickly drove out the rebel. He fled southwards with a band of followers and managed to create for himself a small principality in the Tihamah with his capital at Mokha, from which the Imam was powerless to remove him. Turkce Bilmez then demanded the surrender of Aden, sending a mission which the Governor received with courtesy before slitting the throats of most of its members at a banquet. In June 1833 Muhammad Ali informed the British that he intended to attack Mokha. When no objection was raised, the attack was made and Turkce Bilmez was expelled. The British now realised with alarm that the Egyptians were the masters of the whole eastern coast of the Red Sea from Bab al-Mandab to Aqaba. In August 1837 the Governor of Bombay Sir Robert Grant wrote, "I think that it will be absolutely necessary to have a possession of our own on or near the Red Sea."

Muhammad Ali was not merely a conqueror but a business man whose policy was to monopolise the trade of every area which came under his power. As his arch-enemy the Foreign Secretary Lord Palmerston said, "like all countries Egypt has rich and poor. The rich is Muhammad Ali and the poor is everyone else." The Pasha took formal control of the coffee trade and excluded all competitors. He started to expand inland, and in the summer of 1837 he bought Taizz from its Governor, a treacherous uncle of the Imam.

The British take Aden

In September 1837 Muhammad Ali was warned that the British regarded Aden as within their sphere of influence, and he formally denied that he had any designs on it. In that same month the British administration in Bombay realised that a pretext for forcible intervention could be found. The previous January an Indian dhow flying the British flag, the *Duria Dowlat*, had been wrecked off the coast of Aden, its cargo looted and some Indian ladies on board insulted. There was evidence that there had been collusion for purposes of fraud between the dhow's captain and the Aden authorities but Grant urged that as a punishment the town be occupied. His superior, the Governor General was not prepared to go quite so far, and instructed that the Sultan should first be given a chance to make reparation; perhaps an agreement for a coaling station might be negotiated. Haines was sent to exact restitution, which he succeeded in doing after finding that some of the goods were being sold from the Sultan's own warehouse. Most of the cargo was restored and the Sultan agreed to pay for the rest.

Haines had been ordered not to regard this as the end of the incident, but to proceed to offer to buy Aden from the Sultan of Lahej. He was helped in this by the Arab's fear that Muhammad Ali might seize it without any payment, and his hope that in conjunction with the British the port might be developed into a rival to Mokha. In January 1838, therefore, the Sultan agreed to cede Aden for an annual pension of 8,700 dollars, and wrote to Haines "I have given my seal that Aden is yours." However, he wished to maintain his jurisdiction over the Arab residents, a stipulation to which Haines objected, and negotiations dragged on. At the end of the month the hot-headed young son of the Sultan failed in a plot to kidnap Haines and repossess the document of cession. Haines sailed for India, warning the Sultan that he would return. He also sent a message to the Egyptian commander in the Yemen, saying that Aden was now a British possession, and cautioning him against any interference. Despite this, Muhammad Ali told the Consul General that if the British wished merely for a coaling base he was quite prepared to take over Aden and give them one: he was informed with some asperity that Great Britain was strong enough to look after her own interests.

The British administration in Bombay regarded the attack on Haines as "a most happy incident", which showed that the Sultan was "little better than a common marauder" and proposed that "we should be allowed to take possession of the port of Aden as a compensation for the insult offered to the British flag". It was clear to them that Aden needed "civilised rule", and for their purposes its possession was "most essential", both as a coal depot for all seasons of the year and as a potentially impregnable military base which might otherwise be taken by the French or the Russians. The Governor General replied that he could not authorise its capture without the permission of Whitehall, which was slow to make up its mind.

In October the Bombay administration decided to act without awaiting the approval of their superiors, and sent Haines back to take possession of Aden. The Sultan, seeing that he had only a single ship and knowing that the British had just suffered a disaster in Afghanistan, began a protracted correspondence. Losing patience, Haines menaced, "You write of the British Government as if you were speaking of some petty Shaikhdom...Would you play with a lion as with a cat?" He ordered a blockade. In November one of his small boats was fired upon, and to avenge this "shameful and cowardly attack", he called for reinforcements. When these arrived he decided to take the town by storm which he did on 19 January 1839. He reported that his losses, including wounded, were fifteen men, while the Arab casualties were 140.

The Turks in the Yemen

In 1840 after years of relentless British pressure, Muhammad Ali could no longer avoid submitting to his Ottoman overlord, and as part of the settlement, he had to withdraw his troops from Arabia. This withdrawal left Yemen in chaos, as each tribal leader asserted his independence. The Imam was powerless and could not prevent the looting of Sanaa, so he sent an envoy to Aden in 1841 to request protection. In 1843 he asked that an officer be sent to reside with him as his adviser and again in 1848 he asked for help: Haines, now Political Agent, had to refuse.

The Sharif of Abu Arish occupied the Tihamah and demanded that the British should evacuate Aden. His methods of extortion were ingenious; once he built an enormous grain chest and invited twenty-five of the leading merchants of

Mokha to inspect it: they were all locked in until they signed over a tenth of their property. British Indian traders suffered particularly and after an insult to the flag, the Ambassador at Constantinople was instructed to complain. The Turks sent an officer to investigate but, well-bribed, he merely recommended that the Sharif be appointed a Pasha on condition of paying tribute to the Sultan.

For some months in the winter of 1840 yet a third force was in the field. A fanatic proclaiming himself the Regenerator of the Faith seized control of Taizz and Hujariyyah. He promised to abolish all taxes, to drive the infidel from Aden and invulnerability to sword and bullet to all his followers. It was a sign of the anarchy of the times that 12,000 men joined his banner, and it took a major effort by the Imam to defeat and kill him.

The Imamate itself became an object of strife, with four holders in seven years. It was not until 1848 that one emerged who was strong enough to bring the Tihamah and Hujariyyah under some form of control. By then, however, it was too late: the Turks had decided to reassert control of the country. In April 1849 they took Hodeidah, and so began a stay that was to last for seventy years.

Although at the beginning each had little more than a toe-hold, for the first time there were now two imperial powers, the British and the Ottoman, in South-West Arabia, each with its own tradition and methods of government. It was inevitable that they should seek to expand inland from the coasts and that the areas that came under their control should be developed in different ways. There had always been the dualism of Zaydi and Shafai, but after some years the Shafais were divided between the two regimes and started to change according to their areas. It was also inevitable that the two Empires should clash.

Chapter Three

Two Empires in the Yemen

Aden under Haines

The capture of Aden was particularly welcome to the British, coming as it did at a time when the hopes pinned to an alternative overland route to India by means of the Euphrates had diminished. The Bombay administration marked its approval of Haines's action by presenting him with a sword worth two hundred guineas. However, within a few months, in October 1839, Sir James Rivett Carnac, Grant's successor as Governor, questioned the expediency of retaining the port, writing that "it was a bad move and will be a constant source of expense and trouble to us". He considered that now the immediate objective of keeping out the Egyptians or the Americans had been achieved, it would be preferable to hand Aden over to the friendly Sultan of Muscat. However, although it had not specifically authorised the capture in the first place, the Whitehall of Lord Palmerston would never contemplate hauling down the flag once it had actually been hoisted, and Bombay therefore had to bear the continued cost of keeping Aden.

Keeping Aden was not without its difficulties. Haines's first preoccupation was to erect fortifications sufficient to repel any attempt at recapture. Simultaneously and by the judicious use of intrigue, he worked to prevent the Arabs from uniting against the intruder in their midst before these defences were ready. Within a month Haines concluded Treaties of Friendship with his immediate neighbours, the Abdalis of Lahej, the Fadhlis of Shuqra and the Aqrabis of Bir Ahmad, as well as with the more distant Sultanates of Hawshabi, Lower Yafa and some of the Subayhi tribes. Another early objective was the creation of a highly efficient intelligence network based on the Jewish communities resident in most South Arabian centres; quite soon Haines was receiving quick and accurate information from as far away as Sanaa and Mokha.

The local chiefs also appeared to wish for peace. In March a British soldier who had wandered outside the town was murdered, and the Sultan of Lahej paid a visit to express his regrets. In June he concluded an agreement that in return for a monthly subsidy of 541 Maria Theresa Dollars (a sum equivalent to the one that he had lost through not keeping his original undertaking to sell Aden), he would maintain friendly relations and encourage trade. However it appeared that the Sultan too was buying time, in order to form an alliance with his traditional enemies the Fadhlis. In November 1839 the two tribes mounted a joint attack upon Aden. Haines' defences held and they were repulsed with some 200 casualties. In May 1840 an assault by 5,000 men was also unsuccessful, as was another on the same scale in July, when the tribesmen tried to outflank the defences of the Isthmus by going round them on the sand when the tide was out, only to be forced back by naval gunfire. Haines wished to march inland to teach the Sultans a lesson, but was forbidden by Bombay to take any offensive action without permission. The Sultans, however, had had enough, and the last serious attack on Aden was made in August 1846 under the leadership of a religious fanatic and some 2,000 tribesmen that he had attracted by promises of invulnerability and loot.

Haines did not only see the value of Aden in purely military terms. He realised that it could be developed into a place of great mercantile importance, opening up "the rich towns of Hadhramawt and Yemen". This required real vision, for, as he wrote of the area before its capture, "its trade is annihilated, its governor imbecile, its tanks in ruins, its water half-brackish, with deserted streets and still more deserted ports". For the explorer Wellstead a few years before, it had consisted of "a few minarets tottering to their fall" in an atmosphere of general ruin. Haines officially reported that there were ninety dilapidated stone buildings, not a single one fit for European habitation, housing a population of 600, of whom 250 were Jews and fifty were Banyans. There were no bricklayers or carpenters in a *suq* which a Sapper officer found "the most confined and dirty I ever entered, consisting of a single alley about four feet wide and seven or nine high and perhaps twenty yards long, the whole covered over and obscured by rags" with "an unendurable smell".

Haines was confronted with enormous difficulties. Firstly he held the not very impressive appointment of Political Agent. He was therefore not a Governor and *ex-officio* Commander-in-Chief with full power over military officers, who regarded his plans for commercial development as unsuitable for a fortress. Secondly Haines was, of course, a sailor and not a town planner or an accountant, but he was given no trained assistants in these fields. He had to do all the work himself, and even to send to his masters a hand-written copy of every letter sent or received, certified by himself as a true copy. It is not surprising that in the fifteen years that he held the post he took no leave, apart from six weeks due to illness. Finally, he had no influential friends to act on his behalf with senior administrators, who tended to regard him as an obscure nuisance in a distant outpost.

Haines started to lay out his town, generally called "Camp", in what the *Asiatic Journal* described as "the crater of Etna enlarged and covered with gravestones and the remains of stone huts". There were hyaenas in the ravines and the area abounded in scorpions up to eight inches in length. Despite the large numbers of local Arabs who came to find work there was a shortage of hands for the heavier tasks. Convicts were brought in from Bombay to make the roads, and when in 1848 some urgent repairs were needed on the fortifications, 3,000 contract labourers had to be imported from India. The rising prosperity of Aden, coupled with the troubles in the Yemen, brought in more Banyans, so that parts of the Settlement resembled an Indian rather than an Arab town. Somalis also arrived in considerable numbers, and made walking at night difficult by sleeping in the streets. In seven years the population had risen to 25,000, of whom 16,000 were Arabs and 1,300 Jews, although these figures were estimates as it was impossible to make an accurate count of the women. There were 600 Indians, all male, and seven resident Europeans including two women. The Portuguese, who did not figure in the statistics as

Europeans, numbered 136, and the balance was made up of troops and camp followers.

Haines provided the services of a modern town, and by November 1842 he was able to write "I am happy to report that the populace of Aden have commenced building permanent shops and houses" – a development expressing confidence which he encouraged with specially low rates. The first Post Office was opened in 1839, when shortage of staff made it the responsibility of the Civil Surgeon. Visitors tended to shudder when they recalled the Prince of Wales Hotel, despite its thirty rooms and billiard table, for its numerous rats, cockroaches and lizards prevented a comfortable night's sleep. Other amenities included a Catholic Church, some "divine sheds" for Anglicans, a Hindu temple, a Masonic Lodge, a theatre and "a commodious jail" which contained a gallows and whipping post. An experimental garden was started, and bamboo cottages were erected for summer residence by Europeans. After six years in charge of public health the Surgeon Malcolmson stated "without fear of contradiction that a more healthy station does not exist in any of the British colonies".

Haines wrote of the local Arabs that "their youth is spent in the study of dissimulation and intrigue and their older age in practising these vices" but in reality he seems to have had a great affection for them and an understanding of their mentality. He wrote "let them feel that you are their superior in tact, intellect, judgment and activity of purpose, that their secret thoughts are known to you, that your information is sure, secret and correct and that you are prepared to counteract their designs" – a policy of bluff that his successors usually tried to carry out as long as there were Britons in Aden. It was easy for the Government of India to write of "the extreme inexpediency of interfering in any manner in the disputes of the chiefs...(we) only retain Aden for the purpose of protecting our depot of coal, not for that of promoting intervention in the affairs of the neighbourhood chiefs" but Haines, in the field, found himself constantly involved in matters of local politics. He had to conduct diplomacy with the Imam of Sanaa and the Sharif of Abu Arish while trying to divert the export of coffee from Mokha. Nearer home he played tribal politics with a masterly hand, and in his later years he worked closely with the

Sultan of Lahej, whose pretensions to being a "super-chief" he did not discourage, using him as an intermediary for dealing with others.

Haines was partly a romantic visionary, and partly a shifty intriguer obsessed with the idea of building up his creation. He used any means to hand, and over the years his administration took on the local Arab characteristics of exaggerated hostility to opponents and excessive reward to friends. One of the ways that he did this was through the Treasury which acted in effect as the only bank in the port. Through the Treasury he made advances which could not be justified or explained. A check of the accounts revealed irregularities and a deficit of £28,000 for which Haines was held responsible. He was recalled to Bombay, and although he was acquitted on charges of fraud and embezzlement, he spent six years in a debtors' prison from which he was released only a few days before his death.

Aden at mid-century

The dismissal of Haines amazed the local tribes. They had come to regard him almost as one of their own Sultans, and some unrest in the hinterland ensued. Haines' policy of paying a stipend to the Abdalis on condition that they kept open the trade routes caused jealousy amongst the other tribes, particularly the Fadhlis, who claimed that their share did not reach them. Since the dawn of Arab history until today the means by which a Yemeni tribe draws attention to its grievances is to cut the roads. This the Fadhlis proceeded to do, making it impossible for people to go in or out of Aden. A French visitor, Gobineau, had hoped to travel outside Aden, but heard that a few days earlier one Englishman had been killed and two others seriously wounded in an ambush. The Fadhlis also gave shelter to a man known to have murdered a British officer under circumstances of great treachery. Haines' successor, Colonel James Outram, the famous "Bayard of India", conducted a sharp, successful campaign to punish such outrages.

In 1856 Outram's successor, Brigadier General Coghlan, became the first top official to pay a state visit to the interior when he went to stay at Lahej. The Sultan, however, grew increasingly resentful of the British practice of dealing directly with other tribes, since this diminished his own importance, and to show his displeasure, he cut the roads into Aden until, as he put it, "the Government shall come to its senses". In February 1858 the Sultan seized caravans of goods belonging to British subjects and then moved his forces to Shaykh Othman from which he could control all routes into Aden and the wells upon which the Settlement depended for its water. Coghlan marched out of Aden at the head of the garrison, and although the Abdalis fought well, they were forced to retreat with about forty casualties. The British then blew up the fort at Shaykh Othman and the Sultan sought a reconciliation.

Coghlan looked beyond the immediate neighbourhood. As he was anxious to have allies in the rear of the perpetually troublesome Fadhlis, he entered into relations with the Lower Aulaqis and the Naqibs of Mukalla and Shihr, all of whom agreed to suppress the slave trade. In 1863 his successor, Mereweather, marked a further stage of British involvement in the affairs of the hinterland. He accepted an invitation to mediate in a dispute about the succession to the Sultanate of Lahej: it had become clear to all claimants that the Sultan was absolutely dependent upon Aden's recognition and consequent subsidy. Three years later, after a quarrel between the Abdalis and the Fadhlis, the latter cut the roads into Aden in order to attract government attention. Mereweather reacted strongly. He took the British forces further out of Aden than they had ever been. They blew up forts in the heart of Fadhli territory and later destroyed the Sultan's palace in Shuqra. Other signs of activity beyond the fortress walls were the opening of a school for the sons of tribal notables in 1856, although this proved short-lived, and the purchase of a rest-house in 1869 for up-country visitors.

In an age which saw Livingstone and Burton exploring Africa and Sturt and Eyre Australia, it is astonishing that no serious attempt was made to learn about the hinterland of South Arabia. Visits to Lahej were not uncommon, but only one European penetrated more than fifty miles from the coast in the half century that followed the capture of Aden. This was Baron Adolf von Wrede, a Bavarian soldier who had served in the Greek army. He landed at Mukalla in 1843 declaring him-

self a Muslim, although people soon realised that he was a
European. They sought information from him on such matters
as the number of eunuchs that Queen Victoria maintained at
her court, and whether it was true that the Czar had a bodyguard of 700 cannibals and was himself seven yards tall with a
single eye in the middle of his forehead. He reached Sif in Wadi
Du'an where he was taken for an English spy. The people were
frightened by the recent capture of Aden; moreover they suspected that since two Naval officers had copied inscriptions at
a coastal site, their crop failures had been due to the evil eye.
They demanded that von Wrede should be put to death. He
was dragged before the Sultan who contented himself with
looting his baggage and returned him to the coast. Geographical journals of the period contain only one other account of a
venture into the interior – that made by Major Miles of the
Residency staff into Wahidi country in 1870. He recorded that
there was universal equality of wealth in Habban – all were
wretchedly poor and even the Sultan whose writ did not run
beyond the town possessed only a single slave and no furniture.

In Aden itself prosperity continued to grow. An account of
the 1870s described Camp (Crater) as having 2,000 houses
while new quarters were growing at Tawahi (Steamer Point)
which had 300 stone houses and at Maala which consisted
mainly of matting huts occupied by Somalis "whose savage
instincts are essentially predatory and decidedly bellicose".
Hunter, the Assistant Resident[1] whose account we have just
quoted thought that "the morality of the inhabitants of Aden is
not of a high order" and particularly disapproved of the Jews
who washed only once a week and looked very dissipated as a
result of their indulgence in home-brewed spirits. He noted
that there was an average of 75 prisoners a day in the jail.
"Financially speaking" he wrote, "Aden is a heavy burden on
India" costing £150,000 a year of which most went in the
maintenance of a garrison of one British Battalion, an Indian
Regiment, three Batteries and 100 sabres of the Aden Troop
which had been raised in 1865. A scheme for a railway linking

---

[1] Coghlan and his successors until 1931 had the style of Resident.

Crater, the Isthmus and Tawahi was considered in 1861 but came to nothing: an Anglican Church was erected in 1864, an aqueduct brought water from Shaykh Othman after 1869 and from 1870 a cable station facilitated communications with London and with India. Aden had been a free port since 1850 and the opening of the Suez Canal in 1869 brought an enormous increase of business and in three months of 1870, 88 steamers entered the harbour, buying amongst other things 3,700 fowls, nearly ten tons of beef, seven tons of mutton as well as 69 bullocks and over 1,000 sheep on the hoof. A quarter of a million camels a year entered Aden bringing goods.

Before this the prospect of a canal through the Isthmus of Suez had led to an increase of European activity in the area and this had worried the authorities in Aden and their masters. The French had taken a spasmodic interest in the Red Sea since the eighteenth century. In 1734 Admiral La Bourdonnais attempted to buy the peninsula of Shaykh Said, the extreme southwestern point of Arabia and in 1805 they contemplated occupation of Kamaran. Forty years later there were rumours that they were seeking bases either at Mokha or Massawa and in 1849, when the Turks occupied Kamaran, the French tried to make arrangements to use it. In 1852 British intrigue amongst the Somali tribes prevented the French from establishing themselves at Obock and even managed to secure for themselves a foothold in this area. The Somali coast was of great importance to Aden for, right up to the withdrawal of 1967 it supplied its population with meat and was its main source of labour.

In 1856 and 1857 French warships were active in surveying both sides of the entrance to the Red Sea and it was believed that if the Canal were indeed opened, they would attempt to occupy the island of Perim. The story was often told that French warships on just such a mission put into Aden but, when their purpose was discovered, the Resident made their officers so drunk that their sailing was delayed until the British had raised their own flag on the island. Whether or not this is true, Perim was occupied in 1857 and a lighthouse erected there.

In 1862 with Perim secure and British interests protected on the Somali coast, no further attempt was made to block the French acquisition of Obock which took place in 1862, but then it was feared that they were scheming to buy Buraykah from the Aqrabi Shaykh. Since Buraykah was a mere ten miles across the bay from Aden, the British could not tolerate this and they opened negotiations to buy it for themselves. Eventually they paid £30,000 and the village became known as Little Aden.

In 1868 Gladstone formed his first government and he proved to be less concerned than his predecessors about the route to India. "An average delay of about three weeks to our military communications with Bombay", he said, "hardly makes the difference to us of life or death." However, when a Marseilles firm, suspected of acting for the French government, bought Shaykh Said from the local Shaykh, Whitehall was thoroughly alarmed. It was only two miles across the water from Perim and its possession, together with a base on the Somali coast, would have made it easy for the French to block the Red Sea. The Turks were encouraged to say that the Shaykh had no right to sell it, and when in 1870 the French arrived to occupy it, the mustering of a Turkish force made them withdraw hastily. This scare led to a reappraisal of the fortifications of Aden, which were subsequently greatly strengthened.

The Turks in the Yemen 1849–1872

In the spring of 1849 the Turks occupied Hodeidah. After a few months spent consolidating their position in the Tihamah, their commander felt strong enough to move to Sanaa, after concluding a treaty with the Imam. Their agreement provided that the Imam should continue to rule the territory that he controlled but should acknowledge the sovereignty of the Ottoman Sultan. He should retain more than half the revenue, with the rest going to Constantinople, and should accept a garrison of 1,000 Turkish troops in Sanaa. These conditions infuriated the citizens of the capital. They imprisoned the Imam, massacred all the soldiers that they could catch and besieged the rest in the citadel. The Pasha, mortally wounded, managed to purchase a safe-conduct for the rest of his men, who retired to the Tihamah.

These events ushered in twenty years of anarchy in the capital; during this time, according to the estimate of the French epigrapher Joseph Halévy who visited it in 1869, the population declined from 200,000 to around 50,000. The tribes of Arhab sacked the city on several occasions, and Halévy reported that half the buildings were in ruins. The Imamate was powerless, and the title was in dispute between several contenders. In 1862 the merchants of Sanaa effectively claimed independence for their city by electing one of their number to manage its affairs. When finally an Imam did emerge he took no part in politics, living in seclusion in the old Zaydi stronghold of Shaharah.

At first things were no better in the area nominally under Turkish control. There were constant murders of tax collectors, the reprisals for which sparked other tribal revolts. Isolated garrisons were massacred and the roads into Mokha and Hodeidah were constantly being cut. There were frequent clashes, often amounting to pitched battles in which the Turks' Arab auxiliaries usually deserted and joined in the looting. The opening of the Suez Canal, however, transformed the situation, for the Turks were then able to move reinforcements by sea and strengthen their armies in Arabia. Asir was conquered, the Tihamah brought under control and in April 1871 Sanaa was reoccupied by troops made almost welcome as a relief from anarchy. Ahmed Mukhtar Pasha, the Governor, made no attempt to subjugate the warrior Zaydi tribes of the Hashid and Bakil. Instead he turned his attention southwards.

The Anglo-Turkish clash of 1873

At first the British welcomed the increased control of the Turks to the north, feeling that it would be easier to deal with a "quasi-civilised" power rather than with unstable tribal or religious leaders. Soon, however, they became worried: there appeared to be no obvious limit to the Ottoman Pashalik of Yemen, which three centuries earlier had embraced both Aden and the Hadhramawt. The authorities in Aden had not really thought out how much of a hinterland they needed to protect the Settlement, and they received no directives from India or

London. They therefore had no clear policy, but circumstances caused them to drift vaguely towards expansionism. In the summer of 1871 a series of agreements was made with various Subayhi leaders who undertook to keep security on the roads and to return any plunder, in return for monthly stipends which varied from 25 Maria Theresa Dollars up to 40. The following year a new Amir of Dhala sought and was accorded British recognition.

During 1872 the Turks completed the pacification of Hujariyyah and their tentacles started to stretch out into what the British now regarded as their own territory. Reports were received in Aden of the Turks' intrigues with the Subayhis and then in October 1872 the Hawshabi Sultan was summoned to Taizz where he made a formal submission to the Sublime Porte. In the same month the Abdali Sultan received a letter from Ahmed Mukhtar Pasha setting out the view that as a Yemeni he was an Ottoman subject and inviting him to acknowledge this. In December the tone changed to a peremptory command.

The British were now alarmed. The Ambassador at Constantinople was ordered to discuss the problem with the Grand Vizier who said, reassuringly, that although the Porte officially regarded Lahej as part of the Yemen, he would instruct Ahmed Mukhtar Pasha not to take any further action there. At the same time the Government of India drew up a list of nine tribes (referred to as "Cantons") which it regarded as being in the British zone of influence. These tribes should be protected against external aggression in return for an agreement not to have any relations with other powers and to submit their internal disputes to the British for settlement. The tribes concerned were the Abdalis, the Fadhlis, the Aqrabis, the Hawshabis, the Amiris (Dhala), the Alawis, the Subayhis, the Yafais and the Aulaqis. The Ambassador was instructed to pass this list on to the Grand Vizier with the request that British interests in these tribes should be recognised and that they should be left alone. This was not in international law the declaration of a Protectorate, but it came very near to being one.

Whatever instructions he may have received from Constantinople (and communications were not easy), Ahmed Mukhtar

Pasha continued his forward policy. In May 1873 Schneider, the Resident in Aden, reported that the Amir of Dhala had submitted to the Turks, given a hostage and accepted the status of an Ottoman official. Soon afterwards came news that the Alawi Shaykh had also given a hostage. More serious still, the Turks took advantage of a quarrel in the Abdali ruling family to espouse the cause of the Sultan's recalcitrant brother and to send troops into Lahej under the pretext of protecting his interests as an Ottoman subject. Throughout the summer diplomatic pressure at Constantinople was tried without success; the Turks still refused to withdraw. The Foreign Office grew frantic at the thought that the India Office might get Britain into war with its old ally Turkey. The situation became ever more confusing because, at least in theory, it was now possible for Whitehall to control the actions of its subordinates by means of the telegraph. The system was, however, still in its infancy and no one knew exactly what was happening. In the past the man in the field would have solved the problem with his opposite number and then written home to recount his actions: now independent initiative became much more difficult.

At the end of October Schneider was authorised to send troops to Lahej to protect the Sultan but not to attack the Turks, and he marched out with 300 men. It was not, however, until December that the Turks finally left Abdali, Hawshabi and Alawi territory, and it took another three years of diplomatic pressure to get them out of Dhala.

The events of 1873 are of great importance in Yemeni history because for the first time South Arabia was formally divided into two distinct territories separated by a boundary, which, although not yet delimited, was apparent to the tribes and recognised by international agreement. Secondly, the British had in effect established a Protectorate over a large part of the hinterland, far beyond what was required for the immediate defence of the Aden base. Gladstone might write that "there is every imaginable objection to the proposed protectorate. It involves the most indefinite obligation. It binds us to support those over whose conduct to others we have no control", but a process had started that would prove impossible to reverse for nearly a century.

Consolidation into two Yemens

Although the Turks had withdrawn from certain areas as a result of British pressure, they did not retract their claim, as successors to the Khalifate of the Prophet, to sovereignty over the whole of Arabia as the cradle of Islam. This remained a constant threat to the British, and so did the possibility that any discontented notable might accept the suzerainty of the Turks and invoke their intervention within the Protectorate. The Aden authorities therefore moved to consolidate their position with a system of formal Treaties of Friendship and Protection with the surrounding tribes. Qishn and Socotra came first in 1886, and then in 1888 there was a whole series of which those with the Aqrabis, Lower Aulaqis, Fadhlis and some of the Wahidis were the most important. In 1895 a second batch included the Alawis, the Hawshabis and the Lower Yafais.

These closer relationships with tribal chiefs led to a growing involvement in the hinterland, where attempts had to be made to settle local quarrels in order to prevent the Turks from interfering. Apart from the Lahej oasis, the area was of practically no economic value but the cutting of trade routes to more prosperous places could be a considerable nuisance so British officials found themselves dealing with disputes by mediation or by force. Attempts were made to end friction over frontiers between the Abdalis and the Fadhlis, between the Fadhlis and their other neighbours and between the Abdalis and the Hawshabis while in 1886 the Aden Troop moved out to help the Sultan of Lahej against the ever predatory Subayhis.

Need to forestall the Turks led to British concern in the Sultanates far to the east. In 1850 an Ottoman attempt to capture Shihr and Mukalla was defeated but in 1867 they showed a renewed interest in an area which had been a scene of constant fighting and intrigue as Arabs, mostly of Yafai origin, who had grown immensely rich in the service of the Nizam of Haiderabad struggled for control. By 1873 the brothers Abdullah and Awadh ibn Umar al-Qu'aiti seemed sufficiently established to make a Treaty abolishing the export of slaves and their position was formally recognised by a Friendship Treaty of 1882 and a Protectorate Treaty of 1888.

Even after these Treaties the outside world knew little of the unique civilisation of the Hadhramawt. Nearly a thousand years earlier Sayyid Ahmad ibn Isa, a descendant of the Prophet, had overcome both pagans and heretical Muslims by preaching and by force. He settled in the Wadi where his progeny multiplied and dominated the area as a spiritual aristocracy. There was little local wealth to support them and their tribal followers so many of them had to seek their living abroad, either in Zanzibar or more frequently in the East Indies. Usually they married before setting out in search of fortune but their wives never left the Wadi: often they raised other families abroad and then, in retirement, sometimes forty years after their departure, they would return and reclaim their first brides. The money that they sent back supported a cultured, almost academic community, but one that, cemented as it was by religious leaders, was fanatical and not disposed to welcome infidels.

In the year 1893, however, three Europeans did succeed in entering the Wadi. The earliest was a learned German, Leo Hirsch, who was the first to see the three main cities of the interior. In Shibam he found surprising wealth with Italian soaps, French candles and Dutch porcelain in the *suq*; in Saiwun he was received by a courteous and well-educated Sultan who discussed European politics with intelligence; in Tarim a fanatical mob called for his blood. Hirsch was followed by the enterprising couple of Theodore and Mabel Bent who wrote the first readily available account of the Wadi. They found the slopes studded with castles reminiscent of the Rhineland, and brought back many tales of folk customs and local life. It was, however, another forty years before further travellers entered the Hadhramawt.

The Bents travelled also amongst the Fadhlis and the Yafais where once again they were reminded of mediaeval Germany, for each community had to be constantly on the watch against attack. All along the tracks they noticed cairns marking the places where a tribesman had fallen in action. The Lower Yafai Sultan ordered them out of his country when they refused to give him a gun.

As the Bombay government had warned that any trader who entered the hinterland did so at his own risk and few were sufficiently foolhardy as to do so, the only British travellers were occasional Political Officers but their duties increased with greater involvement in tribal affairs.

A Political Officer who left a vivid account was Wyman Bury who travelled in disguise under the name of Abdullah Mansur. Of the tribesmen he wrote "the lowest type, indigent, churlish, treacherous and grasping – a pariah preying on the weak and filching from the strong…Still, with all his faults, he can die like a lone wolf when his time comes. His gamut of emotion is a simple octave, religion at one end and avarice at the other, the latter an absorbing passion which influences most of his deliberate acts and thoughts". Their rulers were little better for the Lower Yafai Sultan was "impenetrably wrapped in a fit of the sulks almost amounting to monomania…many believed he was actually insane" while the Amir of Dhala was "a kindly and (to outward semblance only) simple old man with a sweet, pensive smile…a wily old strategist". It must be remembered however, that none of these Chiefs was of the magnificence of an Indian Rajah for even the Sultan of Lahej, dignified in 1896 with the title of His Highness and a salute of eleven guns and Knighted in 1902 had a revenue of merely 1,50,000 Rupees (just over £10,000) and an annual stipend of nearly 40,000 Rupees more. The Fadhli Sultan, the next most important in the west had a revenue of 20,000 Rupees and a stipend of 4,320. The Sharif of Bayhan had little but his monthly stipend of $30.[1]

Few boundaries in South Arabia are well defined and even today there are still clashes over grazing rights, the ploughing of disputed land and over the division of water. When the tribes on one side of an undelimited frontier were the subjects of one Imperial Power while their neighbours were under the protection of another, such minor local incidents could escalate into an international confrontation. In March 1900 a Yemeni tribal chief, probably assisted by the Turks, occupied a

---

[1] These stipends were however greatly prized, partly as a symbol of status and secondly because there was little actual money in an area which operated on a barter system. As late as the 1950s this writer remembers a tribal notable begging him for a dollar to buy tea and a transistor battery for otherwise he would have had to sell a goat to raise the cash.

fort called al-Darayjah which the British regarded as being within Hawshabi territory and thus within the Protectorate. For more than a year negotiations and complaints succeeded one another but the Turks refused to leave. In July 1901 Hawshabi tribesmen attacked the fort but were repulsed and this time it was the turn of the Ottomans to protest. The British lost patience and in the same month a force of 500 men was sent to expel the invaders. British and Turkish regular troops fought a pitched battle which left the British masters of the fort.

Both sides started a race to collect those tribes which did not obviously belong to the other. The British entered into negotiations with the Rassassi Sultan of al-Baydha, taking some time to discover that he was insane, and concluded Friendship and Protection Treaties with Bayhan, the Shaibis, the Upper Aulaqis and some of the Upper Yafais. Simultaneously the Turks were active in Upper Yafa and in Amiri country where they established posts on Jabal Jihaf, in an area which was particularly sensitive as it contained numerous villages of uncertain allegiance. In order to remove the danger of further incidents, London and Constantinople agreed that the frontier should be delimited and a joint Commission assembled at Dhala in February 1902. At first progress was slow, for the Ottomans reiterated their claim to the whole of Arabia and denied the legal justification for any boundaries at all. Later they reduced their demands, merely demanding the cession of certain districts. The British argued that some 550 square miles of Hujariyyah were really Subayhi country and protested about systematic obstruction. Frequent reference to distant capitals meant that the actual survey did not start until March 1903. It had covered 150 miles from Bab al-Mandab to the Upper Yafai border when the party came under fire from the tribes and the Turks refused to continue. Even then their officials declined to sign the maps without express orders from the Sultan which were finally given, after a threat that the Royal Navy would be used to prevent Constantinople from sending any more troops to Arabia.

The British showed their determination to maintain their position on the frontier. Troops and a Political Officer had been stationed in Dhala since March 1903 and showed every sign of remaining in a place which gave healthy respite from the heat of Aden. An agreement of 1904 gave the Amir an extra $100 a month to pay 50 men to keep open the roads through his territory. However, the advent of a Liberal Government in London in December 1905 put an end to a forward policy which was absolutely opposed by the Secretary of State for India, John Morley. He refused to allow the building of a sanitorium in Dhala and brought back the Political Officer and the troops. In 1904 there had been bids for a concession to build a railway from Aden up to Dhala but this was viewed by Morley as a means of expansion and therefore vetoed: he even refused to allow a line to go as far as Lahej. He instructed Aden to "avoid like fire any intervention in the rows and quarrels of the gentry of the unruly hinterland" and again stated in 1909 that the British Government "do not propose under any circumstances that can be foreseen" to act beyond the territory of Aden. He ordered that no attempt should be made to disarm the tribes and that no punitive action should be taken for past breaches of the peace, and finally that there should be no fresh protectorate treaties. This meant an end to expansion on the frontier, although under his successor a "tidying-up" treaty was made with the Audhalis.

Relations with the Turks improved and, during the war of 1911 when the Italians blockaded the Yemeni coast, the Aden authorities permitted the passage of mail through Lahej. One of the most far-sighted officials in the Residency, Colonel Jacob, submitted a memorandum in May 1914 urging the need to prop up the Ottoman position in the Yemen, by helping to preserve their pact with the Imam and by mediating in their quarrels with the Idrisis of Asir who had achieved virtual independence. He even suggested that the Turks should accept the services of British officers to reorganise their administration, and he was himself prepared to resign his commission to undertake this task. This idea was too revolutionary for Whitehall and was anyway overtaken by the outbreak of war.

The events of the early years of the century set the seal upon the clash of 1873 and led to the situation as it is today. From this time onwards one could no longer use the word "Yemen" as a synonym for "South Western Arabia", for now two distinct entities went their separate ways and developed in very different fashions. The Yemen was definitely divided by a frontier which had international validity, although it was accepted reluctantly by the authorities in Sanaa, who never formally surrendered their claim to the whole. The southern portion based on Aden, which had occasional hopes of gaining some profitable areas from the north, was in general content with the situation.

Aden before the First World War

The period before 1914 was one of great prosperity and boom, particularly for the bunkering trade, which although Aden had to compete with Perim, amounted to 165,000 tons in 1891 and constantly increased. The foundations of the Port Trust in 1888 took the affairs of the harbour out of the hands of the officials and put them into those of the leading merchants, with a consequent increase in efficiency. A similar devolution of power led to the creation of the Aden Settlement Board in 1900, which had powers over building, water and electricity. Several schools were founded, both government and private, and a new class of educated Adeni Arabs started to emerge, although all skilled labour continued to be imported from India or the Far East.

The picture, however, was not entirely rosy. Brigadier General O'Moore Creagh, VC, the Resident from 1899 to 1900, wrote that "the swindling that went on was appalling" and that Aden was not really a free port because of the monopolies involved. He found the military equally bad for the fortifications had been neglected and guns could only be repaired in Bombay which meant that they were out of position for a year at a time. The political affairs of the hinterland, according to Creagh, were run by "an evil-looking rascal of mixed Arab and Persian origin" who blackmailed the chiefs and put in fraudulent expense claims. So low had the reputation of the Settlement fallen that when in 1899 the Viceroy, Lord Curzon learned that twenty soldiers of the Royal West Kents had publicly raped a Burmese woman, he ordered that the Battalion should spend two years in Aden: the *Contemporary Review* felt this "a disproportionate punishment".

There was still confusion in official minds as to the role of Aden. The military regarded it purely as a fortress and disliked the presence of a large native population within its walls. In order to move some of them out Shaykh Othman was bought from the Abdali Sultan in 1882 for $25,000 and an increase in his stipend. The Foreign Office, which had discovered during the events of 1873 the difficulties involved in dealing simultaneously with Constantinople and with Calcutta by means of the India Office, proposed that the control of Aden should be transferred to the Colonial Office to make communications easier. The India Office, although always pressing London to pay a higher proportion of the expenses of Aden, was unwilling to relinquish control, and successfully resisted the proposal at Cabinet level in 1874. The suggestion was discussed again in 1890 and 1901, but the question of who should pay always caused deadlock.

The Turks in the Yemen up to 1914

For twenty years after their reoccupation of Sanaa in 1871, the Ottoman authorities were fortunate in that the Imam of the Zaydis was a man of piety rather than of politics, content to perform his religious duties. The country was reasonably quiet, exhausted by a generation of anarchy. For a period the tribesmen, armed with their old *jezails*, felt themselves outclassed by the modern rifles of the Turkish army, which could also call upon machine-guns and field artillery less cumbersome than that of earlier campaigns. The authorities started to make better use of Arab auxiliaries, raising four Battalions from the hill tribes and using them for intelligence duties and tax gathering. Yemen was used as a place of exile for officers of suspect politics or dubious morals. Thus men of great ability were occasionally found in the garrisons, although others were almost comically corrupt: travellers told of escorts who had to be paid to go away and one Governor was said to make money out of selling promotions to ranks as low as that of Corporal.

Heavy smuggling of arms in the late 1880s put the tribesmen on more equal terms with the authorities and in 1891 a tax-gathering party from Luhayyah was ambushed and annihilated. The revolt spread quickly, with rumours that the whole of Asir had risen. These events coincided with the assumption of the Imamate by Muhammad ibn Yahya Hamid al-Din who took the name of al-Mansur Billah, in conscious echo of his ancestor Qasim who had started the sixteenth-century insurrection against the Turks. He quickly became the focus of a great surge of nationalist sentiment as he fled out of range of the Turks to the first Zaydi stronghold of Sada. Soon the whole country was in flames. In the highlands only Sanaa where 2,000 Turks resisted a tribal force of 6,000 for several months and Amran remained under Turkish control. Even the Shafai south came under the Imam and this enabled him to receive smuggled weapons from the Sultan of Lahej, to the great resentment of the Ottoman authorities who suspected there was connivance from Aden.

The Imam set out the cause of his revolt in terms which could have been exactly those of Qasim three hundred years earlier or of his son Yahya just over a decade later. "Officials were not giving Allah His due, nor respecting His laws nor those of the Prophets of Allah, but they have rather set up unto themselves a religion that was offensive to the sight of Allah and antagonistic to His laws, committing every kind of transgression and leading to the participation therein of those of our people who came in contact with them, violating Allah by drinking wine, obscene relations with males and every kind of fornication; they have oppressed the weak, insulted and degraded the noble, until posterity was corrupt, and the word of the Jews and the Christians rose high, and the Kurds and the Ethiopians ruled the people. They have discarded every regard for the faithful, and lost every feeling of benevolence and pity towards the Muslims." A thousand years after the arrival of the first Imam al-Hadi ila'l-Haqq, his descendant thus still proclaimed the complete symbiosis of Zaydi doctrine and Yemeni nationalism.

Constantinople appointed an exceptionally tough and ruthless Pasha, Ahmad Faizi, who offered money for rebel heads and gave his troops absolute freedom to sack and pillage. Three hundred villages were burned, and Sanaa was relieved by means of a march that astounded military opinion throughout the world: artillery was man-handled over roadless mountains which rose above 8,000 feet. The Imam retired to the north.

The Turks then began an attempt to apply the reforms that were being introduced throughout their Empire as it struggled to modernise itself. Secular schools were opened, regular government offices staffed by officials expected to wear European dress and other innovations that we shall mention below started to appear in Sanaa and other large centres. Most offensive of all to a conservative and religious-minded people was a new code of civil law based on western concepts, brought in to replace the old Shariah law which stemmed from the Prophet. In 1902 there was a series of risings which confined the Turks to Sanaa, the Tihamah and Hujariyyah, but they lacked leadership and co-ordination and fell apart, enabling the authorities to regain their grasp.

In 1904, however, a leader did appear. The Imam Muhammad was succeeded by his son Yahya, who was to be the dominant figure in the Yemen for over forty years. In the old tradition, a rival candidate demanded a theological duel, but Yahya, strong in the support of the Hashid tribe (from which his mother came) and the Bakil, could afford to ignore the challenge. He wasted no time in calling for a national revolt against the occupying forces and the most serious rising so far began.

In November 1904 the new Imam and about 15,000 tribal followers started to besiege Sanaa, aided by captured artillery that was exceptionally dangerous because it was so inaccurate. About 3,000 fresh Turkish troops arrived at Hodeidah and fought their way up to Sanaa, but there they could do no more than join those already locked up inside. The Turks starved: they were reduced to eating dogs and cats and a horse fetched $400 as meat. There was a fear that the revolt might spread throughout Turkish Arabia and the situation was so desperate that for once Constantinople reacted quickly. From all over the Empire, from Albania to Kurdistan, troops were mobilised, ships were hired from Odessa and Marseilles, and by April it was estimated that there were 50,000 regulars in the Yemen. In the meanwhile a garrison of 1,200 at Hajjah had been starved into surrender, Ibb, Qataba and Yarim had fallen and the forces of the Imam had again reached the boundaries of the Aden Protectorate, enabling the Sultan of Lahej to send in arms and even a machine for minting coins. At the end of April Sanaa itself surrendered to Yahya, who gave a safe conduct to officials and their families.

The Turks continued to build up their army and the veteran Ahmad Faizi Pasha, now aged about 75, travelled by night and day across Arabia to take command. In June it was estimated that the Turks had lost 20,000 men since the start of the rising and that their forces had grown to over 80,000 rifles, 500 sabres and 15 Batteries; 3,000 local camels were acquired and 3,000 mules brought in from Anatolia. In August Ahmad Faizi advanced on Sanaa, which he occupied without resistance because the Imam had the difficulty which has beset so many leaders of Yemeni tribal forces – in the moment of victory his men had dispersed homewards to enjoy their loot. Yahya retired to the mountains of Shaharah with the Turks in pursuit, but he had enough strength left to inflict a bloody defeat upon them. After that the war took on a desultory character: the Turks were unable to concentrate an army sufficient to overcome him because so many of their men were scattered in garrisons. In 1909 Yahya managed to capture the Marib area and early in 1911 he mounted another siege of Sanaa which held out for two months before relief arrived.

Simultaneously with the fighting continued spasmodic negotiations, as successive Pashas alternated harsh measures with attempts at conciliation. The Imam still regarded the Ottoman Sultan as responsible for the defence and foreign policy of the Islamic world as a whole, and was prepared to leave these matters in his hands, but at the same time denied his right to intervene in the religious affairs of the Zaydi community. The Imam demanded that justice should be done according to the Shariah, that he himself should appoint the judges and administer the *awqaf* (funds for religious purposes) and that only those taxes sanctioned by the Qur'an should be collected.

In 1911 after the second siege of Sanaa, threatened by the Italian seizure of Tripoli and the outbreak of new wars in the Balkans, the Turks were so anxious to remove troops from the Yemen that they accepted the Imam's claims. Under the Treaty of Da'an the country was effectively divided; the Imam controlled the highlands as far south as Taizz, and the Turks continued to administer the Tihamah. In his zone the Imam was supreme in legal matters, while the more mundane work of government was left to the Ottomans: he also received £30,000 a year which was the first charge upon the revenues of the country. This agreement, contained in an Imperial *Firman* proclaimed in Sanaa in September 1913 amidst great rejoicings, worked surprisingly well. As time went on the Imam started to increase his influence in the political sphere and he was sufficiently satisfied to remain loyal to the Turks throughout the war, despite British efforts to purchase his allegiance. Indeed, he welcomed the Ottoman presence as a guarantee against his own turbulent subjects, and in 1919 he made the most determined efforts to force them to remain.

One historian has calculated that in forty years of Turkish occupation nearly half a million men died on each side. Despite this there was very considerable material progress in the major centres, the effects of which spread out some way into the countryside. The Turks were always warriors rather than tradesmen, and they allowed much of the commerce of the country to pass into the hands of foreign merchants. By 1900 there were 100 resident Europeans in Hodeidah, which boasted a water condenser, an ice factory and stone jetties. Postal and telegraph services linked it with the main centres of the Yemen and with the rest of the world and in a further bid to improve communications a railway to Sanaa was projected, which would have cut the length of journey from six days by camel to less than one. In October 1909 a survey party reported that it would cost about £2 million and in May 1911 the first sod was cut. Another line linking Hodeidah with Taizz and Dhamar was also approved but neither plan was ever to get very far. In addition to the shortage of money there was a great lack of security even in the neighbourhood of Hodeidah, and the original survey party had to be protected by an escort of 850 armed men. A German traveller and an Italian vice-consul were murdered in a deliberate attempt to embarrass the authorities; the Zaraniq, the most warlike tribe of the Tihamah, charged a Turkish Battalion £1 a head for permission to pass through their territory in 1913.

Sanaa itself was greatly modernised under the occupation. Carriages appeared in the streets, Turkish officers wobbled on bicycles, a band gave concerts and a weekly newspaper was published. In 1888 two Italian brothers opened a firm and by the end of the century Greeks ran cafés and shops which sold goods from western Europe. The Turks started an industrial school where Arab boys could learn a trade, a military school and two more schools for civilians where education was free. They built a modern hospital and a pharmacy. An American missionary who had travelled widely regarded Sanaa as next to Baghdad the most flourishing city of all Arabia: indeed it reminded him of Cairo and was clearly as advanced as the majority of towns in the Balkans or Eastern Europe. The fact that the Sanaa of the 1950s seemed a museum piece was not the result of centuries of neglect but of a conscious decision by its subsequent rulers to hold the twentieth century at bay.

South Western Arabia in the First World War

From the beginning of the century it was becoming increasingly apparent that there would one day be war between Great Britain and Imperial Germany, and that when this happened Constantinople would follow the leadership of Berlin. For years before the outbreak of war, far-sighted men like the archaeologist Hogarth were building intelligence networks in Turkish Syria; several months before the declaration a force was organised to invade Mesopotamia and troops moved to protect the Suez Canal against possible attack. Only in South Western Arabia did the British authorities make no serious preparations for war and no one seems to have foreseen that the Turks might cross the frontier. Whitehall and Simla were too busy to pay much attention to a distant outpost. On the spot first a sick and then an incompetent Resident remained supine.

The Turks were known to have about 14,000 men in the Yemen but only a third of these could be spared from garrison duties; the number of men in the Aden fortress was slightly less. To defend the frontier the British would have had to move a strong force to Dhala, and they lacked both the men and the mobile artillery to do this, leaving the responsibility instead to the Sultan of Lahej, who was given rifles, ammunition and encouragement to enlist mercenaries from the fighting Aulaqi tribes.

Intelligence gathering across the frontier was also left to the Sultan and clearly the British knew little of what was happening in Sanaa or Taizz. Some authorities argued that the Imam, as a friend of the Abdali, would prevent any invasion of his territory while others thought that the Turks would not dare to move out any troops for fear that he might revolt: a third school believed that he could be made into an ally by a promise to recognise him as independent sovereign of the Zaydi areas. In the event he made no secret of his intention of remaining loyal to his pact with the Turks.

A few days after the outbreak of war the Imperial authorities decided to take advantage of the fact that an Indian Brigade was passing up the Red Sea en route for Egypt, and used this force to attack the Turkish position at Shaykh Said which menaced the island of Perim, so important for its coaling and cable facilities. Forts were captured and destroyed and promptly reoccupied and rebuilt. The Aden authorities had not been consulted and indeed condemned the operation as folly in that it achieved nothing beyond alienating the Imam who resented what he saw as an act of aggression against his territory. Early in the New Year he expressed his annoyance by attacking the town of al-Baydha, which Aden regarded as being within the Protectorate and saved by the timely despatch of rifles and ammunition.

In the spring regular Turkish troops crossed into Dhala and occupied Jabal Jihaf where they remained stationary. A month later the Viceroy thought that they would go no further, Whitehall wondered if it might be possible to spare part of the Aden garrison for operations in Somaliland while the Sultan of Lahej disbanded some of his mercenaries. In fact the Turkish commander, Ali Said Pasha, a most accomplished soldier and diplomat, used the time to win the allegiance of the Hawshabi Sultan, to enlist irregulars from amongst the Yafai and Subayhi tribes and to attempt to subvert the Fadhlis and the Hadhramis.

The terrain and the need to stay within reach of water meant that the Turks could only advance along Wadi Tuban, but no attempt was made to fortify any of its defiles. On 1 July 1915 the Turks moved into Hawshabi country and two days later they brushed aside in an hour without casualties the Abdali forces from a position that the Sultan had promised to hold for two days. The same evening the Aden Moveable Column of about 1,000 men set out to encounter them across thirty miles of trackless desert. The collapse of the Lahejis necessitated a forced march and the men of the young Welsh Territorial Battalion and even the Indian troops were unable to stand the over-powering heat. Many died in the sands and those who managed to reach Lahej were in little condition to fight. Their equipment, including water and ammunition, was carried on camels led by Subayhi tribesmen, who gleefully deserted with their loads, happy to take revenge on the Abdali Sultan. There was a night of confused hand-to-hand fighting in Lahej after which the British, fearing encirclement, staggered back to safety. They had lost all their equipment and machine guns, and some of their artillery. More than 50 were killed in the fighting while another 30 perished from heatstroke, and many more were permanently invalided. Amongst the casualties was the Sultan of Lahej, who had been mistaken for a Turk and killed by an Indian soldier.

The enemy were too exhausted to attempt a pursuit, but so complete was the rout that there was no attempt to defend Shaykh Othman, despite the importance of its wells and the fact that guns installed there could dominate the harbour. Aden itself bristled with heavy guns but as they all pointed seawards they were of no help in the crisis. There was no serious possibility that the Turks could have captured Aden, as they would have had to cross the Isthmus in the teeth of ship-borne gunfire before assaulting the mighty fortifications. However, there is little doubt that the British officials panicked, talking of a last-ditch defence of Steamer Point. The Resident, who had already made enemies, was chosen as scapegoat and summarily replaced, while the authorities in India hastened to put on record that they had never agreed to a sortie outside the fortress area. A tough, cool General, Sir George Younghusband, was summoned from Egypt with the alarming news that "The Turks are on the golf-course" to bring reinforcements and restore morale.

Younghusband succeeded in his objectives. A few days after his arrival he carried out a counter-attack which bundled the Turks out of Shaykh Othman. He proceeded to turn the town into a fortress. It was surrounded by a perimeter fence manned by pickets and posts were created in an arc reaching round to the Abyan beach, keeping the Settlement out of artillery range. The Turks located their headquarters in Lahej and guarded it by a similar arc of strong points. Between the two lines was a belt of about six miles of no-man's-land into which both sides sent patrols, laid ambushes and moved forward their guns for brief bombardments. This stalemate, with about 1,800 British and 5,200 Indians on one side and 2,500 Turks with a varying number of irregulars on the other, continued for over three years. The British objective was to keep the Turks so occupied that they did not have leisure to interfere with the rest of the Protectorate, while Ali Said Pasha sought to keep up an impressive façade which would deter a major British attack or a revolt in his rear.

Life in Aden continued in a surprisingly normal fashion, despite the presence of a besieging army less than twenty miles away. Prices rose, but wages grew even more quickly. Over 1,600 vessels a year entered the harbour and from the hinterland came a daily average of 200 camels, bringing fruit, vegetables and firewood from the enemy-occupied zone, returning laden with kerosene, rice, sugar and occasionally whisky for the Turkish officers. Both sides collected customs duties on these transactions. The British soldiers had an easy life compared with their brothers in the trenches of Flanders or in the mountains behind Salonica, and the Turks, completely cut off from their homeland after the Arab Revolt of June 1916, responded to the leadership of Ali Said Pasha by keeping their morale until the end. No military supplies ever reached them and all that Constantinople knew of their activities was what was published in the British press.

Younghusband's original instructions were to reoccupy Lahej immediately, but he argued that it would be unwise to attempt another venture across the desert in the heat of summer. Reluctantly the Government of India accepted his view, although they were acutely conscious of the damage to British prestige all over Arabia caused by the failure of the protection promised to the Abdalis. They continued to press for an advance but London stubbornly refused to make any more troops available. The authorities in Aden urged that the opportunity should be taken to advance to Taizz, establish a protectorate over the whole of Hujariyyah and build a railway linking Aden, Taizz and Hodeidah. Their view was that, as Colonel Jacob minuted, "this fertile area should properly be ours". The India Office supported the suggestion, but the War Office declined to provide the two Divisions that would have been required.

In advocating this large-scale annexation of territory, the Aden authorities expressed their conviction that if the Turks were expelled from the area, the Shafai population would welcome British rather than Zaydi rule. They observed that although the Imam did practically nothing to help the Ottoman government, he refused to take any effective action against it. Unable to drive the Turks from the Protectorate by force, the British hoped to stir up rebellion behind Ali Said's army and opened negotiations with potential trouble-makers. The most obvious of these was Sayyid Muhammad Ali al-Idrisi, who had turned the vague spiritual overlordship of his family in Asir into something resembling an independent and organised state. He had led several uprisings against the Turks before the war and preceded the Sharif of Mecca in making an alliance with the British in the hope of adding the Pashalik of Yemen to his domains. Aden had at first hoped that it might be possible to persuade him and the Imam to make common cause against the Turks, but it was clearly impossible to reconcile their ambitions and a choice had to be made. In view of the inactivity of the Imam and of British aspirations in Hujariyyah it was natural to prefer the Idrisi so in March 1917 Aden was authorised to make him a monthly subsidy of £7,000[1] to hire tribesmen to fight the Turks with the unenforceable proviso that he would not use them to pursue his private quarrel with Yahya.

The Idrisi managed to build what Aden called the "Confederacy", paying leaders of the Hashid and Bakil tribes and notables opposed to the Imam on personal or political grounds. As usual there was disagreement between Whitehall

---

[1] This sum shows that considerable importance was attached to the Idrisi for Ibn Saud was receiving merely £5,000 a month.

and Delhi as to what action was required: India considered that if the Confederacy were supported but failed, the Imam would be alienated for all time while London argued that if the Confederacy succeeded and had not been helped, the British would have no friends and moreover there was a possibility that the Idrisi might turn to the Italians for aid. The Imam did not advance his cause by sending an arrogant letter to Aden in July 1917, demanding that all Southern Arabia except Aden should be handed over to him, that the Idrisi should be removed from power and that the British should have no contact with anyone in the Yemen except himself. In exasperation Aden discussed the possibility of sponsoring a rival Imam but finally the opinion prevailed that "Yemen appears to be working up for a general internecine struggle and we should wait and see who emerges *de facto* winner"; the Confederacy should be given "just enough encouragement to prevent collapse" for there was no point in assisting the Idrisi to expand his territory at the expense of the Imam, who might possibly prove a friend once the Turks had been expelled.

Between September 1917 and February 1918 there was a series of skirmishes in which the British lost nearly 300 men without making any progress. The war as a whole was in a most critical state, because the collapse of Czarist Russia had freed more German Divisions for an offensive in France, Italy was in disarray and the Turks were holding more firmly in Syria and Mesopotamia. It was therefore decided at a conference in Cairo, under the chairmanship of the High Commissioner Sir Reginald Wingate, to make another attempt to win over the Imam, if necessary at the expense of the Idrisi, who appeared to be doing little to earn his subsidies. The Resident was instructed to write to Yahya offering to ensure his supremacy in Yemen, to give him arms, a subsidy equal to that which he had received from the Turks and a port so that he should have independent access to the sea. The Imam replied in May with a list of twelve demands which mostly repeated those of the previous July, except that he apparently envisaged that the Sultan of Lahej should be permitted to deal directly with the Aden government. He would require, he wrote, ammunition, a subsidy, armourers, a guarantee of no British interference in the Yemen and the prohibition of "the import of spirituous liquors, wanton pastimes and all munitions except those intended for his own use". By this time the whole situation of the war had changed. The Allies were clearly heading for victory and could afford to attach little value to the support of the Imam. Wingate therefore ordered that a temporising reply should be sent.

The spring and early summer of 1918 were quiet on the Aden front and in August *The Times* printed the first communiqué for six months with the heading "A Forgotten Corner of the War". A couple of actions in October, however, showed that the Turks were still well-equipped and supplied with ammunition and fighting as resolutely as ever. More serious than the fighting, though, was the influenza epidemic which cost the British 176 men in November alone.

Although the Ottoman Empire signed an armistice with the Allies on 30 October, Ali Said Pasha refused to surrender without direct orders from Constantinople, which he did not receive until early in December. He then came into Aden to a hero's welcome, bringing 174 officers, 2,481 men, 221 irregulars and 159 women and children. For the British authorities his departure from South West Arabia merely substituted a new set of problems.

Chapter Four

Aden and the Hinterland 1919–1959

The Imam tries to reunite the Yemen

The events of the war left the British and the Imam Yahya deeply divided by mutual suspicion. The British felt that by not assisting them against the Turks, Yahya had failed in his moral duty and they were convinced that he had designs upon the Protectorate. The Imam naturally remembered the British intrigues with the Confederacy, resented their preference for the upstart Idrisi and feared that they would encourage the pretensions of their ally the Sharif of Mecca to set himself up as the King of all the Arabs. He was angry, too, at the British occupation of Kamaran and other islands which he claimed as part of the Yemen.

The first actions by both sides did nothing to decrease their hostility. Yahya did all that he could to obstruct the evacuation of Turkish forces for which the Armistice provided, claiming that they had outstanding debts which should be settled before leaving, although his real object was to persuade as many as possible to stay to serve him as soldiers and as administrators. The British warned him that "future territorial benefits will depend upon his course of action", but he merely issued a formal order forbidding the surrender of Ottoman regiments. When they did move from such places as Dhala, Upper Yafa and Hawshabi, Yahya replaced them with his own men.

The British felt that they needed a base in the Yemen from which to enforce the evacuation of the Turks and also to secure the return of civilian internees which included 12 Englishmen, 160 Indians and some Greeks. There were other considerations too: throughout the war the Foreign Office and its officials in Cairo were haunted by the belief that its Italian allies, who already controlled nearly 500 miles of the south-western shore of the Red Sea, had designs upon the eastern coast which it was imperative to forestall. Finally, a British position in a port such as Hodeidah, cutting the Imam off from the outside world, might provide the cheapest and easiest way of compelling his withdrawal from the Protectorate.

For these reasons, therefore, in December 1918, after brushing aside limited resistance from the Turkish forces, British troops occupied Hodeidah and fought off an attempt to expel them. The Imam wrote to King George V protesting at the seizure of territory which he claimed had been owned by his ancestors for over 1,000 years, and he wrote also to the French, American and Italian governments. Nevertheless, in March 1919 the British authorities in Cairo discussed the possiblity that Hodeidah should be kept permanently, and they considered the possibility of replacing Yahya with another Imam. Aden on the other hand recommended that Yahya should be supported and given Hodeidah, and that Salif with its valuable salt industry should be retained instead. After a prolonged policy debate the traditional view of the Government of India prevailed: "What we want is not a united Arabia but a weak and disunited Arabia split into little principalities as far as possible under our suzerainty – but incapable of co-ordinated action against us, forming a buffer against the powers in the West." It was decided that, apart from some minor frontier adjustments in the Protectorate, no further Arab territory should be annexed and that the Imam and the Idrisi should be reconciled and numbered amongst Britain's other Arab satellites. Colonel Jacob was instructed to go to Sanaa to tell Yahya what was expected of him.

Although two of the objectives for the British occupation were soon achieved – the detainees were released and some 10,000 Turkish troops left the Yemen and Asir – a new reason for remaining arose. The rivalry between the Imam and the Idrisi led to a race to secure the allegiance of the areas once directly ruled by the Turks and in this the Idrisi, as a Shafai, was the more favoured. By mid-1919 he had collected hostages from most of the tribes of the Tihamah. The Imam also moved down from his mountains and occupied Zabid, making it clear that the contestants would fight for possession of the country's main port. The people of Hodeidah themselves wanted neither the Imam nor the Idrisi, and petitioned for the return of the Turks, an Egyptian ruler or even permanent British occupation.

In the summer of 1919 the tribes, desperate to capture arms to resist the Imam, twice attacked Hodeidah, suffering about a hundred casualties. So fearful were they that Colonel Jacob was going to Sanaa to urge Yahya to take them over that they detained his mission at Bajil about thirty miles inland from Hodeidah, holding it from August until December. A threatening overflight by the RAF, the first time that aircraft were used for police purposes in Southern Arabia, produced sporting targets for marksmen rather than instilling fear. The Imam's attempts to secure the release of Jacob's mission were rebuffed, and it was the Political Officer in Hodeidah who eventually freed the party in return for a ransom. The impotence and unpopularity of the Imam in the area had been made manifest, so when a year later it was decided to evacuate Hodeidah, a representative of the Idrisi was allowed to take possession. Naturally this sequence of events since the war had deepened the Imam's hostility towards the British.

On occasions Yemeni troops looted villages near Lahej and when, in an attempt to prevent this, the British established a post at Nawbat Dukaym where the three main roads from Dhala, Mawiyah and Taizz converge, it came under fire. A further case of worry was the news of French and Italian interest in the Yemen, which was shown by a series of visits by traders and concession seekers. The British therefore decided to make another attempt to reach a settlement with the Imam. They offered to recognise his sovereignty over Lahej and Hadhramawt as well as the Yemen, a subsidy, arms, help to develop ports and railways and mediation in any disputes that he might have with Britain's other friends, provided that he did not have dealings with any other power. He would also keep much of the territory within the Protectorate that he was then occupying. He accepted presents, including a Ford motor car and welcomed Jacob, although he declined to allow a permanent envoy to reside in Sanaa. After nearly a year of negotiations he hinted that he might agree with most of what the British offered. He stipulated, however, that a Treaty must include a promise to protect him against any attack by a European or Arab state – a commitment that the military authorities in London were unwilling to undertake.

During these proceedings it was learned that Yahya was intriguing in Bayhan, Yafai and Qutaybi country, but Whitehall decided to overlook this for the sake of obtaining a Treaty. In November 1923 the Imam's envoy said that all British treaties in Southern Arabia were invalid, as they had been concluded either with the Turks, who were usurpers, or with tribal chiefs who, as Yemeni subjects, were not independent powers. Although he would forego his claim to Aden itself, Yahya insisted that he should appoint the judges throughout the Protectorate, nominate an overseer of revenue in each Shaykhdom and settle tribal quarrels, although he was prepared to confirm existing chiefs in office subject to their good behaviour. At the same time the Imam's forces, under Sayyid Abdullah al-Wazir, moved across the disputed border to occupy al-Baydha and the Audhali Sultanate. The British reacted by distributing arms to loyal tribesmen and by building an airstrip near Shuqra from which they could operate against the invaders.

This pattern of clashes and simultaneous discussion continued throughout 1924 and part of 1925. In July 1924, the Imam was troubled by tribal revolts; although he did not withdraw his claim to sovereignty, he offered to share influence over the coastal states while he would continue to occupy the northern part of the Protectorate. In February 1925 there was heavy fighting around al-Baydha; it was reported that 800 Yafais armed by the British and 400 Yemenis had been killed in a battle in which the RAF had participated. In March the Upper Aulaqi Sultan called for help, claiming that the Yemenis were fighting unfairly by ignoring guerrilla tactics and merely "rushing like hungry dogs, shouting for revenge and using the name of the Imam Yahya as their battle slogan. They all fire at once and never stop until their objective is reached, utterly unmindful of the loss of life". The Audhalis evacuated their women and children to Aden, and even Lahej seemed in such danger that the Sultan brought his family into Crater. In a move to stabilise the situation a Squadron of bombers was sent to Aden and was frequently in action. However, in November

1925 the Foreign Office admitted that these strikes had "not proved entirely successful and HMG are anxious to use every effort to establish permanent conditions in the hinterland without recourse to armed force".

In the meanwhile the Imam had driven the Idrisi from Hodeidah. Whitehall, worried about a dramatic increase in Italian influence, decided to send its greatest expert on Arab affairs in another attempt to make a settlement with the Imam. Sir Gilbert Clayton arrived in Sanaa in January 1926 and although he established cordial personal relations with Yahya, no progress could be made. Nothing could remove the difficulty that the British wished to discuss the details of a frontier which Yahya considered did not exist: to the British "Yemen" meant that area which had been ruled by the Turks, while to Yahya the word indicated all that had ever been under the sway of his Himyarite ancestors. He rested his case on the invalidity of all the Treaties concluded by the British, adding for good measure that they had been obtained through bribery, and intimidation.

Clayton was left with the impression that although the Imam himself might have made an agreement, he was unable to convince some of the more xenophobic notables: the situation remained unchanged. In July 1927, in response to an attack in the House of Lords on Britain's "ignominious position", a government spokesman had to admit that it was "unsatisfactory from almost every point of view". The Yemenis were occupying the whole of Amiri, Qutaybi, Alawi and Shaibi country, half of Audhali and tracts of Upper Yafa and Subayhi, where their men had penetrated within forty miles of Aden. The War Office calculated glumly that it would take an entire Division of 15,000 men and an expenditure of a million pounds to drive them back over the frontier. However, in the autumn of 1927 the Air Ministry claimed that the RAF could perform the task infinitely more cheaply, and the Cabinet decided to give it the chance.

Within a matter of months the RAF had its opportunity. The Imam's commander at Qatabah arrested or kidnapped two Protectorate notables and ignored a demand for their release. The Yemenis were presented with an ultimatum, and, after 48 hours' warning, Qatabah was bombed on five occasions in

March. The Imam asked for a truce. The truce was accorded, and eventually extended until June, when his request for a prolongation was refused and a new ultimatum issued. For a fortnight there was a series of raids, including one on Taizz, and then Yahya gave way. The Shaykhs were released and all Yemeni troops withdrawn from Dhala. Jacob condemned the bombing as "ignorance in action". It had been hoped to split the Imam from his Shafai subjects, as British officials trained in India where the difference between Sunni and Shi'i was more marked, tended to exaggerate the difference between Zaydi and Shafai. In the event, the British action served to unite the two groups in apprehension of annexation. However, the Chief of the Air Staff, Trenchard, pointed out that the Yemenis had been expelled from much of the Protectorate without a single British casualty at a total cost of £8,567. When there was criticism of the method employed, an Under Secretary assured members of the House of Lords that "the bombing was done in the most humane way possible".

The question then arose of repeating this type of military action, in order to secure the evacuation of Audhali country, where the Sultan called for help to liberate the higher part of his territory. Whitehall, by then under a Labour government, decided that ground operations would be useless without bombing, but as the government felt that this would antagonise the League of Nations, it continued with vague negotiations.

There was some sympathy for the Imam on the part of the British. A former Governor of Bombay said that he had legitimate grievances, particularly over Hodeidah, and that he had been "treated rather as a naughty schoolboy". A former Minister referred to him as "a very enlightened chief who wishes to open trade with us", and suggested that he might possess oil. Visitors to Sanaa, such as the American-Syrian writer Amin Rihani and Colonel Jacob, reported that the Imam would like peace, but he feared that to conclude a formal Treaty would so enflame public opinion that his throne would be endangered. He was said to be ready to accept an independent Protectorate, provided that he could appoint the judges and that appeals should be heard in his Shariah courts – a thing which often occurred in practice. In return he would be prepared to conduct all his trade with Britain, despite tempting offers from

Italy, Russia and America. In July 1930 the Colonial Secretary said that relations with the Imam were extremely friendly, but that he showed no readiness to make a Treaty based on mutual recognition of sovereign rights – the only basis acceptable to London.

In the early 1930s there were occasional Yemeni forays across the frontier which were usually ended by the threat of bombing: later it was suggested that these forays were the actions of unruly tribesmen or incompetent officials rather than deliberate policy. By the spring of 1933 Yahya foresaw the strong possibility of war with Saudi Arabia, and he decided to end the trouble on his southern flank. Writing that he was confident of the Chief Commissioner, Colonel Reilly's "humane and excellent qualities, perfection and high learning", he invited him to Sanaa and accepted as a precondition that he should evacuate Audhali and release the forty youths of notable families held hostage at al-Baydha. Whitehall suggested that Reilly should demand a permanent representative at Sanaa but accepted his advice that the Italians would want the same privilege: for the same reason he decided not to press the RAF request for airfields at Sanaa or Hodeidah.

After six weeks of discussion the Treaty of Sanaa was concluded in February 1934 and recognised the *status quo*. Britain saluted the Imam as King, which was a significant raising of his status, and dropped its claim to al-Baydha while Yahya tacitly accepted the Anglo-Turkish line of 1905, although in his own mind he was merely allowing HMG to administer what he still regarded as his own. In deference to his old claims there was to be no further demarcation, and no boundary pillars were erected. It was decided that the settlement should last for forty years and then be discussed again. Each side appointed a Frontier Officer empowered to settle minor matters on the spot.

Some weeks later Colonel Lake, Secretary for the Protectorate, went to Sanaa to exchange ratifications. He reported that he was received at Hodeidah by the Port Governor (formerly barber to the Imam) and escorted into the capital by cavalry to the strains of a band playing "Pop goes the weasel". This marked the real end of Yahya's thirty-year campaign to reunite the southern lands once ruled by his ancestors although he never abandoned the dream of doing so: a period of generally peaceful coexistence was ushered in.

Aden and its political development

It took nearly twenty years after the First World War to determine the constitutional position of Aden. In July 1917, while leaving administrative affairs under the control of Bombay, London took charge of military and political matters; the direction of the campaign was given to the War Office and the Foreign Office, through its High Commissioner in Egypt, dealt with political questions. The Viceroy "agreed gladly to the transfer of Aden and the Hadhramawt to the London Foreign Office"; the India Office merely commented that as Aden was part of British India it would presumably have to be disannexed. However, there was a feeling in Whitehall, particularly among the armed services, that administration of territory was not an art in which the Foreign Office was skilled. It was suggested that Aden could be formed into a single unit with British Somaliland, and that the responsibility for it should be handed over to the Colonial Office. At the time indeed, the Colonial Secretary, Winston Churchill, was gathering all Middle Eastern affairs under a single umbrella and even the Prime Minister, Lloyd George, thought that he had taken over Aden. Eventually it was decided that the Colonial Office should only control the hinterland, while all that concerned the Settlement of 75 square miles should once again be dealt with by the government of Bombay.

This situation was obviously extremely confused and unsatisfactory. It resulted, as Colonel Jacob said, in an administration that was "apathetic and fifty years behind the times". Periodic questions in Parliament merely produced the answer that the matter was still under consideration. It was not until the spring of 1927 that yet another compromise emerged, under which Bombay still administered the Settlement while all its political and military affairs were taken over by Whitehall. The Government of India, not that of Bombay, was to contribute £250,000 a year and one-third of the political and military expenses up to a maximum of £150,000. A baffled MP

73

inquired as to the advantages of dual control by London and Delhi but was apparently satisfied by the answer that "It is necessitated by the local circumstances." It was further agreed that the Colonial Office and India should alternately nominate the Resident – the Treasury having decreed that to appoint a Governor at an annual salary of £2,775 "appears to throw a needlessly heavy charge upon the tax-payer": a Resident was £500 cheaper. There was certainly no excess of European officials for in 1930, outside the Secretariat, there were only the Chairman of the Port Trust, the Judicial Adviser and the Chief of Police.

Economy continued a main preoccupation of Whitehall and when in 1928 the newly appointed Resident complained that the furniture in Government House was hired from a local firm and that he needed some heavy glass and china-ware as the strong winds often swept his dining table bare, he found himself engaged in a protracted correspondence. Finally, having satisfied itself that the local insects would not eat an oak table, Whitehall authorised the expenditure of £120. Eighteen months later, after weighty deliberation, the Treasury agreed to the monthly sum of 5 rupees for a sweeper at Perim lighthouse and another 30 rupees for the purchase of disinfectants.

In 1932 this unwieldy administrative structure was simplified: Bombay ceased to play a part in any but judicial matters, and the administration was placed directly under Delhi. The Resident, Colonel Reilly, changed his style to that of Chief Commissioner but this was clearly only a temporary measure, for it was becoming ever more evident that, with increasing intervention in the Protectorate, it was impossible to separate Aden from its Hinterland. The possible future independence of India was being discussed and Whitehall wished to have undivided control over so important a base – a view which was shared by the Service Ministries despite the extra expense that it would involve. The Colonial Office supported the demand of the Arab population of the Settlement that they should not be ruled by an Indian government presumably dominated by Hindus. The Indian community, on the other hand, opposed any change, and as early as 1922 an MP had said that "the Colonial Office stinks in the nostrils of the people of India." The Central Legislature of India unanimously condemned the severance of Aden, while a distinguished Parsee presented a Memorandum that Indians had been in Aden long before the British and that its prosperity had been built largely by their efforts. He argued that Somaliland had been ruined by its transfer to the Colonial Office, merchants had left and Indian administrators replaced by expatriate Britons at double the salary. Indian fears were calmed, however, partly by the provision that legal appeals should still be heard in Bombay and partly by a declaration that "no racial legislation or segregation would be permitted". Various administrative details had to be cleared up – Reilly was concerned that there were not enough local lunatics to justify an asylum and persuaded India to continue to take them on repayment – and then in 1937 all control passed to the Colonial Office with Reilly as Governor. His instructions forbade him to make Ordinances for divorce, currency, import or export duties or additional taxation, interfere with military discipline or make any regulation involving racial discrimination. He was given an Executive Council whose advice he was expected to take although he could overrule it provided that he reported the matter to the Secretary of State: he alone decided which matters it should discuss.

Formal control from India thus ended after nearly a century, but its influence was to linger on through officers and clerks trained in its traditions. In 1839 Aden had been one amongst hundreds of tumble-down fishing villages on the shores of Arabia, but by 1939 it was perhaps the most flourishing town in the Peninsula, although, as a distant outpost, it had never attracted much solicitude, and even less investment, from the Government of India. Its success was due to the efforts of individual officers and merchants from the sub-continent; that success had, however, been purchased at the cost of separating it completely from those parts of the old Himyaritic state which were still under the Imam. Aden's way of life and of thought had altered, and even its local dialect, with English and Hindustani words taking strange Arab forms, was totally different and almost unintelligible to citizens of Sanaa or Taizz. Despite the increasing participation of Arabs in its commercial and political development, these divergences were to be enhanced rather than diminished.

The war prevented any further constitutional advance, but

in 1945 the old Settlement authority was replaced by the two townships of Fortress and Shaykh Othman, run by Boards appointed by the Governor. They collected taxes on property, *qat*, and vehicle and building licences which they made over to the Colonial government, which in turn was responsible for water and electricity and made other funds available for amenities. In January 1947 a Legislative Council was inaugurated with all its members nominated by the Governor: four held seats *ex-officio*, and there were four other officials and four non-official members representing various interests but not employed by the Crown. The same year saw the end of the last formal link with India, when appeal cases were transferred from Bombay to the East African Court at Nairobi. Nevertheless, rupees continued to be the currency until 1951.

In 1949 elections were held in Aden for the first time. The composition of the Fortress Township Authority was changed to consist of four nominated officials, three nominated unofficial and three elected members. Candidates had to be British subjects, although voters could be of Adeni or British birth with two years' residence or of foreign birth with five years' residence, and had also to meet certain financial qualifications. Thus the electorate was very small: only 5,000 out of an estimated population of 70,000 possessed the franchise. However even so limited a measure transformed the situation: politics had come to Aden.

There had never been any evidence of serious discontent with British rule before December 1947, but in that month a three-day general strike was called to protest against what was regarded as a pro-Zionist policy in Palestine. A state of emergency had to be declared, the Fortress Commander took over responsibility for security and after locally raised troops had proved to be of uncertain loyalty, Royal Naval parties were landed. Aden saw its first bomb and in the riots 33 Arabs, 4 Indian Muslims, 1 Somali, 78 Jews and 6 unidentified people were killed. The official *Annual Report* stated that it was not until February that the situation returned to normal.

After this, anti-British sentiment was often expressed in the myriad private clubs where Adenis used to spend almost all of every afternoon chewing *qat* and gossiping with their friends. Amongst the more physically active some football and sporting clubs took on nationalistic colours, but the prospect of elections meant the formation of organised political parties. In the early 1950s three such groups with distinct policies could be identified. The Aden Association, which was led by the Luqman family and published its own newspaper, called for the eventual independence of Aden within the Commonwealth through co-operation with the British: it numbered long-resident Indians and Somalis amongst its members. Secondly, the South Arabian League (SAL) advocated union between Aden and the Protectorates to form an independent state which the Sultan of Lahej, the party's principal backer, aspired to rule. The third group was the more radical United National Front (UNF), which demanded union with Yemen, Muscat and the Protectorates as a republic.

A more effective force than these groups, which were little more than debating societies, was about to emerge. Sir Tom Hickinbotham, Governor of Aden from 1951 to 1956, wrote that in the 1930s the condition of Arab labourers was "disgraceful": coolies were herded into sheds with only the sea for washroom and lavatory and with no hope of holidays or social benefits. Workers were, however, so anxious to keep what jobs they had that there was no serious unrest amongst them until 1948, when employees in the Port went on strike to obtain wage increases similar to those given to Government staff and rendered absolutely necessary through post-war inflation. The harbour was paralysed and it became clear that there was no machinery for dealing with such problems. Therefore in 1949 the Government created a Labour and Welfare Department and a Labour Advisory Board: neither of these had any formal representatives of the workers for none existed. The *Annual Report* for 1951 and 1952 commented that they had "no conception of labour organization or of collective bargaining" and that there was only one Trade Union which represented eleven European harbour pilots. This situation was to change with dramatic suddenness.

Two Arab Unions, including one for Forces civilian employees were founded in 1953 and by December 1956 the total had grown to 21 of which 16 represented the staff of individual companies. In that year official statistics showed that there had been 70 disputes in which 28 per cent of the working population had been involved: 210,000 working days had been lost compared with 338 the previous year. The leaderships, reported the Deputy Labour Adviser to the Colonial Office, had "a childlike ignorance of industrial procedure...able to expound complaints but unable to suggest remedies". Sometimes there was a strike before any demands were formulated and one leader told this writer that if he did not from time to time call for a strike, his members would think that he spent his day drinking in the Crescent Hotel (as indeed he did). Some young men quickly grasped the fact that a career in Trade Unionism would open to them ways to power which would normally have remained closed on account of their poor education or mean social standing and they politicised the movement through simultaneous membership of the United National Front. The non-industrial nature of much of the agitation was shown by the refusal of the Trade Unionists to participate in a Labour Joint Consultative Committee and in demands for a curb on immigration with the complaint that a hybrid rather than an Arab community was being formed. Meanwhile the British Trade Union Congress sent out worthy but naive representatives to explain how things were done at Transport House.

In 1953 the Township Authority was made into a Municipality with six nominated members (including two Europeans), twelve elected Arab members and two elected Indians. Thus for the first time local people formed a majority on a public body. Two years later there was an important change in the balance of the Legislative Council, which was enlarged to eighteen members of whom four were nominated unofficial members and five were elected.

The greater role now open to Arab politicians stimulated further demands, and through the mouth of Hassan Bayoomi the Aden Association called for self-government, a majority on the Legislative Council, recognition of Arabic as an official language, more senior posts for Arabs and curbs on immigration. Nationalist sentiment was still more provoked in May 1956 when the Under Secretary for the Colonies, Lord Lloyd, informed the politicians in most pro-consular tones "that it would not be reasonable or sensible, or indeed in the interest of the Colony's inhabitants, for them to aspire to any aim beyond that of a considerable degree of internal self-government...the importance of Aden both strategically and economically within the Commonwealth is such that (HMG) cannot foresee the possiblity of any fundamental relaxation in their responsibilities for the Colony." British officials on the spot, who tended to regard the Aden Association as "the loyal opposition", were aghast at this curt refusal of further discussions which, they felt, would only provoke hostile feeling. Two months later, for the first time since 1947, there was bloodshed on the streets of Aden when a mob of 2,000 attacked a police station to attempt the release of three men held inside for leading an illegal procession: three of the assailants were killed. The year 1956, with its labour unrest and bloodshed, would anyway have been a bad one for the British authorities, but it was made much worse by the disastrous invasion of Suez in the late autumn. Even in areas which had incontestably benefited from the British presence the tribespeople identified themselves completely with Nasser and the Arab cause and were delighted at his success, for everyone believed that there had been collusion between the Western Powers and Israel. The British had been regarded as both moral and invincible, but this image was now tarnished for all time.

There was less labour unrest in 1957, but considerable dissatisfaction was caused when, at the request of the unofficial Members of the Legislative Council and to the great detriment of the Aden revenue, the Governor issued an order forbidding the import of *qat* on which many of the labourers spent a large proportion of their wages. The addicts were able to avoid this by travelling a few yards out of the Colony into Abdali country where they continued to chew as before, although at rather higher cost. The prohibition was so ridiculously ineffective that it lasted only for a few months, although it left behind a feeling of resentment. During the year the young nationalists consolidated their grip on the leadership of the Aden Trade Union Congress (ATUC), in whose higher councils scarcely a manual worker could be found. The political nature of their interests was shown by their refusal to discuss labour matters with the government and by attacks on non-Arabs, including Indian families that had been resident in Aden for generations as "T.B. germs". The ATUC newspaper, *al-Amil*, became the

79

main voice of opposition, and it became difficult to distinguish between the ATUC and the UNF. Oblivious to all of this, stolid British TUC chieftains came and expounded such mysteries as working to rule and affiliation to ICFTU.

Two events early in 1958 made the ATUC even more overtly political. In February the Imam Ahmad announced that the Yemen would be associated with the new union of Egypt and Syria, thus acquiring some respectability as an Arab nationalist. Demands were heard from the Aden labour leaders for unity with a Yemen in which it was inconceivable that they could continue to enjoy such liberty: they started to talk of "the occupied south", and for the purely tactical reason of acquiring a stick with which to beat the British, the ATUC became in effect a Yemeni nationalist movement. The second event was the announcement of a constitutional advance which would give the elected members of the Legislative Council a majority under the chairmanship of an independent Speaker instead of that of the Governor. Elected members of the Council, too, were to join the Executive Council in charge of the main civilian subjects of Labour, Local Government, Health, Education, Public Works and others. It was clear to the ATUC leaders that they would have no share in this because the bulk of their supporters, migrant Yemenis from the north who had flocked to Aden to obtain work or to avoid oppression, had no votes: they therefore determined to try to destroy the Council even before the elections which were due in January 1959.

Given the number of different ethnic groups within the population, the problem of the franchise was considerable. In 1955 the total number of inhabitants was 138,000 of whom nearly 37,000 were Adeni Arabs. The immigrant Yemenis numbered 48,000 and immigrants from the Protectorates 19,000. There were also over 15,000 Indians, over 10,000 Somalis and nearly 5,000 Europeans, most of whom were English. There were also under 1,000 Jews.

The ATUC started their campaign in April 1958 with a 24-hour strike against the immigration policy and against any franchise for citizens not of Arab birth. Bombs were thrown and in May a state of emergency was proclaimed. Events reached a climax in November when after the arrest of two journalists there were two days of rioting in Crater. The Governor reacted strongly: 240 Yemenis were rounded up and bundled across the frontier while 560 others were arrested; in the House of Commons the Colonial Secretary said that the situation, which he considered an attempt at intimidation rather than a statement of industrial grievances, had been "handled with great skill". Delegates arrived from Transport House to talk about contracting in and contracting out.

Encouraged by the strident support of Nasser's propaganda broadcasts, the ATUC continued to denounce the new Constitution and to call for a boycott of the elections while offering no constructive alternative. Intimidation on the day of voting (this writer recalls seeing gangs of bully-boys on the streets) kept the poll down to 27 per cent, although as a result all the candidates returned were moderates. The Union leaders at once denounced the Council as illegal and incited their followers to ignore its existence.

The social and economic development of Aden 1919–1959

The forty years that we have sketched were also times of drastic transformations in the economic and social spheres. The income of Aden rose from £66,000 in 1921 to £140,000 in 1937 and to £4 million in 1955. Its credit was good, and in December 1953 a loan of £1,300,000 was raised in London for investment in a power station, telephones and water.

Before the war there were only two industries – salt, which produced about 80,000 tons a year and employed 750 regular and 550 casual workers, and the building of dhows, of which five a year, of cargo capacity of 200 tons each, were built in Maala. The whole situation was transformed in 1952 by British Petroleum's decision to build a refinery at Little Aden, at a cost of £45 million. Within a few years the population almost trebled as work became available and other small industries started to meet the increased needs. Nearly 2,000 Arabs were employed at the refinery, and another 800 worked at bunkering the ships which took advantage of the cheapest and most efficiently supplied oil on the Far Eastern and Australasian routes. In 1957 only London, Liverpool and New York handled more ships. This, combined with the cheap goods available in the traditional free port, brought nearly a quarter of a million shoppers a year into Aden *suqs*, where new stores opened to take advantage of the general prosperity. The airport at Khormaksar became an important staging post, and other first class hotels competed with the Crescent which had opened in 1932. The number of banks increased annually, and so did motor vehicles, of which there had been about 400 in 1933.

By the end of the 1950s the social services were more advanced than those of many European countries. The Queen Elizabeth Hospital at Khormaksar was recognised as one of the finest in the Middle East, while the government and the refinery made cheap housing available.

Education expanded dramatically. In 1921 there were 359 boys in Government schools, and as late as 1942 the Education Department consisted only of a Director and two junior clerks with no one to replace any of them when they went on leave. The budget for 1942/3 was £9,194. By 1948 the number of school children, now including girls, had risen to 4,000, and it reached 10,000 in 1956. Schooling was free up to the age of fourteen and over fifty students were receiving higher education abroad at Government expense. Educated Adenis started to demand literate wives, marriages took place later and with subsidised housing young couples could start life in their own homes instead of often spending years with their parents. There was a change, too, in the attitude of youth, which started to take an interest in events outside their own sphere and followed the press of other Arab countries and in particular that of Egypt. Partly to counter hostile propaganda and partly to provide an outlet for local talent, Aden Broadcasting Service was created in 1953 and attracted great support, receiving 500 letters a day from its listeners. Listening to their fellows, the Adenis started to acquire a sense of a distinctive culture of their own, a culture that grew annually more unlike that of their northern brethren, which remained so static.

Another event of the late 1950s was to bring yet more great changes to Aden. The Suez invasion showed that it was no longer possible for Britain to depend upon flying troops from a central reserve in the United Kingdom to emergencies in the

Far East or Australasia, as the independent countries of the Middle East or Africa could refuse permission for their territory to be over-flown. The Defence White Paper of 1957, presented by Duncan Sandys, therefore planned that east of this potential barrier there should be increased numbers of men at strategic points available as mobile reserves. Aden was chosen as one of these bases; a new command structure was created which removed it from the command of the Middle East Headquarters in Cyprus and placed it directly under London. Its Chief, an Air Vice-Marshal, also controlled British land forces in the Arabian Peninsula and the naval elements in the Gulf.

The number of service personnel in Aden increased four-fold in three years, with striking effect upon the economy. By early 1961, of the 62,000 people employed in Aden 11,640 worked directly for the forces, and a large proportion of the 21,000 with domestic jobs were with service families. Many of the 7,000 in the retail trade depended upon purchases by the troops and their dependants while the 1,700 in the refinery, the 5,600 in the Port and the 5,000 in light industry profited indirectly.

The social results of this influx were less happy. Before that time most of the small number of resident Englishmen had expected to spend many years in the area. They lived amongst the Arabs, at least some of whose language they usually learned, took a deep interest in local events and mixed easily with the people many of whom they regarded as close friends. There had been no atmosphere of segregation as the communities shared the few bars and restaurants or met on terms of equality in each other's houses. The newcomers in the services, on the other hand, who knew that they were in Aden only for a limited period, clung together in British enclaves and declined to mix with the Arabs whom they tended to regard with suspicion or contempt. Their very numbers made them conspicuous; the British ceased to be just one more thread in the tapestry that was South Arabia and started to stand out firstly as aliens and then as an army of occupation.

Since 1839 every decade had increased the differences between Aden and the rest of South Arabia, but in few decades had the process been as rapid as in the 1950s. Whereas North

Yemen had if anything regressed in the forty years since the Turks had left, Aden had changed practically out of recognition: with its booming prosperity, large expatriate community, political parties, free press and atmosphere of bustle and business, it had come to present a striking contrast to the somnolent cities of the north.

The Aden Hinterland 1919–1959

The pre-war Protectorate Treaties had served their purpose in halting the Turkish advance, but they had resulted in the preservation of a mosaic of feeble and fragmented states. The rulers of these states varied from the Shaykhs of Upper Aulaqi claiming descent from those Shaykhs of Ma'an who had resisted the Romans in BC 24 and the Lower Yafai Sultan, whose family was of similar antiquity and who was believed to incarnate the soul of the Yafai people, to the Atafi Shaykhs, who were described by the first travelling Political Officer, Lord Belhaven, as "a small family of half-destitute goat-keepers". Some were originally from other areas, such as the Qu'aiti Sultan of Mukalla whose Yafai forbears had conquered the country in the previous century, and the Sharifs of Bayhan, descendants of the Prophet who were accepted as mediators between warring tribes rather than as rulers. In the old South Arabian tradition, succession was not by primogeniture but by election within a hereditary group either by its own members or on a wider tribal basis. "Once elected", wrote Belhaven, "both chief and tribe are subject to each other's will, and this is the ancient blending of feudalism and democracy." In the case of the Audhalis an agreement between the Sultan and the tribes, based on a customary law far older than Islam, was put in writing. This underlined the fact that the tribes were allies rather than subjects of their chiefs. They had contact with their "rulers" only when it was to their advantage to do so; otherwise they resisted or ignored them.

The direct rule of a Sultan usually extended only over those to whom they extended protection, the detribalised people of the towns and the labourers on their lands. There was little money to pay soldiers who were themselves no better armed than the tribesmen: one Sultan told this writer that if he offended a tribe beyond endurance, his life would be in danger every time that he stepped out of his house. A ruling family, or *dola*, might have many branches, each one with definite rights, sharing the profits and the losses of government amongst themselves on a strict basis dictated by custom or written agreement. The houses of the *dola* might have their own relations with the tribes separate from or even opposed to those of the Sultan, and, as each member was a potential Sultan, the acquiescence of the stronger personalities had to be gained before any action could be taken. A further curb on the rulers was provided by the existence of independent communities, descended either from the Prophet or from the pre-Islamic saints mentioned in the first chapter: these, too, had their clients amongst the tribes and, as they often claimed magical powers, they might carry more weight than a Sultan.

British policy had long been to keep down expense by avoiding, as far as possible, entanglement in the affairs of the interior and by making no effort to change the situation. For more than a decade after the war they continued to treat the area in the tradition of the Indian North West Frontier, purchasing good will by giving small presents and subsidies to local leaders and interfering not at all even when internal feuds led to murder. They made no attempt to administer the area, to assert authority or to better the lot of the people; this non-intervention was generally acceptable to independent-minded tribesmen who knew of no other way of life. The government, they said, was a milch cow but one that should remain tied up in Aden. This policy, described by the Resident Sir Stewart Symes as one of "aloof indifference diluted with bribes", had indeed the advantage of being very cheap: in 1930 the Protectorate cost the British taxpayer £30,000 and 2,600 rifles which were distributed to various notables.

One crime, however, did bring government retribution, and that was interference with the main trade routes. Offenders might be banned from access to Aden *suqs* or have their stipends stopped and if these methods failed, recourse was had to bombing, particularly after the RAF took over responsibility for security in 1927. The future Lord Portal of Hungerford, who commanded in Aden from 1934 to 1935, described one such operation against the Qutaybi tribe, some of whose members had been proved guilty of banditry against Yemeni caravans, although they were paid to keep the roads open. An ultimatum that the actual criminals or approved hostages should be handed over and a fine of $500 paid was sent by hand and also dropped over the villages – when this produced no response, the house of the Shaykh was destroyed. Still they did not surrender so the area was "blockaded" from the air, with bombers constantly overhead to prevent the tribesmen from ploughing their lands; delayed action bombs were dropped for nearly two months until the approach of the rains made the offenders give way. There had been no Government casualties and only three among the Qutaybis who were killed trying to take a bomb to pieces. The blockade system could produce unexpected results for on one occasion the RAF decided to seal off a valley by destroying the only road and no houses were damaged: the Qutaybis thought this due to inaccurate bombing and sent a stiff note saying that such inefficiency lessened their faith in the ability of the British to protect them.

Sir Bernard Reilly has said that such collective punishment was "understood and not resented by tribesmen" and, in the experience of this writer this statement, although so apparently strange, is absolutely true for a tribe is a group which expects to share benefits and losses, advantages and disadvantages. It is difficult for those who have not lived amongst the people of South Arabia to understand that what the toughest warrior really fears is the scorn of his womenfolk whose tongues are vicious and fanatical guardians of the honour of the tribe and its solidarity and will readily humiliate a man in public on the least suspicion of cowardice. If, at considerable expense, a punitive expedition had been sent by land against the Qutaybis, the men would have been compelled to resist with probable loss of life on both sides and intensification of the trouble but it constituted no loss of face to give way to a force that was both irresistible and unassailable. One old rascal whose career of crime had spanned three decades cheerfully told this writer that he had had four houses bombed, twice writing to the RAF to congratulate them on their good shooting, and each had been rebuilt rather better than before with financial aid from the Government: he bore not the slightest malice. People who knew little of Arabia constantly protested that bombing of villages was inhumane but in fact it was for decades the best method of control for there was very rarely loss of life, houses were easily rebuilt and no one had valuable property to lose. A tribe knew that once some of its members had sinned, it would be punished and it wanted to get this over without losing face.

This point is so important that it is worth illustrating with a personal experience. This writer, compelled to punish a village did so by means that can only be described as deceitful. Their women and their neighbours who would have reviled the fighting men if they had meekly accepted chastisement, sympathised with them for being the victims of such a dirty trick and no face was lost. The men gave this writer a particularly splendid lunch on his next visit.

A first attempt to take more positive action in the Protectorate occurred under the Residency of Sir Stewart Symes who wrote "the territory in general presented an unedifying example of the principle of individual liberty which precluded the possibility, except by coercion, of carrying out any measure for the common welfare". He tried, therefore, to bring about some sort of stability by calling a conference of Rulers which met at Lahej in 1930. Eighteen Protectorate chiefs attended and Symes hoped that they would agree to combine to defend the frontiers and to take joint action against wrongdoers: by establishing peace it would be possible to move towards a policy of social and economic development with money spent on public services rather than on doles to notables. The experiment was, however, premature and mutual jealousies proved too strong for the creation of any effective union.

Nonetheless there was increasing intervention in the Protectorate throughout the 1930s, as officers went into areas which had seen no Briton since Wyman Bury thirty years before. Wing Commander Rickards travelled throughout the Protectorate laying out more than forty landing grounds, often at the request of local people who appreciated the possibility of an air link with Aden. The use of aircraft conferred great benefits in evacuating the sick or wounded to hospital or bringing in urgent supplies, but reliance upon them meant that roads were neglected and no money was made available for their development. The existing railway which extended to Lahej went into disuse, and no attempt was made to make one from Aden eastwards. Therefore, although there was swift and easy access to Aden, travel within the Protectorate was always difficult and often dangerous up to the very end of the British period.

In November 1933 Sir Bernard Reilly, wishing to lessen the dependence of the government on the Sultan of Lahej for work in the Protectorate, applied for funds to appoint a Political Officer to promote development, work for internal security and to assist the RAF on the ground. The man chosen was the Honble. A. Hamilton (later Lord Belhaven). "Ham", as an outsider, was often accepted as a mediator and his arrival in an area was seized upon as an excuse to settle old feuds "as a favour to the government" and thus without loss of face. The majority of disputes in the Protectorate have always concerned land or the use of water, that most precious of commodities, so each agreement meant that some new area could be cultivated in peace.

In November 1934 Reilly urged that as the frontier question had ended with the Treaty of Sanaa, attempts should be made to establish security within the Protectorate. He obtained £500 a year to form groups of Tribal Guards to police the trade routes within their own territories. Subsequently he raised another force, the Government Guards, to escort the Political Officer and other officials anywhere in the Protectorate. As the Aden Protectorate Levies had been formed in 1928 to protect airfields, there were now three military establishments in which a tribesman could earn money in a way which brought him honour and respect, and at the same time could learn that there were other ways of life than that which had come down unchanged from his ancestors. For the first time, also, he came into daily contact with comrades from outside his own immediate family circle.

Reilly also had schemes for social welfare. He created a group of medical dispensers and appointed an Agricultural Adviser in 1937. Progress was made with education, and in 1935 a College for the Sons of Chiefs came into being so that future tribal leaders might receive some education and come to know their peers. Shortage of staff slowed down progress during the war but in 1941 the first boys from the Western Protectorate were sent abroad, to Gordon College in Khartoum, for further education. Schools were opened in Dhala and in Shuqra and the one at Lahej had 100 pupils by 1943. An Education Officer for the Protectorate was appointed in 1944 but always encountered resistance from the tribesmen. They suspected that their children were being held as hostages, and they resented the absence of children who were needed for their labour on the land or guarding the flocks. Often when this writer pressed people to allow their sons to be educated, he would receive the reply that they had already "given" one boy to the school and that was enough.

These events were, however, on a small scale compared with what was happening further east. It has already been remarked that it was necessary for many of the inhabitants of the Hadhramawt to earn their living outside the Wadi, and in the 1930s it was estimated that nearly 100,000 men were working abroad, some of whom had become immensely rich. The most successful of all were the Sayyids of the al-Kaf family of Tarim who were believed to own property in Singapore worth about £25 million; Reilly heard that they paid £50,000 a year in taxation.

It has also been noted that very few of the Hadhramis remained abroad. Their aim was always to make sufficient money to buy or to improve a family property in the Wadi despite the terrifying lack of security there. Armed tribesmen robbed the townsfolk and the peasants, and quarrels over the loot led to frequent killings and consequent blood feuds, which lasted for generations. A man might well be killed in revenge for a murder committed by an uncle a generation before. An Arab sociologist found that there were people in Huraydah in Wadi Amd who had not dared to leave their houses for more than twenty years as their enemies kept constant watch. It was often impossible to cultivate the fields, even with armed guards; at Ghurfah a system of trenches had to be dug to enable the labourers to reach the date plantations which in other places could be tended only by women. The Qu'aiti Sultan of Mukalla and the Kathiri Sultan in Saiwun scarcely exercised any control outside the walls of their capitals, and only in places where there were communities of Sayyids, who could use their religious prestige as descendants of the Prophet, was there anything which approached a peaceful existence. Prominent amongst these Sayyids was Bubakr ibn Shaykh al-Kaf, who used his great wealth to do what the Sultans could not. He minted his own coinage, and he settled blood feuds by payments from his own pocket. He tried to pacify the Beduins by building schools, digging wells and by sending missionaries to groups that were still semi-pagan. He built a road from Mukalla on the coast up to the Wadi Hadhramawt, and as all who travelled upon it were his guests they had their expenses paid. Motor cars were stripped down, loaded upon camels and reassembled in Tarim where Rickards in 1933 saw a rally in which 75 vehicles took part. It was natural that Sayyid Bubakr and those who had seen the orderly life of South East Asia under Western rule should contrast this with the anarchy of their homeland. Indeed, as early as 1927, a group of Hadhramis in Singapore held a meeting to discuss the insecurity of the Wadi. Sayyid Bubakr took advantage of rare European visitors to send messages begging the British to establish a presence.

In March 1933 Sir Bernard Reilly became the first senior British official to visit the Wadi and in the following year he sent Harold Ingrams to make a report on the situation. In 1936 Ingrams returned and, working in close co-ordination with Sayyid Bubakr who did much of the negotiating and most of the paying, established what became known as "The Peace of Ingrams" – a general truce which was in the first instance to last for three years. The settlement had been laborious, for more than 1,400 signatures were required from prickly and truculent tribesmen, but the results were immediately apparent. Secretly all welcomed the chance to make peace without loss of face: a rifle was no longer the most essential item of dress for a tribesman and was rarely seen in public. The roads became safe, agriculture started to flourish and a special department was established to deal with Beduin problems. According to Ingrams the value of agreements was now widely recognised. An agreement was concluded amongst the Sayyids of Shihr that none of them would allow their wives to spend more than $10 on a dress or $2 on a tea party.

Other changes followed the conclusion of peace. In 1937 the

Qu'aiti Sultan became the first ruler to sign a new form of Treaty based upon a pattern existing in Malaya. He bound himself to accept a Resident Adviser "and for the welfare of the state to accept his advice in all matters except those concerning Muhammadan religion and custom". The Aden Protectorate was divided into a Western half (WAP), with a British Agent based in Aden, and an Eastern one (EAP) with the Resident Adviser in Mukalla. Ingrams was the first to hold this post and in 1939 he concluded a similar Treaty with the Kathiri Sultan.

It is proposed to discuss Advisory Treaties later in this chapter so here it is sufficient to say that Ingrams used his position to start to organise a government with which the British subsequently interfered little in matters of detail. Security was maintained by the creation in 1938 of a British-officered force, the Hadhrami Beduin Legion. Recruitment into its ranks assured a tribesman of regular pay, medical care and education for his children. Efficient collection of taxes raised the revenue from 630,000 rupees in 1934 to 15,00,000 in 1944. In 1934 the only officials in Mukalla were a Wazir, a Treasurer, a Commander-in-Chief and a doctor, but by 1944 there were twenty administrative departments largely staffed by Sudanese and Indian Muslims. *Naibs* (Deputies) were sent out to govern provinces and Administrative Officers dispatched to towns. In 1944 a State Council with non-official members made its appearance and a similar body was created in the Kathiri Sultanate. The two states started to issue their own postage stamps in 1942.

Social progress was shown by the increase in the amount of money made available for education. In 1936 the Qu'aiti Sultanate spent 6,000 rupees (£450), but by 1944 the sum had risen to 1,54,000 rupees which represented 10 per cent of the state revenue. Over 130 girls attended Mukalla school. A Secondary School and a Teacher Training College followed and a School for Qadis helped to reduce the government's dependence upon foreign employees. In 1934 the expenditure on health was 5,500 rupees, which covered little more than the salary of a Doctor who served mainly as personal physician to the Sultan: in 1944 it had risen to 74,000.

Once the tribesmen had hung up their weapons, there was little insecurity in the EAP, although in 1945 a tribal leader with ambitions for independence had to be suppressed by a powerful force. Occasionally the Beduins became restive, since they feared for their livelihood as they saw lorries replacing camels for the transport of goods. In 1955, for example, five villages were bombed after a force of soldiers had been surrounded. In this incident there was no evidence that the troubles had been instigated from outside. However, in the following year, while Britain and Saudi Arabia were at loggerheads over the Buraymi Oasis in Oman, King Saud attempted to create subversion amongst the Hadhrami tribes, distributing rifles and dollars lavishly to any who would take them. In May 1956 a troop of Saudi tribal guards who were escorting an American oil exploration team crossed the border and were forced to surrender by the RAF and the HBL.

Most of its inhabitants believed most firmly that there was indeed oil in the Wadi, but it was never found in sufficient quantities to justify the enormous expense of operations over such difficult country and so far from the sea. The area, however, flourished in other ways, particularly after the start of a scheme to assist the farmers to install pumps. Health units and schools spread and in 1950 Town and Village Councils gave the local people a say in their own affairs.

Mukalla grew and prospered and showed its sophistication by engaging in politics. Soon there were two parties: the Hadhrami Party, which in alliance with the Sayyid Party of Tarim wanted a union of the two Sultanates, and the National Party which stood for Qu'aiti particularism. The National Party achieved prominence in 1950 when, as a protest against the appointment of a Sudanese as State Secretary (Chief Administrative Officer), its members attacked the Sultan's Palace: martial law was declared after a dozen people had been killed and later a special court sentenced some seventy people to jail. Apart from these incidents, the EAP presented a peaceful and untroubled contrast to its western neighbour, where stormy events were taking place.

At first the WAP also had progress to report. The wartime problems of shipping obviously made it imperative that the area should grow as much of its own food as possible, so in 1941 the Director of Agriculture obtained a grant of £10,000 to buy seed and oxen. This was advanced to the farmers of Abyan, a naturally fertile place but one where generations of feuding between the Fadhlis and the Lower Yafais had made cultivation hazardous. To prevent the recurrence of such tribal fighting in an area of economic importance the government considered it necessary to play a more active part in the affairs of the Protectorate and to establish at least a rudimentary form of administration. In the 1930s Ingrams visited the Fadhli Sultan and found him counting the Treasury, which was contained in an old tin box which went everywhere with the Ruler, even being carried on his knee when he went to Aden by taxi: something more formal was now obviously required.

The result was a series of Advisory Treaties similar to those concluded with the Qu'aiti and Kathiri Sultans. The Colonial Secretary defined their objective as helping the local people "without in any way interfering with their own administration, without in any way sapping their self-reliance" but, as we have seen, there was no local administration and indeed there were hardly "states" in any normal sense of the word. British Political Officers, assisted by handfuls of Government Guards, were sent up-country to persuade the rulers to establish some sort of administrative machinery. Their task was formidable for first they had to convince the chief that the sole object of the government was not his personal enrichment and then to work with what officials there were, men often corrupt or illiterate but usually from the *Dola* and thus impolitic or even dangerous to dismiss. The British officer had no executive power and could work only through persuasion so what he could achieve depended almost entirely upon his own personality and the relationship that he could establish with the Arab authorities: that so much was done is proof of the ability and character of many of those who served in the WAP.

If a Political Officer quarrelled with the Ruler, his position could become very difficult for although the Treaty bound a Sultan to accept the "advice", formally given, of the Governor of Aden, this could only be done after consultation with the Colonial Secretary and thus was machinery too ponderous to be used except in matters of very major importance. Life could become awkward for the officer for everyone knew that while their Sultan would remain, the Briton would disappear on leave or posting and it was obviously foolhardy to antagonise a permanent authority in order to ingratiate oneself with a transitory one. There was a feeling, too, that a Sultan, however evil, was a fellow-Muslim and one of their own folk while an officer, however benevolent, was an unbeliever and an outsider. A Chief who had held power for decades knew infinitely more about the area and had the all-important background information about personal, family and tribal relations and was able very easily to put pressure on anyone that he believed was working against him by helping or informing the British officer. A junior officer who rashly became involved in a dispute with a Ruler who had given loyal service in the past would be unlikely to find himself supported by the higher authorities in Aden: certainly none would expect to survive the enmity of the Sharif of Bayhan or the Audhali Sultan. It was possible to depose a Ruler who had broken his Treaty but this could only be done if a more suitable member of the *Dola* could be found and were willing to take office: deposition therefore was very much a last resort for the Government. Sir Kennedy Trevaskis who was intimately associated with the area for thirteen years, has written of "travesties of government (which) tax the weak, buy off the strong and keep what is left over for themselves" but there can be no doubt that they were Arab states under Arab rulers: the WAP was never a British colony and officials who had served a regular apprenticeship in administration in India or Africa often gave up in despair at the problems that they encountered. The main British hold was the need that the rulers felt for protection against what would have been the oppression of the Imam if they had been left on their own and the fact that the British alone could provide them with arms and money. The states of the WAP were very far from ideal but, to quote Trevaskis again, "they did shield the majority from the far more brutal injustice of tribal anarchy".

Small though the British presence was in the WAP, it enraged the Imam who still regarded as his own all the territory of South Arabia. After the Treaty of 1934 relations were cordial for a time and the Imam sent one of his sons as a representative at the Coronation of King George VI and allowed a British Medical Mission to establish itself in Sanaa. However, the Order in Council which established the Protectorates applied not only to the area which the Imam had tacitly accepted as being under British control but extended also to the Hadhramawt and the district of Shabwa in which there was believed to be oil: neither of these places had been mentioned in previous negotiations and Yahya saw this as a breach of faith and an annexation of territory over which he claimed sovereignty. In 1938 Yemeni irregulars occupied Shabwa but were expelled by force. The Imam complained of this, and of the erection of a fort at nearby al-Abr where, he said, a well had been dug by his ancestors a thousand years before. It was, he claimed, "part of our old and original country", and he rejected any compromise such as neutralisation as "illogical, unreasonable and unjust". Other moves that the Imam regarded with apprehension were a British advance into Subayhi country in 1940 when there was a possibility of an invasion by Italian forces from Ethiopia, penetration into Dathina in 1943 and the conclusion of an Advisory Treaty with the Sharif of Bayhan in 1944. Seeking support for his position, he enlisted the help of the newly-created Arab League, which in June 1946 "pledge(d) its support to Yemen in its stand towards the Protectorates disputed with the British government", although it hoped that the matter could be settled by friendly negotiation.

Relations became worse after the murder of Yahya in 1948, a crime which his son Ahmad blamed upon Yemeni political dissidents sheltering in Aden. Ahmad did, however, receive the Frontier Officer, Seager, in May when he requested an extradition treaty and a supply of arms, and in November 1948 he invited the Governor of Aden to discuss formal diplomatic relations which would have ended the anomaly of Great Britain's being represented only by an Arab Political Clerk living in Hodeidah far from the seat of government. Whitehall agreed to a most unusual arrangement, by which the Governor of Aden should be accredited as Ambassador to Yemen while a Foreign Office man took up residence in Taizz as his deputy. This, however, came to nothing, for the following year there was a serious frontier incident when the RAF destroyed a fort which the Yemenis had recently built within territory claimed by the Sharif of Bayhan. A visit of British oil prospectors to Shabwa appeared to the Imam another violation of past agreements and caused further protests.

The Imam appealed to the Arab League which, while referring to the Yemen's "lawful rights" welcomed the prospect of
direct negotiations in London. The old impasse – that the
British wanted a detailed settlement of a frontier which the
Yemen claimed should not exist – caused prolonged discussions. These, however, eventually resulted in a *modus vivendi*
which was signed in January 1951. It was agreed that the *status
quo* should not be changed, that resident diplomatic representatives should be exchanged, and that a joint commission
should be established to deal with frontier disputes; moreover,
Britain promised aid with development.

This agreement did not last long because of a fundamental
difference of interpretation of the meaning of the *status quo*: to
the British it meant maintenance of the existing frontier, while
to the Yemenis it meant that there should be no changes made
on the Aden side of them. The Governor, Sir Tom Hickinbotham, felt that the British government should do more for
the people under its protection. At the time it was spending less
than one and a half pence a year per head on the people's
welfare, so he inaugurated a vigorous forward policy with
emphasis on social services. By 1955 there were 27 schools in
the WAP, excluding an Intermediate School at Zinjibar which
took boarders from outside the Fadhli Sultanate. Modern hospitals were built in Lahej and on the Fadhli–Lower Yafai
border, and such impetus was given to Abyan that it became an
enormous and flourishing enterprise with increased Arab participation in its management. Cotton cultivation there, as well
as in Lahej and in Lower Aulaqi and Dathinah, brought new
wealth in cash and consequently a much wider choice of goods
in the *suqs* of the hinterland. Roads were built or improved to
carry greatly increased traffic and Town Councils were established in Zinjibar and Jaar. The Yemeni Frontier Officer, the
wily Qadi Muhammad al-Shami told Hickinbotham that the
Yemenis disliked these measures because "the more uncivilised
the Protectorate, the less trouble we shall have when we take
over", but it was the political advances which more upset the
Imam.

Hickinbotham was anxious that those states which had not
yet agreed to Advisory Treaties should do so before the Imam
could establish any influence over their rulers. When it

appeared that Ahmad was taking an interest in the Upper Aulaqi Sultanate, he was warned off by an Advisory Treaty in May 1952 and another was concluded two months later with the Audhali Sultan. Shortly afterwards when the Sultan of Lahej, who consciously modelled himself on King Farouq and who used to invite his guests to stroll in his garden without informing them that there was a lion loose in it, had to flee from his capital after tying two of his cousins to a tree to use for revolver practice, the British extracted an Advisory Treaty as the price of recognition from his brother and successor, Ali ibn Abd al-Karim. Ahmad regarded this, and the fact that to prevent possible disorders British troops had been sent to Lahej, as further breaches of the *status quo*: his protests were disregarded.

Ahmad was irked by the fact that the British were advancing into "his" territory while retreating elsewhere in the world: the withdrawal from Abadan had just taken place and negotiations for the evacuation of the Suez Canal Zone were far advanced. He was particularly worried by the increase of British influence in his Audhali and Aulaqi neighbours and the project of linking the two states by a road which he believed was being constructed to carry away the mythical oil of Shabwa, which he regarded as his by right. He therefore determined to prevent the building of the road by subverting the tribes along its proposed route, warning them that it would be the prelude to the loss of their independence which they should defend with arms and money which he would make available. This message proved irresistible, and in December 1953 the Shaykh of the fierce Damani tribe of Audhali with at least sixty of his warriors crossed into the frontier town of al-Baydha which they used as a base for raiding the Protectorate, shooting at government buildings, destroying crops and ambushing the roads. They were soon joined by any tribesman, with a grievance, or who had lost a law case, who knew that they would be welcomed with arms, money and the prospect of excitement in return for putting a member of his family as a hostage. The following year some of the powerful Rabizi tribe of Upper Aulaqi, incensed by the unfortunate killing of their chief's aged aunt by the APL, joined the rebels.

We have seen that to resist firstly Turkish and then Yemeni

encroachments the British had made a series of Treaties with local Rulers, appealing to and upholding their spirit of tribal independence; and by 1954 there were over fifty Chiefs in direct touch with Aden. The result was a collection of non-viable petty states wholly dependent upon the British for protection and financial support: in the WAP only Lahej with a population of 39,000, a revenue of £¼ million, a Constitution, Agricultural Courts and a Regular Army (described by Hickinbotham as "a sorry collection of ragamuffins") had any credibility. Hickinbotham felt that the time had come to reverse the old policy of relying upon tribal particularism and, by reviving the idea of a federal union, to create a South Arabian nationalism to stand distinct from Yemeni nationalism as represented by the Imam. He therefore invited the Chiefs of the WAP to Government House in January 1954 and all except the half-crazy Upper Aulaqi Sultan and the Hawshabi attended.

Federation was clearly in the interests of South Arabia (it was obviously absurd, for example, that goods in transit should pass through four customs posts in a hundred miles), but the Rulers were presented with a rigid scheme, which, owing to the interference and advice of Whitehall, bore little relation to local conditions. Fiercely independent and mutually jealous Chiefs were expected to surrender most of their power and responsibilities, and to become instead members of a Council of Rulers under the Presidency of a British Governor. There was to be an Advisory Legislative Council, which would in due course be elected, and an Executive Council under the chairmanship of the British Agent. The Governor would retain control of defence and foreign affairs while the Federation would deal with customs, health, communications, postal services and education, using the British Political Officers in the states as its executive arm. The Sultan of Lahej expressed the general sentiment when he told Trevaskis that the proposals were "surrender terms dictated to a defeated enemy" which would turn South Arabia into a conventional colony. In the light of history it is clear that the right objective had been sought in the wrong way, for the Rulers should have been told that if they could agree amongst themselves to form a federal union, they would eventually be able to look forward to complete independence. It was unfortunate for them that a

Federation did not come into being in 1954 before opposition to it could crystallise at home and abroad: the years immediately following saw growing Arab nationalism and then Suez, which made every British initiative automatically suspect and increased both Nasser's prestige and his readiness to meddle. There would have been no ATUC to lead the opposition to Aden's merger with the WAP and subsequently to poison its relations with other Arab states and with the Labour Party in Britain, and the Federation might have acquired a self-confidence that the later union never achieved. At least the Colonial Office learned a lesson, and when the idea of a Federation was revived in 1956, it told the Arab Rulers that they should work out the details for themselves although the British government would help.

The Imam saw in these proceedings a further breach of the *status quo*. He feared that a successful new state might act as a magnet for discontented Shafais. He succeeded in involving the Arab League – which could hardly be expected to welcome a potential new member whose Head of State had been appointed by the Colonial Office – in his protests that the Rulers were being forced into a union abhorrent to them. The League sent a mission to investigate, but it was told by the Lower Yafai Sultan that there had been no pressure and that he would unite with the Yemen only if that country made substantial social progress. The League, however, passed a resolution warning the Chiefs against co-operation with British colonialism, and stating that they should do nothing that would "violate their nationalist and Arab spirit and alienate themselves from their Arab brothers and in particular Yemen".

Energetically prodded by Yemeni officials, the dissidents increased in numbers and activity. In the summer of 1954 they were responsible for 281 incidents in a fortnight. Trouble spread to Dathinah after an unstable local Shaykh looted a lorry and declared his adherence, as an independent state, to the Arab League. The Rabizis became so effective that they compelled the government to withdraw from parts of Upper Aulaqi and caused the APL to mutiny to avoid further encounters. The RAF went into action against Lower Aulaqi tribesmen who had cut the roads and refused to pay a fine. The only way that the British could prevent men going off to Yemen to receive arms and money was by distributing similar bribes to stay at home and soon the WAP bristled with rifles: opportunities were taken to pay off old scores and anarchy spread through parts of the area. The security forces, particularly the Government Guards and the Political Officers working closely with them, were stretched to the extreme, but they managed to prevent a complete collapse of law and order. The Yemeni Frontier Officer, Muhammad al-Shami, who had orchestrated much of the unrest, met the British Agent and offered peace in return for a formal withdrawal from Upper Aulaqi. Cairo Radio did its best to increase the troubles by announcing great successes for forces that it presented as struggling against colonialism. This writer recalls hearing Cairo Radio announce the wrecking of the Aden Railway by heroic partisans, although in fact the railway had not operated since 1930 and the Italians claimed to have destroyed it in 1940. He heard also of his own death at the hands of the forces of liberation and later was given lunch by the man who had received a reward for killing him.

The Protectorate rulers began to worry whether the British government would consider the effort to defend them worthwhile despite Treaty obligations. A Minister from the Colonial Office, Henry Hopkinson, who was the first Minister ever to visit Aden, tried to set their minds at rest by assuring them that London would be unlikely to abandon an area where several million pounds had been invested in a new refinery: the Sharif of Bayhan, a man with an unparalleled skill in putting a devastating question with an air of innocent simplicity, asked if rather more had not in fact been invested in the Suez Canal. Lord Lloyd repeated these promises, but the Sultans still foresaw that they might not be honoured after a change of government in Whitehall: the Sharif told two visiting Labour MPs "What we really fear is the British Socialist Party."

Early in 1957 more than 50 incidents occurred in a month as fighting flared up in the Dhala area, while Cairo Radio started to refer to the Protectorates as "Occupied South Yemen" and the Arab League declared its support for "the lawful struggle of the Yemen to liberate all its territories". The Imam talked of inviting Russian volunteers to defend him against colonialist aggression and arms from Czechoslovakia began to arrive; T34 tanks, 37mm anti-aircraft guns and mortars appeared to replace the artillery left behind by the Turks. These new weapons led to an increasing involvement of British service personnel with the Arab forces who had no armour or artillery and could not readily co-operate with the RAF in attacking targets because of language difficulties and lack of training. The Imam's dependence upon Communist supplies alarmed the Saudis, who prevailed upon him to send his son al-Badr to London in November, but no agreement could be reached.

In the spring of 1958 the activities of the dissidents attracted the attention of the world's press when a force estimated to be up to 1,000 strong besieged a British Political Officer in a mountain fort, at a time when bombs were being thrown in Aden. The situation in the Dhala area seemed very critical and in a bid to reduce the pressure, the British gave arms and money to the Audhalis and Bayhanis to carry out reprisals on the Yemen. Every day forts on both sides of the frontier were attacked and vehicles could move only with strong escorts: pitched battles developed and often British and Protectorate forces and Political Officers invited aggression so as to have an excuse to call for help from the RAF, a weapon that the Yemenis could not effectively counter. Egyptians, and probably Russians, were actively promoting trouble and the Governor of Aden, Sir William Luce referred to "two powerful influences, both hostile" while, with a charming lack of realism, a Labour MP called for the spread of Trade Unionism in the WAP.

However, at the end of 1957 a confidential government document recorded that the most dangerous of the dissidents was not a tribesman on the frontier with a rifle but the premier chief of the WAP, Sultan Sir Ali Abd al-Karim of Lahej. He had rejected the unification proposals of 1954 not because he was against a united South Arabia but because he aspired to head it himself: he seems to have seen himself both as Kaiser and as Bismarck, bringing about a union under the domination of Lahej as the Second Reich had formed around Prussia. He resented the way that the British had come to regard other rulers, such as the Sharif of Bayhan and the Audhali Sultan as his equals and sighed for the old undisputed preeminence enjoyed by his father. He attempted to assert himself by interfering in other states, supporting candidates in disputed elections in two of the Aulaqi lands, encouraging the Lower Yafais to complain about the Abyan Board and trying to secure the dismissal of the Fadhli Naib.[1] He spent freely in an attempt to win adherents throughout the Protectorate.

His main weapon, however, was the South Arabian League, led by his close associate Sayyid Muhammad al-Jiffri, which called for the departure of the British and for the creation of an independent state under Sultan Ali. Jiffri was banned from entering the Colony but received hospitality at Lahej to carry on his propaganda work. Even more worrying for the British authorities was the Sultan's very evident support for Gemal Abdul Nasser, whom he had met on the pilgrimage in 1955. Nasser supplied school teachers and other advisers until Lahej became, in the words of an official report "an outpost of Egyptian subversion". People in the town thought that Ali would defy the Governor and announce his adherence to the UAR, but the British struck first. In April 1958 they entered Lahej to seize the three Jiffri brothers, the two most politically active of whom escaped and only the third (who later told this writer that he did not think that he was important enough to be arrested and so had not fled) was captured. Sultan Ali went to London to protest and almost immediately afterwards the whole Lahej Regular Army deserted to the Yemen, taking with it the contents of the State Treasury. The Sultan ignored formal "advice" to return and so was declared in breach of his Treaty and deposed. A former Labour Colonial Secretary agreed that the action was regrettable but necessary.

For a moment the situation looked extremely critical. It was possible that the Laheji deserters might proclaim themselves an army of national liberation and invade the Protectorate, possibly supported by Russian tanks rumoured to have been seen in the area. The Lower Yafai Naib had already become dissident and was in the mountains with some of his tribal guards and the contents of his State Treasury, so there were powerful enemies poised on both the east and west of Aden itself. British reinforcements were brought in from Kenya and the Life

---

[1] The Fadhli Sultan spent much of his time in a canoe, shooting at fish with a Bren gun and the effective ruler of the state was his cousin and Deputy (Naib) Ahmad ibn Abdullah who later replaced him as Sultan.

Guards arrived to establish a camp in Subayhi country. However, there was an anti-climax for all was quiet: the deserters drifted back, Lahej acquired a new Sultan and after a meeting between British and Yemeni officials in Ethiopia, aid to the Protectorate dissidents appeared to diminish and their activities across the border decreased. At about the same time six of the Protectorate Rulers announced that they had agreed to form a Federation.

Chapter Five

Yemen under the Mutawakilite Kings 1919–1962

Yahya conquers a country

When Yahya ibn Muhammad Hamid al-Din was recognised as Imam late in 1904 he was little more than a local religious leader and an arbiter of tribal disputes, but he was a man driven by the ambition to unite under his sway all those lands which had once been ruled by his Himyarite and his Zaydi ancestors. We have seen that his first action was to call for a revolt against the Turks occupying the country and that this led to seven years of warfare until the Treaty of Da'an in 1911 left him the effective ruler of the highlands as far south as Taizz, although he remained the chief of the Zaydis rather than a Yemeni national leader. During the war he refused tempting offers to repudiate his agreements with the Turks but, as they moved out, his men started to fill the vacuum.

Yahya's right-hand man, Sayyid Ali ibn Ahmad al-Wazir, took over the Shafai areas of Hujariyyah and, as we saw in Chapter Four, moved beyond them across the border of the Aden Protectorate. Although the Imam held part of the area until the end of 1933, his rule was never accepted: British protection was preferred as it brought subsidies rather than taxation, and the tribesmen resented the Zaydi habit of treating the Shafais as a subject race. He was, however, left in possession of the Rassassi sultanate of al-Baydha, whose former chief spent the rest of his life in chains in a dungeon.

While his forces were encroaching southwards, the Imam simultaneously moved westwards into the Tihamah and towards the Red Sea, where the departure of the Turks had left large regions unadministered. Both the Idrisis of Asir and the Zaydis raced to fill the gap, and it appeared that the Idrisis might win the larger part because, as Shafais, they were the less unwelcome. By the middle of 1919 they had collected hostages from most of the tribes and in February 1920 their forces were within a day's march of Sanaa. The following year, on the departure of the British, they occupied Hodeidah. The Hashid and the Bakil whom the Idrisi had cultivated during the war were also in the field on his side, and so were the tribes of Arhab and the Zaraniq of the Tihamah. Yahya's position looked precarious, particularly when Taizz declared for his opponent. Fortunes fluctuated, but after the British discontinued his subsidy in June 1920, the Idrisi started to run out of money and was unable to pay his allies, who did not hesitate to change sides. The British tried to mediate but Yahya implacably maintained that the whole coast line up to the Hejaz was his by ancestral right.

In March 1923, Sayyid Muhammad ibn Ali al-Idrisi, a man whose skill in manipulating his descent from the Prophet and whose mastery of tribal politics enabled him to match Yahya on equal terms, died. He was succeeded by a boy of only sixteen. The family fortunes began to decline as internal quarrels flared into civil war, and their position was still further weakened when, as a result of King Hussayn of the Hejaz meddling in the affairs of Asir, Ibn Saud occupied much of its northern region. Finally the British decided to abandon their wartime ally in favour of an attempt to do a deal with the Imam and withdrew what little support they had been giving. In March 1925, Yahya was able to occupy Hodeidah and the coast up to Midi.

In the meanwhile Yahya had been fighting on other fronts. Each major tribe in the Yemen was practically a little independent state with its own Chief, its fighting men, its customary law and markets, and none accepted interference from anyone in its internal affairs. The Imam had in effect to conquer them, partly by exploiting tribal rivalries and partly with his small regular army. During the war the Hashid and Bakil had allied themselves with the Idrisi in return for money and arms, and when he could no longer pay them they continued to fight against Yahya in defence of their tribal law, resisting his attempts to impose the Islamic Shariah. It needed a series of campaigns and considerable subsidies to bring them back to their traditional alliance with the Imamate and their role in fighting for him against other tribes. In 1924 the tribes of the Jawf in the east revolted and the Imam was besieged in Sanaa.

The following year the Zaraniq of the Tihamah petitioned the League of Nations for recognition as an independent state with a capital at Zabid. When this was ignored, they sought British protection, which was also refused. They rose in arms and won several victories, and it took a year's ruthless campaign by Yahya's son Ahmad to bring them to heel. Such was his ferocity, added to his reputed magical powers, that Ahmad was nick-named "al-Jinni" (the Demon). He showed similar harshness in repressing a revolt in Jabal Barat. By 1930 the country was effectively conquered, and Yahya proceeded to consolidate his rule by holding hostages from the tribes and placing small garrisons in potential danger spots. He was so successful that in 1933 the delegates from Aden travelling up to the capital for the negotiations for the Treaty expressed astonishment at the security and order which prevailed, in striking contrast to the anarchy of most of the Aden Protectorate.

With both Zaydi and Shafai areas under control and his southern border secured by agreement with the British in Aden, Yahya felt ready to absorb Najran which had been ruled a thousand years before by his ancestor, al-Hadi, and also the northern Tihamah still under the increasingly feeble sway of the Idrisis. These objectives were almost certain to lead to a clash with Ibn Saud, who by the Treaty of Mecca published in January 1927 had taken Asir under his protection. With extraordinary presumption, the Imam was confident of victory: indeed he was reported to be discussing the alterations that he would make to the Haj when he took Mecca. When, therefore, the Idrisi chief quarrelled with his new overlord, Yahya was quick to exploit the situation by offering him shelter and help in an attempt to drive out the Saudis. As a further provocation, in April 1933 Crown Prince Ahmad moved into the unadministered area of Najran, perhaps in pursuit of dissidents, and demanded submission from the tribesmen. When Ibn Saud sent an embassy to protest, Yahya refused to see them and kept them practically as prisoners. Ibn Saud was still conciliatory and offered to negotiate over the frontier question, and possibly even to accept Yemeni rule over Najran, but Yahya with his usual intransigence insisted that he should have the whole of Asir.

In April 1934 there were armed clashes on the borders but once again Ibn Saud tried to obtain a peaceful settlement, even agreeing that Yahya might continue to give hospitality to his Idrisi opponent provided that he restrained him from political agitation. Yahya, however, remained blindly obstinate, and two Saudi armies started to move. One force under Crown Prince Saud soon became involved in the mountains and made little progress, while the other, under the future King Faysal, advanced inexorably southwards through the Tihamah. By the middle of May Faysal had captured Hodeidah but although he occupied several other towns, he made no attempt to cross the mountains that lay on the road to Sanaa. Ibn Saud was uncertain of the attitudes of the two neighbouring great powers, Britain and Italy, and was not prepared to run the risk that they might intervene to save the independence of the Yemen. Moreover, he was understandably cautious about involving his troops in country as unfamiliar as the mountains of Raymah and Harraz. He therefore offered peace on generous terms which the Imam grudgingly accepted, surrendering his claims to Asir and Najran by the Treaty of Taif, which was negotiated in July by the future King Khalid and Sayyid Abdullah al-Wazir.

Thus within six months Yahya had signed two Treaties, which marked the end of his dream of regaining all the lands of his ancestors. Despite his obstinacy and his courage he had been forced to realise that both his neighbours were stronger than he was and that in future he would have to confine his activities to the government of his own country.

The administration of the Yemen under the Imam Yahya

We have seen that during the thirty years that followed the First World War some initial steps were taken in Aden towards popular participation within an orderly government of the colonial pattern, and some form of rudimentary administration was brought to the Protectorates. There were divergences, too, in what was happening in different parts of the dominions of the Imam. These can be divided into Sanaa with its neighbourhood and the Zaydi districts to the south, the Shafai areas of Hujariyyah and Tihamah and finally the northern mountains of the great Zaydi tribes.

In the first group, Yahya, while never neglecting the theocratic attributes of his ancestors, ruled as a temporal and absolute king. From his immediate predecessors he had inherited neither an army nor a civil service, and he had to create both, with the help of some 900 Turks whom he had persuaded to stay behind. Some of the Turkish officers were still serving in the 1940s when the traveller Freya Stark described them as "grizzled old men of infinitely pathetic dignity" with sabres and patched uniforms. Before that Yemeni cadets were sent to the Military College in Baghdad, but Yahya soon realised that their loyalty might be undermined by what they saw abroad and preferred to start his own officer school with training provided by imported instructors who were easier to control. The regular army, perhaps 18,000 strong, was recruited from the traditionally allied tribes of Hashid, Bakil and Khawlan. Service was for life, although an old man was permitted to retire if he could produce a replacement. Pay was about ten shillings a month, out of which the troops had to buy such necessities as ammunition, but they received presents on great occasions. In the old Arab tradition they chanted songs as they marched, calculated to inspire fear in their enemies, although some spectators found the sight of tribesmen dressed in indigo dye performing the goose-step remarkably comic. There was also a militia in which every man in the country should theoretically receive military training, but administrative difficulties prevented it from being effective. Yahya also had problems with equipment and Clayton in 1926 saw a Company marching to fight the Idrisi with its entire baggage carried by four camels and two donkeys. Although there was later an arsenal producing 4,000 rounds a day, Freya Stark regarded the artillery as "a museum of military rubbish".

Initially, too, the remaining Turks performed administrative duties, often in such routine posts as running the telegraph system. The most important of these, Muhammad Raghib, who had been in the Ottoman diplomatic service before the war, acted as adviser on the outside world to the Imam who had never set foot outside his own mountains and in his eighty years never even saw the sea. Other officials were recruited from the traditionally literate classes – the Sayyids, the descendants of the Prophet and the Qadis, the hereditary class of Zaydi administrators and scholars. Foreigners sometimes described the Qadi Abdullah al-Amri, the most important of Yahya's advisers, as "Prime Minister", just as they regarded Muhammad Raghib as "Foreign Minister", but neither held any kind of independent executive authority. Later there was a Council, consisting mostly of Sayyids, who bore the title of Ministers but as there was no corps of trained bureaucrats, their Departments exerted little influence over the everyday life of the citizen. All power was centralised in the hands of the Imam, and although it was easy for the sophisticated to attack this as tyranny it satisfied the average Yemeni, who felt that he had the right to have his individual problems personally considered by his Ruler.

There can be no doubt that Yahya felt deeply responsible before God for the welfare of every one of his people, and that this responsibility could not be delegated. This made him extremely accessible to his subjects: he spent two hours a day sitting under an umbrella speaking with anyone who wished to approach him and receiving written petitions as he walked around the city.

European visitors have described him at work, squatting on the floor as endless streams of often grubby little pieces of paper, rolled up like cigarettes, were brought in. These might be a request for admittance to hospital or for permission for a school to buy chalk or from one of his sons to borrow a motor car or to discharge a dead soldier from the army, as well as more weighty matters: each received his careful scrutiny, and he either wrote or dictated a reply which he "signed" in the manner of his Himyarite ancestors by dipping his finger in a bowl of red ochre and running it along the text. At times a slave would enter with a pile of silver dollars which had been collected in tax, and the Imam himself would count it and make payments. The American-Syrian writer Amin Rihani thought that "his one-man government, with all its rusty gear, could not under the circumstances be better run by the president of an American corporation".

The traditional appearance of an Islamic state was preserved and the main event of the week was the leading by the Imam of a solemn procession to the mosque every Friday. A committee "encouraged virtue and restrained vice", and strict interpretation of the Shariah saw that the Quranic punishments of amputation of a hand for theft and stoning for adultery were enforced. As a result of such measures all visitors found that there was so little crime that they were very rarely needed. Minor wrongdoers, such as wine-drinkers, were led around the *suqs* with a drum on their backs which a crier beat as he announced their offences and invited the people to revile them. The Imam imprisoned one of his own sons for drinking alcohol, although some said that his arrest was caused by unprincely behaviour in riding a bicycle. In the historic fashion of his ancestors, Yahya felt a special responsibility for protecting the Jews and for harrying the Ismailis.

Occasionally Yahya broke Zaydi custom. The most important instance of this was his attempt to secure the succession for his son Ahmad instead of leaving it to the choice of the *ulama*. From 1927 onwards he used bribery and threats to prevail upon leading figures, and particularly upon potential candidates, to swear an oath of loyalty to Ahmad – an innovation that was greatly resented. He was also the first Imam to write the leading articles in the official newspaper. When the Americans presented him with a radio transmitter he used it for moralistic preaching and political propaganda.

The Shafai areas where there were villages rather than tribes were divided into provinces ruled by Amirs who represented the Imam. The provinces in turn were split into smaller districts. In the early days the Amirs were often Sayyids, but Yahya knew only too well that any of them could claim the Imamate if they felt strong enough. Therefore, whenever possible, he replaced them with his own sons, while the subordinate posts were held either by Sayyids or members of the Qadi class. Nearly all the officials, which in practice meant the local governor, the tax-collector, the judge and their clerks, were Zaydis, dubbed "Junkers" by Amin Rihani, and they had little doubt of their total superiority to the people that they controlled. Shafai soldiers had proved unreliable in the wars against the Idrisi and Ibn Saud, so in each district there was a detachment of Zaydis who kept order and collected taxes, billeting themselves on a village and feeding at its expense until all was paid. They also supervised the forced labour which the people had to provide to build roads and to maintain government buildings, and the requisitioning of animals for official purposes. A further means of control was the detention in Sanaa of hostages for the good behaviour of the tribes. It was always understood that these boys, usually about 2,000 of them below the age of 15, would be punished if their relatives misbehaved, but in the meantime they were better fed and certainly better educated than they would have been at home.

Much the same system, although in practice less harsh, applied in the Zaydi areas to the south of Sanaa. In the areas where his writ ran, Yahya's rule was rough and severe, but it was the only method that was suited to a naturally turbulent nation whose weaker members were able to enjoy the advantages of a security denied to their neighbours in the Aden Protectorate before the Ingrams peace. Everyone knew where they stood and today, after long periods of subsequent anarchy, people may still be found who regret its passing.

In the areas north and east of Sanaa where the great Zaydi tribes had their stronghold, there was hardly any administration at all. Hostages were held in Sanaa – nearly one third of the whole male population of some Jawf tribes was detained – but effective power was in the hands of the shaykhs. They however were restrained by tradition, local religious leaders and the need for popular support for their actions. Yahya realised that it would be futile to attempt to destroy the tribal system so he concentrated upon making of it the best use that he could, subsidising important leaders and trying to influence the elections of Chiefs. He endeavoured with little success to introduce the Shariah law in place of tribal custom and to persuade litigants to come to his courts. The payment of certain taxes is, it will be recalled, a religious duty in Islam, but the northern tribes assessed themselves and paid what they thought fit. Throughout Yahya's reign, therefore, the Hashid, the Bakil and their peers remained as they had always been, allies rather than subjects of the Imam.

Foreign relations under the Imam Yahya

In the days before the discovery of oil in the Arabian Peninsula the Yemen was one of the few states that was basically
self-supporting. So, whereas his neighbours Ibn Saud of Najd,
King Hussayn of the Hejaz, the Idrisi Sayyid of Asir and the
Sultan of Muscat were dependent upon British subsidies, the
Imam Yahya could live off his own. He was fiercely determined not to accept the slightest restraint upon his freedom,
however much this might cost: he told one of his confidants
that he would rather eat straw than submit to any external
influence. He believed that India and China had been colonised
because they had given commercial concessions to foreigners
for these concessions had subsequently been used to justify
military occupation: therefore, although he believed that there
was oil in his dominions he refused to permit any exploration.
When a visiting Envoy asked why he had not accepted the offer
of $2 million from an American company for prospecting
rights, he replied by posing the question "How much more
would it cost to get them out again?" He discouraged alien
visitors and the few European residents found it very difficult
to travel: one told this writer that for each excursion out of
Sanaa they had to apply for permission which Yahya was far
too courteous to refuse – he merely gave it too late for it to be
of any use.

Yahya's policy, then, was to keep his country isolated,
conceding as little as possible in return for his limited needs.
His first necessity was arms and ammunition to keep his forces
in the field against his numerous enemies. These, of course,
included the British, who stood between him and control of
the lands that he claimed to the south. His first choice as an ally
was the United States, but his request for recognition in 1919
remained unanswered and a subsequent goodwill visit by the
US Consul in Aden produced nothing concrete. Despite his
misgivings, therefore, as to the extent of their ambitions (as
long ago as 1917 some of their newspapers had claimed the
Yemen as a future possession), Yahya turned towards the
Italians whose position in Eritrea made them neighbours from
whom arms could easily be procured. The Italians responded
with alacrity for they had been politically active in the area

since the opening of the Suez Canal and they had tried to acquire Socotra and had intrigued in the Hadhramawt. During their war with the Turks in 1911-2 they had supplied arms to the Idrisis, forging links which continued after the armistice, to the alarm of the British, and seeking concessions to exploit the salt of Salif and the oil of Farasan. London believed, too, that Rome was bribing Yahya's councillors, seeking to exacerbate Anglo-Yemeni relations and encouraging him to expect their support in his territorial ambitions. In August 1926 they became the first western power to conclude a Treaty with the Imam whom they recognised as King of the Yemen, without making clear whether or not they accepted his definition of the country as including the Aden Protectorate and Asir. The following year they received the first Yemeni delegation to visit Europe. Meanwhile they actively supported one of the candidates in the Asiri civil war.

There had been Italian merchants at Sanaa since 1883, but after the war there was a persistent effort at commercial penetration. By 1925 the Italians had a practical monopoly of the trade of Hodeidah where they started to build a modern hospital and an airfield. They also installed radio links which enabled Yahya to communicate with his officials in the provinces. They were prepared to supply weapons and technical advice in return for preferential treatment for Italian firms. The Italians sold the country its first aircraft in 1925, putting these arrangements on a more formal basis by a secret treaty in 1927. Their other activities included training Yemeni pilots, giving boys schooling in Eritrea and enlisting Yemenis in their colonial forces. They maintained a presence throughout the 1930s when they had several diplomats and doctors (including the personal physician of the Imam) in the country, and an Italian controlled the military arsenal and directed what engineering projects there were.

For some years the French, also neighbours with their base at Djibouti, competed in the supply of arms but an ambitious plan to develop Mokha was rejected because Yahya refused to countenance their importing a large number of foreign workers which he saw as the first step towards colonisation. The French thereupon dropped out, a German mission in 1927 had no result and in the same year America again declined to establish relations because of its lack of interest in the area. The Russians were more forthcoming, and in 1928 signed a treaty which resulted in diplomatic representation at Sanaa, some doctors and a trade delegation at Hodeidah which tried to undercut western commerce, particularly in kerosene. However, they had little political success and in 1938 the whole mission was recalled and purged. A commercial agreement with the Netherlands in 1933 and a Friendship Treaty with Belgium in 1936 were little more than scraps of paper; even the very limited Italian influence came to an end in 1943 when the Imam broke with the Axis powers.

While European powers failed to establish close relations with the Imam, the independent Arab states were hardly more successful. In 1931 Yahya made a Treaty with Iraq which was to provide military assistance and training for Yemeni officers, and after the war of 1934 relations with the Saudis were very good. They even survived an attempt on the life of Ibn Saud, which many believed had been instigated by Yahya's son Ahmad, and an invasion of Yemeni territory by a survey mission led by the explorer St John Philby. In 1936 the Imam joined in a regional pact directed against Zionism in Palestine with Saudi Arabia and Iraq: this was a sort of forerunner of the Arab League which the Yemen joined upon its foundation in 1945.

In 1944 the Yemen protested to the United States about its support for the Jews in Palestine and at the same time asked for help in its border disputes. The following year the American Consul in Aden arrived on a goodwill visit and was told that the only country which could be relied upon for disinterested support was the United States: other informants said that there were vast natural resources in iron and oil waiting to be exploited. Washington consulted London and finding that Whitehall had no objections, established formal diplomatic relations.

Two years later the Imam sent one of his sons to Washington with requests for modern arms and a credit of $2 million. These were politely delayed, although a promise was made to consider help in developing Hodeidah. The Americans told the British that they had no special interest in the Yemen but agreed to sponsor it for the United Nations, which it joined and where it could show its Arabism by collaborating with its fellows in a strong line on the partition of Palestine.

The opposition to Yahya

Towards the end of the 1930s clandestine opposition towards the Imam and his system of rule began. Despite his attempt to keep his realm in complete isolation, putting difficulties in the way of those of his subjects, particularly Sayyids, who wished to travel abroad and even excluding newspapers published in other Arab countries, Yahya was unable to prevent those who did get overseas from comparing the progress that they saw with the stagnation that existed at home. Shafai merchants, many of them in Aden, resented the monopolies of trade exercised by the Imam. The Zaydi Sayyids and *ulama* were disturbed at Yahya's preemption of the succession for his son Ahmad. These factors meant that, although different groups had divergent objectives, there was for the first time political discontent in the Yemen: in the past there had been trouble enough but it had come from aspirants to the Imamate or from tribes with grievances.

The first stirrings of the new spirit were found among the young intellectuals and took literary shape with poems and pamphlets. A group discussing reforms placed its hopes in the Crown Prince Ahmad but after they caught a revealing glimpse of his harsh authoritarianism, its leaders fled to Aden in 1944. They were all members of the religious and intellectual aristocracy, Qadi Muhammad Mahmud al-Zubayri, Sayyid Ahmad Muhammad al-Shami and Shaykh Ahmad Muhammad Nu'man, a Shafai from the most influential family in Hujariyyah. They became known as the *Ahrar*, the Free Yemenis, and they won the support of the local politician Muhammad Ali Luqman whose newspaper *Fatat al-Jazirah* (The Youth of the Peninsula) gave them a platform which they exploited so effectively that the Imam, unused to public criticism, asked the British to restrain it.

These attacks continued, and so, in April 1946, Yahya sent his son Ahmad to Aden in an attempt to win back the *Ahrar*. Ahmad was once a personal friend of many of the *Ahrar*, and still had some lingering reputation for liberalism. He gave an interview to *Fatat al-Jazirah* in which he promised to open up the country in the way that they demanded, exchanging diplomatic missions with other Muslim countries, exploiting the mineral resources with the help of foreign technicians and spreading education. Many of the *Ahrar* were delighted, hailing him as the Saviour of the Yemen. They even overlooked the extremely menacing behaviour of his bodyguard who nearly perpetrated a massacre when Ahmad, who had insisted on watching a football match, was accidentally struck by the ball. Others, however, suggested that they should ask for more, and finally three demands were formulated: firstly, that there should be a Constituent Assembly; secondly, that Yahya should appoint a government of technicians and capable administrators; finally, that all the Imam's sons should be excluded from office. It was obvious that these terms could only have meant the end of the power of the Hamid al-Dins and that they could only be rejected.

With financial support from Yemeni merchants in other countries, the *Ahrar* bought a press and started to bring out their own newspaper, *Sawt al-Yaman* (Voice of the Yemen) and a series of pamphlets by Zubayri and others which were circulated in the towns of their homeland. They carefully refrained from attacking either the Imamate as an institution or the person of Yahya; they concentrated instead upon the abuses of the system, saying that the country had been better governed under the Turks and contrasting its backwardness with the progress that they saw in Aden. They were anxious to avoid charges of being British agents or opponents of Islam, and they therefore cultivated good relations with the Muslim Brothers whose leaders Zubayri and Nu'man had met in Cairo and who obtained publicity for their cause in the Arab press throughout the Middle East. They saw themselves as a pressure group to bring about a consultative form of government which would give educated youth a share in power through a constitution to which they attached great hopes: indeed they declared that it would take the Yemen from misery to happiness in a single day. They also exposed abuses such as those of the taxation system, which they claimed was exploited by corrupt officials and then wasted by the Royal Family.

The movement received an unexpected supporter when the Imam's ninth son Ibrahim defected to Aden and joined them. In the meanwhile they made secret contacts within the country and indeed within the inner circle of Zaydi grandees. The most important of these was Sayyid Abdullah al-Wazir. He had been a trusted general and administrator, but as he came from a family that had held the Imamate and was himself well qualified to claim it by birth and achievement, he resented as unconstitutional the presumption that Ahmad would follow his father without election. He and his brother had also recently been deprived of lucrative governorships in favour of Yahya's sons. A more disinterested supporter of the move for change was one of the most influential of the Imam's advisers, Sayyid Hussayn al-Kibsi who, frequently representing his country abroad, had come to realise its backwardness. Another was an Iraqi Colonel, Jamal Jamil, who had once headed the mission to train Yemeni officers and then remained behind as Director of Public Security in Sanaa. They were joined by an exiled Algerian businessman, al-Fudayl al-Wartalani, whose travels abroad enabled him to act as a link between the *Ahrar* in Aden, his fellow Muslim Brothers and the conspirators in Sanaa.

At the end of 1947 Wartalani united the aims of the various groups in what was called the "Sacred National Pact", which provided that Abdullah al-Wazir should succeed Yahya as a "Constitutional, consultative and legitimate Imam to follow in word and deed the Qur'an, the Traditions of the Prophet and the practice of the pious ancestors." The traditional duty of an Islamic ruler to consult his people was interpreted in the fashion of the Muslim Brothers to justify proposals for the establishment of something resembling western democratic procedures. There should be firstly a Provisional Consultative Assembly and subsequently a Constituent Assembly which could not be overruled or dismissed by the Imam, and to weaken the conservative tribal chiefs it was provided that two-thirds of the members should come from the towns and that Yemenis resident overseas should have places. It is most probable that Sayyid Abdullah, as traditional and as haughty a Zaydi aristocrat as Yahya himself, would have disregarded these conditions once he was firmly in power and felt it safe to do so, but for the moment he promised to be bound by them.

As Yahya was an octogenarian and in failing health, the conspirators first decided to await his death from natural causes before seizing power. In the meanwhile they tried to enlist support from the Arab League, and Sayyid Abdullah, who was on friendly terms with Ibn Saud who may still have suspected Ahmad of attempting his murder, ascertained that the King would have no objection to his succession provided that it were achieved by legal means. However, early in 1948 the plotters started to fear that Yahya had learned of their intentions and would take action to prevent them. They believed that he was about to summon Crown Prince Ahmad from his provincial governorate of Taizz, either to rebuke him for his ruthlessness or to have his support in case of trouble: they therefore decided upon assassination. Some tribal malcontents were engaged to do the actual killing, and there was probably a plan for the simultaneous murder of Ahmad.

In mid-January an attempt was made upon Yahya's life. At first the conspirators thought the attempt had succeeded, and they dispatched a pre-arranged signal to Aden before they learned of its failure. The *Ahrar* there gleefully published the "news" that Yahya was dead and that Sayyid Abdullah was the new Imam – they even gave a full list of his Cabinet. Naturally Yahya demanded an explanation from Abdullah al-Wazir but was apparently satisfied that he knew nothing of any plot and with his public statement acknowledging Ahmad as successor to the Imamate.

A month later, on 17 February 1948, Yahya was out for a drive in the country when he was ambushed and machine gunned to death. He fell trying to shield a young grandson, and his adviser Qadi Abdullah al-Amri died with him. Abdullah al-Wazir, who according to one story had watched the deed through binoculars, seized the palace and hastily announced Yahya's death from a heart-attack, and his own succession. One of the Princes managed to send a telegram to Ahmad in Taizz telling him what had happened. At once the Crown Prince left the city with about 180 faithful soldiers and a bag of gold. Meanwhile in the capital two of the Princes trying to restore the situation were murdered by the Iraqi security chief, Colonel Jamal Jamil.

The *Ahrar* hastened up from Aden to claim their inheritance. Ministerial posts were given to Zubayri and Nu'man, the first Shafai to hold one, while the renegade Prince Ibrahim was made President of the Consultative Assembly. Sayyid Abdullah tried to win internal support by releasing all hostages and announcing a pay-rise for the army and a programme of school and hospital building. At the same time he reformed the system of taxation. His Foreign Minister al-Kibsi sent telegrams to all the Arab states inviting recognition, carefully neglecting to state that Yahya had been murdered. Abdullah also hoped for help from the British, to whom he sent a telegram expressing the wish for "unlimited co-operation". The General Secretary of the Muslim Brothers arrived and gave the coup the blessing of his movement, while the Arab League decided to send a delegation to investigate the situation.

Meanwhile Ahmad with his small force had marched unopposed through the Tihamah, where he had been helped by the Governor of Hodeidah, and joined some of his brothers at Hajjah where he was popular for he had once been its generous governor. His brother Hassan, who was well-known in the tribal areas, organised a force from the Hashid and Bakil; another Prince was active in the east. The army was shocked when it was learned how Yahya, their spiritual leader and the national hero of the resistance against the Turks, had died; it made no effort to defend the new regime. Tribesmen shared the same sentiment and deplored the breach of the oath to accept the succession of Ahmad. They were further stimulated when the Crown Prince, short of money, let it be known that he would have no objection to their looting Sanaa when it had been captured.

Yahya's meanness had led to rumours that he had built up an immense war-chest which the conspirators hoped to seize to finance their new regime. Their failure to find it, if indeed it existed, meant that they were unable to buy support and they started to split among themselves, finding that even Abdullah al-Wazir was unable to provide positive leadership in the developing crisis. They attached great hopes to international recognition through the Arab League Mission. Much time was spent in devising a new national anthem to greet the Mission and ordering cutlery for its formal reception, but it never arrived. Ibn Saud, horrified at the murder of a fellow monarch, invited it first to Riyadh for discussions and kept it there while Ahmad's forces moved on to the capital which fell on 14 March.

Ahmad, who had already declared himself to be the Imam, was officially recognised as such firstly by the *ulama* of Sanaa and then by foreign powers. The leading conspirators were imprisoned in Hajjah, except for Zubayri who was abroad on a mission to Ibn Saud. Abdullah al-Wazir, Jamal Jamil and some others were brought back to Sanaa for public execution: their heads were displayed for more than a week. Sanaa was given over to Ahmad's tribal supporters, who removed everything that they could carry down to doors and window frames.

The coup, the first to take place in the Arab world after the Second World War, failed largely because of the revulsion caused by the murder of Yahya and the general sympathy with Ahmad. Unpopular though Ahmad was, in the eyes of tribesmen he was seen to be avenging a personal wrong. Sayyid Abdullah was not cynical enough to disavow the murder and punish its perpetrator while profiting from it himself. His appointment of young men to places of responsibility and the bringing of Shafais into power alienated many whose support he needed, and religious and tribal leaders who had taken an oath to obey Ahmad upon his father's death were uneasy at the idea of breaking it. The new government failed to gain any control outside the city of Sanaa, and never won the support of the army. Kibsi's declaration that foreigners would be brought in to help the revolution alienated the still xenophobic populace, to whom the *Ahrar* were anyway suspect as agents of the British authorities in Aden.

The new regime failed likewise to attract any external support for there was not yet a Gemal Abdul Nasser ready to intrigue and interfere abroad in pursuit of his own ambitions. There was also a fundamental weakness which would anyway have broken up the conspirators: Sayyid Abdullah really wanted no more than a change in the personnel operating the system without any basic transformation in it; the *Ahrar*, for all their hopes of a new and ideal world, had no power base in a country which could only be dominated by the tribes and by the army.

The reign of the Imam Ahmad

Ahmad never forgave the people of Sanaa for their acquiescence in the murder of his father and perhaps he feared their resentment after the tribal looting that he had permitted, so he resumed his old residence at Taizz and revisited the capital only once. Except in matters of detail he ruled much as Yahya had done, showing the same enormous knowledge and intuitive understanding of the country, the same careful attention to the welfare, particularly the spiritual welfare, of his people, and the same harsh repression when it appeared necessary. From his youth he had set out to inspire fear – the story was often told that he slept with a rope tight around his neck so that his eyes bulged and terrified beholders. The credulous repeated that the Hamid al-Din family could command the services of *jinns*, that Ahmad had been seen to throw down a bundle of twigs which was instantly transformed into snakes, and that he had descended a well to wrestle with a demon for a treasure with which he had emerged after a struggle so titanic that his beard had turned white. This treasure and other bullion and jewels were said to have been put in secret hiding places by slaves who were then slaughtered so that they could not disclose them. The whole atmosphere of the Yemen during Ahmad's reign was thus totally different from the bustling commercialism of Aden or the developing Protectorates.

The coup of 1948 had made Ahmad distrustful of his people so he was much less accessible than his father had been. To counteract this, he let it be known that any telegram sent to him with a prepaid answer would receive his personal attention: a witness saw him deal with 200 in a single session. Like his father he conceived it his duty to concern himself with every detail of administration, authorising each purchase of an airline ticket or the issue of ammunition for his troops. He would have felt it dereliction of duty to have done otherwise, and anyway it was difficult to delegate any question involving money to corrupt and underpaid officials: so widespread was the malversation that a foreign visitor heard that the Minister of Finance had himself been caught and condemned to attend his office in shackles for a few days.

Originally, grateful for his actions in 1948, the Imam

appointed his brother Hassan as his Deputy in Sanaa and gave him the empty title of Prime Minister. However, he later realised that many would prefer his brother to his son Muhammad al-Badr as his successor, and he sent Hassan to represent Yemen at the United Nations and himself assumed the Premiership. Two other brothers held portfolios, as did Badr, but there was no Cabinet in any western sense – each Minister dealt only with the Imam and the actual administration was so limited that the Minister of Agriculture was reported as saying that the whole of his Department travelled on his donkey.

Ahmad's residence in Taizz and his mistrust of the Zaydi grandees made him more sympathetic to the Shafais than his father had been, despite suspicions that Hujariyyah had hoped to secede in 1948 and possibly unite with the Aden Protectorate. He appointed Shafais to high positions, including the Governorship of Taizz, and often himself led the prayers in their manner rather than in that of the Zaydis. He spent his winters near Hodeidah, which his father had never seen. He built a hospital there and encouraged its growth to prosperity.

Like many of his ancestors, Ahmad was a poet of taste and distinction, often exchanging stanzas with his adversaries. He could be moved by verse and several of the conspirators of 1948 who had been imprisoned in a dungeon in Hajjah obtained their release through lines which won his approval.

Although more distrustful of his own subjects than Yahya had been, Ahmad was much more accessible to foreigners. Indeed, he enjoyed talking to visiting doctors and engineers and showed considerable understanding of their work. He put fewer difficulties in the way of Yemeni youths who wished to go abroad and there were several hundreds at foreign universities by the end of his reign. He had no objection to his subjects importing electrical machinery and vehicles, as he collected heavy taxes upon them, often as much as the original cost, and even, tongue in cheek, told a would-be entrepreneur that he was quite free to open cinemas provided that he made no charge for admission.

Ahmad wished to develop the roads, hospitals and schools of his country but was hampered by a shortage of money: at his death only £8 million was found in his treasury. This poverty led to another relaxation in the policy of isolation – a positive search for foreign aid. Early in his reign Ahmad requested American assistance to build a modern port at Hodeidah, applied for investment under Point Four and for technical help from the United Nations. He gave concessions to the West Germans and to the Americans to search for oil and, finding no other patronage, accepted Russian technicians for Hodeidah harbour and Chinese labourers and a loan of £10 million to build a road from there to Sanaa. By the end of 1958 there were 500 Russians and 1,000 Chinese employed in these tasks. The story is told that when they had finished and applied for payment, the Imam replied that he did not like the work and that they might take it away again if they wished.

Ahmad realised that the invention of the transistor radio made it impossible to keep his people in ignorance of what was happening abroad and did his best to exploit the modern media. In January 1957 he invited a party of foreign journalists, sent them to Qatabah where he stage-managed a battle so that they might witness some British "aggression". He even gave an unprecedented press conference, at which *The Times* correspondent noticed "the stark gleam in his protruding eyes…he spoke in rapid gasps, pulling at his black-dyed beard". Yahya had regarded the person of the Imam as too sacred ever to be photographed, but portraits of his son were seen in the newspapers.

Events such as this and the increasing number of foreigners in the country were deeply disturbing to the more old-fashioned – the Yemen was still a profoundly conservative society. Education was still entirely Islamic and classical, there were no schools for girls, and in the hospitals all the female nurses were foreigners. Over half the children died before they reached the age of five and most were kept dirty to avert the evil eye. There was only a single Bank in the country and, apart from one textile factory which never succeeded owing to the intrigues of the local import merchants, there was no industry. Foreigners were unwilling to invest in a land where there was little security, what local capital existed was unenterprising, there was no infra-structure, government monopolies were restrictive and Ahmad feared that manufacturing would lead to Trade Unions with the consequences that he could see in Aden. The Jews were practically the only skilled artisans in the country, but all except a handful had left upon the creation of the State of Israel: Yahya once said that they had been in the Yemen for 4,000 years.

By the mid-1950s most of the old *Ahrar* were at liberty again. Although some accepted government appointments, others continued to work against the Imam while, as we have seen, some conservatives deplored what they regarded as the unseemly haste of modernisation. It was, however, from neither of these political wings that there came the first serious attempt to topple Ahmad from power. It is possible that his brother Ismail, who had been imprisoned for drinking, contemplated a coup in February 1950 but nothing came of it. In April 1955, however, the Imam disciplined the Chief of Staff and some of his soldiers for brawling with villagers. Incensed, the Colonel besieged the Palace and called upon Ahmad to abdicate in favour of his brother Abdullah. Abdullah had close links with the Americans whom the Imam distrusted because of their support for the British in Aden. Ahmad submitted and, remembering the widespread revulsion caused by the murder of Yahya, the conspirators hesitated as to what to do with him. While they vacillated, Ahmad's son Badr hastened off to the family stronghold of Hajjah to rally the Hashid to his father's aid. However, before they arrived, the Imam had regained control of the situation. There are various stories as to how he did it, the most picturesque being that he seized a machine gun from a sentry and charged out of the palace firing from the hip; another is that he bribed the guards to release him and subsequently fined them the same amount as a punishment for their conduct. Yet a third, told to this writer by a man who claimed to have taken part in the events, gives the credit for the reversal of fortune to his own tribe, the Ahl Muhammad of Hujariyyah. Many of its men worked as "boys" in Aden and as the leave season had started they were at home. They had been paid good wages so all had modern rifles and, being cooks, were well-fed and tougher than the average under-nourished Yemeni. When they learnt that there was trouble in the city they hurried in, anxious to join the winning side, but were misinformed as to which it was. Told that Ahmad was coming out on top, they attacked the rebel soldiers, who were no match for the fighting kitchen-boys.

This abortive coup was no revolution, merely a traditional attempt at changing the person of the Imam, but it had significant results. The first was that despite the desire of many of the family that Hassan should succeed him, Ahmad felt that Badr deserved appointment as Crown Prince. He announced this, saying that it was at the request of the people although it was against Zaydi traditions and upset many of the *ulama* and other conservatives. Secondly he never fully trusted the army again and although it may not be true that he always slept with vital parts of its tanks under his bed, he was unwilling to let it have equipment which would make it clearly superior to the tribesmen on whom he felt that he could rely: many of the modern weapons that were later imported were never issued. Ahmad personally supervised the public beheading of the Chief of Staff while Prince Abdullah and another brother Abbas who had joined the plot were more discreetly executed in Hajjah.

Yahya had always refused to have close relations with any foreign power and this was another of his policies that was reversed by Ahmad. He permitted a few resident Ambassadors and maintained his own abroad. After the British began their forward policy in the Aden Protectorate, where he was convinced that there was oil, Ahmad started a definite search for allies. Early in 1955 he joined in a security and military pact with Egypt and Saudi Arabia, known as the Treaty of Jedda, and as part of the agreement the Saudis gave him a considerable sum for the purchase of arms while Nasser refrained from any active support of the *Ahrar* exiles in Cairo. Shrewdly, however, the Imam realised that the greatest danger to his position was the expansionist ambition of Egypt under the banner of Arab Nationalism and that the threat of Communism was remote: he decided therefore to reinsure himself by entering into relations with the Soviet Union. Early in 1956 he concluded a trade agreement by which Russia would supply agricultural equipment, building materials, wheat and rice in return for coffee, fruit and hides and later in the summer he sent Badr, now his principal roving Ambassador, to Moscow. A trade treaty was made with East Germany, China was recognised and students were sent to Czechoslovakia: *The Times* warned that the Imam was playing with fire and gullibly admitting forces that he would be unable to control. Weapons arrived from the Eastern Bloc, although their acquisition was mainly a matter of prestige for they were too sophisticated to be maintained by the Yemeni armed forces.

Although Ahmad had taken the opportunity to show his Arabism during the Suez crisis by allowing 21,000 Yemeni citizens to volunteer for battle alongside the Egyptians, the Saudis started to worry that he was giving Communists access to the Peninsula so they persuaded him to send Badr to London to make another attempt to settle the frontier problem. Nothing was achieved and declaring "We are Russia's friends", Badr went on to Bucharest, Belgrade, Moscow and Peking, which he reached in January 1958, boasting that he had signed ten pacts with four Communist countries. After this the Russian press sacrificing as usual truth for political expediency always praised Ahmad as a progressive and anti-imperialist hero, and upon his death Khruschev declared that he "had made a worthy contribution to the cause of consolidating the political and economic independence of the Yemen".

Early in 1958, 35 people were arrested after another attempt on Ahmad's life and the Imam decided upon a masterstroke to disarm all but the most conservative of his opponents: he announced his adherence to the newly-formed union of Egypt and Syria. The armed forces of the two countries were to be united under the command of the Egyptian Field Marshal Amr and they were to follow united foreign, economic and educational policies. There was to be a Federal Council made up of equal numbers from each partner and supreme authority was to be vested jointly in Nasser and the Imam, who thus retained a veto in everything affecting the Yemen. From the beginning the arrangement was obviously a farce: Nasser was embarrassed to find himself yoked to so disreputable and reactionary a ruler but was unable to reject what was presented as a step towards Arab unity. It seems that only the simple-minded Badr, who had fallen under Nasser's spell during his visits to Cairo, took the union at all seriously.

Although the Cairo propaganda machine was thus prevented from attacking him openly, Ahmad had few illusions about the sentiments of Nasser towards his regime. When in January 1959 pamphlets against him, signed "The

Free Officers" (the title of the movement that had overthrown King Farouq), were discovered in circulation, he expelled the Egyptians who were training his forces. Three months later, Ahmad, who had been receiving morphine as a pain-killer for the arthritis from which he suffered, found that he had become addicted. He departed to Rome for a cure, to the consternation of many of the Zaydi *ulama* who were uncertain whether prayers would be valid in the unprecedented absence of an Imam from the country. His arrival in Europe, accompanied by at least thirty ladies from his harem, reputedly the most important of his hostages and the greater part of the treasury in the form of gold bullion, was a godsend to journalists who reported with fascination upon the doings of the party and upon the scimitars and muskets of his guards. They declared that the party rejected beds in favour of sleeping upon the floor and it was even said that Ahmad, lying upon a pile of cushions, showed his immense strength by inviting a doctor to stand upon his outstretched hand and raising him up in the air.

Badr was left in charge of the country. He was convinced of the need of Egyptian help to secure his own succession against the claims of the more conservative Hassan, whether or not his father ever returned. He also genuinely believed in the principles proclaimed by Nasser, in Arab nationalism and in the need for the support of the masses. He broadcast speeches about ending the rule of a corrupt clique, purged many of his father's advisers and he had himself hailed on the radio as "The Treasure and Hope of the Nation", personally reading out many telegrams which praised his liberalism and generosity. A group calling itself "The Young Sayyids" formed around him and advocated changes; there were also some elements who hoped for full-blooded Nasserism, extreme nationalism and a republic. Badr promised rapid development and, more practically, a 25 per cent pay-rise for the army. In the meanwhile he recalled the Egyptian officers expelled by Ahmad and even appointed one of them Director of Security. He started an airforce training centre with Egyptian instructors and brought in doctors and teachers who were at the time recognised throughout the Arab world as agents of Nasser's subversion, propaganda and intelligence service.

Events were soon to show that it was Ahmad, however, who

had the more realistic notions as to how the country had to be governed. It was found that the money for development and for the army simply did not exist and the pervasive Egyptian influence was greatly resented: a high official who defected to Aden told the British Agent Trevaskis that while Cairo declared that it loved the Yemen as a sister, it really desired her as a concubine. In June there were reports of unrest in the army and two unpopular Qadis were killed in Taizz. Badr had to admit that there was trouble and that it was no longer possible to be lenient and sympathetic towards wrong-doers. Finally he was ready to resort to traditional methods by bribing the Hashid and the Bakil to come to his aid.

In August, however, Ahmad announced himself cured and upon his return the unrest subsided almost instantly. We need not accept the tale that as he landed at Hodeidah he cried, "There has been a request for a Constitution," and, brandishing his sword, continued "This is the Constitution," but certainly, in a Quranic phrase he said that he would "cut off right hands and left feet" and would tolerate no more "nonsense". Heads rolled and he once again sent the Egyptians away, accusing them of being "tools of a foreign power". There were rumours that he had put Badr under arrest but in October he broadcast to the nation that the *ulama* had asked him to confirm the succession and he called for support for the Crown Prince, praying that he would help the poor and oppressed and stand for the ideals of Islam.

During this period Ahmad made one most uncharacteristic political mistake. He resented the loss of the money paid to the Hashid, and he invited their Shaykh Hussayn ibn Nasser al-Ahmar to come with a safe-conduct to discuss its restitution. After a furious altercation he ordered the beheading of the Shaykh and his son and although normally his executioners waited to see whether his rage would cool, this time they acted at once. There can be little doubt that afterwards the Imam deeply regretted a deed which stained his reputation and alienated the traditional supporters of his dynasty.

The fiction of the union with Egypt grew more evident, despite a letter from Nasser to Badr in January 1961 in which he hoped for reconciliation and the restoration of closer links; when Syria defected in the following September, Ahmad seized the opportunity to declare that he too was leaving. In November 1961 he published a poem ridiculing Nasser with wit and elegance, to which the less literate dictator was only able to reply by making the Imam Number One of the Cairo Radio series "Enemies of God", calling for his overthrow and making a formal breach of relations.

Despite Ahmad's toughness, the country was evidently changing. In 1960 there was urban unrest and 1961 saw the first strike and the first civil disobedience in the Yemen as the economic realities and political ideas of the outer world started to penetrate through the old walls of isolation. In March 1961 there was yet another attempt to kill Ahmad, who was left for dead in Hodeidah with four bullets in his body. His assailants naturally lost their heads but so tough was the old Imam that he survived for more than a year. However, he reverted to morphine to combat the pain, and gradually let power slide into the hands of Badr. On 19 September 1962 he died in his bed at the age of 63.

A decade after his death this writer had the opportunity of visiting Ahmad's palace, now a museum but still pervaded by his immense personality, and found himself powerfully reminded of our own King Henry VIII. Both were men of gigantic physical strength and overwhelming force of character, fierce, unscrupulous and merciless rulers when only these qualities could hold undisciplined people in check. Both were capricious rather than wantonly cruel, both were theologians and writers of distinction, both were intensely patriotic and determined to resist the slightest foreign encroachment. Neither had the least doubt of the superiority of their nation over the rest of humanity and both were determined to preserve and foster their original genius and, although deeply conservative, did not refuse to profit from all innovations. Both lived in constant danger of revolt or assassination and neither could afford to delegate substantial powers. Ahmad would have been at home in the European Renaissance, ruling a kingdom rapidly emerging from the Middle Ages: history was to show that with all his faults he at least gave the country a stability and security which it has never since regained.

Chapter Six

The Federation of South Arabia

Birth of a new state

We have seen that the attempt by Sir Tom Hickinbotham to create a Federation in 1954 failed because a group of Rulers, largely unprepared and with no tradition of mutual co-operation, was suddenly confronted by a proposed constitution which, while doubtless admirable from the point of view of a political scientist, bore little resemblance to the facts of life in Southern Arabia. Moreover, the proposed constitution held out no prospect of existence as an independent state. During the following three years several important events took place which made some form of unity appear more attractive, provided that it could be obtained on terms which were negotiated and not dictated.

From 1955 onwards there was a great revival of Yemeni subversion and of direct attacks across the frontier and in June 1956 the Frontier Officer at al-Baydha, Qadi Muhammad al-Shami, told a visiting journalist that the natural boundaries of his country ran from the Red Sea to the Arabian Gulf, including both Protectorates. At times Bayhan, Audhali, Dhala and Lower Yafa all came under attack and some form of co-ordination amongst the affected rulers was obviously necessary. Their apprehension was increased by the constant propaganda of Cairo Radio after 1956 which ceaselessly proclaimed that the British would be expelled from the Arab world. While the rulers did not really believe this, at the back of their minds, and in particular that of the Sharif of Bayhan, was the fear that a future Labour government might voluntarily depart, leaving them in the lurch with no prospect other than that of piecemeal absorption into the Yemen. The succession of

Crown Prince Badr was unlikely to be long delayed: as he was known for his Nasserist sympathies, this would bring the Egyptians to their doorstep and add to their danger. There had also been the attempts of Sultan Ali Abd al-Karim of Lahej to dominate the Western Protectorate. Thirdly, exploration for oil had started again in the Hadhramawt which was unlikely to share its wealth unless a partnership had been agreed in advance. Fourthly, the Abyan scheme had shown the advantages of inter-state co-operation and despite the meagre help afforded by the Colonial Development and Welfare Fund there had been advances in communications, agriculture and marketing which were not inconsiderable by local standards and which made internal boundaries an increasing anachronism. Finally there was discreet pressure from British officials and hints that financial help would be magnified if there were a union.

In June 1958 a party of Rulers, amongst whom the Sharif was the most eye-catching, came to London to put the idea of a union to which all of South Arabia could ultimately adhere. It would be an Arab state with its constitution only in Arabic, although the state would be in close association with Britain. It would need British support in troops and in money; the Sharif hoped for £20 million in the first year while the Audhali Sultan, the total revenue of whose state was £41,000 of which £25,000 came from the sale of arms, asked for £1 million for his population of 15,000 souls, At once the Secretary-General of the Arab League called upon all his members to unite to destroy the idea and Egypt and the Yemen were vociferously hostile. The Foreign Office was worried about this reaction and the Treasury dubious about increased expense but they were forced to give way to pressure from the Colonial Office and from the Ministry of Defence, at this time under Duncan Sandys, which was anxious to have a more secure perimeter around the Aden base, then growing daily in importance.

The result was a Treaty signed in February 1959 by the Governor of Aden, Sir William Luce, and the Rulers of six states of the Western Aden Protectorate, Bayhan, Fadhli, Aulaqi, Dhala, Lower Yafa and the Upper Aulaqi Shaykhdom. Starting with a declaration that "the Federation desires to develop ultimately into an economically and politically independent state in friendly relations with the United Kingdom", it specified that all previous agreements between Britain and the component states should continue in force and it extended British protection to the Federation as a whole. The British remained fully responsible for the conduct of its foreign affairs but could not make agreements about the frontiers without consulting the new government, which also bound itself to "accept and implement in all respects any advice given by the UK in any matter connected with the good government of the Federation" although the Rulers could express their views before this formal "advice" was given. London promised to provide financial and technical aid to help social, economic and political development and in particular the maintenance of a Federal Army and of a Federal National Guard (which was in fact the old Government Guards, control of which was handed over to the new administration), while the British maintained the right to station troops outside the Aden base.

As the Treaty was signed, the Queen sent a message of goodwill to the new state and *The Times* regarded it as "an important step towards finding a permanent solution", referring also, perhaps less felicitously to "the need to gather the sheep more or less into one fold". The Colonial Secretary spoke of future independence although he declined to set a date and the Fadhli Naib declared that the union would be based upon democratic principles, social justice and equality.

The new state started with daunting problems. It had no natural resources to provide an independent flow of revenue and was thus almost totally dependent upon external aid: in July 1962 *The Times* reported that Britain was paying 85 per cent of its expenses. Secondly it had to win acceptance in a sceptical world which saw it as yet one more British manoeuvre to make colonial rule look respectable through an artificial federation at a time when those of Central Africa and the West Indies were clearly falling apart. Thirdly it had to come to terms with those states which were not members and in particular with Aden which was still, of course, a Crown Colony. Finally, and perhaps most difficult of all, it had to establish institutions which worked: relations between the centre and the component parts are notoriously complicated in federations.

We have often remarked upon the spirit of fierce independence which characterises the South Arabian Arab: there has never been a tradition of accepting the judgement of one's peers and gracefully agreeing to abide by the decision of a majority and so, to preserve everyone's face, some form of unanimity must be found even at the expense of endless wrangling and compromise. No tribal leader would accept the superiority of another so it proved quite impossible to endow the new Federation with such a normal institution as a President: sovereignty was therefore embodied in the Cabinet, the Federal Supreme Council, with a rotating Chairman who changed monthly and thus made any continuity impossible. No Ruler could possibly accept exclusion from the Federal Supreme Council and therefore he had to be a Minister. Although this was not too serious a matter in the early days, finally there were sixteen members and the Cabinet became unwieldy and expensive with artificial portfolios. A further disadvantage was that a Cabinet consisting entirely of hereditary Sultans and Shaykhs automatically attracted hostility from professional democrats.

We have also seen that the Sultans were basically war leaders, guarantors of peace and arbitrators of disputes but definitely not administrators, and with few exceptions they had neither the training, the mentality nor the taste for detailed control of a government department. The spread of schooling to the WAP had been so recent that there was a very limited number of educated men of tribal birth capable of holding responsible posts so that these fell into the hands of people from Aden Colony, while the most senior of all were held by British Advisers attached to the Ministries. Whereas on their home ground the Rulers had held a great advantage over the British Officers because of their intimate knowledge of the country, now they were baffled with civil service procedure, and many became little more than rubber stamps in the hands of men who despite all their loyal and sincere devotion to building up the Federation were nevertheless still on the staff of the Colonial Office and thus ultimately responsible to Parliament at Westminster and not to their Ministers. Naturally no Minister, in his capacity as a Ruler, would permit any other Minister to interfere in his state nor willingly surrender any source of revenue. Finally what strength the Sultans had came from their close contact with their people and as Ministers in a faraway capital, they tended to lose this. These weaknesses might perhaps have been overcome if the Federation had been granted more than a decade of life and in particular if it had survived until a new generation could take over.

The Federation started without an office, without even chairs and tables, but in September 1959 it took a great step forward with the laying of the foundation stone of its own capital, al-Ittihad (The Federation) set deliberately outside the confines of Aden Colony. At the same time Lahej joined and three more states, Dathinah, Lower Aulaqi and Aqrabi, acceded in February 1960. Increased grants from London meant real progress in education, health and communications and in 1962 HMG spent £4 million on security in the area – this ensured that practically every tribal family had at least one member with a good and regular salary. An official report of 1960 admitted that "not much is known about mineral wealth" and although the Overseas Geological Service undertook a survey the following year, it found no evidence of significant deposits. However, cotton production boomed, with nearly 50,000 acres under cultivation in 1962 producing £1½ million worth of lint and seed. Attempts were made, particularly in the Fadhli Sultanate, to associate the people more closely with public events by creating councils. Although at first the members were nominated, elections for membership were introduced later – however, as the majority of voters carried rifles, elections had to be regarded as festivities rather than political contests.

The Imam regarded the creation of the Federation, like every other change in the Protectorates, as a breach of the Treaty of 1934 and refused to recognise its existence: in June 1959 his representative declined to enter into negotiations about frontier disputes when told that the Ministers of the new state would take part officially. However, deteriorating relations with Egypt and internal worries made Ahmad less inclined for adventure on the border and after a visit by Sir William Luce to Taizz in July 1960, relations were better than they had been for many years, leading even to the secret exchange of security information. Two prominent Yemeni exiles were expelled from Aden: Ahmad Muhammad Nu'man was told to leave in the summer of 1960 and in January 1961 the left-wing Muhsin al-Ayni had to move on to Cairo where he acted as representative of the ATUC.

The 1957 Defence White Paper envisaged that Aden, with Singapore and the United Kingdom itself, would be one of the three major military bases that Britain contributed to the world-wide system of western defence, for no major war east of Suez without allies was contemplated. However, in British minds, if not in those of all her allies, Nasser was the greatest menace after Russia and Whitehall strategists still foresaw the possibility of having to defend the oil-fields of the Gulf by force. The value of the new base was quickly demonstrated when British troops were in action in the summer of 1957 in support of the Sultan of Muscat against rebels in the Jabal Akhdar, in operations which showed the importance of the ability to move a force quickly before unfriendly powers had had time to organise opposition in the United Nations and other vocal circles. Troops could be acclimatised and equipment tested under Arabian conditions and early in 1960 the Royal Naval Amphibious Warfare Squadron was moved from Malta to Aden, where it was joined by a Royal Marine Commando and a squadron of a cavalry regiment with Centurion tanks.

Between 1957 and 1959 the service population of Aden increased four-fold, which led to overcrowding and slumlike conditions. From the end of 1959, with the ominous forecast by the *Daily Telegraph* that an immense increase in military building was normally the prelude to an evacuation, work started with such vigour that soon new flats were being completed for service men at the rate of one every sixteen hours. Messes, clubs, offices were started and in 1960 two major schools were opened. When in 1961 it became apparent that Kenya, where very much more had been spent, was about to become independent, the Defence Ministry crystal-gazers decided to undertake the biggest construction project in their history, to turn Little Aden into an enormous base with a £5 million cantonment for 2,500 soldiers, 1,000 women and children with workshops, schools, a church and a sportsground. The Minster of Defence, Harold Watkinson, was quite categoric that this time it was forever, saying in Parliament on 28

February 1961 that "we do not propose to leave the Arabian Peninsula and our treaty obligations there". With Cyprus now independent, Aden was easily the most important base between the UK and Singapore.

There was, however, a threat to its security developing as quickly as the base itself expanded. We have seen that the ATUC, drawing most of its strength from migrant workers who as Yemeni citizens were without a vote in Aden, had called for disruption of the Legislative Council elected in February 1959 and from then onwards it increased its use of strikes as a political weapon. In 1959 there were 84 strikes, causing the loss of 150,000 working days amidst an atmosphere of growing tension and indiscipline as the employers hit back with lockouts. The Trade Union newspaper, *el-Amil*, profiting from a freedom of the press rare in the Arab world, became ever more openly political and ever more vituperative. It was clear by early 1960 that the ATUC was by now less concerned with improving the lot of the labourers than with furthering the careers of its leaders through the expression of Yemeni nationalism – a sentiment that was more anti-British than pro-Imam, from whose harsh rule most of its members had fled. At a public meeting on 10 February 1960 the ATUC Secretary-General, Abdullah al-Asnag declared his "belief in a United Yemen...One nation, one Yemen...No North, no South but one Yemen...No Legislative Council. No Federation...There is only one Yemen, the occupied part of which must be liberated."

The Government tried to work with the ATUC in its industrial capacity and invited a retired TU official from London to report how it would be possible to have unions which were effective but yet would operate within a set of agreed rules: the ATUC refused to meet him. There were thirty strikes in the first half of 1960 and the Minister of Labour Hassan Ali Bayoomi said that at a time when Aden was looking forward to increased control of its own affairs, it could not afford industrial chaos. In August 1960 the Governor introduced the Industrial Relations (Conciliation and Arbitration) Ordinance which provided for compulsory arbitration before a strike or lockout could legally take place. It also safeguarded against the misuse of union funds for political purposes and established wage councils to make recommendations concerning the pay and conditions of the workers. *The Times* regarded it as "an extreme measure" but one that was justified by years of prolonged irresponsibility and on the day on which it was debated in the Legislative Council, a general strike closed down the harbour, the airport, shops and restaurants. Thanks largely to the efforts of Bayoomi it passed by 13 votes to 8 after a debate in which some of the Members walked out. The government offered to suspend application of the measures in return for a promise that the ATUC would work for industrial peace but met a decided refusal.

There was a diminution in the number of strikes but the ATUC attempted to intensify the struggle by enlisting support abroad and opening offices in Cairo and London where it prepared Questions for left-wing members of the Labour Party to ask in Parliament: this link which grew progressively more intimate was to prove of great importance while the Federation lasted. In January 1961 Bayoomi accused the ATUC leaders of aiming at dictatorship and of putting the whole future of Aden in jeopardy: in particular he charged that they were trying to obstruct the progress towards independence by inviting the United Nations to take over the administration.

The British authorities considered the possibility of neutralising the turbulent elements in Aden by merging the Colony with the Federation and after a report by the new Governor, Sir Charles Johnston, in March 1961 and a visit by the Colonial Secretary, Iain McLeod, in April, the decision to do this was formally taken in May. The reasoning was clearly stated by the Prime Minister, Harold Macmillan, in his diary, when he wrote that "the real problem is to use the influence and power of the Sultans to help us keep the Colony and its essential defence facilities". A few days later on 16 May he wrote that "the line should be to merge the Colony with the Federation of Rulers and give as much power as we can to the Sultans who are on our side". The value of the base was shown once again a few months later when it proved an essential staging-post for moving troops to Kuwait whose new independence was threatened by Iraq.

Quite apart from British military interests, a merger was

obviously to the ultimate advantage of both Colony and Federation for economic, geographical and historical reasons. On its own Aden was a port without a hinterland while the Federation was a hinterland without a port, although, of course, it was theoretically possible that it might create one of its own which would bypass Aden and reduce it to ruin. Neither had the potential to be a credible independent state without the other. Bayoomi, who emerged as the leading politician in favour of union, assumed that Lord Lloyd's denial of any possible independence for Aden would lapse upon merger with the Federation, whose eventual independence was written into its Treaty with London, and the recent British action in relinquishing control over Kuwait showed that they were prepared to loosen their grip upon the Peninsula. The Colony had ample money, but as Bayoomi said, not even a revolver of its own for defence, whereas the Sultans had few funds but numerous fighting tribesmen who were feared by the Adenis since the Government Guards had attacked a police station to release one of their comrades: they needed a voice in the control of this force. The Federalis – the term used by the British population to mean the Rulers and their officials – were alarmed at the possibility of a government in which the ATUC had great influence emerging in their rear and thus squeezing them between two states controlled by hostile Yemenis.

The necessity of a merger was thus obvious, but there were serious problems to be overcome. Firstly the Federation itself was not accepted by the rest of the Arab world and was the object of unremitting attack by the radios of Cairo, Baghdad and Sanaa, carried into every household by the transistor set. Secondly the people of Aden, apart from an occasional picnic at Lahej, hardly ever ventured into the Protectorate and were profoundly ignorant of conditions there, blandly assuming them to be barbaric: they had great difficulty in communicating with the tribesmen and not infrequently this writer found himself interpreting between an Adeni and a Beduin. There was also the problem of the future of the Hadhramawt, with whose enterprising merchant communities the Adenis felt that they had far more in common than they did with the peasant farmers of the WAP, and with whose alliance they hoped to outweigh the rest of the Federation. Another difficulty was financial, for Aden depended upon its status as a free port while customs duties were the main source of revenue in the Federation; also, the Adenis did not wish to have their money spent in the hinterland. Less obvious was the fact that some of the British officials on the spot were opposed to any merger, those concerned with the Colony wishing to keep out the beggarly Federalis while those in al-Ittihad were worried about the impact of wily Adeni politicians on the virgin WAP. Finally there was the sheer technical difficulty of reconciling two completely different political systems: the Federal Ministers held office by right of birth and each appointed six members to a docile Council while Aden had a Legislature with an elected majority to which its Ministers had to answer.

A glance at the Aden press for the first half of 1961 shows that the possibility of a merger was then hardly a burning issue. There was little news of what was actually happening in the Federation but considerable detail about immoral practices near the wall of the Maternity Clinic, about an ox that had gone mad in the *suq* and kicked an old woman in the jaw and about wild dogs in Maala. There were complaints about bus conductors winking at purdah ladies, noisy drunkards, careless student cyclists, the smell of rubbish dumps in Crater, postcards sold to tourists that made Aden look ugly and the practice of Hindu Doctors in automatically giving purgatives to all patients "thus deviating from a noble and humane task". Although most of the leading politicians controlled their own newspapers, they did not for the moment use them to air their views on the future.

When the political debate did open towards the middle of 1961 the merger of the Colony and the Federation was unanimously accepted amongst the Aden politicians who, indeed, saw themselves with a larger stage upon which to act. Asnag even attacked the British Government for what he called a separationist policy, dividing the port from its natural hinterland and he applied for permission to open Trade Union offices throughout the Federation despite its absence of industrial workers. The veteran Muhammad Ali Luqman wrote that the Federation and Aden formed a single unit. Bayoomi never had any doubts and the religious leader Shaykh Bayhani prayed for a successful merger. Only the South Arabian League, a tattered remnant with its leaders in exile, was opposed to amalgamation.

Hoping to profit from this general agreement, in the autumn of 1960 just before his departure, the most statesmanlike Governor that Aden ever had, Sir William Luce, recommended that the Colony politicians and the Federalis should be left by themselves to negotiate upon the terms for a merger. This policy, which naturally involved the grant of independence to Aden horrified Whitehall, and, in particular, the Ministry of Defence, jealous for its base, but it was almost certainly the only way in which the merger could have been achieved without serious opposition but, through lack of vision, London allowed it to slip.

It was unfortunate that Luce left at this stage and was succeeded by Sir Charles Johnston, a distinguished member of the Foreign Service, the staff of which is not trained to govern Colonies. Diplomats are sent to a post to perform a specific task and then move elsewhere regardless of the ultimate results while a Colonial Service officer, knowing that he might well live with the effects of his actions for the rest of his career, was bound to take a longer view: a diplomat, too, tends to regard a signature on a piece of paper as concluding a matter while anyone who knew South Arabia understood that it was by no means decisive. A Colonial Service officer, like a parish priest, was prepared to fight his superiors in the interests of his people while a Foreign Service officer, like a Jesuit, was so loyal to his masters' greater interests that he was prepared to be callous about individual cases. Whitehall should have made every effort to persuade Luce to continue to serve.

Even if Luce's plan had been adopted, there would have been formidable difficulties. Although those who boycott an election deserve little sympathy when they complain about the result, it was easy to attack the credentials of the Aden politicians who had been elected by only 27 per cent of the possible voters. The franchise anyway did not include the single largest group of the population, the 48,000 immigrant Yemeni workers: the ATUC had more members than the total that had gone to the polls. It would, however, have been extremely difficult to have held new elections for there was no agreement upon the franchise: old political leaders like Luqman and Bayoomi strongly objected to any system which would put power in the hands of non-Arabs, even of Aden residents of long standing with British passports, while Asnag naturally wanted votes for all his Yemeni supporters. Luqman and Bayoomi were unwilling to discuss a merger until this matter had been settled, while Asnag declared that while he would not form a party to oppose it, he did not support the Federation in its existing form.

In June 1961 some of the Federal Ministers went to London to discuss the accession of Aden and the future of the Federation for which, the Sharif repeated, independence was the ultimate goal. Shortly afterwards the Colonial Secretary invited the Aden Ministers to join the talks, but he made a major mistake in treating them as the sole representatives of political opinion in the Colony and in not insisting that Asnag and his colleagues should also have a chance to state their views. The two sets of Ministers agreed upon the need for a merger and decided to leave the details to be worked out upon their return home.

There was considerable dissatisfaction in Aden amongst those who had not been invited to the meeting and for the first time opposition to the merger started to form. Asnag said that the Federal Ministers were "imperialist dolls" and that those from Aden represented no one; Luqman argued that the negotiations for such a significant step as the entry of Aden into the new state could only be carried out by Ministers freshly elected on a franchise confined to Aden Arabs. By the autumn it was clear that several members of the Aden Legislative Council, including the Minister of Education, Abdullah Saidi, were dubious. However, Whitehall was anxious to take advantage of the severe blow to Arab nationalism and the personal prestige of Gemal Abdul Nasser brought about by the defection of Syria from the UAR and to hurry through the merger as quickly as possible: intense pressure, including threats and bribes, was brought to bear upon the recalcitrant members, who were vulnerable as businessmen with lucrative contracts with the government. Simultaneously the Federalis pressed for a speedy conclusion. They were not convinced that the authorities were in earnest as they had not seized the opportunity of a technically illegal strike, called with little industrial grievance to test the government's nerve, to crack down upon the ATUC.

In January 1962, therefore, opening a new session of the
Legislative Council, Sir Charles Johnston indicated that the
government was convinced in principle of the desirability of a
merger. However, a few days later everything was over-
shadowed by a bitter and hysterical strike which started in the
Girls' Secondary School, where it was alleged that British
teachers discriminated against Arabs in favour of Hindu and
other students. Other colleges joined in and every family in
Aden was affected as wild scenes took place. The authorities
managed to exploit the situation to discredit Saidi to the advantage of the pro-merger Bayoomi, and empowered him to make
concessions, previously denied to the Minister of Education,
to settle the strike. Nevertheless, they were alarmed at the
evidence of the extreme volatility of the whole Aden population, including the educated classes.

As an inducement to Aden it was announced in April that
London would give the Federation a block grant of £5 million
over the next three years. The Federation itself changed its title
to the Federation of South Arabia, as the previous style which
included the word "Amirates" would no longer have been
appropriate. In May agreement between the two sets of Ministers was reached on most points, leaving the final details for a
conference in London under the chairmanship of Duncan
Sandys, now Colonial Secretary. Abdullah Saidi formally dis-
sented, and was dismissed from office.

The support that Saidi attracted showed that the Ministers
did not reflect the opinion of the majority of the people of
Aden. While supporting the Federation as an ultimate ideal,
many Adenis did not want it until conditions in the old WAP
had risen nearer to those in Aden. Others disliked the way in
which it was being forced through. Luqman departed to lobby
the United Nations – his fare, it was said, paid by the US
Consulate in Aden. Asnag, unmoved by the bait that the
Labour Ordinance might be repealed if he kept quiet,
announced that he was forming the People's Socialist Party
(PSP) to oppose the merger. His newspaper said that the union
would be resisted until the end and, for the first time, called for
the closing of the base and the evacuation of all British personnel. He was greatly encouraged by the support of two Labour
MPs, one of whom referred to "the Tolpuddle Martyrs of

Arabia" and talked of "many grave indignities imposed on the people of Aden" while the other promised that "we shall be your representatives in Parliament": the two attended a meeting at which it was said that 10,000 people had assembled to denounce the merger and beamed genially but uncomprehendingly while a female firebrand declared her willingness "to spit at the Queen" and her hope that "the streets would run with British blood". Asnag was supported, too, by messages from the ICFTU and by the Egyptian propaganda machine which quoted the Labour MPs with relish and referred to "stark imperialism" and "puppet ministers and papier maché Sultans".

Sir Charles Johnston, however, said that the merger was an inevitable necessity and that it was too important to be obstructed by opposition. Although the Legislative Council, elected before the Federation was born, had naturally no popular mandate for a merger, he refused to bring forward the elections due in January 1963, saying that there was not enough time and that in the general atmosphere of intimidation, the British government had to accept responsibility and could not shift it on to the shoulders of the electorate. He declined, also, to pressure the Hadhramawt into joining or to ensure an election in the Federation where, as he urbanely put it, "they have their own special democratic system".

The main problem was whether Aden should be regarded as merely one of 13 states or as the equivalent of the other 12. The conference lasted three weeks during which Sandys kept both sides working until past midnight relentlessly cajoling and bludgeoning. Finally, almost out of sheer weariness, the Arab participants reached agreement, in order, they declared, "to bring nearer the achievement of full independence to which we attach the highest importance". The British government obtained its principal objectives, its sovereignty over Aden was not affected and it reserved the right to remove Aden or any part of it from the Federation "if it considers this desirable for the purpose of its world-wide defence responsibilities". The authority of the Governor, now restyled High Commissioner, was to prevail over that of the Federation in matters of defence, foreign affairs and internal security; the latter, although theoretically a Federal matter, was "delegated" to the High

Commissioner. Aden Colony achieved a measure of constitutional advance. A Chief Minister was to be appointed, on whose advice the High Commissioner would normally act except in the reserved matters. On the Legislative Council the ex-officio members were to be replaced by others elected by the existing members, although this naturally hardly increased its representative character. Aden was given a special grant of £$\frac{1}{2}$ million to meet transitional expenses. Furthermore, if after six years two thirds of the Council members so demanded, it could leave the Federation. Aden was to have four Ministers on the Federal Supreme Council and 24 out of 84 members on the Federal Council, a change in the quorum which ensured that the body could still function if all the Aden members decided to boycott it. Technically it all looked very nice, "an ingenious formula" said *The Times*, but it was surprising that Sandys, with all his experience, should have expected it to endure, obtained as it was by coercing and bribing unrepresentative politicians and blessed by the full-hearted consent of practically no one.

According to Bayoomi's newspaper, the returning Ministers were received with "fireworks, applause and love". However, to prevent any expression of popular opinion the life of the Legislative Council was extended for a year, thus ruling out an election before the formal accession date of 1 March 1963. Abdullah Saidi declared that he would oppose the merger by all constitutional means for the Federation "with 26 Imams" was "a pure autocracy under the whip of the British Agent". Asnag, encouraged by statements like that of the Labour MP Fenner Brockway that the union would be "regarded by all Arab states as an act of political aggression" and that of the Socialist International which declared it "against the will of the democratic forces in the area", talked of "destroying the Legislative Council" and of "dragging the Ministers in the streets".

The Aden Ministers tried to convince the people in a series of broadcasts. Bayoomi said that if it did not join the Federation now "on the most favourable terms", it might have to beg its way in later. Muhammad Husseini, the new Minister of Education, maintained that the base "was the largest single source of employment" and others argued that industrial troubles were ruining the country and that the merger would cost Aden nothing. There was, however, an atmosphere of violence for, denied access to the radio and excluded from the Legislative Council, the opponents of the merger had no other means of making their views heard. A few days before the Council debate Asnag was jailed for a fortnight for leading an illegal procession, thus removing him from the scene to the mutual satisfaction of the government and himself. When the Council met on 26 September there was a general strike and a riot in which British troops hurled tear gas bombs, the police killed a rioter and Bayoomi's newspaper and party headquarters were set on fire. For the first time a woman was arrested and she was later sentenced to ten weeks' imprisonment. Two newspapers, including that of the ATUC, had their licences withdrawn for "incitement to racial hatred".

The Members of the Legislative Council were torn between intimidation by the government and the menaces of the street mob. Finally, of the twelve elected Members only four voted in favour, so that the motion was forced through by five official and six nominated Members. The following day occurred the coup in Sanaa which overthrew the Imam al-Badr, and Sir Charles Johnston later commented that he was "pretty certain" that if it had been debated two days later the resolution would not have been passed. One is astonished that he could ever have believed that a settlement reached in such a way could have survived in a situation so completely transformed.

Asnag and the PSP were freed from the embarrassment of supporting unity with a Yemen ruled by the Imam Ahmad and Republican flags appeared in many streets. Muhsin al-Ayni, now Foreign Minister of the Yemen Arab Republic (YAR), declared that all Adenis were entitled to Yemeni citizenship. Asnag told a journalist "at heart I am a Yemeni" and that there was no further chance that Britain would be allowed to keep the base. There were reports that some of the Aden Ministers had changed their minds and rumours that even Whitehall was having second thoughts, as a delegation of Federalis hurried to London to urge non-recognition of the new government in Sanaa and firmer measures against local dissent. The Sharif of Bayhan, more practical, stayed at home to organise the smuggling of arms to the royalists and to use his great influence in the eastern deserts on their behalf: within a few days his activities were being denounced by Sallal, the new President, and by the ATUC.

The possibility that the merger might still be halted and the arrival of the Egyptians in the north kept up the excitement in Aden during the autumn. In October there was a series of illegal strikes which were followed by the deportation of nearly 100 workers and the imprisonment of Asnag and two of his colleagues. On 13 November, voting on party lines, the House of Commons approved the merger after a debate in which Sandys contemptuously dismissed the PSP demand for unity with Sanaa as "no more than an emotional expression of Arab nationalism by people who know that there is no risk of Britain's agreeing to it." For the Opposition Denis Healey attacked "the tying of Aden Colony...by far the most politically advanced territory in Arabia to the reactionary shaykhdoms" and asked why if the base were purely to defend the Gulf it could not be moved there at the expense of its wealthy Rulers. He repeated the call for new elections before the merger took effect although it was obvious that this would mean indefinite delay and that the Federalis could not be expected to agree to renegotiate a treaty already signed. This demand was echoed by the Aden Minister Muhammad Husseini who resigned and received a scornful letter from Sandys pitying him for his inability to resist intimidation. The ATUC reacted to the Parliamentary debate by calling a general strike, which most people agreed was less effective than usual.

In January 1963, after his strength had been still further increased by the election by the Legislative Council Members of four new colleagues to replace the official members, Bayoomi was appointed Chief Minister and the merger finally took formal effect. *The Guardian* gloomily forecast disorder until it broke up again; while *The Times* more optimistically referred to the "reintegration" of Aden and its hinterland and pointed out that the treaty was, after all, mainly of Arab workmanship. A few days later four Adenis joined the Supreme Council, one of them receiving the important Ministry of Finance. For the first time the Federation had a Foreign Minister, Shaykh Muhammad Farid al-Aulaqi, a man of great ability who combined descent from one of the oldest tribal families in Arabia with an education at Oxford.

A Foreign Minister was certainly needed. Relations with the YAR were becoming extremely strained as the Sharif of Bayhan continued to help the royalists despite Nasser's attempt to persuade the British to recognise the new regime in return for the dropping of its claims to the south. Early in November Sallal, however, referred to "the occupied south" and threatened to carry the war to "the ageing and ailing colonial empire" of Britain which he called "a hideous old woman." Muhammad Farid's first action was to protest that Sallal was inciting Federal dissidents to lay mines; later there were further frontier clashes and air incursions. Meanwhile, Sallal appointed a Minister for Southern Yemen Affairs. At the end of February he complained to the United Nations that there had been flagrant aggression by the British, called on "the brothers of the South to take revenge" and closed the frontier.

The second problem for the new Foreign Minister was that after the merger the United Nations started to take an interest in the affairs of South Arabia. In November the representative of the mentally unstable dictator of Iraq declared that the union had taken place against the will of the people, who should be permitted to join the YAR; other delegates too were convinced by the propagandists of the PSP. No one listened to Muhammad Farid as he attempted to explain the situation. It seemed that every country was entitled to express its views upon the problems of South Arabia except the legitimate government of the country, and no one wished to trouble to study the merits of the case. In May the Special Committee on Colonialism decided by 18 votes (of which only one was from a country where an opposition was permitted to exist) to 5 that the people of Aden should be permitted to "decide their future under free and genuinely democratic conditions" and that a Sub-Committee should visit the area to investigate. As *The Times* said, if the Committee members "were collectively activated by a dispassionate search for the truth", there would be a case for admitting them but it was clear from the beginning that they were only interested in facts that would permit them to treat the British government as a criminal: they were therefore refused entry to South Arabia and had to confine their activities to Cairo and Sanaa where, naturally, they only heard what suited them. In July the Sub-Committee of five recommended new elections, although only one of the countries represented had themselves held free elections in the previous decade.

Meanwhile, there was considerable progress in South Arabia itself. Three more states had joined the Federation, a national currency was arranged, and 36 senior military posts passed from British to Arab hands. New roads were built, hotels and post offices appeared and in 1963 there were over 200 students from the Federation receiving higher education in Britain. Muhammad Farid expressed himself satisfied with the financial aid promised by Whitehall and the statement of the Ministry of Works that during the next three years £30 million would be spent on the base meant that prosperity would continue. The capital al-Ittihad with its gleaming cars and modern buildings started to look like Kuwait – the only difference was that they had been bought not from oil revenues but from the pockets of the British tax-payer.

In the summer of 1963 there were two important changes in the *dramatis personae*. Hassan Ali Bayoomi died, leaving a gap that was never completely filled. Amongst Adeni politicians he had the greatest understanding of the problems of the Protectorates and he had the firmest faith in the future of the Federation which had been considerably shaped by his toughness in standing up to both the British and the Federalis. His strength of personality meant, however, that his colleagues were minor figures; other leaders such as Luqman and Asnag, who never forgave Bayoomi's part in the Labour Ordinance, could not work with him and were forced into opposition. His successor, Sayyid Zayn Baharun, was a leading merchant who fully understood that Aden's prosperity depended upon the base and upon trade, but who knew very little about the Protectorates. The second figure to leave the stage was Sir Charles Johnston. He was replaced by Trevaskis, who was suspect in the eyes of many Adenis because of his decade of close association with the Federalis. During these years he had incurred obligations difficult to disregard to Rulers such as the Sharif of Bayhan and the Audhali Sultan.

Baharun soon showed that he did not attract the same aversion as his predecessor, and he achieved a considerable success in bringing together a seven-man committee, free from British influence, to discuss the franchise for the next election. Although even the PSP agreed to take part it seemed impossible to find a formula that would satisfy everyone: each party advocated giving the right to vote to its supporters on ethnic grounds while ignoring other criteria. There was still opposition to Indians and Somalis, however many generations their families had lived in Aden, and the British were unwilling to give concessions to the immigrant Yemenis who had no permanent stake in the Colony and who were simultaneously citizens of a potentially hostile state. The announcement that there was no intention of postponing the elections beyond April 1964 made the matter urgent. A constitutional conference was arranged in London for mid-December, at which Baharun let it be known that he would request £30 million a year as rent for the base.

Again there was no question of involving the PSP leaders in the discussions and at a night-time meeting on the beach, they decided to wreck the conference. On 10 December one of their members threw a grenade at Khormaksar airport just as the Ministers and officials were leaving for London: an Indian woman in transit was killed outright, a Deputy High Commissioner, George Henderson, who had gallantly shielded his chief received fatal injuries and Trevaskis and the Fadhli Sultan were amongst fifty others who were wounded. A state of emergency was declared and some 200 Yemeni workers who did not happen to have money handy to bribe the police were deported and 55 were detained, including all the top leadership of the ATUC. Those arrested were kept in grim prisons in the WAP, whence there were soon complaints of torture and which the press, to its concern, was not permitted to visit. A delegation of Labour MPs came out to commiserate with the perpetrators rather than the victims of the outrage and found themselves greeted with stones from tribesmen who resented this attitude. Sanaa Radio referred to the "hero" whose "sacred hand" had thrown the grenade and Cairo also supported this act of terrorism. The grenade had effects which were to last until the end of the Federation. The British now tended to see all opposition as terrorist and the urban population as an unpleasant rabble in stark contrast with the decent men of the hinterland, whereas the strength of Labour support for Asnag and his colleagues encouraged them to believe that if they could hold out until there was a change of government in Whitehall, power would be handed to them on a plate. The whole constitutional process was delayed for six months, which meant that it was not complete when the British General Election occurred. The Federalis' distrust of the city mob increased, although the Audhali Sultan was quoted as saying that with 150 tribesmen he could wipe out the whole national-ist movement; the politically conscious Adenis were horrified at the incarceration of some of their number in the jails of the "feudal sultans". An Adeni Minister resigned, a Member of the Legislative Council said that conditions were worse than in Hitler's camps and they asked Trevaskis to intervene on their behalf: when he refused it increased their tendency to see him as an ally of the Federalis against them.

The day after the grenade had been thrown, the General Assembly of the United Nations passed a Resolution, num-bered 1949, which called upon the British to repeal all laws which restricted public freedom, to release all political prison-ers and "to cease forthwith all repressive action against the people of the Territory". It said also that there should be a provisional government after a general election, to be held on the basis of universal adult suffrage and supervised by the United Nations, and that the early removal of the base was "desirable". In April they called for the end of the state of emergency and re-established a Sub-Committee to keep in touch with the situation.

In the meanwhile there was an outbreak of tribal dissidence in the Radfan area where the tribes, nominally part of the Amirate of Dhala, had long ignored the Ruler. He in turn had made little effort to interfere with them. Now, however, as a result of the lavish British help to the Federalis, he had grown rich and the tribesmen felt that some of the proceeds should have been passed on to them. Therefore, in the old tradition, they cut the roads, and although a minor scuffle on 14 October was later declared to mark the start of the national struggle for independence, their first major exploit was an attack by some 200 tribesmen on a fort at Thumeir. Compared with the Upper Aulaqi and Damani troubles of 1955 or the Dhala operations of

1958, this unrest was on quite a small local scale. In the past such incidents would have been put down by an experienced Political Officer, some Government Guards and perhaps bombing: now, however, conditions were different.

There was now a shortage of experienced Political Officers; the two best, Johnson and Henderson were dead and most of the others had been absorbed into the expanding government machinery of al-Ittihad, where they served as Advisers to Ministers. Air control and the bombing of villages, although long proved to be the best deterrent, were felt to be out of keeping with the progressive trends of the age and there was reluctance to employ them, while Aden now swarmed with army officers anxious to win their spurs and to justify their existence at a time when defence cuts were in the air. Finally there was a new and aggressive policy on the part of the Egyptians occupying the Yemen, exemplified by Gemal Abdul Nasser who, speaking at Port Said on 23 December pledged that "the UAR will place all its potentialities for the liberation of Aden and the Protectorates from British imperialism". Groups of Egyptian Intelligence Officers were installed in frontier towns like Qataba and al-Baydha and took charge of the recruitment, training and equipment of dissidents.

Early in January some 200 British troops were in action in Radfan and their commanders deliberately set out to court attention. "The trouble-shooting reporter" of *The News of the World* "cabled from the sun-baked wilderness (where) no European had dared to penetrate" that "the dreaded wolves of Radfan (were) lean, wild-eyed, gun-toting killers", fighting the British to earn bride-money. This publicity was extremely good for army recruiting, and several decorations were awarded but it attracted much unfavourable scrutiny of the Federation from outside and encouraged the Egyptians to continue to support subversion once they knew that the eyes of the world were upon the area.

Although on 16 January 1964 the elections which were due to be held in April were postponed, the situation in Aden rapidly reverted to normal. The detainees were freed and Baharun brought forward a measure which was unanimously approved by the Legislative Council on 3 March, giving the franchise to males over 21 years of age who had been born in

Aden, or were naturalised and resident there, who could speak Arabic and who had never held any other passport. This effectively disqualified thousands of British and Commonwealth subjects, immigrant Yemenis and even citizens of the Federation who had not acquired sufficient residence. Apart from some shots fired at a group of opposition politicians having a quiet drinking session on the beach, safe from the prying eyes of their constituents, and a single grenade incident, there was no terrorism for several months after the airport incident.

Meanwhile the war in the Yemen was continuing, and, despite official denials, the Aden authorities turned a very blind eye to the activities of the Sharif of Bayhan in supplying arms to the royalists, caring for their wounded and stirring up trouble behind the Egyptian lines. The British delegate at the United Nations might say that the United Kingdom had "scrupulously" carried out a policy of non-intervention but everyone in South Arabia knew that this was not true. Indeed, it was deemed perfectly logical for the British to assist those fighting the troops of Gemal Abdul Nasser. It was not however surprising that the Egyptians should hit back and on 13 March two of their aircraft attacked a Beduin settlement with machine guns and incendiary bombs and a fortnight later one of their helicopters fired on a fort held by the Federal Guard. The Federal Government invoked the defence treaty and demanded retaliation and, after a warning, a fort at Harib just across the frontier was destroyed by RAF fighters with the prior approval of Whitehall.

There was an immediate international outcry and in London some of the Suez passions were stirred. *The Daily Herald* spoke of "a mindless zombie in Whitehall" who had authorised the attack and of "third division Kitcheners" while *The Observer* pointed out that the Sharif was within his rights in calling for action but that he was Britain's "most demanding ally" who alone could obtain military violations of the UN Treaty without exhausting the normal resources of peacekeeping. Denis Healey later said to Trevaskis that the attack on Harib was "our biggest mistake" and Trevaskis added "In retrospect I believe that he may have been right." Although justified from the local standpoint, it harmed wider British interests and it also alienated many officials of the Foreign

Office who complained privately that the country's Middle Eastern policy was being made by the Sharif and resented being blamed by international opinion for supporting him: some were to pursue the Federalis with considerable vindictiveness. The attack diverted attention from the far more blood-thirsty activities of Nasser in the Yemen, and there was a feeling that without the Imam the country was now "respectable" and should not be made the victim of a more powerful neighbour.

The YAR complained to the UN and demanded the closure of the Aden base. Relatively impartial delegates, however, shared Adlai Stevenson's difficulty in understanding what exactly had happened on a frontier which each side complained that the other was constantly violating. Eventually a mild motion was passed, deploring the British action and all other attacks and asking the Secretary General U Thant to use his good offices to settle outstanding issues. Nothing came of a British suggestion that the UN should do something practical like delimiting the frontier, and the Colonial Committee voted routinely by 19–3 for the immediate independence of Aden.

Opposition to the Federation

In April 1964, on his first visit to Sanaa, Gemal Abdul Nasser declared that "we swear by Allah to expel the British from all parts of the Arabian Peninsula", but even before that his agents had reactivated the troubles in Radfan. The first series of operations had had an ill-defined political objective – the troops had moved in, the dissidents had withdrawn and then the troops retired: nothing had been achieved and it was simple for Egyptians to claim a victory over the forces of imperialism. In March there were 24 shooting incidents on the Dhala road and in April 22 incidents. There were reports that the dissidents were organised in bands of up to 300 men, with uniforms and equipped with bazookas and automatic rifles. The Federalis would probably have been content to leave the area simmering but the military authorities in Aden yearned for what one of their Brigadiers was to call "a tactical exercise with tribesmen" and to test training and equipment. The Prime Minister, Sir Alec Douglas-Home, justified operations by saying that subversion was "encouraged and sustained from the Yemen". The action, which involved the use of 1,000 pound bombs and the burning of crops, caused political storms and *The Guardian* declared that the Federation had "dragged HMG from folly to folly". Over 70 journalists including an intrepid lady, sent home their stories and the tale that British soldiers had been beheaded by the dissidents produced a spate of headlines.

Despite editorial forebodings that Radfan would prove to be Britain's Vietnam, the fighting lasted only six weeks, during which the military authorities doubtless learned some lessons. The Egyptian propaganda painted a picture of a defenceless people resisting enormous forces trying to compel them into allegiance to the reactionary rulers of a state to which they had never belonged. On 19 May the Arab League "deplored the brutal British aggression and the war of extermination exercised by the British imperialists against the national strugglers in defiance of the UN Charter, principles and resolutions, as well as the sacred right of people to self-determination" and followed this not inaccurate picture of what the Egyptians were themselves doing in the North by a call to Afro-Asian countries "to positively contribute to the consolidation of the just revolt in the Occupied Yemeni South". When all was over Denis Healey declared that "the troops have done their job magnificently" and drew the conclusion that "the Aden base is necessary to Britain's role in Africa and the Middle East", sentiments with which his leader, Harold Wilson concurred.

The Constitutional Conference, which had been delayed by the airport bomb was now urgent. As Sandys said, the arrangements of 1959 were out of date while Baharun thought that the method of governing needed altering "from A to Z". Trevaskis advocated that only essential British controls over foreign affairs and defence should be maintained, that sovereignty over Aden should be ended, that there should be a large grant for rapid development, and that a definite date should be set for independence which would be followed by a guarantee of defence against external aggression. Like Luce's last proposals, this was a statesmanlike act which might have saved the situation but once again it was too radical for Whitehall, where, despite the limitations of its political understanding, the Ministry of Defence had a disproportionate voice.

After a month of pounding the Ministers, Sandys was able to state on 7 July that it had been "decided radically to reshape the Federal Constitution on democratic lines". Independence would come in 1968 and in the meanwhile the civil service would be completely arabised. There would be a President and a Prime Minister and a National Assembly formed after direct elections in urban areas and indirect elections in tribal territory, a system which had already worked in the Fadhli Sultanate. However, under the pretext that the talks were government to government, no attempt was made to insist on the participation of the PSP leaders, although one had said recently that they would consider Britain's retention of the base. Abdullah Asnag was not consulted although he was in London. Despite this he had long talks with Labour leaders, in which he convinced them that he was a moderate democratic socialist, struggling against Rulers who were automatically dubbed feudal and reactionary, although no one quite knew what this meant in the context of South Arabia: in particular he impressed upon them that there could be no progress while Trevaskis remained. Unwisely the Federalis made no attempt to put their case to potential Ministers in the next British government, although they did try to make friends abroad with Muhammad Farid announcing that the new state was being viewed with some sympathy by the Rulers of Jordan, Kuwait and the Lebanon. Routinely the Sub-Committee on Colonialism denounced the changes and so did the Arab League, despite a message from Muhammad Farid that independence would range a large and well-trained army by their side.

Just before the Conference ended, the Fadhli Sultan, one of the original Federalis, defected to Egypt where he denounced Sandys for his "haughtiness, rudeness and threatening language". His flight attracted excited headlines but had little practical effect in South Arabia, although it was exploited by Nasser in an attempt to unify all the forces opposed to the British in Aden. The Fadhli Sultan held meetings with the exiled Sultan of Lahej, with Asnag and with previously unheard of local groups such as the Free Bayhanis, the National

Hadhrami Conference and the Youth of Yafa, trying to knit them all together under the title of the National Front for the Liberation of Occupied South Yemen (NFLOSY). Although Nasser was most conciliatory early in July in an interview that he gave to Messrs Stephens and Seale of *The Observer*, saying that he had no objection to an independent South Arabia if all concerned agreed or even to the retention by the British of "a military staging-post", which he distinguished from a "base", a month later Seale was reporting that Egypt had decided upon "an all-out war of liberation".

Nasser now aimed to show that Aden was ungovernable without his acquiescence. To do this he made use of the Aden members of the Arab Nationalist Movement, which under the leadership of George Habash was based on Beirut, and combined extreme Marxism with an equally extreme nationalism. It recognised no Arab boundaries and established clandestine groups in secret contact with the leadership, which was always ready to use violence to achieve power. The founder of the Aden branch, which called itself the National Liberation Front (NLF), was Faysal Abd al-Latif al-Shaabi, a man with numerous personal grievances who worked in the Federal Ministry of Commerce and Industry. Its membership included trade unionists dissatisfied with Asnag, several members of the police and armed forces, junior government employees whose educational lack of success did not promise them a bright future, intellectuals with ideological commitment and teachers and students at Aden College. Their link with Cairo was provided by Faysal Abd al-Latif's cousin, Qahtan al-Shaabi, a former member of the SAL who while working as an Agricultural Inspector at Lahej had defected with government funds.

Nasser had lost confidence in Asnag who was basically a man of words rather than of actual violence, whose support in the ATUC was waning, who knew nothing of the hinterland and who anyway was prepared to wait and see what would happen when his Labour friends came to power. Nasser preferred the tough tribesman Qahtan whom he had once appointed as head of the projected National Liberation Army (NLA). Although internal feuds had caused the NLA to fall apart, Qahtan had contacts with men who were prepared to fight, and he was able to arrange for grenades to be thrown in

Aden and for a rocket attack in August which damaged the Legislative Council building. Journalists and government servants received letters warning them that murder awaited those who collaborated with the British, and two newspaper offices belonging to Federal Ministers were burned. Meanwhile an Egyptian officer at al-Baydha was reported by Sanaa Radio to be distributing mines and grenades and to be training Protectorate dissidents as parachutists. Qahtan's communiqués, broadcast by Cairo, claimed the opening of new fronts in Dhala and in Dathinah.

The elections for the Legislative Council were to be held in October and Asnag, perhaps fearful that he might himself be elected and thus be seen working with the British or that he might have to make promises that he could not fulfil, called for a boycott. A sign of his declining influence was that two of his supporters, including one Khalifah Abdullah Khalifah who was still detained upon suspicion of throwing the airport bomb, announced themselves to be amongst the 47 candidates for 16 seats. The importance of the election was attested by the large sums of money spent by some of the candidates and it was said that two wealthy Indian brothers, who had passed their necessary examination in Arabic, cut banknotes in half, giving one to a voter and telling him to return for the other portion if they were elected. On polling day there was a single grenade thrown but 76 per cent of the 8,000 voters went to the polls. For the future of South Arabia, the simultaneous election in the UK which brought in the first Wilson Government was far more significant.

The Aden poll was headed by the Chief Minister Baharun and by Khalifah, who obtained about 98 per cent of the votes and whose immediate release from jail was demanded by the other Members, ten of whom indeed suggested that he should be appointed Chief Minister. Asnag, conveniently forgetting that he had called for a boycott, claimed that nearly half of those elected were his supporters and although it quickly became clear that the new British government did not intend to abandon the base, he had hopes of coming to some agreement with it. No one took any notice when the UN Sub-Committee of supposed experts on the area, failing to notice that the side that it had supported had won, called for fresh elections.

Aden was obviously one of the most pressing problems for Anthony Greenwood, a leading member of the Society for Colonial Freedom and of the Anti-Bloodsports Society who had taken over from Duncan Sandys. He was confident that reason and moderation would prevail. As a gesture of goodwill he swept aside the objections of the Federalis and ordered the release of Khalifah and he made little secret of his view that he regarded Baharun as an irrelevance and Asnag as the real leader of Aden. The Labour government, remembering how it had been his ally at the time of Suez, naively thought that Nasser would be grateful and not oppose their efforts but he realised that a deal between Greenwood and Asnag would cut the ground from under his own feet and increased his support for Qahtan; hoping, as Patrick Seale reported, to mount "an offensive to bring the Federation to its knees within three months."

Greenwood arrived in Aden on 26 November 1964 amidst an outbreak of terrorism which he realised had been "specially laid on for my visit": he described it as "brutal and senseless". It was directed against British service men and their families and claimed 5 deaths and 35 wounded in a single weekend. He travelled widely in the area for ten days, and when he left he emphasised that the British government would stand by the pledges made by its predecessor to maintain the base and to grant independence not later than 1968. Nevertheless he gave the impression of a fresh approach for he "succeeded in un-freezing local attitudes" in the words of Patrick Seale, persuading both the Colony politicians and the old Federalis to accept "a unitary state on a sound democratic basis". There would be a common executive, judiciary and legislature, a single citizenship elected on a common franchise after a transitional period: the details were to be worked out at a Constitutional Conference to be held in London in March 1965, although working parties of Ministers were to start at once.

Greenwood's purpose was to give the Federalis some say in Aden while allowing the Colony politicians scope throughout the old WAP. Despite the opposition of Cairo, it was welcomed by Asnag who regarded it as "in line with the UN proposals". Time was however to show that when they had had the opportunity to consider the detailed implications the

Federalis came to regard the plan as too drastic, while the Adenis felt it gave them too little. As a symbol of the new age, Trevaskis, who was identified in most minds with the more unpopular measures of the previous government, was dismissed. He was replaced by Sir Richard Turnbull, who had played a considerable part in bringing Tanzania to a peaceful birth. Almost simultaneously Asnag announced that he was giving up his post with the ATUC and it was generally believed that he did this at the request of Greenwood to depoliticise the unions.

These developments were viewed with great hostility by Nasser, who regarded it as essential for his prestige that the British should not peacefully hand over power but should be seen to have been driven from the Arabian Peninsula through his efforts. He had no wish that South Arabia should become an independent viable state under any auspices but his own, or to provide too great a contrast with the troubles that he was encountering in the north. He therefore determined to increase the terrorist campaign, until, as Radio Sanaa announced on 27 December, there was a "blood-bath".

Nasser's Intelligence Officers drew up a well-thought-out plan for operation by Qahtan and his terrorists. The first essential was to wipe out the Police Special Branch and other organisations engaged in security. This was so successful that five officers were murdered in six months: others were frightened by threats to kill all who collaborated with the British and were not too zealous in their duty. The second feature of the plan was to stir hatred between the local population and the British troops. This was started by the throwing of bombs, one of which killed an English girl at a teenage Christmas party and another wounded children at an army cinema. The soldiers reacted roughly, and even people who were basically pro-British turned hostile after brusque searches. Trade suffered as some areas became unsafe. The third objective was to keep the security forces at full stretch up-country by making trouble in as many places as possible. A surrendered terrorist appeared on Aden Television describing his six month course in guerrilla tactics and photographs were shown of Egyptian-made booby traps fashioned out of school satchels and thermos flasks. Even the American Ambassador in Cairo came to realise that "the

Egyptians may have been directly involved in bombing incidents".

Nasser regarded it as essential that the proposed Constitutional Conference should be aborted and when the NLF announced that it would kill anyone attending "the conference of treachery", the Aden politicians had little doubt of their ability to do so. The SAL declared that as the meeting would be "between master and servant", they would not attend. The more adroit Asnag formulated conditions for his presence that he well knew would be unacceptable. Even the Federalis made difficulties, with Muhammad Farid contending that they would not participate unless the states of EAP took part as full members – this with their hopes of finding oil they were unwilling to do.

The argument over the role of the Hadhramawt led to a clash between the Aden government and the Federalis, as a result of which Baharun offered his resignation to the High Commissioner. Turnbull not perhaps the most tactful of men made little effort to make him reconsider. It was unfortunate that he did not understand the pressures on Baharun or realise that he was one of the few Colony politicians who really believed in Federation. It was equally unfortunate that Turnbull saddled himself with a successor who was bound to prove more difficult. His choice was Abd al-Qawi Makkawi, who was known to be opposed to the Federation. He was an employee of the famous Red Sea trading firm of Besse, appointed a director when the business felt that it needed an Arab for the sake of its image but wished to have one, according to Aden gossip, who was not intelligent enough to be a nuisance.

From the beginning it was clear that Makkawi knew that it was impossible to work both with the British and the terrorists, and that he had little doubt which was the more dangerous to offend. He appointed Khalifah Minister of Finance and in his first public statements he declared that he would work for a complete revision of the Constitution, votes for Yemenis who opted for citizenship, the end of colonialism, the repeal of the Industrial Relations Ordinance, "restoration of general liberties" and subsistence allowances for the families of detainees. When a series of terrorist attacks led to the imposition of a curfew, he publicly dissociated his government from the decision, accusing the British troops of "acting like madmen" in spreading panic by snatching people from their beds. One of his supporters even suggested that the bomb throwers were really Englishmen in Arab dress. Makkawi said that he could make government impossible, and one of his Ministers threatened "we can create anarchy if we find that Britain does not wish to respond to our demands". Towards the end of April he demanded the early closure of the base and the full implementation of UN Resolution 1949, which although formulated by a group which had never even set foot in Aden, he regarded as a magic panacea for all problems and as an incantation which could be used whenever he was pressed to do something positive. When the Supreme Council criticised the Resolution, Makkawi's men walked out.

As the March Constitutional Conference had gone by default, the Wilson government made the first of many attempts to find someone to solve the Aden problem for them. The previous Conservative cabinet had regarded any attempt at involvement by the UN as mischievous but naively Greenwood thought that its intervention might be helpful. He announced in mid-May 1965 that he had invited its participation in a commission to consider an appropriate constitution for a unitary state which would become independent in 1968. The UN, however, regarded constructive activities as opposed to meddling no part of its work and refused to help. Greenwood still pinned his hopes to a commission with international representation and stated in July that the former Chief Justice of the Sudan had agreed to join two Englishmen on a visit of several months to Aden. Makkawi, however, had little difficulty in persuading the Sudanese government to get their citizen to withdraw and to prevent the other two from coming, he declared that he would ban their entry as "undesirable immigrants": what Sandys called "a futile attempt to shelter behind an international commission which has no authority" thus collapsed in ignominy for Greenwood and triumph for Makkawi.

In the meanwhile, with continual clashes in the hinterland and occasional violations of the frontiers, terrorism in Aden continued. In 18 months after the airport grenade, 5 Britons and 14 Arabs had been killed and 150, mostly British, injured.

Cairo declared that "killing imperialists is a legitimate act and one of the chief aims of the revolution." The NLF claimed responsibility for all these actions and in June 1965 the High Commissioner declared it a terrorist organisation and assumed powers to combat it. Suspected members could be detained, anyone convicted of assisting them could receive a maximum of ten years in jail, while minor acts of support might be punished with up to three years imprisonment. Makkawi immediately denounced the new measures and so did a body recently formed in Taizz. This was the Organisation for the Liberation of the Occupied South (OLOS) which was an amalgamation of the SAL and the PSP: Asnag had come increasingly to realise that his old Labour friends were not going to instal him in power in Aden. The NLF did not join the organisation for it was always adamant that its aims could only be achieved through violence, while the OLOS did not despair of gaining success through political means although it by no means ruled out terrorism. Both these groups still existed entirely through Egyptian support, while Makkawi did not dare to appear less nationalistic but could only live from hand to mouth, with no real party or policy of his own, scoring points off the British and in the words of *The Times* "playing the game of obstruction for all that it is worth".

In an effort to get things moving forward again Greenwood came unexpectedly to Aden at the end of July. Once again it seemed for the moment as if he had achieved a surprising success: he told the press that "a crisis had been averted" and that a working party would meet in London the following week to plan for a full Constitutional Conference in December. Despite Qahtan's threat that anyone attending would be regarded as a traitor, both Makkawi and Asnag arrived. It soon became clear, however, that they had come merely to obstruct, for they refused to take part in any discussions unless all their demands for total and immediate acceptance of the UN Resolution and on the base were met. There was no possibility of agreement and the talks collapsed. Asnag disingenuously explained that "the British had terminated the talks for reasons best known to them".

By the mid-1960s Britain had shed most of its old colonial Empire but always there had been a Nehru, a Nkrumah, a

Kenyatta or a Makarios around whom a new polity could form: in South Arabia there was no commanding figure. Neither Asnag or Makkawi knew anything of the hinterland where anyway, as "suq-rats", they commanded not the slightest respect. The NLF leadership was clandestine, and none of the Federalis had any following in the Colony. The one figure with sufficient personality and political skill to act on a world stage, the Sharif of Bayhan, had ceased to play any role since the fall of his friend Trevaskis. Whitehall still, however, clung to its hope that someone could settle the Aden problem for them and its next unlikely candidate was Gemal Abdul Nasser. It was argued that since Nasser had suffered reverses in the Yemen he would be happy to make peace: in fact, the opposite was the case, for he needed some success to counterbalance his defeats, and Aden, where he had already invested much time and money, was the most promising location. London decided to send George Thomson, a junior Foreign Office Minister, to Cairo, amidst a series of leaks that perhaps after all it might be possible to give up the base in favour of a staging post.

Soon after the Ministers had returned from London, Sir Arthur Charles, the Speaker of the Legislative Council, became the eleventh Briton to be murdered. Although Taizz Radio broadcast a communiqué from the NLF claiming responsibility and adding that all British officials would be "shot one by one like dogs", Charles had been both deeply respected and very popular – in private Makkawi and his Ministers expressed their regrets. The High Commissioner, however, pressed them to do so in public and despite the comment of *The Daily Telegraph* that they were "rebellious, criminal, craven or ineffective" it was difficult not to sympathise with one of their Members who asked "who will protect those who do condemn? [the murder] Every Member of this Council is exposed to assassination and we will not be surprised if one of us is killed after leaving the Council." Far from blaming the NLF for the murder, Makkawi called for its recognition as a legal political party and said that it should have a voice in negotiations. Another Member of the Council declared that "we cannot gain our rights except through the use of arms". Turnbull thereupon dismissed Makkawi, suspended the Constitution, and imposed direct colonial rule.

Independence and the British withdrawal

Makkawi, despite his statements that "the whole Aden people will stand as one in the face of British imperialism" and that the government "had lost its mind" in dismissing him because he had refused to act as its puppet, was surprised and glad at escaping from office with a whole skin. Trevaskis regarded the suspension of the Constitution as "an unprecedented act of despair" and disastrous in its timing, for, if Thomson had been able to reach an accommodation with Nasser, it would have been unnecessary; if he had failed, it could have been done after his visit to Cairo. However pressure from the Federalis and even more from the Service officers in Aden, whose morale was low in the general uncertainty about the future, proved decisive. The British had once had the option of either making the Federation work by giving it whole-hearted support or of coming to terms with the opposition but now, despite a lingering hope that Asnag might still co-operate, they had little choice but to rely on the Federalis. It had become clear that neither they nor their opponents wished to form a coalition to share power but wanted complete control. There therefore seemed to be nothing for HMG to do but to hang on in the vague hope that something would turn up to save the situation. Whitehall hoped that perhaps his setbacks in the Yemen might cause Nasser to withdraw and thus deprive the opposition of its principal support, or that eventually democracy might seep into the Federation making it generally acceptable. Lord Beswick, the Under Secretary dealing with the area, told Muhammad Farid that "you must build up a popular regime and this will enable you to stand against any outside threat" and "what we want from you is a more liberal attitude in order that we can rally UN support", but he had no practical advice as to how this might be done.

Nasser contemptuously refused to see Thomson but his officials did meet a party of Federal Ministers, telling Muhammad Farid that the UAR was not "against shaykhs, sultans or any Arabs in South Arabia but was committed to rid the area of British imperialism". They demanded a promise that the base would be closed but the Federalis replied that this would be a matter for an independent South Arabian government.

Soon after the failure of the working party in London and even before the dismissal of Makkawi, the Federal Supreme Council invited Sir Ralph Hone, who had been Constitutional Adviser to the government of Kenya and on Central Africa, and Sir Gawain Bell, a former Governor of Northern Nigeria, to visit Aden to advise on constitutional changes. Their report was presented at the end of January 1966, envisaging what they called the "United Republic of South Arabia", an ingenious compromise between a federation and a unitary state with Aden, no longer a Colony, as its capital. There was to be a Council of States and an elected National Assembly, a President with limited powers and a Prime Minister, responsible solely to the Assembly, who should select a Cabinet in which no Ruler could hold a Ministry. It was a blue-print for a liberal democracy which in an ideal world should have satisfied everyone, but of course it had little appeal for groups striving for absolute power. Asnag, indeed, denounced it even before publication as "naked aggression against the rights of the people" and, produced as it was just before the Defence White Paper, which settled the fate of the area, it was still-born.

Terrorism in the autumn of 1965 was carried out partly by a few highly skilled and trained assassins and partly by indiscriminate hired bomb throwers whose efforts were often as dangerous to themselves as to others: youths paid a few shillings often forgot in their excitement to remove the pins from their grenades. British families were a particular target and in mid-September a bomb was thrown in the lounge of the airport where children were waiting to fly back to England after their school holidays. The arrest of 79 NLF men on 23 September revealed that they had prepared maps showing where some of the 300 British families lived in Crater, and a later haul produced weapons and explosives with Egyptian markings. British-run schools were closed and bars and cinemas placed out of bounds. Officials were made to feel that they were never far from Nasser's attention and some received letter-bombs. Pressure was kept up also on the local people and when seven Aden newspaper owners were threatened by the government with closure if they continued to print terrorist communiqués, they replied that they had been threatened with death by the NLF if they did not. On 1 October Asnag was quoted as saying that "we are in a state of semi-war. We recommend our members to use any means, violent or non-violent, to show their resistance to British rule." This call was followed by nearly a fortnight of the worst rioting that Aden had ever seen in which Federal forces had to help to keep order, tear gas was used against school boys and girls and British troops had to fix bayonets. Over £250,000 worth of damage was done. At the end of the year it was calculated that 48 members of the security forces, 60 civilians and 115 terrorists had been killed: it was a terrible figure, even if it did not quite match the NLF claim that they had killed 1683 soldiers and destroyed 18 aircraft.

Despite the troubles, it was a period of considerable prosperity in which cultural and economic life flourished. It was rather unfair of Philip Goodhart to say in the House of Commons that as a centre of intellectual sophistication Aden was comparable to Millwall, for the Colony had acquired a good museum, a TV service and there were 24 periodical publications. For the first time an Arab was appointed to the Supreme Court and policewomen appeared on the streets. Great blocks of flats, often built by Ministers to rent, replaced the old shanties in Maala, and competition for labourers meant that wages were high. Up-country rifles flowed in an apparently unending stream: issued to favoured tribesmen for £3, they could easily be sold for £60, and some of them ended up as far away as the Congo. The Federal forces, so large now that nearly every group benefited, were the best paid in the Peninsula apart from those of Kuwait. The Federation as a whole became accustomed to a standard of living which it had not earned and which was not justified by its own resources, for it was kept up by British subsidies. In 1965 aid amounted to £17 million and the Federal Minister of Finance stated in August 1966 that 75 per cent of the revenue came from HMG. In addition a further £14 million was spent locally by forces and civilians.

The government paid particular attention to the expansion of education upon which it spent 20 per cent of the budget apart from military costs. There was full universal primary and intermediate schooling in Aden and places at secondary schools, which provided a better training than those of richer countries like Libya and Kuwait, were opened to competition. Evening classes, co-educational for the first time, were available for those who had not achieved examination success. In 1965/6 there were 268 students from the Federation, amongst whom was the daughter of Makkawi, receiving higher education in Britain, and this figure included 60 at Universities. Rural districts received intermediate boarding schools and even a backward area like Wahidi had a girls' school. School Health Officers were appointed and as late as August 1967 there were still advertisements for headmasterships of new schools.

The hinterland was also given seven major hospitals and malaria was almost eradicated. Particular attention was paid to communications, with a bitumen road up to Dathinah under construction, postal services were introduced, villages were endowed with fresh water systems and electricity came to many places. Dathinah held local elections and Agricultural Co-operatives and a Cotton Producers' Federation looked after the interests of the peasants. New crops were introduced and training courses arranged for fishermen. Only in industrial development was little done, for it was difficult to create new manufactures without a protective tariff which would have ended the free port upon which so many depended for their prosperity, and there was a shortage of skilled labour. In view of the general boom, Makkawi's statement that the British had neglected the country and that he would do more in two years than they had in 130, seems particularly silly.

The advent of the Labour government in October 1964 did not at once change the defence policy that had been laid down in the Duncan Sandys White Paper of 1957, despite the fact that Richard Crossman, who had become a member of the Cabinet, remarked earlier that "the defence of the scattered remnants of a great Empire may be more burdensome than the defence of its earlier unity". Harold Wilson in particular felt that there was a vocation to continue to maintain Pax Britannica and that the important special relationship with the US was justified by the fact that the British could, through their world-wide bases, achieve things impossible for the other Allies. There were also commitments to defend Singapore and Australasia and on 16 December 1964 the Prime Minister told the Commons that "we cannot afford to relinquish our world role – our role which for shorthand purposes, is often called our 'East of Suez role'". This could only be maintained if there were a base in the Arabian Peninsula which, anyway, was felt necessary to safeguard the oil fields of the Gulf upon which the UK was still completely dependent.

In a period of inflation the government wished neither to increase expenditure nor reduce commitments, but this was becoming impossible. As the financial crisis worsened it was obvious that something would have to be cut and many in the Labour Party felt that if economies were necessary, they should fall upon defence rather than upon social services and doles: some no longer wished to pay the price of a world role and East of Suez was costing £320 million a year. In particular the closing of the Aden base would save £200 million a year and it was easy to argue that there was something rather ridiculous in an impoverished country with its out of date aircraft hanging on there while its international influence was tangibly declining. Terrorism meant that more troops were now employed in guarding their families than were available for service outside the base. Despite this, as late as November 1965 Lord Beswick said after a visit that he was sure most people wished the base to remain.

However as Wilson's support for the Americans in Vietnam became more unpopular with his left wing, he felt that something had to be done to appease them. Optimists in the Foreign Office believed that Nasser and his followers would be so gratified and convinced of British goodwill by an announcement of an impending departure from Aden that they would immediately call off their campaign of terror. There were comforting thoughts in the Ministry of Defence that uninhabited islands in the Indian Ocean or increased facilities in Bahrain could take over Aden's role and provide all the fun of building new bases. It was, however, as Philip Darby wrote, "in the offices of the Treasury that the retreat from the world role began" and by the end of 1965 it was decided that the defence budget for 1969/70 had to be cut from £2,400 million to £2,000 million. In January 1966 Denis Healey and the Foreign Secretary went to Washington in the forlorn hope that the Americans would make good the deficit, but they returned with empty hands. When, therefore, the Defence Review was presented on 22 February, Healey announced that when South Arabia became independent by 1968, Britain would not retain military facilities there.

Lord Beswick, who in November 1965 had gone to Aden to tell the leaders of the Federation that the British would stay, returned before the publication of the White Paper to announce that they would leave. The Audhali Sultan, Chairman of the Federal Supreme Council, remarked bitterly in reply that this was "dishonourable". "For years," he declared, "we have borne the abuse and vilification of much of the Arab world because we believed that the British government was our true friend...(but now it) finds its own self interest to desert its friends and leave them in the lurch" and "the whole Arab world will regard us as fools for having placed so much reliance on the solemn word of the British government." "You are economising," he said, "at the expense of the lives and prosperity of other people." He pointed out that the agreement contained no provision for unilateral abrogation and another Ruler compared the Federation with a trapeze artist whose partner had unexpectedly gone on a lightning strike. The Sultan of Lahej told a journalist that they had believed that whatever British government was in power, its word would be honoured and indeed that this had been promised by Healey himself the previous year: how could the oil states, he asked, be sure that pledges however solemn would not be sacrificed to political expediency.

Just as Asnag and his associates had made contacts with Socialist politicians while that party was in opposition, now the Federalis sought friends amongst the Conservatives. Before the White Paper was debated, Trevaskis wrote to *The Times* that independence without a defence agreement while 65,000 Egyptian troops were on the northern frontier would be a "mockery" and that Sandys had "given a solemn assurance that a defence agreement would be concluded to provide continuing British protection" for "to launch South Arabia into independence without assuring it of any adequate defence against external aggression would be an act of bad faith and cynical irresponsibility". Healey at first tried to brush the commitments aside by saying that the government to which

they had been made "has now disappeared" but had humi-
liatingly to concede that the pledges had of course been given
to the Federalis and not to the suspended government of Aden:
he then tried to deny that there had been any "ratting" on
British promises, although he agreed that the previous June he
had promised to honour the treaty commitments. Labour
spokesmen, inspired by Wilson's dictum that "the lawyers can
get out of this treaty", argued that an independent South
Arabia could no longer expect the same consideration as a
protectorate and that obligations would lapse, while Conservatives spoke of "a breach of faith", "humiliation" and
"sheer stupidity", warning that terrorism would soon strike at
any new base in Bahrain and that a vacuum would be created
into which Russia, China or Egypt would step. They pointed
out that a valuable bargaining counter to get the Egyptians out
of the Yemen had been thrown away and when Nasser was on
the brink of defeat "we have given an injection of new life into
a discredited dictator". After the Audhali Sultan's speech to
Beswick had been leaked to the Tories, the battle was resumed
with Sandys accusing the Prime Minister of having "grossly
misled" the House of Commons, in reply to which the Foreign
Secretary, Michael Stewart, could do nothing more convincing
than accuse him of being "mischievous".

The almost simultaneous publication of the Hone-Bell Report and of the Defence White Paper announcing that the
British would leave Aden meant that the original objectives of
the nationalists would be achieved and that there was no further "need" for terrorism. However the evident abdication of
responsibility encouraged further violence. Nasser wished to
see the British depart with the maximum of humiliation so as to
regain the prestige that he had lost in the Yemen; moreover,
rival groups began to dispute the inheritance. Although both
were supported by the Egyptians, – in July 1965 Faysal Abd
al-Latif told the NLF Executive Committee that "until now
we have been totally dependent on the financial support which
is offered by the UAR" – there were real differences between
the NLF and the OLOS of Asnag and Makkawi. The latter was
predominantly a party of the educated Adeni bourgeois with
some remnants of the North Yemeni labourers who had been
recruited by Asnag into the ATUC and followed Nasser impli-

citly while the NLF, drawing much of its strength from the tribal hinterland, was at lower levels becoming increasingly Marxist. However, in January 1966 the Egyptians forced an amalgamation of the two under the composite title of the Front for the Liberation of Occupied South Yemen (FLOSY) and in March Makkawi announced that he was Secretary General of a twenty-man revolutionary council with its headquarters in Taizz to which all anti-imperialists could adhere. Qahtan al-Shaabi refused to accept this arrangement and was imprisoned in Cairo.

Aden was now in the position that more of its leaders were in exile than at home participating in events, and the Federal government started to seek reconciliation with as many of them as possible. In April a group of Ministers went to Beirut where they met some of the tribal dissidents, including the former Fadhli Sultan who agreed to return, but Asnag and Makkawi who had promised to be present were frightened from doing so by the Egyptians. Later the South Arabian League came back, saying that Hone-Bell was worth study and calling upon the Arab League not to support FLOSY: the Egyptians responded by closing its offices in Cairo and Taizz. In May, as a further gesture, the Federal government announced that it would accept the UN Resolutions by which its opponents set such store and called for a conference of "all who care for the homeland" to discuss its implementation. The EAP, still relatively untroubled, refused to take part; the High Commissioner declined to press them to do so and therefore the initiative collapsed.

The Federalis came to accept that a military base under British sovereignty would constitute an embarrassment to an independent country for, as the Audhali Sultan said "it not only marred our reputation but also created an iron curtain between the Federation and other Arab states". However, there was clearly a vital need to replace the aircraft, armoured vehicles and heavy guns with which the British had supported the Federal forces. Early in June after a South Arabian mission had been in London, it was announced that London would contribute £5½ million for the expansion of the local forces and increase its annual subsidy by £2½ million for three years after independence. The army would be expanded from six battalions to ten and aircraft would be supplied. Turnbull said that although this would be a small force, he did not think that the independent Federation would be exposed to foreign aggression, but if it were it could defend itself until the UN came to its aid: perhaps he had not heard that that body had not been very successful in the north.

The value of UN assistance was shown at the end of July when two aircraft from the YAR attacked the town of Naqub near Bayhan, wounding some children with shells of Russian origin. The matter was discussed by the Security Council where the Egyptians asserted that the British had faked the incident to assist Israel while the Yemeni delegate, Muhsin al-Ayni claimed piously that "my country has always been the victim and never the perpetrator of aggression". With British prompting, the New Zealand Delegate suggested that the UN should send a mission to investigate but the idea that the UN should act impartially or try to find out the truth instead of uttering routine condemnations of imperialism was considered outrageous by the Russian Delegate. Naturally nothing was achieved.

Even before the attack on Naqub, the Federalis and their Conservative supporters were urging the need for a British commitment to continue to defend the area after independence. Indeed in a debate on 11 July 1966 Reginald Maudling, the former Colonial Secretary asserted that there was already "an absolutely clear and binding undertaking to help the Federation after independence" and the former Prime Minister, Sir Alec Douglas-Home, declared that this could only be ended by the mutual consent of both parties. In reply Michael Stewart, the Foreign Secretary, argued that after independence there would be a different state with which Britain was under no obligation to enter into a defence agreement. The Federalis, in a series of meetings, pointed out the weakness of this claim and the Audhali Sultan said that they would need an assurance of defence for as long as the Egyptians remained in the Yemen. They would not be able to assure their own internal security before the middle of 1968 and there was a real possibility of a civil war in which FLOSY might invoke intervention which the Federalis would not be able to ward off because they had no air force. The Sultan said that there would be little use in appealing to the UN after an invasion and was so insistent that Stewart was driven to snap "do not talk so much about the British forsaking your country". After George Brown succeeded Stewart, he tried to persuade them that they would not be accepted as independent members of the UN if they had a defence treaty, an argument that they disposed of by pointing out that the existence of such treaties caused no one to doubt the independence of Malaysia, Singapore, Kuwait or Libya: they were hardly reassured when Brown told them "you are on my conscience".

Terrorism became increasingly sophisticated in Aden. Incidents involving point-blank shooting and electronic mines began, in addition to haphazard grenade throwing. June was the worst month so far with 8 killed and 50 wounded and in the whole of 1966 there were 45 deaths and 538 injuries in 500 incidents.

Acts of terrorism could be divided into three kinds, Firstly there were those directed against Arabs who collaborated with the authorities. In February 1966 FLOSY threatened to kill anyone who accepted a nomination to the Supreme Council and in April it published a list of 162 people who were to consider it a final warning. In the same month the Minister of Defence, the Sultan of Lahej, narrowly escaped when a mine was detonated under his car, in August a newly elected Adeni member of the Federal Council was murdered and some months later there were bazooka attacks on the houses of Ministers. Other victims ranged from a Deputy Permanent Secretary of the Federal government to a clerk in the fire brigade.

Secondly there were attacks supposedly on British personnel and their families, although in practice any westerner was at risk: a woman tourist from a passing ship, a German business man and an American seaman were among those killed. Social life became restricted after two English ladies died when a servant concealed a bomb in a cabinet and the High Commissioner called on the British community to avoid giving parties and to consider whether they really needed servants. He himself nearly lost his life on 11 February 1967 as just before his arrival for the celebrations of the National Day a mine was found in the place where his helicopter was to land: it was later learned that this had been put there by a FLOSY member who worked as a driver for the Intelligence Office.

Most numerous of all incidents were those in which the NLF and the followers of Asnag fought for supremacy. In February 1966 Asnag's successor as President of the ATUC was murdered, two months later the General Secretary of the Bank Employees Union was killed by a FLOSY man and then the pro-NLF President of the Civil Aviation Union was seriously wounded by a grenade. The rivalry was made more obvious when in December 1966 the NLF formally announced that it would carry out its "revolutionary responsibilities" independently of FLOSY, which it regarded as merely an Egyptian puppet. The increasing predominance of the NLF was shown in January 1967 when it called for a general strike in memory of the day on which the British had seized Aden 138 years before and although the ATUC and FLOSY disavowed the call, there were major riots. The next month saw the murder of one of the former Ministers in Makkawi's government and the following day an explosive device killed three of the sons of the ex-Chief Minister. Their funeral was a highly emotional event in the course of which two men were beaten to death. To protect its supporters, Egyptian Intelligence officers trained a special group of FLOSY members which was known as the People's Organisation of Revolutionary Forces (PORF).

Many of the Aden Police, knowing that the British were going to leave, were naturally unwilling to make enemies amongst the ruthless men who would probably be their future masters; others, including an Inspector, actively supported the terrorists for ideological reasons. Not infrequently, therefore, wounded terrorists were sheltered in police stations and they or their weapons were moved through search cordons in police vehicles and even launches which other security forces were not permitted to check. In November 1966, in the third such incident in five months, a police sergeant was seized by the Irish Guards as he threw a grenade at their patrol.

As the Aden Police proved increasingly unable and unwilling to combat terrorism, the Federalis begged that they should be allowed to do so with their own troops which they still believed to be loyal. In April Muhammad Hassan Obali, the Adeni who had been appointed Minister of Education, claimed that the Regular Army could restore order in a fortnight if given a free hand. Their case was supported by Duncan Sandys in a letter to *The Times* of 6 March in which he urged that responsibility for law and order should be transferred to the Federal Government as soon as possible for "it is essential that they gain some experience of this difficult task while British advice and support are still available". The High Commissioner combatted this view, arguing that as their methods were unlikely to be gentle, it would be better if Britain were no longer even formally responsible and anyway that he could not share the control of security while British lives were still at risk. Turnbull refused even to hand over Shaykh Othman where the European population was minimal, and in the meanwhile he would not put a single policeman or vehicle at the disposal of the Federal government, who thus had no authority outside al-Ittihad. The Federalis accused him of abdicating control to the terrorists in the January riots, saying "you keep us out and let the terrorists in": the NLF and FLOSY were collecting taxes to finance their activities while people known to be loyal to the government feared for their lives in Crater.

Turnbull, who cordially disliked the Rulers whom he described as "a bunch of bonnet lairds", refused to help them himself or to press their case upon Whitehall. The Federalis pleaded that the situation needed Arab measures but these he firmly refused to countenance. The Federalis felt that pressure on the Egyptians to cease support for the terrorists could be brought to bear through the Sanaa government by deportation of Yemeni workers or by sending Yemeni merchants resident in Aden to explain the situation. Nevertheless Turnbull said that the only proper course was to make representations through the American Embassy which represented British interests in Sanaa. After the murder of one of their colleagues, the Federalis closed the frontier so as to divide the Yemenis from the Egyptian terrorist masters by destroying the trade of Hujariyyah: after a few months Turnbull forced them to reopen it. The Federalis discovered the presence in Aden of four well-known terrorists who were preparing to lead the riots in January but were told that they could not be arrested because they had not yet rioted. Obali, who managed to reopen the schools in the face of a FLOSY boycott by organising schoolboy gangs who took on the FLOSY gangs, was rebuked by the High Commissioner. When the man who had sent a letter bomb to a senior British civil servant and then returned disguised as a woman to Aden to organise further acts of terror was captured, he was quickly released by Turnbull on the orders of Whitehall: the Audhali Sultan complained that "you release one of our most vicious enemies and we are not consulted". In the face of the High Commissioner's attitude, the self-confidence and prestige of the Federal government gradually ebbed away.

The main burden of maintaining security, therefore, fell upon the shoulders of the British troops. One Battalion in six months searched 35,000 Arabs and 8,000 vehicles in the course of which they captured 12 grenades and 6 pistols: this small return reflected their lack of good information despite, or more likely because of, a multiplicity of Intelligence Officers whose reports often coincided because they had in great secrecy and with much self-congratulation all paid the same lying agents. However, the greatest problem for the troops was the refusal of their political masters to recognise that there was an actual emergency which could only be dealt with by methods inapplicable in normal circumstances. Families should have been sent home, relieving their guards for security duties, and the death penalty made automatic for anyone caught carrying weapons. The soldiers came to feel that even if they caught a terrorist he would not be punished, while they themselves would be if even in good faith they killed a suspect who later proved to have been innocent. The use of bayonets even in self defence was forbidden, and for many months they could shoot only after they themselves had been fired upon. Until April 1967 they were not allowed to pursue even an identified sniper into a house unless accompanied by a policeman and if they saw a man with a rifle go into a mosque, they had to ask an Arab soldier to go in pursuit and invariably he returned saying that he could not find the suspect.

Another problem that the security forces had to face was a well-orchestrated campaign accusing them of ill-treatment of suspects. The Egyptian Intelligence Officers told their recruits that they would not be tortured if they were captured but they were to claim that they had been, for then the onus of disproof would rest on the British. Their propaganda denounced "Torturer Turnbull and his gang of Sadists" while the ATUC called a strike to protest against British brutality. In October 1966 Amnesty International published a report by a Kurdish gynaecologist resident in Sweden in which various forms of maltreatment were described in detail: it was a remarkable document for this expert claimed to have investigated 300 cases in five days – which would have worked out at five an hour in a 12-hour working day. He could hardly have checked the accounts very thoroughly.

However even such unsubstantiated allegations needed investigation and George Brown appointed a distinguished barrister to go to Aden. He spent a fortnight preparing a report which was published just before Christmas showing that there had been some limited amount of wrong-doing. However both the Foreign Secretary and the Conservative spokesman agreed that the troops had shown remarkable restraint in a situation in which 36 of their comrades had been killed and nearly 200 wounded in terrorist attacks. Undeterred, in February 1967 the founder of Amnesty claimed that the news of the killing of 50 Arabs by British soldiers had been suppressed by the censors – a story found to be completely without foundation. During his visit he refused to take the slightest interest in the atrocities committed by the Egyptians a few miles away. The endless stream of allegations meant that British investigators had to devote almost as much time to investigating one another as they could find for interrogating suspects.

In November 1966 the Foreign Office, displaying a naive optimism rarely encountered since the simpler mediaeval saints vanished from the earth, reverted to the idea that UN intervention would be helpful. The UN agreed to send a mission despite the declaration of FLOSY that its arrival would be resisted and the lives of its members in danger unless it recognised in advance that FLOSY "alone has the right to determine the fate of the people". The FO pressed the Federalis to accept it which they did reluctantly, saying that it should not be intimidated by any "foreign-controlled group". However when it became known that the mission would consist of representatives of Venezuela, Mali and Afghanistan, the Federalis became alarmed that its composition was dangerous. To

Muhammad Farid's complaint that "not one member was even neutral", the FO soothingly replied that "Venezuela and Afghanistan were not hostile", and that they should congratulate themselves that Tanzania had not been included and that a South American rather than an African was chairman: the visit would be "constructive" and it was inconceivable that they would refuse to talk to the government of the country. Sandys warned that the mission was "nothing but an exercise in anticolonial and anti-British propaganda, likely to make the situation worse". FLOSY threatened "exceptional violence" during its visit which the NLF announced that it would boycott unless it undertook not to meet the Federalis. The prospects of its success were thus hardly favourable.

In July 1966 Sandys had asked whether the British government "think that (they) can force independence unilaterally on South Arabia whether they want it or not? It is quite clear that they do not", but early in 1967, perhaps now having misgivings about the UN mission, Whitehall attempted to do this. In February Muhammad Farid and Girgirah, one of the few Adeni politicians to show real faith in the Federation, came to London to say that it was useless to discuss independence without a guarantee of protection, for they still had no air force and they would not be able to ensure internal security until the middle of 1968: independence would also be impossible without the accession of EAP which Turnbull refused to pressure into union. On February 27 George Brown amplified earlier statements by promising that the British would provide an air component "sufficient to deter the kind of incident that has happened in the past", and on 10 March *The Times* reported that the British would retain the Khormaksar base for a limited period after independence.

Brown's proposals were given formal shape by George Thomson who flew to Aden without warning on 17 March. He offered independence in November, this would be followed for six months by air cover provided by a Royal Naval aircraft carrier. From London's point of view this had the merit of making the presence of troops to guard the planes unnecessary. The Federalis were taken by surprise and felt that HMG was weakening and that intransigence would gain them more concessions. They stood out, therefore, for independence in the spring of 1968, a defence treaty and the indefinite retention of British troops, arguing that they would not be able to rally support if people thought that they were to be sacrificed to the Egyptians after six months. Despite Muhammad Farid's hint that they might seek Russian support if abandoned by the British, Thomson said that HMG had the duty and the right to decide the date of independence.

The UN mission arrived in Aden on 2 April, announcing that it would remain for a few weeks but it became clear at once that three more perverse and preposterous figures could not have claimed to represent the collective conscience of mankind. They refused to recognise the existence of the Federal government, a reasoned letter from the Chairman of the Federal Supreme Council did not receive the courtesy of an acknowledgement and they were prepared to talk only to the British and the terrorists. Aden was in chaos, deeply flooded by the heaviest rains in memory, while there was savage fighting between NLF and FLOSY supporters in which about twenty people were killed. The mission lived in a fortified hotel which they left only once. They hoped to interview the detainees at Mansourah camp but the prisoners refused to speak to them and yelled abuse so that they left in dismay in a helicopter which attracted some bullets. They then decided to broadcast an attack on the Federal government, questioning its legality, without realising that the Federal authorities controlled the radio station and naturally refused to let their statement go out. Now in a complete fury, the mission decided to leave after only four days, making hysterical scenes at the airport with the Afghan shrieking "You British are bloody sight contributing to the bloodshed in the world more than anyone else" – a remark which well illustrates the spirit in which the UN mission had approached its task.

Sir Alec Douglas-Home regarded the performance of the mission as "totally discreditable and petulant", while, for the Liberals, Jeremy Thorpe "deplored the non-judicial manner in which this delegation has gone about its work". George Brown tried to save something by inviting it to London to discuss its complaints, although he admitted that he was puzzled by their claim that the local British authorities were unco-operative. At the same time he announced that a senior Minister, Lord

Shackleton, would go to help "the heavily stretched authorities" in Aden.

Lord Shackleton, his hand strengthened by a statement from Denis Healey that the last British troops would not necessarily leave before independence, spent more than a month in the area, visiting EAP and other up-country areas. He broadcast an appeal for all parties to come forward and discuss how to establish a broadly-based government to preside over the transition to independence, for Britain's policy now was "unite and quit". His main difficulty was that FLOSY and the NLF were only prepared to negotiate on condition that everyone else was excluded from the talks but he had secret meetings with the NLF and more public ones with the SAL; an attempt to contact FLOSY through Tom Driberg MP failed as a result of Egyptian pressure on Asnag and Makkawi. Like Thomson before him, he could not persuade the Federalis to accept independence on British terms, although the offer was improved to independence in January 1968 and air cover for nine months. However, the South Arabians, having won these concessions, stood out for more. They said that an off-shore air force directly controlled from London was not enough, and asked for the stationing of four Battalions for four years. Muhammad Farid said that a unilateral Declaration of Independence by London would be "a complete betrayal".

Naturally the FO could not admit that its own fatuous error in involving the UN had caused the fiasco, so a scapegoat had to be found. The obvious candidate was Sir Richard Turnbull, whose position had anyway been undermined by the arrival of Lord Shackleton. His departure was greeted with glee by the Federalis and by many British officials who felt that his deference to the armed forces had deprived the young Federal government of any chance to learn to stand on its own feet. His successor, Sir Humphrey Trevelyan, was a veteran Ambassador with long experience of difficult postings. Brown explained that the transition to independence needed the presence of a diplomat to carry out the policy of an orderly withdrawal of British forces, consultation with all concerned and especially the UN for the establishment of a broad-based government and the leaving behind of a stable and secure state.

While Trevelyan was assuming office, King Faysal of Saudi Arabia was paying a State visit to London. Since the early days of the war in the Yemen he had had close links with the Federalis, with a bond of joint enmity to Nasser, and as time went on they came to depend upon him more and more for support and advice. After the Defence White Paper of 1966 he told a party of Ministers that although he had no personal ambitions in the area, he would be prepared to take the place of the British if they left. In the meanwhile he advised them to follow Nasser's method of making big and impressive promises and then not implementing them: his opinion that they should accept the UN Resolution proved decisive and he recommended constitutional reforms that would seem democratic even if they themselves continued to hold the actual levers of power. He thought that he had sufficient influence in EAP to persuade the Sultanates there to join the Federation and that he could rally some support for them in the Arab League. His brother-in-law and closest associate, Kamal Adhem, suggested to them that they should not seek a formal defence agreement with Britain but should reach a secret understanding that troops would remain as long as the Egyptians stayed in the Yemen.

Faysal prevailed upon the Federalis to meet the dissidents in Beirut in April 1966 and his pressure brought about the return of the South Arabian League, which had long depended upon him for financial support. In November the Ministers saw him again and he said that he would try to overthrow the Qu'aiti Wazir, "a traitor who spoke only in the name of street urchins" who for Egyptian money was hampering a merger. He also advised, however, that the Federalis should put their own house in order before attempting to absorb EAP.

In January 1967 the Cairo newspaper *al-Ahram* published what is called "a very compromising document from Faysal's office in the Cabinet building in Riyadh" which showed that the Saudis and the British were working closely together over South Arabia. Faysal, said *The Voice of the Arabs* "has put his hand in Britain's sinful and criminal hand stained with the blood of millions of Arabs and Muslims". A further quotation will show the tone of the Egyptian propaganda of the time: "Faysal has committed a crime that goes beyond treason, subservience and deviation. If it is said that there is no misdeed beyond blasphemy, then this in itself is blasphemy."

On his State Visit, the King, in the words of Harold Wilson "gravely urged us not only to leave military units in the area but to accept a binding military commitment to use them to defend the new South Arabian state against attack or infiltration from UAR-inspired Arab nationalism". In most of the Gulf States, he continued, there were seditious groups ready to act when Nasser ordered and "unless we held firm in South Arabia, the Gulf would be subverted within months". Faysal argued that as 80 per cent of its population were not South Arabians, Adeni opinion was not important, and said that he was ready to help in the area if needed. In the meanwhile he thought that there was no point in trying to appease Nasser, for "agreements signed one day are violated the next".

Before Trevelyan could settle in, the whole situation in the Middle East was transformed by the crushing defeat of the Egyptians in the Six Days' War which began on 5 June 1967. In Aden riots broke out, and as the British were believed somehow to have helped the Israelis, there were attacks on British and Jewish property and sabotage of oil installations. Nasser, now reconciled with Faysal, was reported to have withdrawn 15,000 troops from the Yemen and the threat of his intervention in the South was sensibly diminished.

Encouraged by this weakening of the Egyptian position, Whitehall decided to follow the advice of King Faysal, reinforced by that of Lord Shackleton. Thus on 19 June George Brown, who a few days before had been described by Crossman as "appallingly uncertain of himself about the Aden policy", gave the most definite pledge yet for the future defence of the Federation. Independence would be on 9 January 1968 and a force of bombers would be stationed indefinitely on the island of Masirah where they would be within easy reach of the mainland; a strong fleet including a carrier would remain in the area for six months, detailed to repel any aggression. There would also be a further £10 million given in military aid, including eight Hunter fighters, radar, armoured cars, artillery and a Military Mission. The Conservatives were delighted, Sir Alec Douglas-Home said that it seemed as if the Foreign Secretary had defected to them, and Duncan Sandys thought that he might almost have been listening to himself speaking. The Labour supporters were aghast but Crossman recorded that "George is genuinely and passionately determined to get out of Aden at all costs and this package is solely designed as a cover for this operation."

The very day that reports of Brown's statement appeared in the press, Aden suffered its worst crisis. Some three weeks earlier the five Battalions of the Federal National Guard (formerly the Government Guards) were merged with the Federal Regular Army to form the South Arabian Armed Forces (SAAF); the General commanding the Middle East Forces sent the congratulations of their "British brothers in arms". The decision may well have made administrative sense on paper but its results were catastrophic. Two dissimilar forces, with different roles and traditions, were amalgamated without proper study of possible consequences. A decade under Army officers had turned the FRA into an imitation of a British regular Battalion with its theoretical abstention from politics, its separation of ranks, its formal discipline and its practice of living in large units divorced from its surroundings. The FNG on the other hand had been raised to assist Political Officers and was being stationed in small forts where officers and men messed together and discussed politics and mixed with the local people. Up-country, in a small station, the Arab officer or some old soldier often acted as a surrogate Political Officer, and discipline, although excellent on the battle field, tended to be casual in daily life.

The British officers responsible for the amalgamation had not properly considered a fair distribution of the highest posts amongst the two hierarchies that had co-existed, and they tended to find the FRA more congenial. Many of them, ignorant of South Arabian conditions, did not understand the importance of maintaining some sort of tribal balance and they allowed the two most senior jobs to go to members of the Aulaqi tribes, which also provided the Quarter Master and seven out of the ten Battalion Commanders although they consisted merely of 28 per cent of the force. By judicious promotions, their domination would have been secured in perpetuity so members of other tribes, headed by four Colonels, organised a petition to the Minister of Defence. The

Commander of the Armed Forces, as was natural in a British regular officer, treated it as a matter of military discipline and rather than trying to settle the matter in the Arab way by discussion or appointing mediators, suspended the four Colonels.

On 20 June some of their men started a disturbance and when they saw some British troops who were in fact returning from range practice, assumed that they were coming to restore order and opened fire upon them killing seven soldiers. In the hysterical atmosphere that followed the Six Days' War it was easy to believe that the British were firing on Arabs on behalf of Israel and the trouble spread to al-Ittihad, where mutineers briefly occupied government buildings.

Later in the day the Armed Police in Crater feared that a routine patrol which they saw approaching was coming to attack them and they shot it up, killing thirteen British soldiers amongst scenes of wild brutality. The evening came with Crater no longer under government control and with an uneasy calm elsewhere.

For thirteen days the most densely populated part of the Colony, ringed with British troops, was cut off from the rest of Arabia while the Federalis urged that their troops would probably mutiny again if ordered to move in. The authorities even considered leaving it alone but its proximity to the vital Khormaksar airfield might have endangered the forthcoming withdrawal of British troops. The area was therefore occupied in a surprise move by night without resistance. The leading nationalists had already been smuggled out in an ambulance with a police escort.

The collapse of the Federation

The events of 20 June destroyed the credibility of the Federal government, not one of whose Ministers had tried personally to confront the mutineers: furthermore, when peace was restored they declared themselves satisfied with an apology and made no attempt to purge disloyal elements from the Armed Forces. The problem for the British was that they had no legal right to overturn the Federalis, whose members could have gone home and made trouble in their own states, and there was nothing, anyway, with which to replace them. Although the Hone-Bell Report had been published in January 1966, the excitement caused by the Defence White Paper and the worries over the future had meant that for months it was not even discussed and matters were allowed to drift along. At last, in October, Turnbull had recommended that an Adeni should be appointed Prime Minister to replace the rotating Chairman and that one-third of the Ministers should be from the Colony, while those that were not should have an Adeni deputy. In December the Federal Supreme Council established five committees to study a new constitution but when broad agreement emerged in February, there was still no consensus as to who should be its head. The hereditary leader of the area, the Sultan of Lahej, lacked personality and was basically a country gentleman interested in expanding his estates – this he did so effectively that by the spring of 1967 he owned 190 of the 220 irrigation pumps at work in the Lahej Oasis. The Sharif of Bayhan who in his prime would have carried off the position with supreme panache had not been seen in the capital since the fall of Trevaskis although he retained the Ministry of the Interior: in February *The Times* reported that he was being invited to form a government but that he was continuing to be sulky and preoccupied with intrigues with the Saudis and in Yemen. The two most prominent and successful up-country Ministers were the Audhali Sultan and Muhammad Farid, neither of whom would willingly accept the primacy of the other. Amongst the Adenis, Girgirah, the ablest and most articulate, had started to lose his nerve after attacks on his house.

In his first statement Trevelyan said that his aim was a broad-based caretaker government and in order to assist him George Brown in his speech of 19 June said that "we regard a new constitution as essential now". The mutiny gave an added urgency and after intense pressure from the British, the Federalis announced on 6 July that they had appointed the Minister of Information, Hussein Ali Bayoomi, a brother of the first Adeni Chief Minister, to form a cabinet for South Arabia.

Bayoomi started his task with enthusiasm and considerable hopes of success. As a teacher and journalist he had known most of the FLOSY leaders all his life and he realised that they were extremely frightened of the advances made by the NLF. He made contact with the NLF, and Faysal Abd al-Latif proved not unsympathetic to a move which would weaken the grip of the traditional Rulers, although he warned that if Bayoomi were attacked by the Arab media, the NLF was so vulnerable to Egyptian propaganda that it would have to join in the attacks. The tribal defectors including the former Fadhli Sultan were persuaded to enter the proposed administration and the South Arabian Armed Forces, although they declined to provide any officers to hold Ministries, were apparently ready to support him. After a few days he announced that eight important people were prepared to serve under him.

Suddenly Bayoomi's effort collapsed. Sanaa Radio denounced "another British trick", whereupon both the NLF and FLOSY declared that they would kill anyone who took office. Even worse the Federal Ministers started to realise that an effective Premier who could choose his own Ministerial colleagues might well mean that some of them would lose their posts. Therefore, on 27 July, without consulting him, they announced that Bayoomi's mandate to form a government had been withdrawn. Bayoomi complained that in their search for a new image, the Federalis had never been sincere: "the Council was not serious when it asked me to try to form a government. It thought that I would fail, but I succeeded...the Federal government does not want to give up authority to any person or body." However, his inability to win over any of the real nationalist opposition showed that even an Adeni of the Adenis was bound to fail if he had been tarred with the Federal brush.

While Bayoomi's chances had looked hopeful, Trevelyan went to New York to persuade the UN mission that a new era had started and that there was now a constructive role for it to play. The members were not prepared to risk their own persons in Aden again but agreed to go to Geneva and talk even to the Federalis, although they would not recognise them as a government.

After dismissing Bayoomi, without consulting anyone the Federalis proclaimed a new constitution, based on Hone-Bell. However, it was still a Federation of Sultans: upon his return

Trevelyan brushed it aside as an irrelevance. He rebuked the Rulers for their treatment of Bayoomi and advised them to go to Geneva and make the best terms that they could. As he said in his memoirs: "our attempt to strengthen the Federal government had failed. We could do no more for them."

In May 1967 there were still a hundred Britons up-country but by the end of June they had all left, leaving the states on their own without any support. In the second half of August all except Bayhan, the three Aulaqi states and Wahidi were lost to Federal control, with the NLF tending to be stronger in the East while FLOSY did better in the West. The Rulers were mostly abroad and their deputies were so taken by surprise that they had not had time to remove their families or personal possessions – in Audhali huge stocks of arms fell into the hands of the insurgents. The takeover was often managed by small groups of determined men who knew what they wanted; the traditional authorities, on the other hand, suffered paralysis of the will and were leaderless. Many of the peasants, promised the lands of the ruling families, actively supported the revolutionaries, while others felt that it would make little difference to their lives which flag flew over government buildings. Some states fell by violent action: the fort in Dathinah was stormed by several hundred men, and others fell to well-planned coups and luck. It was said that the Kathiri state, some weeks later, was taken over by its football team which declared itself the new government.

On 28 August the Chairman of the Federal Supreme Council said that it had lost control and that there had been "a people's revolt which we cannot oppose". It invited the army to take over power. Deeply divided amongst themselves, the officers refused, and Trevelyan's broadcast a week later that the Federation had ceased to exist was merely a recognition of the obvious.

During all of these events the supporters of the NLF and FLOSY continued to attempt to exterminate one another, with the NLF usually killing three for every one that it lost. After the formal breach in December 1966, the Egyptians pretended that their protégé was the sole nationalist movement and all murders and attacks were "credited" to FLOSY. Meanwhile, the NLF leaders were still detained. In March 1967 the obsequious Arab League passed a Resolution which pledged support to FLOSY as "the legitimate frame of the struggle of the people of the area", but after the June war effective Egyptian help was greatly reduced and the NLF leaders released. During the British absence from Crater the two sides fought it out. The Mayor, a FLOSY supporter, was kidnapped, removed in an ambulance and never seen in Aden again. On another occasion four FLOSY members were machine-gunned as the loudspeakers of a mosque proclaimed that the NLF had condemned them for treason. By mid-August Asnag's old fief, the ATUC, was dominated by the NLF and there was then little doubt as to which was the more effective organisation.

Even before the collapse of the Federal government, the British had obviously been thinking of a successor to it. FLOSY was still completely subservient to the Egyptians – it was clear that if FLOSY took power in Aden, Nasser's prestige, lost in June, would be regained and he would secure a new base to create mischief for the whole Peninsula. The South Arabian League was discredited as a tool of the Saudis and was regarded as almost an adjunct of the Federalis through its close links with the Audhali Sultan. Moreover, it lacked support in the Army and strength on the streets of Aden. There was therefore only the NLF. They were firmly anti-Egyptian and as late as 24 August they complained that Nasser was holding some of their men in Taizz. Trevelyan says that "their enemies alleged that they had Communist affiliations, but of this there was no hard evidence". This lack was presumably due to the poor quality of British Intelligence, for if they had known about the proceedings of the NLF Second Congress at Jiblah in June 1966 or of the third at Khamer in November, there could have been little doubt. In addition, some of its members had received indoctrination in China.

One is puzzled by Trevelyan's statement that "despite all our efforts to get in touch with the NLF, we had no communication with them, even indirect, until the last three weeks before independence" for senior British officials had been in touch with them at the time of Lord Shackleton's visit and may have been before. On 19 June George Brown lifted the ban on them and in July there were further discussions about their possible support for Bayoomi and the revival of the UN mission. A FLOSY spokesman later claimed that the takeover of some of the states by the NLF had been in collusion with the British and in the same month *The Times* reported rumours in Aden that the NLF would take over the government.

On 2 September Trevelyan flew to London and during this visit the formal decision was taken to support the NLF, which was a strange decision if, as he said, there had been no contact with them. In his Diary entry for 5 September, Crossman noted that the "Foreign Office now wants to negotiate with the extreme nationalists, the FLN (*sic*), because FLOSY, the moderate party they'd previously backed, hardly exists now." George Wigg opposed this, saying that it "meant betraying everyone in Aden who had promised to support us". Crossman agreed that this would undermine the Federalists and have a bad effect in Kuwait and elsewhere. However, he accepted George Brown's view that there was no alternative, although he admitted that "the FO has swung in a few months from one extreme to the other". Apart from Wigg there was a general hope that the disappearance of the Federal government would mean the end of the defence commitment. "Anyway," says George (Brown), "we want to be out of the whole Middle East as far and fast as we possibly can".

While Trevelyan was in London, Qahtan al-Shaabi staged a dramatic press conference in Zinjibar for journalists collected by his emissaries from their Aden hotels. Surrounded by cheering soldiers, he declared his willingness to hold talks with the High Commissioner provided that it was accepted that the NLF was "the true representative of the people". He said that members of FLOSY would be able to live in peace under a future NLF regime which would brook no interference from Egypt or from the UN, and that while he believed in union with the YAR there was no immediate prospect of this taking place.

Trevelyan responded in his broadcast of 5 September by agreeing that the Federation had ceased to function and by recognising the nationalist forces as representatives of the people. He welcomed the readiness of the NLF to talk and although he said that there was no preference for any particular nationalist group, he did not mention FLOSY by name.

The High Commissioner's announcement led to several

attempts to reconcile the nationalist groups, in which the Army played a leading part. On his way to Geneva, Muhammad Farid had stopped in Cairo and reached an understanding with FLOSY which was later accepted by many of the Aulaqis including the majority of senior military officers, although soldiers from the other tribes had more sympathy with the NLF. Anxious to avoid a split in its own ranks, the South Arabian Armed Forces (SAAF) on 6 September called on the nationalist factions to negotiate with each other. The Arab League also offered to mediate, and there were attempts to involve Nasser personally. The Egyptians hoped to secure some share in power for their ever weakening protégés. However, Makkawi, living as ever in a world of make-believe, said that while FLOSY had the right to rule, it would accept "limited participation of some other nationalist elements". A week later he increased his generosity so far as to offer the NLF one-third of the Ministries. The NLF also indicated its willingness to allow some minority FLOSY share in any administration that it might form. At the end of September Faysal Abd al-Latif and Makkawi announced in Cairo that the two had agreed to share power between themselves, excluding all other groups: Faysal even praised the helpful role of Gemal Abdul Nasser. In October Qahtan felt that the position of the NLF was sufficiently assured for him to go to Cairo personally, where after several weeks of negotiations with FLOSY leaders he declared their "full agreement on all subjects".

During September and October the NLF consolidated its position up-country with the all-important assistance of the SAAF, which was still paid and equipped by the British and under the ultimate command of an English Brigadier. On 6 September, Shackleton stated that the "NLF is the real power on the ground" and although three days later he dismissed as "absolutely absurd" rumours that the British were working with it to crush FLOSY, this was in fact what was happening. When the British troops were evacuated from Little Aden on 12 September, control was handed over to an SAAF officer known for his allegiance to the NLF: NLF flags appeared everywhere and no FLOSY supporter dared to challenge them. In the same month the Sharif of Bayhan went to see King Faysal, probably to ask for help and possibly even for the absorption of his state in the Kingdom and soon after he left NLF officers of the SAAF ousted his supporters. *The Times* commented that the Sharif "personifies the question of whether an onus of protection is still on the British" but when the Sharif attempted to return, the High Commissioner decided there was no such obligation. He writes in his memoirs: "we had to threaten the use of British aircraft against an attempt by a man who was still nominally under British protection, to recover his state by attacking across the frontiers the rebels who had usurped his power with the aid of a battalion which we were helping to pay and arm and which was still nominally under British command. We were right to do so." History may not be so smugly complacent that this was an honourable course of action.

With regard to the EAP, Foreign Office staff managed to delay the return of its Sultans from Geneva until the NLF had a firm grip on their states. In October the British provided arms and logistic support for the NLF as it moved in to take over the FLOSY-dominated Aulaqi and Wahidi areas. At this time Colonel Mitchell, commander of the troops in Crater, received hints from senior officials that the activities of the NLF were to be regarded as having their blessing. Finally in November the last action of the RAF in Arabia was to attack FLOSY members on behalf of the NLF.

Meanwhile, although talks continued in Cairo between the leaders of the two nationalist movements, there were outbursts of savage fighting as local groups determined to settle old scores. The more organised FLOSY had a better register of its adherents, so previous neutrals found it easier to claim that all along they had supported the NLF, which anyway appeared more representative of local opinion: FLOSY leaders had been out of the country for years and seemed more concerned with Egyptian than with Adeni interests. Support for the NLF also grew in the SAAF, particularly at Headquarters. FLOSY officers tended to be isolated up-country and were finally the victims of a purge. On 6 November the army formally declared its loyalty to the NLF and its readiness "to strike with an iron hand all conspirators against it".

In August, after 150 British soldiers had been killed, Whitehall decided that Aden was an active-service station.

Almost immediately the withdrawal started, as a Battalion was sent home and not replaced. In September, in addition to Little Aden, Shaykh Othman and Mansourah were abandoned. Incidents continued, however, as the nationalists, although fighting amongst themselves, wished to be seen to have driven the colonialists into the sea. Trevelyan, who had long been preoccupied with the evacuation of the British personnel rather than with the future of Aden, recommended to Whitehall that it was pointless to remain, losing lives, while the NLF and FLOSY decided their quarrels. Crossman in his account of the special Cabinet meeting on 30 October shows that most of his colleagues were delighted at the collapse of the Federation, which "absolved (us) from the whole very expensive military commitment, including bombers and protective screening". George Brown apparently still had regrets but Crossman says: "That the regime he backed should have been overthrown by terrorists and has forced our speedy withdrawal is nothing but good fortune. It now looks as though we shall get out of Aden without losing a British soldier, chaos will rule soon after we've gone and there'll be one major commitment cut – thank God." On 2 November, Brown announced that there would be a final departure at the end of the month, whether or not there were a new administration to take control.

Brown's statement was the signal for a last round between the NLF and FLOSY. This was fought out mainly in the streets of Shaykh Othman and lasted three days, during which at least 100 and perhaps as many as 300 men were killed. Eventually the SAAF moved in with heavy artillery to obliterate the FLOSY strongholds. On 7 November, Brown recognised that the NLF appeared to have the upper hand, and a week later he announced that Lord Shackleton would meet its leaders in Geneva to make arrangements for the handover. On 29 November the last British troops left, and the following day the People's Republic of Southern Yemen came into existence.

The Federation was the bridge which led across from the traditionally anarchic WAP to the modern state of the PDRY. The reasons for its collapse are therefore worth considering. Many of them were not its own fault. With the exception of some enthusiastic officials on the spot, the British government had no interest in the Federation for its own sake. It was created when strategic considerations indicated a need for a base in Aden and abandoned when they did not – the well-being of the inhabitants was scarcely regarded. The emphasis on defence requirements meant that the Federation had abnormal status, for it was neither a completely independent state nor a conventional colony. It was as entirely dependent upon the UK for military and financial support as any colony but the British could not enforce actions upon it. It could not, for example, compel the rulers to come to terms with Asnag or Makkawi when this might still have been possible, or to appoint suitable Ministers or remove incompetent ones, for membership of the Cabinet was determined by the provision that the heads of all the component states had to have posts. Yet the British were able to obstruct the Federalis from taking action in Crater or Shaykh Othman, which might have checked the nationalist movement, or from holding any meaningful negotiations with Egypt. In addition they refused to urge the entry of EAP into the Federation, although its accession would have done much to make the Federation a balanced and viable state.

If more time had been allowed, some of the other difficulties that contributed to the downfall of the Federation might have been overcome. The hostility of the Labour Party would probably have decreased if a settlement could have been reached with the opposition and plebeians could be seen sharing power with the sultans, who themselves would gradually have been replaced by younger and more enlightened men. Similarly the enmity of Egypt and of the Arab League would have diminished if the Federation had developed into an obviously independent state upholding pan-Arab policies. In this connection it was extremely unfortunate that the Rulers were not given enough notice of the proposal to close the base for them to claim some of the credit for the move. If the Arabs had accepted the Federation, the UN would perforce have stopped its meddling. More time would also have brought about a better fusion between the Aden intellectuals, many of whom were always unhappy at the means by which the merger had been brought about, with the increasingly civilised population of the hinterland.

A third group of causes may fairly be blamed at least in part upon the Federalis themselves. From the very beginning to the very end they bickered and intrigued amongst themselves, with none prepared to make any sacrifice of narrow selfish interests for the sake of effective government. No real leader supported by all the others ever emerged: this was in keeping with some of the oldest traditions of Arabia. Nevertheless, their successors overcame the problem. The Federation remained a club of Rulers, and no serious attempt was made to transform a motley collection of tribal groups into communities of citizens of a single state. There was a complete failure to inspire the population with any enthusiasm for the Federation and the government in al-Ittihad remained remote and irrelevant. It had no effective agents up-country and had to rely instead upon the old *dolas*, none of whose members had any training and few any notions of administration, and regarded the Federation as little more than the old regime newly endowed with money for lavish gifts. There was never any idea of founding a political party in the provinces to promote the idea of federation and to act as a link between the people and their Rulers. The surface was scratched with showy symbols of modernity such as hospitals and post offices but nothing was done to modernise the mentality of the inhabitants.

The causes of the downfall of the Federation were not lost upon its successors. The first two groups that we have suggested above were automatically cancelled by the British withdrawal and the achievement of complete independence. The NLF were to tackle the final group with a determination and a ruthlessness which will be seen in the final chapters.

Chapter Seven

The War in the North
1962–1970

During the last few months of his father's life, Badr had in effect been ruling the country. Although many of his family and some of the tribal leaders would have preferred the succession of his uncle Hassan, he had no difficulty in assuming the Imamate. On 19 September 1962 Sanaa Radio broadcast the swearing of allegiance to him by princes and Ministers and carried his proclamation of "new regulations to secure for the citizens their rights in conformity with those of the modern world". All were to be equal, refugees welcomed back, hostages released, no taxation would be levied for the rest of the year and for the first time a list would be prepared to show who was in prison and for what offence. A later decree announced a 40-member Advisory Council, of which half would be elected, Municipalities would be formed and Badr would as Prime Minister spur his government along. Cairo Radio said that Badr would "carry out a Socialist policy" and Nasser, Brezhnev, Khruschev and the Chinese leaders all sent their best wishes.

The elements that had opposed Yahya and Ahmad were still dissatisfied. Although some of the *Ahrar* had come to terms with the government, others maintained their old views. The merchants continued to complain of government monopolies, the Shafais of persecution by the Zaydis and the Qadi class of the pretensions of the Sayyids. The conservatives felt that the progress of innovation was too swift and that Badr had not been properly elected as Imam. On the other hand the young intellectuals were shocked at Ahmad's breach with Nasser whom they regarded as the leader of progressive Arabism, and a thousand students abroad and their elders who had returned saw how their homeland lagged ever further behind other countries. Most of these groups were probably prepared to give Badr a chance and neither singly nor in combination could they have overthrown the regime. This could only be done either by the army or by the tribes – the Hashid, the traditional supporters of the House of Hamid al-Din, were waiting for an opportunity to revenge Ahmad's killing of their shaykh.

Thanks to the presence of a Military Mission and of numerous instructors, the influence of the Egyptians was strong in the army. It has been estimated that they inspired about 80 of the total of 400 officers to form a Free Officers Movement on the lines of the one that had put Nasser in power. This group obtained a promise from Cairo that if it seized power it would be supported against internal enemies and any external intervention from Britain or Saudi Arabia. From the Egyptian point of view, the sooner this happened the better. Badr had not yet had the time to consolidate his personal grip through making his own appointments at every level, the British were in difficulties over the Aden merger and Saudi Arabia was having one of its very rare domestic crises as three of King Saud's brothers defected as a protest against his misrule and talked of a government in exile. Two days, therefore, after Cairo Radio had broadcast Nasser's congratulations to Badr, the *Sawt al-Arab* station there called for his overthrow, declaring that "the Yemenis will write the pages of their history in their own blood, the history of the people of the Yemen whose appointment with fate has arrived".

It seems most probable that the Egyptians forced the officers to strike quickly. It has been said that the Egyptian Chargé d'Affaires warned the Imam that there was a plot against him and then immediately told the conspirators that Badr had discovered their plans and that therefore they must act at once. It is further recounted that Egyptian officers had to help to start the tanks which surrounded and partially demolished the Palace and Badr himself told a journalist that while the shooting was still going on, aircraft already painted in the colours of the new Republic arrived at Sanaa and disgorged Egyptian soldiers.

On the morning of 27 September Sanaa Radio announced that Badr had been killed and that "God supports the Revolution and its heroes…It is everyone's Revolution." Away to the South the Sharif of Bayhan commented to Trevaskis that the coup would mean the end of Egyptian influence in the Yemen: Cairo was better informed. Its Minister of National Guidance, Abdul Kader Hatem, declared at once that Egypt would oppose foreign intervention and the next day formal recognition was accorded. The Russians, too, seem to have known what was happening for they also recognised the Republic and promised to defend it.

Like their Egyptian predecessors, the Free Officers who had carried out the coup looked for a more senior figure to be their formal leader. Their choice, probably at Egyptian instigation, fell upon Colonel Abdullah Sallal, whom Badr had just appointed Chief of Staff despite his involvement in previous conspiracies, for which he had spent seven years in an underground cell. Although he later took credit for its success, it seems that Sallal did not in fact know about the plot in advance. He assumed the Premiership with as Deputy Dr Abdul Rahman Beidani, a German-trained economist and a Shafai whose long residence in Cairo and his marriage to the sister of Nasser's colleague Anwar Sadat had made more of an Egyptian than a Yemeni.

The first declarations of the Republic were that it believed in "God, Arab unity and Arab strength" and that people would not be humbled – all were to be addressed as "Sayyid". It expanded this by promising that it would observe the Shariah, organise the people "into a single popular grouping which will participate in the process of revolutionary construction", reorganise the army, carry out a cultural and social revolution through universal education, practice social justice, Arab nationalism and non-alignment. Its first actions were to raise the pay of the army and to execute three Ministers, two princes and two governors, pointing out as a sign of progress that they had been shot and not beheaded: soon the total condemned rose to more than fifty.

Before the coup, Yemeni officers had spent their lives in conflict or diplomatic dealings with the tribes. Few had any experience of formal administration and fewer still had any training in political science. They had seized power with no plan as to what was to replace the Imamate and the simplest thing seemed to be to make a slavish copy of the Egyptian system of government. They created a cabinet with Departments such as National Guidance and Municipal Affairs, previously unknown in the country, and brought in experts from Cairo to run them. The Ministers themselves had little knowledge of their duties and anyway had no offices so they worked at home: it was said that their main activity was cutting out newspaper reports about the country.

Beidani, who had been put in charge of economic affairs, did at least have ideas of his own and initiated a series of reforms. The land of the royal family, said to amount to 40,000 acres, was confiscated and distributed to the peasants, although the government did not dare to touch the large holdings of tribal leaders whose support was needed. A Central Bank was created and a distinctive currency introduced. Beidani announced plans to develop agriculture and industry and to build up the port of Hodeidah so as to end the country's dependence upon Aden. Economic agreements with Russia brought in experts to help these projects, and Beidani said that he would call an economic conference to discuss them.

From the very first day it was clear that the new regime did not command unanimous support. Amman Radio reported that one of Ahmad's brothers was marching on Sanaa with a tribal force to subdue the "mutineers" as the old Imam had in 1948. Shortly afterwards another brother, Hassan, arrived in Jeddah and, declaring himself the Imam, called for support. Saudi acceptance of his presence showed that he had their backing and this took the practical form of gifts of arms and money. By 5 October a royalist radio station was operating from Saudi territory and three days later came the first reports of arms reaching royalist tribesmen through the Sharif of Bayhan who, according to Sallal, received five million shillings from Riyadh for the purpose. As early as 1 October Beidani accused the Saudis of harbouring rebels and threatened to cross the frontier to carry the war to them – a task manifestly impossible for the Yemeni army to perform alone.

Even if Badr was incorrect in saying that Egyptian troops arrived while the coup was in process, there can be no doubt that aircraft laden with military "experts", arms and ammunition were arriving within three days. On 8 October *The Times* reported that three Egyptian warships were discharging tanks at Hodeidah and that Egyptian-crewed armoured cars were in action near Hajjah. On the same day Western journalists saw Egyptian troops guarding the airfields and on 11 October Egyptian aircraft shelled fortresses inside the Saudi border. It was clear by mid-October that Saudi Arabia, representing the forces of Arab traditionalism, and the United Arab Republic, the self-proclaimed champion of socialism and Arab progress were fighting out their quarrel on the soil of the Yemen with the prestige of both sides totally committed. Haykal, Nasser's trumpeter, said that "Egypt cannot stand aside when it sees reaction devouring a national revolution like a blood-thirsty wild animal." Anwar Sadat, who was the first leading figure to visit the Yemen, pressed its old claims to Najran and Asir which he said Egypt would support with all its strength. Reinforcements moved in and by the end of the month journalists believed that there were at least 10,000 troops. These were regarded as sufficiently important to be visited by Nasser's Deputy, the Commander-in-Chief, Field Marshal Abdul Hakim Amr. The Egyptians were not alone: some Russian pilots were captured flying into the battle zone near Marib in the East.

John Badeau, the American Ambassador in Cairo, has written that it took Nasser three days to decide to send forces to defend the new Republic: if indeed they had not known of the precise timing of the coup, the Egyptian military authorities certainly acted with a speed and an efficiency that nothing in their previous or subsequent record would lead one to suspect. One's credulity is further strained by the statement that Nasser knew so little about the Yemen that he was delighted to borrow "a long out-of-date" economic report from the American Embassy: the Egyptian officers of the military Mission and his own diplomats must have been very idle and it is strange that no one thought of seeking information from the numerous Yemenis living in exile in Cairo. Historians will almost certainly conclude that the Americans were fooled and accept the statement that the Royalist Ambassador made to the UN on 20 December that there had been "a prearranged plan for the invasion of the Yemen, in order to clear the way for the UAR to establish a bridgehead for further aggression throughout Arabia".

The new Republic was extremely anxious to achieve wider recognition than that provided by its original sponsors and in particular to be accepted by the western nations. To woo the British, Beidani disclaimed any interest in Aden, saying that this was a problem for the next generation. This line was accepted by the Foreign Office which thought that a regime dominated by the old *Ahrar* like Zubayri and the Qadi Abd al-Rahman Iryani would be anxious for good relations and that anyway it would need twenty years to put its own house in order, during which time it would be disinclined to add to its problems and might be induced to grant reciprocal recognition of the Federation. The British Minister, isolated in Taizz, was not aware of the lack of control exercised by the new regime outside the main centres or the extent of Egyptian domination. He hoped that the Egyptian influence could be neutralised by friendship with Britain and was a strong advocate of recognition. This was however opposed by the Service Ministries in Whitehall and by the Colonial Office, which accepted the views of the Federalis, supported by the High Commissioner, that the Imamate was a neighbour to be preferred to the Egyptians. In the meanwhile, Sanaa Radio, while fiercely attacking the Sharif of Bayhan for backing its enemies, scrupulously refrained from blaming Britain, which Sallal flattered as "the leader of the world in civilisation and freedom" – although the Sharif could hardly have been acting alone.

On 23 October the British cabinet decided in principle to recognise the Republic. However, before this could be done formally, a message was received from Colonel "Billy" McLean, Tory MP for Inverness, who had on his own initiative gone to find out what was happening. McLean, who knew about guerrilla warfare from experience in Albania, reported that at least half of the country was still controlled by the Royalists and that he had travelled extensively and without difficulty in the eastern areas. In a subsequent article in *The Daily Telegraph* he urged that recognition should be delayed until it was proved that Sallal could stand on his own feet for at present he could not possibly survive without Egyptian help, and his view prevailed. Their hopes dashed, the Yemen Government on 9 November allowed Sanaa Radio to refer to the

"Occupied South" and to call upon its inhabitants to "be ready for the battles we shall wage against colonialism".

The Republic proved more successful with the United States, despite strong pressure against recognition from business interests concerned with Saudi Arabia and the arguments of Crown Prince Faysal on a visit to Washington that President Kennedy should not give his blessing to a regime established as a result of an Egyptian plot. The British Prime Minister Harold Macmillan recorded in his diary for 14 November that he also had urged the President to delay recognition. Kennedy "with his usual charming frankness" had replied "I don't even know where it is", but he felt that recognition could be traded for a withdrawal of Egyptian troops and that Saudi Arabia was endangered by its involvement. Macmillan's views were supported by General de Gaulle.

The American Ambassador in Cairo reported that the coup had received no outside help, while on 21 November the Chargé in Taizz declared that the Republic was "in full control of the country except for some border areas". However, the existence of a Saudi-Egyptian war became more evident as fighting continued. The Saudis broke off diplomatic relations with Cairo, who endorsed Sallal's proclamation of a "Republic of the Arabian Peninsula". After his visit, Field Marshal Amr convinced Nasser that further reinforcements would soon finish off the royalists. Despite Nasser's statement on 23 December that there were 2,000 Egyptian soldiers in the Yemen, most observers put the figure at about 12,000 and the campaign was costing one-third of the country's military budget. In the Delta, where hospitals had been taken over, there were riots of protest at the casualties, which included a Brigadier whose severed head was shown to the correspondent of the *Daily Express*. Early in November the Imam Badr proved to journalists that he was alive and leading the fight back. A month later Dana Adams Schmidt of *The New York Times* reported that the royalists were "slowly closing a ring around Sanaa": it was unlikely, however, that they could hope to take it in the face of Egyptian tanks and aircraft.

However in the State Department it was felt that Nasser was a bulwark against Communism whose face must be saved and that recognition of the Republic would counteract Russian influence and frighten conservative Arab governments into making reforms. It might also lull them into forgetting the consistent American support for Israel. Echoing the bleating of trendy slogans which passed for political thought in "New Frontier" Washington, the *New York Times* stated that the Republic represented "progressive youth – the wave of the future against anachronistic regimes" and would lead to "modern democratic forces (which) will bring the ancient land of Yemen into the twentieth century". Since Alger Hiss there has been no evidence of a Burgess or a Philby amongst American foreign policy makers, but such has been the gullibility and ignorance of so many of them that the Russians probably thought that they were not needed.

Kennedy wrote to the governments of the Republic, Egypt and Saudi Arabia offering his services as a mediator. He pointedly ignored the still legitimate government of the Imam who justly observed "I can only suppose that you have been misinformed", and reiterated his intention to fight on. Although Sallal did not meet any of the normal criteria for recognition, Kennedy formally accorded it on 19 December, assuming that in return he had secured Egyptian withdrawal and a promise of Yemeni respect for previous treaties. Not since Neville Chamberlain had crowed "I have Herr Hitler's word" has a national leader proved such an egregious dupe: as Macmillan pointed out, he paid the price but did not receive the purchase: the US had played its trump but not taken the trick. Nasser's first action was to increase the number of his troops until they reached 28,000 in the spring, publicly to deny on 9 January 1963 that he had promised to withdraw, and, for the first time, to use napalm on undefended villages. Kennedy's response was to increase aid to Egypt, estimated at £200 million in the previous three years, and to give a grant of £12 million for a Cairo electric power project.

The Sanaa government sent a delegation to the United Nations, where naturally the Yemeni seat was occupied by officials appointed by the Imam. The Royalists asked for a mission to ascertain the situation in the country but this proposal was ignored, for as in its dealings with the Federation, the UN regarded facts as unimportant when they conflicted with politics. Ordinary justice demanded that the challengers should prove their case and, as the Jordanians argued, the Credentials Committee was not competent to decide which was the legitimate government. Nonetheless it voted by six to none to install the Republicans. This was subsequently endorsed by the General Assembly by 73 votes to 4, partly due to heavy pressure from the US, anxious to show that it was on the side of progress. Macmillan recorded that in January the Americans strongly supported the Foreign Office's case for recognition, but this was successfully resisted by the Ministry of Defence and the Colonial Office. Therefore on 17 February Sanaa ordered the closure of the British Legation.

The Jordanian Prime Minister, Wasfi Tal, said early in January that American policy in the Yemen was "ignorant and uninformed" and Nasser proceeded to show his contempt for it by launching a major offensive in the month of Ramadan to overrun the areas held by the Royalists. After some weeks Sallal claimed that the Republic "controlled every inch of territory" but it took another six weeks to capture Harib "after a month and a half of fierce battle with the British". In an effort to cut off external intervention, the Egyptians provoked incidents on and within the borders of the Federation and started to bomb strongholds up to 60 miles inside Saudi Arabia which they demanded should be evacuated. Faysal stopped all army leave, ordered a general mobilisation against Egypt and invoked the pledge in a letter from Kennedy dated 25 October promising "full support for Saudi territorial integrity". Macmillan noted with amusement that "the Americans who accepted the threat to Aden and the Federation with some equanimity are now tremendously excited and alarmed about Nasser going for Saudi Arabia and all the vast American oil interests involved". US aircraft were sent to Arabia and Cairo and Sanaa denounced "gun-boat diplomacy" and declared that the promise to withdraw troops would not be implemented while "reactionary aggression persists". The ineptness of American diplomacy meant that it was defending Saudi Arabia with one hand while with the other it supplied the aid without which the Egyptians would have difficulty in continuing their attacks.

American policy had clearly misfired and it turned to the United Nations to pick up the pieces. At the end of February

Ralph Bunche, the American who held the post of UN Under Secretary for Special Political Affairs, went to the Yemen to try to arrange a settlement. Bunche proved as easy to deceive as the majority of his fellow-countrymen involved in the area, was charmed by Sallal and convinced by a visit to Marib, recently captured in the Ramadan offensive, that the Republic was in complete control apart from a few "infiltrators". He added, for good measure, the rather puzzling phrase that the country lived "in the pre-Biblical era". He made no effort to contact the Royalists, so his mission was futile as Faysal declined to receive him. A separate envoy, Ellsworth Bunker, a veteran Ambassador, had therefore to be sent to Saudi Arabia.

Bunker subsequently saw Nasser, and as a result of his diplomatic activities the UN Secretary General U Thant announced on 30 April that Egypt, Saudi and the Republicans had accepted a plan by which Faysal would end military backing for the Imam while the Egyptians started to remove their troops. A United Nations force (UNYOM), paid for by the Saudis and the Egyptians, would supervise a ceasefire in a 12-mile demilitarised zone on both sides of the Saudi-Yemeni frontier. No one thought of consulting the Royalists who actually controlled half of the area in question.

Despite the touching faith of Secretary of State Dean Rusk who declared on 29 May that he expected the disengagement "to be fully effected...within the very next few days", the prospects of success for UNYOM were hardly auspicious. They had not been improved by a speech from Nasser on 21 May that Egyptian troops would remain "until it becomes certain that the reaction that hates the Yemeni Revolution is forced through defeat to contain that hatred in its own heart", while the General commanding his troops in the field estimated that the task might take five years. After further delay caused by a Russian complaint that the operation had not been formally approved by the Security Council, it was not until 13 June that the Swedish General Carl von Horn who had been appointed to command the force arrived in Sanaa.

Even if he had not been endowed with inadequate staff and equipment – at one moment he wrote "we are literally scrounging rations" – von Horn's instructions would have ensured the futility of the mission that he was expected to complete within four months. He was to confine himself to "observing, certifying and reporting" and had no power to compel any disengagement. He was forbidden to recognise the existence of the Royalists so that his surveillance of their area had to be confined to occasional flights. The Egyptians refused to allow him to establish a post at Hodeidah to monitor the departure of their troops. Anyway Field Marshal Amr told him that there was no intention of leaving while Sallal needed support: the agreement was merely that the evacuation should be begun and there was no date set for its completion. The bulk of his men were Yugoslavs who with the close links between Nasser and Tito could hardly be expected to be impartial. Faysal complained that a report that a Saudi convoy was moving 120 mm ammunition was based on nothing more than the fact that some crates had been seen through binoculars at a range of 5 km. Realising the impotence of UNYOM, the Egyptians resumed bombing, although for a time the Saudis continued to keep their side of the pact. Von Horn regarded U Thant's attitude to his complaints as "one of calculated deceit" and resigned after a little more than two months in the country.

At the end of the original period even U Thant admitted: "it cannot be said at this stage that encouraging progress has been made towards effective implementation of the disengagement agreement…No plan for phased withdrawal of UAR troops has been received." Philipps Talbot of the State Department said that it was "bringing the full weight of US influence to bear on Egypt" to secure a withdrawal but that this was impossible owing to the "continuance of tribal guerrilla warfare" which meant that if the Egyptians left, the Republicans would have to seek support from the Russians. The Saudis realised that UNYOM was performing no useful function and decided to stop the financial support upon which it depended. However US pressure persuaded them to change their minds and UNYOM was renewed for two-month periods until September 1964 when the Saudis finally refused to make further contributions. The mission ended, having achieved nothing.

In the meanwhile, although they were hard pressed by the Royalists and completely dependent upon Egyptian backing, the leaders of the Republic quarrelled amongst themselves. At first it seemed that Beidani was Nasser's chosen instrument to control the Yemen, but he started to show some signs of independence and as the old sectarian split re-emerged, Cairo considered it impossible to run the country through a Shafai. Egyptian support therefore shifted to Sallal who had little personal following, for the Shafais disliked him as a Zaydi and the Zaydis, despite his self promotion to Field Marshal, despised him as the son of a blacksmith: he had no political ideas of his own and was quite content to act as Nasser's viceroy. He hailed his master as "the miracle of the Twentieth Century", relied upon Egyptian bodyguards and apparently raised no protest when the Egyptians who controlled the Radio Station excised passages from the tapes of his speeches. Beidani realised that he was losing ground as Shafai representation was cut in the Cabinet and the few remaining members given minor posts, so in January 1963 he sounded out the British Minister about the possibility of London's backing for a breakaway Hujariyyah. When he was rebuffed, he went to Cairo in an attempt to regain his position but while he was away Sallal announced his dismissal. Subsequently he was deprived of his nationality and denounced as an "imperialist hireling, an impostor and a spy". In September he was reported under arrest in Cairo.

Apart from the Zaydi-Shafai division, there were many other problems. Hardly anyone paid any taxes and as a result of Egyptian financial exploitation, including a 25 per cent reduction of customs dues on Egyptian goods and monopolisation of exports, the cost of living had risen by 400 per cent. There was a split between the young progressives and the tribal Shaykhs whose support was vital to the regime and who received the salaries of Ministers as members of the Supreme Defence Council. Nasser himself said of the Yemeni Ministers that "half of them never went to their offices and those that do don't know what to do when they get there". An attempt had to be made to pull things together and after a proposal in February 1963 for union with Egypt, Iraq and Algeria was coolly received, Sallal in April announced an interim Constitution with himself as Chairman of a Presidency Council. Despite a plan for an Advisory Council with 100 elected and 50 nominated members, this interim Constitution was very much in the Egyptian style, enshrining the army as the keeper of the national conscience. Even so, it was greeted by Luqman, the old friend of the *Ahrar*, as "the passport to a new world". The fact that there were five Constitutions before 1967 showed the impossibility of reconciling the fact of Egyptian control with the sentiments of Yemeni national pride.

The Royalists refused to be intimidated. They had the help of mercenaries paid by Saudi Arabia to run their communications and teach them such arts as mine-laying, and they claimed to have some 30,000 men in the field. It was a strange, oddly democratic force, led mostly by Princes of the House of Hamid al-Din, some just arrived from university, to whom every warrior had access. It was impossible to make soldiers out of the urban Yemenis to oppose them and the Republican regular army probably consisted of not more than 3,500 men. It was equally difficult for the government to outbid the Saudis to buy the permanent loyalty of the tribes who happily took arms and money from both sides: one chief boasted that he had received 300 rifles from the Imam and 200 from Sallal. The burden of the actual fighting therefore rested upon the Egyptians, who had about 28,000 men involved by the New Year of 1964. Egyptian propaganda managed to keep news of Royalist successes from the headlines but that January US diplomats in Sanaa could hear the fighting. The tribesmen learned to destroy tanks by stuffing a cloth in the exhaust pipe and killing the crews when asphyxia forced them to emerge. Ambushes were common in a poverty-stricken land; the Egyptian troops were a rich source of watches, shoes and clothes and it was even said that the tribesmen tried to attract them into their area so as to have opportunities of loot.

As their casualties increased, the Egyptians resorted to savage employment of airpower. There were reports that they bombed mosques during prayer times and villages on market day so as to increase the civilian casualties and in July 1963 there was the first evidence of the use of mustard gas, probably supplied by the Russians, which local people tried to combat with iodine and aspirins. The commanding Egyptian General admitted the dropping of napalm, although he was careful to say that it was only upon military targets. Children were reported killed by poisoned food, supposedly destined for garrisons supplied by air. *The Daily Telegraph* printed a leaflet warning that any village which helped the Royalists would be "destroyed and wiped off the face of the earth without hesitation or mercy". The country people retaliated by mutilating Egyptians that fell into their hands, and von Horn heard that while he was there Royalists decapitated 50 Egyptians, slit open their stomachs, and inserted the heads. Some prisoners deprived of nose or ears were sent back to the Egyptian lines where it was said they were killed by their comrades upon Nasser's orders, for their return home would have excited even more revulsion against the war. Another sign of Egyptian desperation was a heavy raid in June 1963 on the Saudi town of Jizan where at least 30 people were killed and the hospital deliberately bombed.

Although *Pravda* referred to the Yemenis as "drug-addicts with barbarous religious practices", the Russians continued to support the Republic and to increase their influence there. Early in 1964 it was estimated that there had between 1,000 and 1,500 "experts" in the country and in March Sallal visited Moscow. Friendship blossomed with a five-year friendship treaty and a pledge of nearly $4 million in aid, arms, pilot training, fishing boats and a road from Hodeidah to Taizz.

Alarmed at this Russian encroachment and hoping to win the war and establish a subservient government before the Arab Summit due in September 1964, Nasser visited Sanaa for the first time in April. He was horrified at the general chaos and ordered a reorganisation of the government which removed much of the executive power from the hands of Sallal. He also commanded that there should be a major offensive. He increased his forces to an estimated 60,000, nearly half the Egyptian army; by August he seemed very near success. The Red Cross denounced "systematic devastation" of the countryside, but the Royalists managed to hold out until the rains came and nullified the Egyptian advantage in vehicles and aircraft.

At the Alexandria summit in early September, Nasser for the first time appeared to make a serious effort to disengage from the Yemen. Faysal, declaring that his "heart brimmed over with love for Nasser" nevertheless refused to make a unilateral renunciation of support for the Royalists and only conceded that the Saudis and the Egyptians should "undertake necessary contact with the parties involved for a peaceful settlement".

Two months later delegations from the Royalists and the Republicans met at Erkowit in the Sudan and agreed to hold a conference to arrange for national reconciliation and a referendum on the future of the country. In the meanwhile there was to be a ceasefire from 8 November and it was understood that up to 23,000 Egyptian troops would be withdrawn. It was soon clear, however, that Nasser had merely been seeking a breathing space and Badr declared that in the first week of the ceasefire the Egyptian airforce had carried out 180 raids. After two postponements it was certain that the conference would never meet, and fighting resumed. In January 1965 the Royalists claimed to have killed 1,000 Egyptians in a week-long battle and in March for the first time the Royalists succeeded in expelling their enemy from an important town when they captured Harib.

Some Republican leaders started to realise that it would be impossible to achieve a peace as between Yemenis while the government was controlled by the Egyptians. The autumn of 1963 saw the emergence of a "Third Force", mainly tribal, which while aiming to retain a Republic, wished to dispense with Sallal and the Egyptian army of occupation. There was some response on the Royalist side, for in April *ulama* from all over the country met in Jawf and called for a constitutional Imamate: the idea grew that both Badr and Sallal should receive generous pensions to leave the country. The aggressive Egyptian actions that led to the failure of the hopes of reconciliation conceived at Erkowit brought matters to a head and in December Shaykh Ahmad Muhammad Nu'man, Chairman of the Consultative Council and two deputy Premiers, Zubayri and Qadi Abd al-Rahman Iryani, the three veterans of the *Ahrar*, resigned as a protest against "corrupt, impotent and bankrupt government" and called for a new Constitution. In February 1965 Zubayri announced the formation of "God's Party" to advocate an Islamic, consultative Republic rather than a military dictatorship and these ideas found favour with a meeting of tribal leaders in Khawlan.

At the beginning of April the murder of Zubayri caused a wave of revulsion which rocked the Sallal government. The continuation of heavy fighting cast doubts upon the only solution offered by the Egyptians – the bludgeoning of the tribes into submission. It was felt that someone was needed who could negotiate with them and win their acceptance. The obvious man was Nu'man, who felt his position strong enough to lay down conditions. He demanded that a national conference should be held in Khamer (about 20 miles north of Sanaa) to discuss peace terms and a new Constitution. Sallal's acceptance of these demands seemed a prelude to his own retirement.

Nu'man, the first Shafai to become Prime Minister, formed a predominantly civilian Cabinet, equally divided between Zaydis and members of his own sect, and including the Hashid leader Shaykh Abdullah ibn Hussayn al -Ahmar and the Bakil chief Sinan Abu Luhum. Following upon the demands of the Khamer conference, he announced a new Constitution which would be a parliamentary democracy with an independent judiciary, and he put an end to the bullying style of Sallal. He tried to involve King Hussayn of Jordan, the Shaykh of Kuwait and the Syrians in peace-making and above all he made approaches to Faysal, to whom as an old-fashioned Muslim with an Azhari background he was much more acceptable than any of his predecessors. In an attempt to win British goodwill he abolished the post of Minister for Occupied South Yemen. Damascus Radio was not alone in seeing his as "no ordinary Cabinet. It (is) a new experiment, imposed by events, the will of the Yemeni people and the common desire of the Arab Revolutionaries to end continuous deterioration."

However, the Khamer conference had called for a People's Army which would replace the Egyptians: thus Nu'man's "Sanaa Spring" was as foredoomed as the "Prague Spring" of Dubcek, for Nasser, like Brezhnev, was unwilling to accept independence in satellites. Sallal was encouraged to form a Supreme Council for the Armed Forces which would effectively take power from Nu'man's government and on 1 July Nu'man resigned saying that "we were surprised by acts and resolutions which were in total contradiction to the letter and spirit of the Constitution". He and his colleagues went to Cairo in an attempt to change Nasser's mind and were promptly detained: others of his supporters escaped to Bayhan.

The new military government was confronted with sweeping Royalist gains, although Amr denied that a single position, however small, had actually fallen to them. Nasser started to see the hopelessness of dealing with people who were Republican by day and Royalist by night. Egyptian troops were strung out along roads in danger of being encircled and Nasser bitterly referred to "my Vietnam". Faysal, seeing his opponent's losses in men and money, was in no mood to help Nasser to extricate himself. Faysal's aid to the Royalists was supplemented by that of the Shah who sent officers to learn to fight a guerrilla war. Nasser, however, showed his characteristic cunning. He started by making up his quarrel with the Americans whom he had publicly insulted seven months before, and then by open threats of war, he frightened them into bringing pressure on Faysal. In his speech on the anniversary of his coming to power he declared that he would not "tolerate indefinitely attacks by Saudi mercenaries", that "there is a limit to our patience" and that he would "liquidate the bases of aggression" and dropped hints that he would invade the Saudi frontier zone through which aid reached the Royalists. On 4 August *The Times* thought that the two countries were "on the brink of war". However, Nasser was careful to be conciliatory at the same time, allowing some withdrawal of his troops and saying that they would all be gone within six months "or even less if we are able to achieve peace".

On 16 August, Nasser swallowed his pride and offered to go personally to ask Faysal for peace and most observers saw this as a humiliation for him. On 24 August an agreement was signed at Jeddah for a ceasefire, to be supervised and implemented by a joint Saudi-Egyptian force. Faysal would stop all aid to the Royalists and in ten months from 23 November Nasser would withdraw all his men. The treaty provided for a conference of 25 Royalists and 25 Republicans to gather at Haradh on 23 November, to establish a government for a transitional period and to organise a plebiscite to be held not later than 23 November 1966. Nasser had to accept the mortification of admitting for the first time that the Royalists were indeed equal parties to the dispute, and his face was only partially saved by Faysal's statement that he had never insisted upon the restoration of a despotic Imam.

As far as is known there were no Yemeni representatives at Jeddah and the agreement was reached by Nasser and Faysal over their heads, practically imposing a condominium. The Royalists accepted it at once but Sanaa showed little enthusiasm and was supported by the Syrians, who were at ideological odds with Nasser. Their newspapers referred to the treaty as "a poisonous spear in the Arab Nation's heart", declaring that "the heroic Yemeni Revolution has been foully murdered and its throat slit from ear to ear". The Russians and the Chinese also used their influence with Sallal against any compromise and supplied more arms.

It is not clear whether Nasser genuinely wanted peace or whether he was once again buying a breathing space to regroup his forces, concentrating on the cities and the Shafai areas. In September he replaced his pro-Communist Prime Minister Ali Sabry with Zakariah Mohieddin, the most pro-Western of his associates and a man who put the domestic interests of Egypt above the adventures of Arab Nationalism. On the other hand, despite an announcement in *al-Ahram* at the end of October that the troops would leave at the rate of 10,000 a month for seven months, very few actually seem to have gone. Anwar Sadat in his memoirs alleges that Field Marshal Amr used the war "as an occasion for personal gain" and to increase the power of the army within Egypt until as Sadat said "Nasser watched what Amr was doing with bitterness and a paramount sense of helplessness", remarking that "the country is being run by a gang of thieves". Certainly the chance to serve in Yemen was welcomed by many officers because of the generous allowances involved, and some observers thought that the return of a beaten army would be the signal for Nasser's own downfall. Nasser however once remarked that he was a man who reacted to events rather than tried to shape them, and it is probable that during the autumn of 1965 he had no clear policy for the Yemen and was waiting to see what would happen.

By mid-October the Royalists had nominated their delegates who were to be led by Sayyid Ahmad al-Shami, one of the old *Ahrar*. After a meeting of the tribes at Janad, the Republicans announced their team under Iryani, another of the *Ahrar*. The two sides met on schedule with two observers each from Saudi Arabia and Egypt to supervise security. The conference lasted for nearly a month but only three formal meetings were held, for, despite pressure from their patrons and even a special envoy from Nasser, the Yemenis could not agree amongst themselves. The Republicans refused to discuss any change in the form of government or to accept the formula of an "Islamic State" which would leave the position unclear and they were adamant that there should be no participation by any of the Hamid al-Din family. The Royalists argued that these matters ought to be decided by the plebiscite which, anyway, should not take place until the Egyptian troops had all left. A further difficulty was that the majority of tribesmen were better off than they had ever been in their lives, able to earn up to £30 a month serving with the Royalists and their leaders courted by both sides: they were in no hurry for peace. The Egyptians tried to help by keeping Sallal in Cairo but General Hassan al-Amri, who emerged as the "strong man", was just as intransigent. On 15 December it was decided to adjourn the conference for Ramadan and to reassemble on 20 February but in fact the delegates never met again.

The dispute between Faysal and Nasser was for leadership of the Arab world and for domination over the Peninsula: the war in the Yemen was a symptom of this rather than the cause. In December 1965 Faysal visited Iran, whose Shah was regarded with particular aversion by Nasser, and following this with meetings with the monarchs of Jordan and Kuwait, started to plan for an Islamic Summit: Nasser saw this as a western-inspired successor to the Baghdad Pact and as an alliance directed against himself. In the same month the Saudis signed an agreement to purchase a major air defence scheme from Britain and the USA. Therefore, although as late as January 1966 the Egyptian press referred to the "concentrated efforts" of the two powers to settle the Yemeni question, relations between them deteriorated sharply. Faysal accused the Egyptians of augmenting rather than diminishing the strength of their forces while Nasser, with his habitual disregard for truth, argued that the Jeddah agreement provided for the withdrawal to start only after the formation of an interim government. On 22 February Whitehall published the White Paper which announced that the British would leave Aden in 1968 and within hours, in a speech so obviously carefully prepared that one suspects that this information had been leaked to him in advance, Nasser declared that "we can stay in Yemen for one

213

year or two, three, four or five years…There was an announcement today that the British had decided to grant independence in 1968. Well, we shall stay there until after 1968." By remaining at least on the borders of the Federation, he hoped to be able to influence the victory of his FLOSY adherents.

In March there was some of the heaviest fighting of the war and on 24 March Nasser left no doubts of his intentions: "we shall support the Yemeni Revolution until it can stand on its own feet and defend itself against reactionary and imperialist plots. We are at present modifying our plans so that, if necessary, we may stay in the Yemen five or more years…we shall reduce the number of our forces and expenditure (and adopt) the strategy of long breath…Shall we surrender to Faysal or stay ten years in Yemen? I say we shall stay twenty years. I now say that we shall strike against whoever intervenes in Yemen…we shall not leave the bases of aggression but shall strike at them." In his speech on May Day, Nasser amplified the last sentence into a promise to help the Yemenis to regain Najran and Asir.

There is no need to detail the events of the next year. The Egyptians pulled back isolated garrisons and concentrated their troops along the coast and in the triangle formed by Sanaa, Taizz and Hodeidah and apart from Sada, left the rest to the Royalists. Yemen was in effect partitioned, although the Egyptians controlled all the main points of entry. After months of diminished effort, the Royalists attacked again in November 1966 and that winter the Egyptians replied by increasing their use of poison gas. In January 1967, 250 people, 95 per cent of the population of the village of Kitaf were reported to have been killed and a Red Cross statement of 21 May said that 318 people had died in three days of attacks. U Thant and the UN managed to find legal quibbles to excuse them from any need to investigate or condemn these barbarities.

For the more effective prosecution of the war, Nasser reduced the Yemeni Republic from the status of a partner to that of a servant, dominated by an army of occupation. In the summer of 1966 General Amri, then Prime Minister for the fourth time, tried to achieve some measure of independence by seeking arms directly from the Russians and this action greatly incensed the Egyptians. Since the arrangement to meet at Haradh, Sallal had been kept as a "guest" in Cairo and in August, after ten months, Nasser sent him back to play the role of a quisling. Amri mobilised troops at the airfield to prevent him from landing, but he found that the Egyptian Ambassador had assembled far stronger forces and was compelled to retire. In defiance of the Constitution, Sallal appointed himself Prime Minister as well as President, although the administration was now completely controlled by Egyptian "advisers". Sallal also started a ferocious purge and amongst fifteen public executions were those of a former Minister, a Vice-President and a Deputy Chief of Staff. The figures for people arrested varied from 2,000 to 4,000, schools and barracks were turned into prisons guarded by Egyptian soldiers and stories were told of the activities of East German torturers. An eye witness described indiscriminate machine gunning of people who tried to hit back at the forces of repression. Amri led a delegation of forty important people to Cairo to protest and the whole party was detained: Sallal asked for their return on treason charges but Nasser preferred to keep them in reserve for possible future use.

Sallal attempted to give some legitimacy to his regime by forming the Popular Revolutionary Union, on the lines of Nasser's own single party, in order "to embrace the whole people...the major stronghold for whose principles all of us would die", but the government so obviously lacked popular support that in February 1967 Tunisia and Jordan withdrew their recognition. Sallal's diplomatic isolation was increased in June when, at the time of the Six Days' War, he broke off relations with America, as did other Arab states. America's USAID officials had already been expelled, accused of killing two Arabs while firing a bazooka at an ammunition dump in Taizz: the State Department, however, failed to learn the lesson that it is impossible to buy the friendship of regimes which are fundamentally hostile.

This situation might have lasted for twenty years, as Nasser forecast, had it not been for the total defeat of the Egyptian forces by the Israelis. Nasser's challenge to Faysal for the leadership of the Arab world collapsed and he was forced to become the pensioner of his former antagonist. In August the

Arab Heads of State met in Khartoum, establishing a Tripartite
Committee headed by the Sudanese Prime Minister, to try to
"enable the Yemenis to unite, live in harmony and achieve
stability in accord with the true desire of the people". In the
same way as two years earlier at Jeddah, this was arranged
between Faysal and Nasser and the Yemenis were not consulted: Sallal vehemently rejected the proposal as "a flagrant
intervention", and refused to accept a referendum. The Royalists were hardly more enthusiastic.

One provision of the agreement was that the Egyptian
troops should leave and this time they did so, sometimes,
ironically, in Saudi ships. In October Republican supporters,
furious at being deserted, attacked the Egyptian Military
Headquarters in Sanaa and several people were killed on both
sides. By early December they had all vanished, having lost
perhaps, thousands. Nasser admitted that it had all been "a
miscalculation...we never thought that it would lead to what it
did": he had apparently expected the operation to last a few
weeks instead of five years. The Egyptian army left behind
mutilated people, ruined villages, destroyed crops, wrecked
vehicles and a burning legacy of hatred.

Before they had even gone, Sallal too had left the stage. He
set off for Moscow to ask for aid and two days later on 5
November, discontented officers, possibly on a hint from
Nasser, seized the government buildings without a shot being
fired in Sallal's defence. He was a man who had inspired neither
liking, trust nor respect; an intriguer and a bully, he was
motivated purely by self-interest. He asked for refuge in Cairo,
which Nasser contemptuously refused, and he then retired
into exile in Baghdad with a pension from the Iraqi government.

He was succeeded by a three-man Council headed by Iryani.
Peace seemed no nearer, however, as the new government
under Muhsin al-Ayni continued the refusal to negotiate with
the Hamid al-Dins or to discuss any alternative to a republic.
With the Egyptians gone, the Royalists gathered their forces
for an attack on Sanaa and early in December Nu'man forecast
that the capital would fall. Iryani felt the need for a "medical
check-up" in Cairo, but General Amri showed his mettle by
assuming office as Prime Minister, issuing arms to civilians and

personally leading the defence. By early January 1968 all the roads into Sanaa had been cut but the Russians flew in supplies of food and weapons, bringing 10,000 tons in three weeks. MiG fighters, too, were reported in action with Syrian pilots and Russian ground crews, but Soviet diplomats were evacuated. It was not until February that the Hodeidah road was reopened with the help of elements from the NLF from Aden. The Republic had survived the departure of some 70,000 supposedly essential Egyptian soldiers.

The failure to take Sanaa showed the lack of co-ordination within the Royalist ranks and led to recriminations which in turn led to disintegration. In the summer of 1968 there appeared to be a split between the Imam Badr, now a sick man who spent much time in hospital in Saudi Arabia, and his cousin Muhammad ibn Hussayn, who had been the most effective of the Princes on the battlefield. The leadership passed into the hands of the latter, but in November the commander who claimed to have killed more Egyptians than any other defected to the Republicans. At the time of the siege of Sanaa, Faysal resumed aid to the Royalists as a reaction to the intervention of the Russians but he realised that to continue it would accentuate the Republicans' dependence upon them. Sanaa's relations with Communist-dominated Aden deteriorated early in 1969; this also lessened Faysal's desire to see the moderate Iryani regime overthrown merely to restore the Hamid al-Dins. In March Iryani said that the Saudis had stopped supplying the Royalists and even before that no more money was made available to employ the mercenaries whose skills were vital.

In May Iryani claimed that the war was over and that not a shot had been fired since December but during the winter the Royalists attacked once more. There was fighting near Sanaa and in the north Sada was captured in February 1970. This, however, proved to be their last throw, for when there was no one to pay them to fight, the tribesmen saw little point in continuing the war.

In March Muhsin al-Ayni, once again Prime Minister, took the opportunity of a conference of Islamic Foreign Ministers in Jeddah to seek from the Saudis alone the mediation which had in the past escaped joint efforts. This proved successful, and in the next month Faysal was said to have "ordered" the Royalists to stop fighting and to have arranged for the return home of all their men, except for the Hamid al-Dins who were doomed to perpetual exile. In May, in the first Saudi aircraft to reach Sanaa since the coup, there returned a large group headed by Sayyid Ahmad al-Shami. He was made a member of the Republican Council, while some of his colleagues joined the Cabinet. This national reconciliation was followed by recognition from Britain and from Saudi Arabia and thus, after nearly seven years of intermittent warfare, the country regained some of the unity and stability that it had had under the Imam Ahmad.

Chapter Eight

The Two Yemens 1968–1972

At the beginning of 1968 for the first time for over a century there were no foreign troops anywhere in the two Yemens: the British had left Aden and the Egyptian army had withdrawn from the North. It was not impossible for an enthusiast to believe that after a break of 250 years the whole of South West Arabia might again become a political unity. Close links already existed between the new NLF regime and the older Republic in Sanaa, which had provided the bases without which the NLF could not have waged their war and had given hospitality to its first three Party Congresses. On the day that he assumed the Presidency Qahtan al-Shaabi declared that "the aim of our Revolution has been since the beginning to unite both parts of Yemen. We are all one people." He appointed one of the most influential leaders, Abd al-Fattah Ismail, as Minister of Yemeni Unity Affairs. The North quickly responded and in the government that General Hassan al-Amri formed for the defence of Sanaa there was a minister with a similar title, replacing the old portfolio of Southern Arabian Affairs. In both capitals there was talk of a "Greater Yemen", which would also embrace Najran, Asir, Muscat and Oman.

On 28 October 1972 Muhsin al-Ayni, Prime Minister of the Sanaa Government and Ali Nasser Muhammad Hassani, Prime Minister of that of Aden signed an agreement in Cairo which provided for a unified single state, with one flag, one capital and one leadership, with single legislative, executive and judicial authorities. By this time however, the North and the South had adopted such divergent stances in home, foreign and economic affairs that not even the most naive enthusiast could believe that the union could become a reality.

Internal political developments

During much of 1968 North Yemen (YAR) had little time for internal politics as its Government had to carry on the war without the help of the Egyptians. The previous November Sallal had been overthrown and replaced by a Republican Council chaired by the Qadi Abd al-Rahman Iryani. The other two members of the Council were his old colleague of *Ahrar* days, Ahmad Muhammad Nu'man, and a rather colourless Shafai, Muhammad Ali Uthman: the former Foreign Minister Muhsin al-Ayni, a man of leftist leanings but strong tribal connections, became Prime Minister for the first time. These arrangements, however, proved of short duration for after a fortnight Nu'man resigned, complaining that the new regime was not prepared to negotiate seriously with the Royalists. He was succeeded by General Hassan al-Amri, who, a fortnight later, also became Prime Minister to take personal charge of the defence of Sanaa.

In the South, on the other hand, there was intense political activity. The new state, calling itself the People's Republic of Southern Yemen (PRSY), came into being, with the High Command of the NLF as its sovereign body. Qahtan al-Shaabi who had headed the delegation to final negotiations at Geneva was nominated as President for two years; he made himself Prime Minister of a Cabinet mostly comprising men who had made their names as terrorists, but whose political opinions varied from Arab nationalism through Baathism to the extreme left. Many had some British training, a few were of tribal origin and Qahtan himself was the only one aged over forty. Qahtan shared with Nasser a type of socialism which eschewed the class war in favour of national unity and believed in combining state and private capital under government direction: he shared also a strong sense of national and personal self-assertion, which had led to his imprisonment in Cairo.

One of the first tasks of the new Government was to create a South Arabian nationality. Thus from the beginning it was stressed that the Republic was a unitary state and no longer a federation of tribes. This was demonstrated at once by the abolition of the old internal boundaries, which were replaced by the creation of six Governorates under officials appointed from Aden, and shown also by the first Ministerial Resolution, which declared a general truce amongst the tribes with effect from 1 January 1968. All bloodfeuds already existing were decreed to have ended and future ones forbidden, with the undertaking that the government would punish transgressions instead of leaving those aggrieved to take revenge. More symbolically, national organisations were set up to cover the whole country: the General Union of Yemeni Women appeared in February and the General Union of Yemeni Workers replaced the old ATUC with its purely local connotations.

The first legal system to apply to the whole area was decreed in the State Security Supreme Court. It could punish with death seventeen offences ranging from inciting hatred of the government to disclosing political secrets or "hesitation, delay or passiveness" in defending the regime. "Disparaging the revolutionary organisation of the NLF", taking or offering a bribe or smuggling could attract jail sentences of up to fifteen years. While the countryside was kept quiet with promises of land reform, a firm grip was established on the towns: an order stated that "the Revolutionary government believes in its citizens being free to express their feelings in support of our Revolutionary Republic...As a safeguard for this the South Yemen Government has now banned demonstrations, public processions and celebrations unless authorised." Other political parties were outlawed, although the pro-Moscow People's Democratic Union (PDU) and a small Baathist group were tolerated, and the Trade Unions were quickly reduced to a subordinate role.

Before the end of 1967, too, the government started its first purge of the security forces. The commander of the army was placed under arrest after holding the post for a fortnight, and the same fate was suffered by the chief of police although he had played a prominent role in assisting the NLF against the British. Seventeen other senior officers were dismissed with loss of pension rights under suspicion of being FLOSY supporters, and further purges took place during the winter. The editorial staff of the government newspaper which had ventured some criticisms was removed.

The NLF began the pleasurable task of punishing those who had served the previous regime. All property belonging to former Rulers and their relatives was confiscated and in January there started a series of secret trials. Six leading Federalis were condemned to death *in absentia* and others who had not escaped received long prison sentences.

In February the Sharif of Bayhan attempted to regain his country and, despite the mismanagement of his Saudi backers, was only driven off after heavy fighting. Makkawi in exile claimed to control 5,000 fighting men and predicted that the NLF would collapse within months as in Upper Aulaqi his supporters, in alliance with members of the former shaykhly family, gained temporary control. The Hadhramawt was being taken over by extreme left-wing groups which formed village soviets and ignored the central government.

In these unpromising circumstances, the Fourth Congress of the NLF assembled at Zinjibar early in March 1968. It became clear that there was a deep division between those who wished to work pragmatically to deal with the numerous problems and those who were prepared to sacrifice everything to the principle of all-out revolution. The latter, led by Abd al-Fattah Ismail, the Minister of Culture, Guidance and Yemeni Unity Affairs, and Ali Salim al-Baydh, the Minister of Defence, inspired by a recent visit from the Palestinian leader Nayif Hawatmah, attacked Qahtan for "pathetic phraseological socialism", for regarding the revolution as "a mere flag and anthem" and as a petty bourgeois. They demanded a new revolutionary situation, based on village soviets, a further purge of "all suspected elements" and the formation of a people's militia of workers, peasants and students; they also reiterated the old calls for "scientific socialism", agrarian reform and the eradication of illiteracy. They wanted Aden to be a centre for the export of revolution, leading a struggle in union with Sanaa against the British in the Gulf and against Israel, as a prelude to the overthrow of all regimes that they disliked. The passing of all these resolutions made it appear that the party, and therefore the government, had moved decisively to the left.

The army was upset by the demand for a militia which would challenge its privileged position. The army had, anyway, a particular aversion to al-Baydh, who had purged its officers, who wished to impose political commissars upon it and who was working to replace British influence and equipment with Russia. So, with the consent of Qahtan, it decided to reverse the decisions of the Congress. On 20 March all ports and frontiers were closed as the army carried out a series of arrests which included most of the leftist leaders and some 150 of their supporters. The NLF High Command invested Qahtan "with all powers to face the present crisis", and on 20 April he reformed his Cabinet, dropping the leftists and affirming that there were no Communists in the NLF.

Some officers purged by al-Baydh were restored and others promoted by him removed. Reassured, the army moved firmly to put down a rising in Abyan of "extreme leftist parasites" and in June to bring back under control the Hadhramawt, where al-Baydh was trying to establish a regime to his own liking. In August the FLOSY hold on Upper Aulaqi was broken after a campaign of calculated brutality which was meant to serve as a warning.

With the support of the army, and of the tribes of Dathinah which comprised 65 per cent of its numbers and who had greatly enjoyed the opportunity of revenge upon their traditional Aulaqi enemies, Qahtan seemed reasonably secure. He was anxious to avoid unrealistic dogmatism and to profit as far as he could from western financial help and from the investment of local capital, but simultaneously he wished to show that he was a man of the left. In October, therefore, he promised that there would be a Legislative Assembly and a new Constitution, although he gave no dates when this would happen. In December he told a rally in Mukalla that the country would continue along the road to socialism.

A new Constitution was also promised in the YAR, where the political situation was not altogether different. The Government there had also fought off a left-wing challenge and was dependent upon army and tribal support, while the return of some of the former royalists introduced another conservative element. The National Council which met in March 1969 re-elected the same three members of the Republican Council and reappointed General Amri as Prime Minister. He announced a programme that was hardly revolutionary: reform of the civil service, improvement of the economy, health services and communications with a special interest in agricultural co-operatives.

In April 1969 there was also a slight change of government in the PRSY. Qahtan apparently bowed to criticism that he appeared to be too autocratic and so handed over the Premiership to his cousin Faysal Abd al-Latif. He wished, too, to attempt to reconcile his leftist critics and so three of them were given posts in the new government: it was to turn out, as Ismail said, that they had joined it so as to be able to overthrow it from within, for in the meanwhile, unknown to Qahtan, the opposition had reorganised. Abd al-Fattah Ismail, the former unskilled refinery worker turned professional revolutionary, had been working closely with Salim Robayya Ali, who had made his name fighting in Radfan rather than by assassinations in Aden. They awaited an opportunity, which the over-confidence of Qahtan provided.

In June 1969 a trivial incident led to an angry exchange between Qahtan and his Minister of the Interior, Muhammad Ali Haytham, as a result of which Haytham was dismissed. Haytham had strong support in the army and amongst the tribes and this he put at the disposal of the disgruntled leftists, who declared that Qahtan had "blatantly violated" the draft constitution by refusing to discuss matters with the High Command of the NLF. He was accused of practising terror and oppression towards progressives and of "individualist inclinations", and was deposed in a bloodless coup which later became sanctified under the name of "The Glorious Corrective Step". He was replaced by a five-man Presidential Council under the chairmanship of Robayya, which included Ismail and Haytham who was appointed Prime Minister. The return to office of al-Baydh, this time as Foreign Minister, gave clear indication that the leftists had won. This was confirmed a few days later by the appointment of a new Executive Committee of the NLF with Ismail as Secretary-General.

Qahtan and Faysal Abd al-Latif were arrested and perhaps 1,200 of their supporters purged. The commander of the army escaped to Taizz, the chief of police was arrested and all the provincial governors were replaced. The NLF High Command was determined to show that it was the supreme authority; in November it announced that it was extending its original two-year period of office for another year, in the course of which a new Constitution would be put to a Parliament which would emerge from local revolutionary councils. Commissars were attached to army units and Haytham declared that the forces would be "re-educated". The recognition of East Germany, quickly followed by a breach of diplomatic relations with the United States and then by the nationalisation of British Banks showed the political stance of the new regime, and this was symbolically confirmed by the abolition of the title of "Mister" in favour of that of "Brother".

Haytham's quarrel with Qahtan had, however, been personal rather than doctrinal, and by the end of the year it was apparent that the struggle between the comparative moderates and the revolutionaries *à l'outrance* had not finally been resolved. Aden simultaneously announced a purge in which twenty NLF members including Qahtan were expelled from the party and a reform of the Presidential Council and of the Cabinet. The two military members of the Presidential Council who had tended to support Haytham against Robayya, Ismail and the increasingly influential al-Baydh, were dropped. Two new Ministers, Abdullah Badeeb, who was generally known to be a Communist, and Anis Hassan Yahya, regarded as a Baathist, took office for the first time. Haytham retained his post at the price of accepting a programme which included rebuilding the armed and security forces "on a revolutionary basis", the "amendment of laws and administrative systems and the development of them in a way conforming with the present revolutionary status", the preparation for the establishment of Popular Councils, a Supreme People's Council, a Constitution and closer relations with "friendly Socialist countries". Military training was started in the schools.

In the meanwhile, in July 1969 General Amri resigned the Premiership of the YAR on grounds of health. After Muhsin al-Ayni had failed to form a government, a rather ineffective engineer named Abdullah al-Kirshimi took office. He was pledged to an austere but non-socialist economic policy, with a total ban on luxury imports, the encouragement of foreign investment and the use of credit to promote development. He remained as Premier for six months and then resigned through frustration at the impossibility of framing a budget that both made financial sense and satisfied the army. Muhsin al-Ayni became Prime Minister again in February 1970, but there was little that he could promise beyond attempts to improve the national finances through more efficient administration and a census to discover the country's economic potential. These minor palliatives were in striking contrast to the sweeping measures being taken in the South, but in practice there was nothing that al-Ayni or any other Minister could do. The main charges on the Treasury were subsidies to tribal leaders and the cost of the army – the two pillars on which the government was totally dependent. In fact al-Ayni's principal achievement was to negotiate the return of the Royalists and the start of national reconciliation.

Crushing its enemies, rather than national reconciliation, was the aim of the Aden government in 1970. There were reports that over 1,000 people were arrested in the first two months of the year and in March a Supreme People's Court in Aden with subordinate Courts in each Governorate were created "to review anti-State activities and offences committed against the safety of the Revolution and peace and order". These courts were not trammelled by ordinary rules of judicial procedure and could try crimes dating back to the beginning of independence over two years before.

A few days after the establishment of these courts the government discovered "a dreadful plot drawn up and maintained by the reactionary and imperialist forces. This plot is not confined to the execution of assassination campaigns only but also aims at having military control over the area." It was said to have included "the blasting of water wells owned by the citizens as well as water pumps of farmers and highwaymanship". Eight men were condemned to death for "betraying the Revolution and the People" in the interests of the Saudis, British, Americans, West Germans and even the Zionists. "Huge public meetings" were assembled to denounce the conspirators and to pledge loyalty to the party. A fortnight later the former Prime Minister Faysal Abd al-Latif was shot "trying to escape."

The Aden government exploited, or perhaps invented, this plot in order to instil a sense of fear throughout the country and this was kept alive by constant references to further conspiracies in the speeches of Ministers and compulsory demonstrations by militants. A great part was played in this by the creation of a People's Militia which had been one of the demands of the Zinjibar Conference subsequently ignored by Qahtan. The Militia came directly under the party and not under the government. After crash courses in ideology, its members were scattered throughout the villages to act as informers, cheer leaders and propagandists. The ideology taught became more overtly Communist: in June 1970 Ismail announced new links with the Russian party, which had promised to help in the creation of party cadres and to provide party scholarships and training courses. The first State Farm was named after Lenin, whose birthday was celebrated with greater publicity than that of the Prophet Muhammad.

With the Militia established, the party turned its attention to the politicising of the security forces. Ismail was categoric that "there can never be any separation between military and ideological education", and he told the troops that there was a "need for the liquidation of obsolete traditional concepts which contravene the responsibilities of the revolutionary soldier who is equipped with political ideology and socialist culture". In June 1970 the Defence Minister announced that "revolutionary military commands" had been formed at all levels of the army to provide "a natural answer to the phenomena of foolhardy revolts aimed at establishing military regimes without progressive, social aspirations", and as part of the process of bringing it to heel, the army was used on road-building, irrigation and other construction work.

The same process was applied to the police. In October the Interior Minister Muhammad Salah Muti stressed the need to change the force left "by colonialism and its stooges" at a parade of 300 men and 30 women passing out after a three month course in police affairs, law and political culture. Six months later he was able to claim that there was now "an organised and regular political classical force, serving the workers and peasants and protecting the objectives and gains of the Revolution".

In order to spread ideology in the rural areas national institutions like the Poor Peasants Union were created, and there was a further attack on tribalism. In November 1970 tribal clubs were abolished "to correct the abnormal social relations between citizens of the single people and remove the barricades which were erected by colonialism and its henchmen". Tribal surnames were forbidden.

To overawe the townsfolk, conversation with foreigners was discouraged and the need for constant vigilance symbolised in the proclamation of the anniversary of the Crater rising, 20 June, as "Security Day". A military member of the Supreme Court declared in October that "the present critical phase passed by our under-developed country demands that we should strike with an iron fist against anti-revolutionary trends in order to ensure stability for the toiling masses through the imposition of the severest penalties on imperialist henchmen and opportunist conspirators and collaborators with the forces of imperialism and reaction in subversive plans aimed at eliminating the Revolution and the progressive gains of the people". He was as good as his word – five of the March plotters including a former Provincial Governor were shot, and one of Qahtan's Ministers jailed for fifteen years. People were called before local committees to explain their political attitudes and there were several reports that these interrogations had led to suicides. By 1972, despite the ban on travelling abroad without special permission, it was estimated that 25 per cent of the population had escaped and sought refuge in neighbouring countries, especially in the YAR. There was no change in atmosphere the following year when few Ministerial speeches were complete without calls for constant vigilance, political mobilisation and training of the masses, and references to "heinous conspiracies" directed against the embattled State. In his May Day speech, for example, Robayya spoke of plots to lay mines, assassinate teachers, burn schools and health units so as to keep the people "hostages of illiteracy, poverty, disease and backwardness".

During 1970 both Yemens proclaimed new Constitutions and a comparison of the documents shows how far the two states had already diverged. An Egyptian and an East German started work in April to draft a document for the South. This was approved by the NLF High Command and, after a series of meetings at which Haytham and other Ministers explained it to militants, it came into force in November. The name of the country was changed into the People's Democratic Republic of Yemen (PDRY) with Islam as its religion and guarantees for private property and the right of inheritance. Despite this all Waqf property (possessions left by testators to provide income for pious purposes) was taken over by the state. All stress was on the working classes and it was declared that "a national democratic revolution is achieved on the basis of scientific socialism". The sovereign body was to be widened beyond the High Command of the NLF to a People's Supreme Council of 101 members, which would have power to determine policy and elect the Head of State and appoint Ministers.

Few had any illusions that the ruling group of the party had any real intention of sharing power or of making any genuine move towards greater democracy. Eighty-six of the 101 members of the Supreme Council were nominated by the government and the remainder "elected" by the Trade Unions. Effective control was in the hands of a Permanent Committee of which Ismail was Chairman and al-Baydh Secretary.

The YAR Constitution was a domestic product, hammered out after a year's genuine debate in which Iryani played a major role; a draft was presented in September which various groups were invited to discuss. The influence of the religious leaders prevailed and the result was that the document started with quotations from the Qur'an and contained a far firmer commitment to the Shariah than any other modern Constitution for it was declared the source of legislation. A Supreme Constitutional Court of *ulama* would ensure that taxes and economic measures were based on Islamic concepts of social justice and that members of the Republican Council should have the qualifications once required of an Imam. The word "socialism" was never used, and the legal and political rights of women left vague. On the other hand the opinions of the educated young were not scorned, for realising that a wholly elected Parliament would be dominated by conservative tribal chiefs, they managed to ensure that one-fifth of the *Majlis al-Shura* (Consultative Council) should be appointed and that a two-thirds majority would be needed to approve legislation. The Constitution was thus a real attempt to find a political system appropriate to the country.

Indirect elections were held and the Council assembled in April 1971, with Iryani declaring that its objective was "to secure for the individual his freedom, dignity and happiness under consultative parliamentary rule". The power of the traditional chiefs was however shown by the election as Speaker of Abdullah ibn Hussayn al-Ahmar, whose tribal support was still essential for any government. As usual Iryani resigned, but was easily persuaded to remain as Chairman of the Republican Council with his old colleagues General Amri and Muhammad Ali Uthman.

Muhsin al-Ayni was replaced as Prime Minister by Ahmad Muhammad Nu'man, who, as throughout his long career, showed that he was a man of words and theories rather than one prepared to tackle difficult problems. In July, after little more than two months in office, he declared himself "unable to shoulder the responsibilities of rule because of the financial difficulties facing the nation", which, he said, could not meet even a small part of its obligations. There was also widespread dissatisfaction at the prevalence of corruption and inefficiency and it was obvious that a much tougher and more realistic man was needed. After a month of drift, General Amri agreed to form his seventh Cabinet, promising an "administrative revolution" to deal with the national problem. As a start he appointed a Supreme Committee attached to his own office to supervise all departments concerned with the economy.

Amri's government lasted a mere ten days before being ended by a ludicrous tragedy. As usually happened in Sanaa, Amri got a wrong number on the telephone and instead of talking to a senior officer, found himself connected with a drunken photographer, who, thinking that one of his friends was playing a joke, answered in kind. Amri, in a fury, sent guards to arrest him and then killed him with his own hands. It was said that President Iryani wanted a public execcution of his Prime Minister but agreed to let him go into exile "for the sake of his health". Amri's post of Commander-in-Chief was abolished, and Muhsin al-Ayni was recalled from the Paris Embassy to form a Cabinet which was still in office during the crisis between the two Yemens the following summer.

In the meanwhile savage in-fighting continued at the highest level within the ranks of the governing party in Aden. In August 1970, Robayya went to China and returned immensely impressed by the cultural revolution, declaring that "a revolution begins to rot when it is taken over by the bureaucrats".

Inspired by Mao, he felt that the transformation of society should start in the countryside and he encouraged peasants and fishermen to seize their means of livelihood, even if this meant bloodshed and anarchy. He urged that as far as possible trade should be conducted only with socialist countries. Ismail, a low-born Hujari, had no support in tribal rural areas, although he had a following amongst the increasing urban proletariat in the towns and an ideological following amongst the indoctrin- ated members of the militia, the airforce and above all in the Party, which he wished to augment by absorbing orthodox pro-Moscow Communists and other groups. Haytham wanted to concentrate on administration rather than politics, to rely on the moderate elements, to hold the loyalty of the tribes and the still largely tribal army and to work at bettering the lot of the people by improving the economic situation. He purged some radicals, declared that there would be no further nationalisation and invited investment from western sources to build new factories and to help to solve what he called the "chronic" financial situation that made nearly half the population unemployed.

Ismail and Robayya joined forces against Haytham despite their own ideological differences, and in July Ismail went to Moscow and presumably obtained a promise of support for the removal of Haytham, who, the following month, was replaced as Prime Minister and as a member of the Presidential Council by the Defence Minister, Ali Nasser Muhammad Hassani.[1]

In October Hassani told a journalist that the policy of his government, "on the basis of commitment to Marxism-Leninism" was to intensify the fight against illiteracy, to dev- elop the social services and to fulfil a three-year development plan. His foreign policy "based on an understanding of the spirit of the age", distinguished between "the forces of libera- tion, progress and socialism" and those of "backwardness, agentry, imperialism and colonialism".

Haytham's supporters were purged. The former Comman- der in Chief was "shot resisting arrest" and the drive to indoc-

---

[1] Despite the formal abolition of tribal names, the reader will find it easier to keep track of "Hassani" than of "Ali Nasser Muhammad" so it is proposed to continue referring to him by this name.

trinate the army was intensified with the foundation of a new Military College and the appointment of a Deputy Minister of Defence for Political and Moral Orientation. "Tribal societies", including such surprising groups as the Girl Guides, the St John Ambulance Brigade and the Aden Butchers Association were dissolved; the climate of terror became still stronger. In October 1971 there were claims that yet another invasion of mercenaries financed by the USA and Saudi Arabia had been repulsed but still more were forecast. Robayya warned that the plots of imperialists and reactionaries "require us to expect the worst eventuality, to prepare ourselves for a long-term struggle politically and militarily, and to strike without mercy all conspirators against the Revolution and its achievements". In October a man was shot for sabotage, in June 1972 another for "associating with organs of the reactionary Saudi government", and in July six more for plotting to overthrow the regime.

Although it was possible that without Haytham the split between the pro-Moscow Ismail and the pro-Peking Robayya might prove deeper than their marriage of convenience, the Fifth Congress of the Party which took place in March 1972 was officially declared to have been "held in a wonderful democratic atmosphere". Robayya later said that it had provided "the basic means of sifting out of the organisation rightist, tribal and family opportunistic elements which constantly impeded the development of relations with the socialist countries". All programmes to transform society in the way desired by the leadership were rubber-stamped with acclamation and all agreed on the importance of ideology in the creation of a "vanguard party". A Politbureau of 31 members with 14 reserves was created, with Ismail as Secretary-General and Robayya as his Deputy; there was apparent harmony as events moved towards the crisis of the summer.

Relations with the Western powers

The western power with which the new government of Aden had most immediate contact was naturally the United Kingdom. Although the British had played a not-inconsiderable part in the NLF's victory over its FLOSY rivals, in the hope that a minority nationalist regime would be easier to deal with than one with close links with Nasser's Egypt, discord started within a few days. With the consent of their population of 78 souls, Whitehall returned the Kuria Muria Islands to their former owners, the Sultanate of Muscat, rather than handing them over to the new Republic: this brought an angry protest from the Aden Foreign Minister and a Note to the United Nations. More serious, however, were the disputes over the aid which the British had promised to the Federation and which the PRSY claimed should be paid instead to itself as the successor government.

On 27 February 1968 the Aden government abruptly dismissed the British experts who had been left behind to assist in the build-up of the armed forces, declaring that the officers concerned would not operate the airforce outside the national boundaries and that this was "a provocation, a meddling with our independence and an interference in our internal affairs". Whitehall expressed its anger at the dismissal; it was further incensed by the putting on trial of rulers and officials who had served the Federation. Thus when the Foreign Minister, Dhalai, went to London at the end of April to ask for a five-year no-strings-attached British grant, his reception was icy. In his May Day speech Qahtan said that the British "instead of paying us a small sum of £100 million, or at least £60 million, in compensation for exploiting our country for 129 years, offered us only £1 million". This million pounds was spurned by Aden so some of it was used instead to pay compensation to the officers who had been dismissed. Qahtan claimed that the attitude of London was a deliberate attempt "to suffocate our people and to topple the progressive regime by the creation of an economic crisis". The expropriation of British firms in the following year still further decreased the possibility that the United Kingdom would provide financial help.

The British were accused of assisting the series of tribal risings against the PRSY and relations grew still worse as the insurgency in Dhofar boiled up: Aden provided bases, training and a staging post for Chinese and Russian arms for the rebels, while the forces of the Sultan of Muscat could hardly have survived without British help. In March 1969 Qahtan complained that the British were continually violating the eastern frontier and were even engaged in bombing. Such accusations were reiterated during the following years, culminating in a statement to the Security Council that a "large-scale invasion" involving aircraft carriers was being planned. The British presence in the Gulf was continually attacked and the Aden propaganda machine spoke of "genocide" and "a wide-scale imperialist reactionary conspiracy aimed at toppling progressive regimes and liquidating the tributaries of Arab Revolution". It was not until the coming of peace in Dhofar in the late 1970s that relations between London and Aden could be said to have improved to the stage where they were merely "cool".

It will be recalled that Whitehall had not recognised the YAR so there were no relations until after the return of Royalists. From the summer of 1970, however, relations became very cordial, with increasing trade and other contacts. The British supplied economic, cultural and technical aid, including an aerial survey and advice on irrigation. The opening of a Bank showed the mutual desire for co-operation.

It was widely believed in Aden that some American officials gave covert aid to the NLF militants while they were still fighting the British and indeed not infrequently the US has thought it astute to try to gain new friends at the price of letting down old allies. If this were indeed so, it profited them little for from the beginning the PRSY saw the hand of the CIA in every attempted coup, tribal revolt, frontier violation and spy ring and as early as March 1968 the US Defence and Naval Attache was given 24 hours to leave the country. On one occasion the government newspaper *14 October* accused the Americans of "planning to entice school boys and girls", of recruiting Muslim Brothers to blow up cinemas, night-clubs and bars and stated as proof that "obsolete love letters exchanged with girls in Cairo were found".

The Aden propaganda organs made much of the links between the USA and its own arch enemy Saudi Arabia, declaring that they were working together to arm, train and pay mercenary invaders. It was no surprise when on 1 April 1970 Aden Radio denounced America as "the sweetest enemy of the Arab Revolution".

In its verbal war the PRSY made much, too, of US backing for Israel, and in September 1969 it called on all Arab countries to break off relations with Washington. It took its own advice the following month, alleging American support for Lebanese army attacks on Palestinian guerrillas and "its continuous plotting". Aden's lead was not followed and neither was its urging in May 1970 that the Arabs should nationalise all American interests and "wage war" against all its products. Later that summer it rejected the Rogers' Plan for a Middle East solution and the following years saw no cessation of press and radio attacks.

American relations with the YAR were broken off during the June War of 1967 and during the siege of Sanaa, General Amri said that the US was the only country still arming the Royalists. The end of the war and the Yemeni rapprochement with Saudi Arabia obviously meant that there were no further grounds for dispute between Sanaa and Washington, but relations were not immediately restored. While Aden rejected the Rogers' Plan, Sanaa gave it a cautious blessing. In July 1972 Rogers himself paid a brief unexpected visit to the YAR; this was followed by the restoration of relations and the start of aid. Aden was darkly convinced that the Secretary of State had gone to stir a war between the two Yemens, as part of its normal policy "to make Vietnamese kill each other and Asians kill Asians".

There is little that needs to be said about relations between the two Yemens and the other major western states. In January 1968 West Germany sent a delegation to Aden to discuss the possibility of aid and later there was a report that a loan of 10 million Deutschmarks would be made. However in June 1969 the new government of Robayya decided for doctrinaire political reasons to recognise East Germany, whereupon, in accordance with its normal practice, Bonn instantly severed diplomatic relations and there were no further contacts between the two countries. A few days later Bonn established links with Sanaa and started to provide substantial aid, undertaking the construction of an international airport and major road works, as well as giving help in military and agricultural matters. It even assumed the burden of organising the postal service.

At the end of the civil war France recognised the YAR and

started to provide some aid, which included a television system – although this was perhaps a luxury in a country largely without electricity. Although Paris appointed an Ambasssador to Aden in 1971 there was little contact between the two countries.

At the beginning of the decade, Italy had been the only western country represented in Sanaa while the others were regarded as hostile or at the best indifferent, but in less than three years all the major western states had Embassies, channelling aid and encouraging investment. Aden, on the other hand, had deliberately cut itself off from western aid and was engaging in virulent propaganda attacks on the countries concerned. At a time of East-West competition, it was possible for a "neutral" to be courted by both sides. This was well understood by the government in Sanaa and their people benefited accordingly: the rulers of Aden were perhaps more principled in taking an ideological approach, but in so doing they rejected much that could have improved the lot of their subjects.

Relations with the Communist bloc

Russia recognised the new government of Aden as soon as it came into existence and within a few days sent a small delegation to establish an Embassy and to give a general blessing to the policies that it had proclaimed. A few weeks later the PRSY Minister of Defence, Ali Salim al-Baydh, went to Moscow to ask for aid, particularly in military matters. It was clear that some agreement was reached for shortly after his return the British officers attached to the army were dismissed and a Russian General appeared in Aden. It thus quickly became apparent that the new regime preferred to range itself with one super-power rather than to practise non-alignment, and evidence of this grew throughout the year. In June Russian warships paid their first call to Aden and the following months arms, mostly light weapons and military vehicles, started to arrive. In August there was an agreement by which Russia would supply military and technical assistance; later in the year an Adeni delegation spent a month in Russia while a Soviet economic group was in Aden for 18 days.

The Kremlin was, however, cautious about becoming too deeply involved in a country about whose stability it was uncertain. The early months saw Qahtan with an army of dubious loyalty, assailed from the extreme left, plagued by tribal revolts and facing the likelihood of an invasion by the old Federalis. Furthermore, whereas the United States had huge surpluses and boundless productive capacity, Russia could only give foreign aid at some sacrifice to its own consumers, and therefore for two years its help was limited to a largely symbolic sum of about £600,000.

Although the Chinese did not immediately open an Embassy in the PRSY it was clear that Maoist thought had considerable attractions for many members of the NLF, who regarded Russia as opportunistic and over-cautious, unwilling to take a real revolutionary line for fear of clashes with America. They felt, too, that the experience of an Asiatic country struggling after a recent revolution to emerge from under-development was more relevant than that of an industrialised European state whose revolution had taken place half a century before. This attitude was manifest in some of the resolutions of the Zinjibar Conference and the Kremlin was gratified when Qahtan succeeded in fighting off the challenge and started to increase support for his government. The Chinese, however, were not deterred and in September 1968 provided a vital loan of £5 million, which saved the PRSY from possible bankruptcy after its failure to extort money from Britain.

From 1968 Russia was determined to show that it was a world power by maintaining a presence in the Indian Ocean. For this it was essential to have the use of facilities in Aden, whose government could play upon fears that it would collapse or be forced to take help from Saudi Arabia to claim aid from the Kremlin. In January 1969 there was a large arms delivery, which included MiG fighters, accompanied by about 50 technicians and advisers. At the end of the month Qahtan was well received in Moscow and returned with a series of promises of co-operation and a gift of 50 fishing boats.

After the "Glorious Corrective Move", the Kremlin felt that it had no option but to work with the new government, despite some doubts that it contained "leftist extremists, cutting corners to establish socialism". Moreover, as Russian advisers were expelled by the Sudanese in 1971 and by President Sadat in the summer of 1972, Aden was Russia's only friend in the area. There were some reports that Soviet military personnel from Egypt had been posted to Aden, but this, like occasional rumours of a base on Socotra, turned out to be untrue.

By the summer of 1972 Russian aid to the PDRY was worth about £12 million a year, and in addition to keeping the country solvent, this aid financed some 30 projects including a power station, a hospital, a dam, fishery developments, a fishmeal plant and a survey of water resources. There were frequent cultural exchanges, including a visit from a Russian circus, and several hundred South Yemenis were receiving training or higher education in the Soviet Union. In July 1970 Russian advisers were posted to the Ministries of the Economy, Agriculture, Works and the National Planning Corporation. In the same month *Pravda* painted a glowing picture of young Hadhramis avidly devouring the works of Lenin and complaining of a shortage of material on scientific socialism. According to *Pravda*, the Yemen had by-passed "the religious-feudal and bourgeois-liberal stages" and passed on to socialism – an accolade which was not accorded to many developing countries.

Part of the price of Russian aid was support for Soviet foreign policy, and Aden and Iraq were the only Arab states to condone the invasion of Dubcek's Czechoslovakia. Recognition was accorded to the Vietcong provisional government and the puppet regime in Mongolia, and suave though vague messages of friendship were exchanged with the Albanian Trade Union Federation.

Relations with the other satellites proved more rewarding; Aden was able to get agriculturalists from Hungary, geologists from Romania and fishermen from Bulgaria. Poland agreed to finance four factories with the requisite machinery, and all these countries in addition to East Germany and North Korea offered training facilities and various consumer supplies. They were not lavish, however for early in 1972 the Foreign Minister Muhammad Salih Aulaqi spent three weeks touring Eastern Europe and returned with a mere $10 million, and even this was in the form of technical assistance rather than cash. The most generous were the East Germans who gave a flour mill, school laboratories, a telephone exchange and a biscuit factory, but, more important to a Communist state, expertise on managing a propaganda machine and the organisation of a political police force skilled in intelligence gathering and torture. They ran also the Institute for the Development of Cadres for the Public Sector and the National Economy.

The Chinese kept a low profile, nagging away at Russian weak spots while providing valuable work in developing roads, airports and harbours. Their work was very visible for it took place all over the country where their experts lived with the local people in tents, whereas the Russians insisted upon living in hotels as befitted Europeans. The PDRY was too small a stage on which to mount some vast project such as an Assouan Dam, but it could easily absorb the numerous small schemes in which the Chinese excelled. Chinese doctors worked in remote villages where no Russian would stay, and they were particularly active in the extreme East and other less attractive places. In total they probably provided more aid than the Russians, and after the visit by Chairman Robayya they promised a further $40 million. Other activities included a strategic road to the Hadhramawt, a textile factory, a fish freezing plant, an agricultural research station and a factory for agricultural and metal implements.

Aden provided facilities for Chinese support of the insurrection in Dhofar at a time when Peking, despairing of winning Arab governments away from Russia or the West, felt that its main hope of influence was through espousing Liberation Movements. China constantly expressed resolute support for the "People's armed struggle in the Gulf", and Robayya was clearly most impressed by Maoism after his visit in August 1970, and for a time he advocated the Peking form of Communism against the Moscow brand supported by Ismail. Amongst many left-wingers, however, the Chinese rapprochement with Washington, based on a common distrust of Russia, caused doubts about the country's revolutionary credentials.

During the first part of 1968, Sanaa was even more dependent upon Soviet aid than was its southern neighbour. For the first time in an officially non-aligned state, Russian airmen supported combat missions against the Royalist besiegers of the capital, and their supply lift kept the Republic afloat. In the autumn, however, when General Amri went to Moscow to ask for more arms so as to finish the war, he did not receive all that he had requested, as his regime appeared to be drifting slowly towards the right. As the South became increasingly anchored in the eastern camp and its relations with the North deteriorated, the Kremlin restricted its supply of weapons to Sanaa, aiming at little more than keeping a customer. When Iryani visited Moscow two years later he spoke of "neutrality and non-alignment", and despite gushing communiqués returned with a promise of a cement kiln rather than of aircraft. In October 1972 Muhsin al-Ayni said that no new equipment had arrived for three years and a few months earlier relations had so far deteriorated that Sanaa found it necessary to deny that the Soviet Military Mission had been expelled. During the actual hostilities, a cargo of arms destined for Hodeidah was diverted to Aden and around the same time a Russian contingency plan for the invasion of the YAR in conjunction with the PDRY came by chance or design into the hands of the Sanaa authorities.

The Russians sent an economic delegation to Sanaa in December 1968 and after that gave aid on a limited scale, helping with a cement factory, giving some medical supplies, improving Hodeidah harbour and the road from there to Taizz. They were, however, unable to compete with the West or with the Saudis and wisely refrained from trying to do so. The East European satellites had little contact with the YAR. The Chinese proved more effective and were very much more popular: their main project was a textile factory, the biggest industrial plant in the country, and nearly 400 of them worked on the road northwards to Sada. As in the South they provided doctors who achieved much with the minimum of equipment and who won many friends.

By the summer of 1972, as we have seen, the YAR could reasonably be described as a neutral country in that it had quarrelled with neither bloc but its sympathies and interests were on the Western side: the attitude of the PDRY was unequivocal – it was definitely in the Eastern camp.

Relations with the other Arab States

Although many of the Arab states had favoured FLOSY, which called upon them not to recognise the NLF Government, the majority proved willing to accept the newcomer. Within a week, all apart from Saudi Arabia and Oman had established diplomatic relations and there was no opposition to its entry into the Arab League. At the end of 1967 King Hassan of Morocco, no lover of left-wing regimes, sent a personal message to Qahtan inviting his participation in the Arab Summit which was due to assemble in Rabat the following month.

For the whole of 1968 the two Republics regarded Saudi Arabia as their most dangerous enemy. President Iryani asked all Arab states to intervene to halt "blatant Saudi aggression", saying that King Faysal had refused to stop aid to the still active Royalist forces which would collapse without his help. By the end of the year, however, Faysal felt that the basically conservative regime of Iryani was one with which he could live and that by continuing to support the failing cause of the Imam, he was merely driving Sanaa into the arms of Aden. In March 1969 Iryani said that the Saudis had stopped supplying the Royalists, but it was not until a year later that Muhsin al-Ayni became the first Republican Minister to be invited to visit the Kingdom. As a result of his negotiations with Faysal, all the royalists except the Hamid al-Dins returned in May 1970, in July the Saudis made their first grant of $20 million and the two countries exchanged Ambassadors.

Faysal had always seen the NLF as dangerous Communists, and he urged the British not to hand over power to them. From the very beginning of the PRSY he regarded the men who had ousted his Federali friends as a menace which he worked to overthrow. In February 1968 he assisted the attempt by the Sharif of Bayhan to regain his country, and he supported other attacks during that summer. His agents were also active in the Hadhramawt, which some people believed that he aimed to annex – if he could have established an oil terminal at Mukalla, he would have been able to avoid depending on the straits of Hormuz. The Aden government hit back as best it could, and in November Qahtan called on the Saudi people to oust their king. Qahtan's successors later claimed that Riyadh had spent

$600 million on support for their enemies. Refugees from the PRSY were paid to be in readiness for an armed return; Saudi funds financed a newspaper in Jeddah and a radio station in Najran which attempted to stir up unrest with claims that Islam was in danger.

The hostility between the neighbours boiled over in an armed clash in November 1969, when the two armies each claimed to have defeated the other in a battle for a border village which might perhaps have been rich in oil. The press reported that aerial dogfights had taken place between Saudi aircraft supplied by Britain and MiGs allegedly flown by Russian pilots. For nearly a week fighting continued until the Saudi forces announced a victory—they asserted that only the moderation of the King had restrained them from advancing as far as Aden itself: in fact, however, internal quarrels had thrown their supply system into chaos.

Three months later, the official PRSY news agency accused the Saudis of plotting another invasion and the charge was frequently repeated throughout the years. In the early 1970s an official speech in Aden was rarely made without a reference to "the reactionary priest-ridden Saudi regime" which aimed at "toppling our revolutionary accomplishments and bringing back our country to the grip of neo-colonialism" in plots with the British, Americans, or occasionally, for good measure, the Zionists. The Radio broadcast the communiqués of the Committee for Solidarity with the Saudi people which accused the monarchy of repression which "takes several ugly forms including stranglement, poisoning and running vehicles over them as well as physical torture which ends in death, blindness and madness."

As early as the Zinjibar Conference of March 1968 the Aden Government pledged its support for "progressive and liberation forces" in the Gulf and from the beginning its assistance was vital to the insurgents in Dhofar. It provided a base from which the rebels could operate and a port through which Chinese and Russian arms could reach them, and it made no effort to give the modern-minded Sultan Qabus of Oman a chance after he replaced his father in July 1970. Aden Radio broadcast the communiqués of the rebels, who would otherwise have been cut off from the outside world, and provided

Commissars to indoctrinate youths who had been kidnapped and brought across the border. There were constant clashes and accusations of frontier violations, and in May 1972 the government of Oman, having complained of an Adeni attack on one of its forts, announced that it had bombed gun positions within the Republic.

In June 1971 Haytham declared that the PDRY would support revolution in the "Occupied Arab Gulf" and promised to defeat all plots "conceived in London, Riyadh or Tehran to divide the Gulf into petty pseudo-emirates, or attempts by these petty states to enter the Arab League or the UN and ignore the will of the people". The following month the infant Federation of the former Trucial States was denounced as bogus and a creation of "Anglo-American imperialism and Iranian-Arab reaction". In August the PDRY refused to recognise the "fake independence" of Bahrain and was the only country to vote against its admission and that of Qatar into the Arab League. Its radio called unceasingly for the overthrow of all these governments and, of the "oil-states", only Kuwait, pursuing its usual policy of buying off potential enemies, escaped attack. Apart from the YAR, Kuwait was the only state in the Arabian Peninsula to maintain relations with Aden and it provided aid after a visit by Faysal Abd al-Latif in April 1969 during his brief period as Prime Minister. There were several subsequent gifts and loans and in August 1972 the two countries established a jointly-owned fishing company.

Sanaa had in the meanwhile adopted a totally different policy, establishing cordial relations with Oman, Bahrain, Qatar and the United Arab Emirates from which it became the first country to receive financial aid. In January 1972 the Deputy Prime Minister Colonel Hamdi went to Abu Dhabi and the visit was returned later in the year by Shaykh Zaid. Iran, always condemned by Aden as an arch-plotter, recognised the YAR after the return of the Royalists and provided technical help. Naturally Sanaa cultivated the friendship of Kuwait, being rewarded by a large loan in June 1968 which was to prove only the first of many.

Throughout 1971 and 1972 King Faysal continued his policy of making Sanaa increasingly dependent upon Saudi financial aid. In March 1971 there was a large consignment of military equipment and buses for schools, in April a printing press and in October two aircraft; these were followed the next year by £1 million for hospital supplies and money to pay the salaries of 250 teachers. The tribal chiefs, without whose support the YAR could not survive, were given Saudi subsidies and there was a general belief that many of the leading Ministers accepted bribes and that senior officers also received their shares.

In return Faysal demanded that a blind eye be turned to his building up on North Yemeni soil an "Army of National Unity" from amongst the numerous refugees who had fled from the South, who were maintained in camps awaiting his signal to move across the frontier. On his own territory he set up the "Army of National Salvation" for the same purpose, and facilitated its work by building garrison towns and roads towards the border. The build-up was intensified after Russia signed a fifteen-year Friendship Treaty with Iraq in April 1972 which, as *The Times* pointed out, gave them a point of pressure on the whole Arabian Peninsula. It seems probable that Faysal encouraged the Omani reprisals of the following month and deliberately heightened the tension on the frontier of the two Yemens during the summer, which will be described later.

In the period that we are discussing both Yemens received aid from the oil-exporting countries of Algeria and Iraq and, after the advent of Colonel Qadafi, from Libya. In 1969 Algeria established Joint Companies both with Sanaa and with Aden to explore for oil, although the one with the North was dissolved in 1972 as the Yemenis failed to put up their share of the capital, and the one with Aden ended in 1976 after the search proved fruitless. Iraq gave cash and aid to improve the harbours of Aden and Hodeidah while Libya helped agricultural development and education in both countries.

Leaders of both Yemens toured other Arab capitals making speeches of goodwill and both followed the general Arab line on Palestine, although Adeni relations were closer because of old links established as fellow conspirators in the Arab National Movement. In October 1969 Aden broke off diplomatic relations with Lebanon as a protest against Beirut's attitude to the Palestinian guerrillas and later with Jordan for the same reason, but Sanaa took little notice and indeed welcomed the first Hashemite Ambassador. Both Yemens tried to exploit the fear that the Israelis would establish bases on the Ethiopian side of the Bab al-Mandeb or on some of the islands, particularly after their tanker *Coral Sea* was attacked as it passed through the Straits.

In November 1970 the leaders of Egypt, Libya and the Sudan, subsequently joined by Syria, announced that they had decided to unite as a "first stage of the projected federation of the four Arab countries and the backbone of the future liberation battle with Israel". In January 1972 Aden offered to join, although Sanaa did not, but no one with the possible exception of Qadafi seems to have taken the matter seriously and nothing further happened.

In the summer of 1972 it seemed that Aden's only real friend amongst the Arabs was Iraq, which had similar close ties with the Communist bloc. There were reports that even Qadafi was turning against Aden. There were rumours that he had been convinced by Makkawi and other FLOSY exiles that the regime of the PDRY was anti-Islamic and in August three men who hijacked an Aden-bound aircraft diverted it to Benghazi apparently expecting a welcome. It was said that the unpredictable Colonel had been persuaded to make over to the militant refugees a consignment of arms previously destined for the government and that this included tanks. As we shall see these matters were, however, overtaken by the clashes of the autumn and the subsequent desire of Qadafi to be seen as the creator of Arab unity.

Economic and social developments

It was obvious from the moment that the NLF took power that Aden would be in financial difficulties for, as Qahtan said, "the colonialist during the last years of his presence created an artificial prosperity". The budget had been about £31 million, of which only £8 million had been raised locally and the balance provided by the British taxpayer: in addition the expatriate community had spent about £36 million on goods and services and provided considerable employment. To make matters worse, the Suez Canal was closed as a result of the June War of 1967, and in February 1968 Qahtan stated that this had already cost £10 million in revenue: the number of ships arriving had fallen from a monthly average of 560 to 115 and the expansion of Hodeidah and the development of Djibouti provided still more competition.

It was hoped that some of the deficit might be made good by the seizure of the property of the former Rulers, but they proved to have been far less wealthy than the propaganda of their enemies had alleged. The only remaining source of money, therefore, was Great Britain and the NLF expected, or pretended to expect that the £60 million promised to the Federalis would be given instead to them. At once, however, Whitehall announced that only £12 million would be made available over the next six months, but owing to disagreements only a minimal sum was actually paid.

The result was, as Qahtan said, "we must prepare ourselves for a long and difficult period in the economic, financial and defence spheres" and in February many government salaries were reduced by up to 60 per cent, although £20 million was still needed to meet expenditure. In June 1968 a special interim tax was levied on the wages of all workers in the private sector and in September the budget deficit was reduced to £8 million from £25 million the previous year: stringent economies had cut expenditure by £17 million and £9 million had been raised in extra revenue. At the end of the month an interest-free loan of £5 million from China staved off the possibility of immediate bankruptcy.

As part of the austerity, the government moved quickly to take control of the economy. In February it set up the first of many National Organisations, taking 51 per cent in a body which was to regulate the import of consumer goods and fixed prices in order to prevent manipulation. Fines and imprisonment were decreed for over-charging or hoarding and penalties for economic crimes became increasingly drastic: in April 1970 a man was sentenced to 15 years for stealing 51 cartons of milk and offering a bribe was regarded as economic subversion, often linked with foreign conspiracies.

In the autumn of 1968 the government started to redistribute land and by the end of March it was reckoned that 14,000 acres had been given out. It was noticeable that none was assigned to anyone who had supported FLOSY or the Federalis, and it was later claimed that rich peasants and corrupt officials had been the principal beneficiaries. No family was allowed to own more than 25 acres of irrigated land and 50 acres of land dependent upon flooding: by creating smaller units these measures decreased efficiency and production.

Under Qahtan, although a Supreme National Planning Committee had been established, there had not been much of a drive towards industrialisation. When Haytham became Prime Minister, however, he set out to encourage foreign capital. A month after the "Glorious Corrective Move" of June 1969, investors were offered tax and rent privileges on condition that they recruited at least 75 per cent of the labour force locally and appointed a citizen to a senior position in management. In October he promised to protect domestic production by duties of up to 300 per cent and he called for foreign participation, remarking that "we have nationalised no one" and offering guarantees and free land to those who would help to transform a service into a production economy.

However, as we have seen, Haytham was not master of the government, and he was unable to prevail over the doctrinaire views of those of his colleagues who put socialist theory above efficiency. In November 1969 his plans to attract foreign investment were shattered when, in order "to liberate the economy from foreign domination", President Robayya announced the nationalisation of 36 firms operating in the fields of banking, insurance, commerce, shipping and petroleum marketing. British, French, American, Indian, Pakistani and Jordanian firms were alike affected and only the BP Refinery which produced 80 per cent of the country's industrial output was regarded as too important to tamper with. The expropriated businesses were given derisory compensation and a fortnight later many of their senior staff were dismissed. Later the Parsee firms, whose names were known to all who had passed through Aden and who had done more than anyone else to build its reputation as a shopping centre, were taken over for "not contributing effectively in the service of the national economy" and for allegedly smuggling out currency.

The assets were seized and others were put under the control of corporations run by the state; in March 1970 five National Companies were set up to administer Internal Trade, External

Trade, Shipping, Petroleum and Dockyards. In January it had been announced that a body would be created to oversee all aspects of the fishery industry and a few days later another significant export, salt, was nationalised. In May public transport was taken over and this was followed in June by the airline. Advertising was declared a state monopoly.

The right to import basic items was restricted to the National Company for Home Trading and all transactions involving foreigners had to be licensed. In December 1970 Aden ceased to be a free port, thus ending a policy which had gone back to the days of Haines, although a free zone for re-export was established. Import duties of up to 25 per cent were imposed in the hope of raising an extra £5 million in revenue. At the same time a decree closed all shops for two days during which traders were to compile and submit a complete list of all their stock, the price of which was then fixed. Any goods not declared were confiscated. Increasing state control caused mounting chaos through excessive demands on a small number of bureaucrats.

Socialist measures were also introduced in agriculture. In April 1970 the first collective farm was established and then a great impetus given to co-operatives which were assigned the land of people who had fled abroad. In November a new land law decreased the acreage that could be privately owned to 20 with permanent and 40 with seasonal irrigation, and *waqf* land was taken over. While this was going on, a great change came over the countryside. As we have seen, Robayya returned from a visit to China inspired by the Maoist concept of agrarian revolution, and the government encouraged the peasants to take over ownership of the land by force. Haytham, perhaps because he wished to ally with Robayya against the more dangerous Ismail, declared in October that it was "necessary to support the iniative which was made by the poor peasants and agricultural workers to take over the farms and marshes of the big landlords as an organised peasant movement after the establishment of peasant committees". Robayya said that they were "merely recovering rights from semi-feudalists and ending all methods of humiliation and exploitation". The official press asserted that this was "the only correct way for clearing the monopolistic-feudalistic relations of production prevailing in the rural areas" and "Land Day" was put in the calendar to celebrate these events. By the beginning of 1972 there were twelve state farms and fifteen co-operatives, with the peasants receiving military training to defend the revolution. The fishermen were encouraged to follow their example, seize their own means of production and form co-operatives.

The government, having frightened off foreign private capital by its policy of nationalisation, attempted to carry on industrialisation with the aid of local investors. In September 1970 it offered free land for factories with cheap water and electricity and customs-free imports of machinery. Local business men, however, also lacked confidence – a few months later the Minister of Finance had to admit that their response had been poor, although they had established a new slaughter house for turtles, thus "opening work for jobless hands", and it was hoped that there would be some light industries such as matches, glass, cigarettes and perfumery. In May 1971, opening a match factory, Robayya said that 80 per cent of the capital involved had come from private sources and that it and other small concerns would be protected.

Ismail, and to a lesser extent Robayya, were however impatient of economic realities and wished to enforce socialism regardless of the cost. After the ousting of Haytham in August 1971 they were able to have their way. Small local businesses, including twelve cinemas, six hotels and all firms making and selling soft drinks were taken over. Robayya declared that there was "still profiteering and opportunism...we shall not allow some to die from indigestion while others die from starvation". In August 1972 privately owned buildings were nationalised without compensation, although each family was permitted to keep a single dwelling. Hassani, the Prime Minister, declared this to be "a triumph for the revolution, ending the exploitation of the people by a group of merchants". More and more enterprising people who could have contributed to the national wealth escaped abroad and Ismail, knowing that many had been FLOSY supporters, looked on their departure with indifference.

With both foreign and local capital driven from the field, there was nothing left to challenge the concept of development directed by the state alone, and this was outlined in a Three

Year Plan published in the summer of 1972. It called for an investment of £40.7 million, of which just over half was to be raised locally and the rest obtained from foreign governments and international bodies. A quarter was to be spent on the creation of new industries, building 30 plants mostly capable of using local raw materials and which were also labour-intensive in a situation where unemployment was reckoned at 73 per cent. There were to be factories for tomato canning, soap, leather-dying, plastics including shoes, textiles, fish meal for cattle feed and cement and it was hoped to raise industrial production by 22.5 per cent. Another quarter would be spent on agriculture, aiming to increase the area of cultivated land by 8 per cent and augment production by 26 per cent by the use of modern methods. There were also allocations for geological surveys. The biggest single item, nearly $\frac{1}{3}$ of the total, was for improvement in communications, in particular, for the building of roads which would both serve strategic aims and facilitate the movement of raw materials to Aden and of finished goods to the hinterland.

The Plan also aimed at preparing for compulsory and universal primary education within ten years; great strides had already been made in this field as the numbers at school had roughly trebled since independence. The party attached great importance to this and to the eradication of adult illiteracy, stressing the need for "a progressive Yemeni nationalist syllabus in education, on a progressive scientific educational basis, to enable the rising generations to rid themselves of the effects of bourgeois and feudal education while arming themselves with an education which will help them to develop a progressive civilised Arab Yemeni heritage" and "combatting all colonialist, feudal and reactionary ideologies which exploit religion in their interest". In the cultural field there was to be a Museum of the Revolution and improved coverage by radio and television "to mobilise the wider masses for the political and economic tasks of the nation". A relatively small amount was allocated to public health, but there had already been improvements: the number of doctors had risen from 26 to 125, of which 33 were Chinese and 15 Russian.

During these years the financial crisis continued. Officials were compelled to "volunteer" to work for one day a month without pay and workers to demonstrate demanding cuts in their own wages, which anyway were often in arrears. To save foreign currency all investment abroad was forbidden, and so was travel, except for those favoured of the Party. Even the elite suffered in July 1972 when the salaries of all members of the NLF "from leadership to base" were reduced and the wages of employees in state enterprises were cut by 33 per cent "at their own request". A Minister received roughly £100 a month and a senior civil servant who had earned £250 under the British now received £80 at a time when prices had soared. These measures were presented as "a new revolutionary gain for the masses to use in their class and political struggle against imperialism, Arab reaction, and mercenaries and agents" and blamed on the former rulers. However, the long-suffering population might be forgiven for finding these excuses rather thin after more than four years of independence.

These years which had seen such a transformation in the economic structure of the South had brought little change in the North. Apart from confiscation of the holdings of the royal family there had been no redistribution of land for there were few big estates apart from those of the great tribal leaders, without whose support the government could not survive. It was estimated that 20 per cent of the cultivated area belonged to the *waqf*, a figure which rose to 70 per cent in the neighbourhood of Sanaa, and none of this was touched. Nearly half the imports were food and there was a severe famine in the summer of 1970, but the government did not interfere except mildly to discourage the growing of *qat* in favour of other crops.

There was no planned attempt at industrialisation, although both foreign and local capital were encouraged to invest with promises that their money would be safe. Development was therefore rather haphazard; however, in 1971 it was estimated that there were 50 private firms employing about 1,400 workers in addition to 21 state-owned concerns with 4,600 more.

The YAR, too, had its difficulties in paying its way. There was a proliferation of low-yielding taxes, some of which could be paid in grain or in cattle and the administration suffered from the over-staffing tradition introduced by the Egyptians.

Visiting a government office one could not but be astonished at the sheer number of people with apparently nothing to do. When Kirshimi was Prime Minister he threatened that those who did not go to their desks would not receive their salaries, but few if any were dismissed. The revenue simply could not match the expenditure, and in March 1970 the financial crisis was so bad that all imports from Aden were banned. In that year, although the official exchange rate was 3 riyals to the £ sterling, it was easy to obtain 15. In May 1971 Nu'man when Prime Minister said that although "if our agricultural and mineral resources were tapped, we should be among the richest countries in the Arab world", there was a budget deficiency of £8 million, the foreign debt was £78 million (of which £51 million was owed to Russia and China) and that exports would cover only a small part of the cost of imports. Only the increasingly close relations with Saudi Arabia enabled the country to survive financially.

Despite these difficulties there were considerable improvements in the lives of many people. In the first ten years of the Republic the number of hospitals increased from 3 to 30, doctors from 2 to 179 and nurses from 16 to 600. Thus some medical care was available outside the main towns. The Egyptians had started some 50 schools, and although many of the teachers left with the army, after two years there was a renewed impetus. Between 1969 and 1972 foreign aid enabled the school population to grow at an annual rate of 32 per cent until there were about 180,000 children, of whom 12 per cent were girls, receiving at least a primary education. In 1970 a University at Sanaa was opened with 61 students and increased rapidly to 120 boys and a girl. In addition there were 1,300 other students obtaining higher education abroad. The YAR had a long way to go to catch up but it was making progress.

We have seen that owing to the shortage of local capital, the development of both Yemens was largely restricted to projects for which they could obtain foreign finance. Many of these have already been mentioned in the sections on relations with the great powers and with the Arab states. International organisations provided some help: for example, the United Nations financed a mineral survey of Aden, the World Bank provided money for road building in both Yemens and the UN Development Programme supported land reclamation schemes in the South. The FAO and the WHO helped both and a timely credit of $45 million from the IRBD helped Aden to keep a crisis at bay in October 1969. Despite all of this the two Yemens remained amongst the poorest nations in the world.

As the two Yemens moved towards confrontation in the summer of 1972, the events of the past few years had turned them into very different states. In the North the end of the war meant that life in the political, economic and social spheres drifted back to very much what it had been under the Imamate. There had been no social revolution, and although the increase in education had weakened the monopoly of the Sayyids and Qadis, these classes still retained much of their influence. The tribal shaykhs, through whom most of the arms and money had been channelled during the war, were if anything more powerful than ever, since the government depended largely upon such magnates as al-Ahmar and Muhsin al-Ayni's father-in-law, Shaykh Sinan Abu Luhum of the Nehm. The predominance of Islam was unchallenged and, despite individual exceptions, the status of women little changed.

In the South the whole of the old social order had been overturned. The tribal chiefs were either in jail or in exile or otherwise deprived of power which was exercised by officials whose standing depended upon position in the party rather than birth. There had been a deliberate attempt to humiliate the Sayyids and other religious personages by forcing them to do manual labour and by compelling their ladies to give up their veils. The regime denigrated Islam whenever it felt that it was safe to do so and party leaders no longer made even a token appearance at religious ceremonies. In March 1971 a statute gave formal equality to women; they worked in the factories and the veil practically disappeared. Early in 1972 the General Union of Yemeni Women expressed the Yemeni woman's "preparedness and the preparedness of her bases to carry arms side by side with the popular police and militia forces and all citizens loyal to the Republic and the Revolution".

In Sanaa the Prime Ministers who succeeded one another had little objective beyond staying in office. They had no political ideals and therefore inspired no loyal followers to form a party and act as their agents in the country. The urban masses had little say in affairs and power was ultimately exercised by the army and the tribal chiefs, who could not but notice what had befallen their counterparts in the South and so were opposed to unity or indeed to practically any change. In the South all was secondary to ideology and the party was everywhere, compelling acquiescence in the policies of the government. The tribes and the army were greatly weakened, although still not entirely without influence. The urban population which was easier to reach and to politicise had more importance than the countryfolk.

In the rural areas of the North the tribes taxed and policed themselves as they had done under the Imams, and the state made no serious effort to administer Khawlan or Jawf. There had been no real redistribution of wealth so, with minor improvements, life went on as before, with the local rich helping the poor as Islam demanded. In the South, on the other hand, an official, usually a stranger to the area, maintained a firm grip with the aid of the militia and an increasingly pervasive political police. Redistribution of land meant that there were no longer any rich and all were dependent upon the state or upon the goodwill of the political appointees who controlled their lives.

Life in the cities of the North maintained its old leisurely way, centring around the afternoon *qat* session, animatedly discussing politics but not doing anything about them. The police were by Middle Eastern standards remarkably easygoing, and there was little interference with the private lives of individuals. Although inflation moved faster and faster, there were no real shortages in the *suq*. In the cities of the South politics were everywhere: there were constant instructions to attend rallies and demonstrations while the police kept a watchful eye on any non-conformist behaviour. In April 1970, for example, 40 youths were arrested for having Beatle haircuts – any interest in the western world was dangerous. Goods in the *suq* were often scarce and government propaganda was always expressing gratitude for some small gift of sugar or medicines from "a friendly socialist state". All in all, the South was more dynamic but the North was happier and more relaxed.

Relations between the two Yemens

Throughout much of 1968 the two Yemens seemed very much in step as their threatened governments struggled for survival and their forces worked in collaboration. In February Qahtan stated that his army would play an active role in the fighting in the North, and Southerners were engaged in the battles to raise the siege of Sanaa. In the same month the PRSY Minister of the Interior, Muhammad Ali Haytham, said that YAR troops had helped in a five-day battle against "sultanic and feudalistic elements" in Bayhan and later in the year forces from Aden cleared the Royalists from Harib and handed back the town to the Republicans. In foreign affairs both Republics were dependent upon Russia for arms and united in hostility to Saudi Arabia.

Administrative measures, too, indicated a special relationship. The two governments did not establish Embassies in each other's capital; instead there were co-ordination bureaux attached not to the Ministries of Foreign Affairs but to those of Yemeni Unity. In April the Aden Nationality Law favoured Northerners by allowing them to acquire citizenship after five years' residence instead of the ten demanded from other Arabs. Northerners were also exempted from the normal requirement of seeking entry visas. At the end of July, the PRSY Foreign Minister Sayf Ahmad Dhalai made the first official visit, meeting President Iryani and General Amri in Taizz, and, after discussing "reactionary and colonialist plots against the two countries", reached an agreement that neither should be used as a base against the other, that they should co-ordinate industrial policies with jointly-owned firms and exchange financial, economic and statistical information. Rhetoric on both sides of the frontier declared that neither revolution would be complete until unity had been achieved: Qahtan, for example said "whoever attacks Sanaa, attacks Aden".

Soon, however, relations began to sour. In March there was a clash in Hodeidah between Yemeni regular forces and an extreme left-wing group which was trying to get control of a shipment of arms: there were strong suspicions that the Aden government was in some way involved but Sanaa did not press the matter any further. During the summer splits and purges within the NLF and the harsh repression of tribal risings caused the start of a flood of refugees from the South, and the difficulties encountered by merchants caused many of them to escape to Taizz and Hodeidah where their tales naturally alarmed their hosts. In August after the defection of the Southern security chief and 200 of his fellow Aulaqis, the Sanaa authorities refused demands to hand them back for vengeance. In November, worried at the easing of tension between the YAR and Saudi Arabia, Qahtan sent a message to Iryani expressing his dismay at the increasing strength of "reactionary elements".

Early in 1969 the split came out into the open. The previous August an extreme left wing officer, a Shafai with strong links with the NLF leadership, attempted a coup against the government of General Amri. The officer, Colonel Abdullah Abd al-Raqib Abd al-Wahhab, head of a special commando unit, came very near to success: there was heavy fighting and several hundred casualties. Amri was forced to revert to the old policy of the Imams and call in the Zaydi tribes and in particular the Hashid of Shaykh Abdullah ibn Hussayn al-Ahmar, upon whose support the Sanaa government became increasingly dependent. Abd al-Raqib, who had been one of the heroes of the defence of the capital, was treated mercifully and merely sent off to Algeria on "an arms training course". In January, with help from the Aden authorities, he attempted a second coup which cost him his life.

These events were the signal for a sharp war of words which Aden began by denouncing the killing of Abd al-Raqib as a crime aimed at exterminating all staunch republican elements. The YAR Foreign Minister, Yahya Jughman, hit back in a bitter speech, accusing the NLF of "horrible massacres" and of being solely responsible for the failure to achieve unity. He said that in December 1967 Sanaa had proposed a National Conference of representatives from both North and South and offered to have a single Ambassador at the UN, a joint diplomatic service and even to accept Qahtan as President of a unified state but had been met with "rigidity, escapism and absolute rejection...Today we are further from unity than we were a year ago. The NLF government has succeeded in achieving in one year what colonialism failed to do in 130.

Imperialism tried to set up a boundary between South and North Yemen, establish a bogus government in Aden and create a new people with a new identity as Southern Yemenis. Imperialism failed in all these things, but its successors, the NLF, has succeeded." Aden was stirring trouble on the borders, he complained, and was plotting to overthrow the Sanaa government.

For some days these polemics continued as Aden retaliated by accusing the YAR of trying to ingratiate itself with Saudi Arabia by training mercenaries on its behalf. A particularly unkind commentator on Sanaa Radio said that FLOSY rather than the NLF had been the true heroes of the struggle against the British, without whose help, and in particular that of the RAF, Qahtan and his gang would never have prevailed. Each Government called for unity while exchanging insults and complaints and was supported by "spontaneous demonstrations" of its citizens. Qahtan, who had been in Moscow, returned to say that "we do not believe in forming a Yemeni regional unity, but we believe in the achievement of an Arab socialist unity". In the middle of February both sides agreed to accept Egyptian mediation. Although the immediate crisis was thus defused, the outbursts had shown the latent hostility, perhaps reinforced by personal jealousies, which had arisen in little more than a year.

Within a month the war of words had started again. When Sallal was overthrown it was announced that a National Council would be established within two years and this body met for the first time on 16 March, and, claiming in effect to be the legitimate government of the whole area, reserved twelve seats for representatives of the South. Aden reacted with fury to this "hostile, imperialistic and reactionary plot" and warned that any of its citizens participating would be liable to the death penalty. Old charges of harbouring armed dissidents were renewed and Iryani was personally accused of trying to liquidate the Revolution by the establishment of an "Islamic State" and of jealousy of the socialist reforms in the South. Sanaa's response was to describe the Aden Government as "an outlaw group and usurpers of authority", while in his May Day speech Qahtan said that "Sanaa workers are in the jails of the government of feudalists, stooges and reactionaries...The masses in Sanaa must understand their responsibilities and overthrow the regime." Amri was accused of being so committed to the Saudis and to the CIA that he could no longer extricate himself.

There were reports of attempted mediation by Kuwait or even by Russia or America, but these came to nothing. However, the overthrow of the prickly Qahtan in June appeared to ease relations between the two Yemens and Iryani professed to see that union was now inevitable. More cautiously Ismail spoke of a common destiny and that winter, as the Royalists made their last efforts, the two moved closer together and Sanaa denounced Saudi aggression against both countries as "an integral part of an imperialist plot".

The apparent harmony continued for much of 1970. A direct telephone link was established, the artistic troupe of Sanaa textile factory performed in Aden, there was co-operation over antiquities, an Aden law provided that any YAR citizen could be naturalised without charge and in May Iryani said that union was vital. In September the two Presidents met at Nasser's funeral where Qadafi urged them to end their "frozen relations" and they agreed to appoint officials to discuss practical details: after a visit from Haytham to Sanaa committees were nominated to establish unified tariffs, a common currency and co-operation in industry and banking were projected.

Despite this, we have seen in earlier sections that with the end of the civil war in 1970 the move of the YAR into the Saudi orbit and increasing dependence by the South on Russia began: from now onwards neither state was fully master of its own destiny. We have seen, too, that the proclamation of the two Constitutions in this year showed how little common ideological ground existed upon which to build a union, and political and economic policies still further accentuated the differences. Yet the ease with which refugees from the South had settled into Taizz and Hodeidah, transforming parts of them into replicas of Aden, showed that the people, or at least the Shafai section of them, were identical. It was not ethnic but governmental differences which made unity so difficult.

At the end of November 1970 there was a sharp deterioration in relations. In its new constitution, the People's Republic of Southern Yemen renamed itself the People's Democratic

Republic of Yemen. The omission of the word "Southern" was an obvious claim to be the legitimate government of the whole area, and the emphasis on "Democratic" was a clear insult to the YAR. Although Sanaa claimed that its desire for unity was so great that it would accept Aden as the capital and adopt its flag, it protested angrily at the new title, which it refused to recognise.

There was no movement towards unity in 1971, during which year the divergence of political attitudes increased. The governments formed by Nu'man in May, by Hassani in August and by Amri in the same month no longer contained Ministers of Unity and an even greater sign of division was the presence in the Sanaa Cabinet as Minister of Foreign Affairs of Abdullah al-Asnag – an inveterate foe of the group which had defeated FLOSY and forced him into exile.

At the end of February 1972 a new crisis arose between the two Yemens as Aden announced that an invading force of 2,000 mercenaries, trained by American instructors, had been beaten back with heavy casualties in the Bayhan area: a few days later it emerged that this was very far from the truth. During the civil war Naji ibn Ali al-Ghadir, the great tribal chief of Khawlan, had been courted by both sides and received enough money and weapons to make himself independent of both Republicans and Royalists, although he had leaned towards the latter: he had no wish for a reduced role when peace came. He acted as a link in passing arms and ammunition from the Saudis on to refugees from Southern Yemen, but he was tricked by the Aden government into believing that they would give him still more to enable him to free himself from any subjection to Sanaa. He therefore crossed the frontier on a safe-conduct and with over sixty of his followers was treacherously killed in cold blood. It was said that the murder was committed by the detonation of mines under the tent where the party was having lunch, and that the object was to frighten other Northern shaykhs from helping the refugees.

Aden feared that thousands of tribesmen would avenge the killing and massed troops on the border which each side started to accuse the other of violating. Ismail toured the "progressive" Arab states hoping to create an anti-Saudi coalition but attracted no support, while the Saudi-financed tribal leaders and YAR officers called for war to destroy the Communist state in the South. Muhsin al-Ayni threatened to resign if this happened but at the end of March he agreed that it was possible if the PDRY "continues air and ground attacks against our border tribes and villages". With Saudi prodding the armed refugees raided back and al-Ayni said that although their presence "embarrasses us", he could not act as a policeman.

President Boumedienne of Algeria attempted to mediate and each side proclaimed its devotion to peace and unity, but clashes continued throughout the summer. At the end of July Sanaa announced that 30 civilians had been killed in al-Baydha by mines placed by saboteurs from the South, eight of whom had been captured and shot. Aden claimed that such allegations were "the intrigues of reactionary forces backed by American imperialism, which fears the development of brotherly ties between the two Yemens". In fact it is likely that on the Northern side local passions had got out of control and that the Sanaa government was unable to moderate them, while the Aden government was prepared to take risks to teach its neighbour a lesson.

The YAR closed the frontier and banned PDRY aircraft from using its air space as relations rapidly deteriorated. The Kuwaitis tried to mediate and early in September al-Ayni said that as a basis for a settlement he wanted a border agreement, a solution for the refugee problem, an end to "Southern Yemeni sabotage", compensation for Northern citizens whose property had been nationalised and for the killing of Naji ibn Ali. Aden asked for a high-level meeting, reopening of the border, curbing of the mercenaries and that troops and tribesmen should be withdrawn from the frontier.

Fighting became more widespread as Aden claimed that there had been a tank invasion against Bayhan and Sanaa complained of air attacks, using foreign pilots, on Qataba where al-Ayni said that there had been "continuous aggression for more than 24 hours". He asserted that more than 100 citizens had been killed and that all that was received from Aden had been "vainglory, obstinacy, arrogance and attempts to evade reasonable solutions". This went on for several days, in the course of which the Northerners occupied Kamaran but an Arab League mediation mission persuaded both sides to agree to a cease-fire on 13 October, to withdraw troops for ten kilometres and to accept patrols from a peace-keeping force. Peace negotiations started and a few days later, to general amazement, the two Yemens announced that they would unite.

Chapter Nine

The Two Yemens 1972–1979

On 28 October 1972, the "two brothers", Prime Minister Muhsin al-Ayni of the YAR and Prime Minister Ali Nasser Muhammad Hassani of the PDRY agreed to set up a unified state. They declared themselves "conscious of the responsibility for the security of the dear land of Yemen and its future generations, desirous of establishing and strengthening the pillars of peace in all parts of our country...anxious to preserve Yemen from the influence of imperialism and neo-colonialism...for the purpose of participating in the struggle for Arab destiny against the Zionist-imperialist alliance". Al-Ayni added that "all who belittle and despise Yemen...were amazed and dismayed when the situation was suddenly transformed from war to accord and unity": he might have added that they would be even more amazed if the union actually worked.

On 24 February 1979 the Radio of the PDRY declared that "the terrorist practices of the regime in Sanaa against the nationalist movement and the sons of the single people have reached unbelievable proportions. The border provocations have escalated." The Radio of the YAR denounced "an ugly model of Hitler represented by the new Nazi Abd al-Fattah Ismail who insists on perpetrating his crimes against peaceful villages...barbarous attacks" with MiGs, rockets and tanks. There were some days of heavy fighting, Arab nations mediated and on 29 March the two Presidents met in Kuwait. The following day they signed an agreement to unite their two countries.

Internal political developments

The Presidency of Iryani

Exactly a month after the signature of the agreement on unity of 28 October 1972, its architect Muhsin al-Ayni resigned as Prime Minister, for it was clear that it would not be possible to persuade political leaders to accept it. The Consultative Council was dominated by tribal chiefs, and they saw what had happened to their peers in the South. Aden demanded the dissolution of their tribal levies which had taken part in the war, and in some cases they received with their Saudi subsidies instructions to prevent the union. Al-Ayni indeed said that many of them wished for a renewal of the war "to please a neighbouring Arab country".

President Iryani, although himself in favour of union, bowed to the conservative majority and appointed as Prime Minister the Qadi Abdullah al-Hajri. He was a personal friend of King Faysal and had a record as a strong Royalist, a Minister under the Imamate, and adviser to Badr. He was also known as a strict Muslim and had been a member of the Presidency Council for some months. His administration included as Foreign Minister Muhammad Ahmad Nu'man, the son of the veteran Ahmad Muhammad, and retained Abdullah Asnag in charge of the economy. The government paid lip-service to the cause of unity: Hajri said that it was urgently necessary, Nu'man denied that al-Ayni had resigned because of Saudi or tribal pressure against it, and al-Ahmar who had a key role as Speaker of the Consultative Assembly asserted that ideological difficulties would provide no obstacle. But in actual fact the government was firmly against unity.

In order to put pressure upon Sanaa, the Aden government provoked a series of incidents on the frontier and far beyond it. They exploited Shafai discontent and trained dissidents in mine-laying in a special Sabotage School in Lahej. In July 1973 the Deputy Commander-in-Chief Colonel Ibrahim Hamdi said that since the agreement had been signed there had been 360 incidents in which 1,000 Yemenis had been killed or wounded. the most important of these was Muhammad Ali Uthman, a firm opponent of union, who had been a member of the Presidency Council since its formation on the fall of Sallal. He was murdered, according to Sanaa, by "elements from across the frontier". The government hit back fiercely: in June some saboteurs were crucified and there was a series of executions in July. Hajri, backed by al-Ahmar and the Chief of Staff, Colonel Hussayn Maswari, exploited the opportunity for a general purge of leftists and in particular to replace suspected army officers.

Iryani, who was genuinely in favour of conciliation and constitutional government, disapproved of these proceedings and he was angered by the chaos engendered by Hajri's ineffectiveness as an administrator. In large areas of Jawf and Khawlan the government exercised no control, taxes were not collected, Ministers pursued independent policies without reference to the Prime Minister and bribery became more necessary than ever to persuade officials to perform their duties. Iryani wanted a powerful single President instead of a bickering Council, effective local administration, which meant weakening the tribal grandees, and an army strong enough to keep the tribes in order. Hajri and the Consultative Council refused to co-operate so in August 1973, as a means of emphasising his own indispensability, Iryani went into voluntary exile in Syria. He was begged to come back and some months later felt secure enough to dismiss Hajri, appointing instead a Shafai technocrat, Dr Hassan Makki, probably to pave the way for the return of al-Ayni and a renewed attempt at union. He took care, however, to reassure the Saudis by bringing back Asnag as Foreign Minister.

The new government had hardly settled in when early in June there were sudden and dramatic developments. As Colonel Maswari later told a journalist, "several saboteurs, attached to a political party in a certain Arab country were arrested...plans to overthrow the regime were also seized": it was no secret that the "political party" was the Baath and the "certain Arab country" Iraq. Iryani, with his normal mildness, wished merely to send proofs of the plot with a protest to Baghdad but al-Ahmar wanted stronger action, threatening that if the army did not take power to enforce security, he and his tribesmen would march on Sanaa to install a government to their liking. Iryani resigned and al-Ahmar, as Speaker technically succeeding him, at once handed over to the General Command of the Armed Forces: without bloodshed, Colonel Hamdi was the new effective ruler. He denied that there had been a military coup and claimed that there had merely been a "corrective step to avert civil war". His first proclamations declared that the army had not expected to find itself in power and was unprepared to deal with a "political atmosphere enshrouded in dense clouds", the "administrative and financial corruption and indiscipline" and the "deviation and disregard for responsibility" which confronted it, and that it had tried to persuade Iryani, whose "wise policies" he praised, to stay in office.

Whether or not this was true, Iryani, having reviewed a guard of honour with his successor, went into exile in Syria and passed from the stage of Yemeni politics. He had deserved well of his country because, combining as he did both Islamic tradition and a desire for progress, he had acted as a transition from the generation active in politics under the Imamate to a new generation ready to take charge. In six years he had presided over both the reintegration of the Royalists within the national life and the start, however halting, of modernisation. In the end, the problem of keeping some sort of balance between the army, conservative tribal leaders and a growing left wing in a situation complicated by Saudi and Adeni intrigues had proved too much for him: a different approach was now needed.

The Presidency of Robayya

The years that followed the signature of the agreement on union saw in the PDRY no diminution of its government's policy of ruling by terror and constant warnings of threats from real or imaginary enemies. In January 1973, for example, Hassani called on the armed forces and the masses to "increase their vigilance and their revolutionary readiness to face all hostile forces". In August 1976 the wording had scarcely changed when he said "vigilance cannot stop for a single moment as long as the enemy continues to threaten our independence and our sovereignty". Citizens were punished for speaking to foreigners without permission and neighbours were encouraged to spy upon one another: indeed, in 1977 it was estimated that nearly one quarter of the population was involved in some form of security work.

Any form of disobedience to authority was severely punished. In 1977, for example, eight farmers were condemned to death for demonstrating against the government's decision to restrict the consumption of *qat*, which was the chief solace of the poor. The sentences were later reduced to fifteen years' imprisonment with the stern warning that "there is no longer room for narrow selfish interests". Political offenders were unlikely to escape so lightly as we can see from the Amnesty International Reports of February 1973 and May 1976. The first stated that in the previous October 60 political prisoners including former Ministers had been shot, allegedly trying to escape. However, as the killings had taken place in three batches, it was impossible to believe the pretext. The second said that it was difficult to estimate the number of political prisoners, which might be anything between 2,000 and 10,000, who were kept in the harshest conditions and sometimes tortured under East German or Cuban supervision. They included many relatives of people who had gone abroad without permission and there were no provisions for appeal or for legal aid. People could be shot under "vaguely-worded statutes" for such offences as attempting to smuggle currency out of the country. No count can be made of the number executed but in six weeks in July and early August 1973 Aden Radio reported seven shot for conspiracy, four for embezzlement and one each for espionage and sabotage. In August 1976 the former Prime Minister Haytham, who had himself helped to build the machinery of repression, put the number at 1,500 in four years. Haytham further estimated that 250,000 of the original population of 1,600,000 had escaped abroad, but even there they were not safe. He himself survived two murder attempts in the streets of Cairo and Muhammad Ali Shuaibi, a well-known anti-Communist author who had written a book *The South behind the Iron Curtain* and was known to be at work on another denunciation of the regime, was found killed in an hotel in Beirut.

In addition many people simply disappeared, leaving their relatives too frightened to make enquiries. Mysterious murders also occurred, as for example in 1973 when a bomb exploded in the car of the Director of Military Intelligence and later another senior officer was found to have been poisoned. Such was the prevailing climate of terror that when in April 1973 the Foreign Minister, six Ambassadors and seventeen other senior diplomats, all generally regarded as moderates and none in the inner circles of the party, were killed in an aircrash, few believed that it was an accident: certainly no credible explanation was provided as to why such a group was visiting a remote village in the mountains.

Repression was given a more formed shape by the creation of a Ministry of State Security in November 1974 in which, a defector reported, East German "advisers" had a prominent role. The police were overtly politicised and the same process could be seen in the army. In January 1973 Ismail wrote in *Pravda* that its "class composition" was changing but a year later Hassani said that there was still a need to purge "slandering and corrupt elements" within its ranks. In August 1974 there took place the first organisational conference of the armed forces branch of the National Front, at which members were instructed to develop their political and ideological activity. By 1977 Hassani was able to report that the army had been "cleansed of reactionary elements and those of feudal origin" and that he had no fears of a military coup.

Particular attention was paid to the building up of an indoctrinated Party Militia. In November 1973 the Central Committee decided to develop it "into a force capable of fighting shoulder to shoulder with the armed forces" and in May 1976 Hassani stressed its importance in "making the popular masses take part in the defence of the revolution and at the same time in the struggle for social and economic construction". They were to be active in mass initiatives, have exemplary attitudes to work and lead the fight against illiteracy. Volunteers were paid by their former employers during their period of training.

Political indoctrination was facilitated by the fact that a decade had passed since independence and a new generation trained in schools dominated by the party was arising. Special classes were established for Beduins in which Marxism was a primary subject and in September 1974 it was decreed that all history books should be rewritten "to spread a progressive culture amongst the masses and uproot imperialist and feudalist culture". Older people were dragooned into attendance at lectures and meetings from which absence brought unfavourable notice. At a higher level, the School for Socialist Sciences developed "ideological consciousness".

There was rigid censorship and in November the Ministry of Information was empowered to "supervise and guide" all printing houses, advertisements, radio and television programmes and to appoint editors. As an example of the attitude of the authorities towards culture we may quote Ismail: "a song should aim at creating amongst the people a new feeling based on revolutionary aesthetics, and not contain any distortion or exaggeration. An emotional song must be able to initiate and develop a spirit of creative activity between men and women" whereas "poetry should reflect the masses' hatred and contempt for all enemies of liberation and progress and depict their love of national independence and social development". Great efforts were made to prevent material regarded as subversive from being brought in from abroad and to prevent contact with foreigners. The Embassies were segregated in Khormaksar and surrounded with a wall, which, according to the local story, was started with either elegant or unconscious irony opposite the East Germans.

There was a drive to bring ideology into the lives of groups such as peasants and women who had hitherto been little affected. The peasants were told that feudalists were responsible for the myth that the private possession of land was a gift from Allah. Women, now hailed as "New Revolutionary Human Beings", "freed from priestly feudalism", were photographed doing arms drill, driving tractors and marching behind such stirring slogans as "Let us firmly and consciously struggle against ignorance and for love of work."

Despite the crushing power of the state, internally its leaders were engaged in savage in-fighting. Diplomats and journalists often commented upon the differences between President Robayya and the party chief Abd al-Fattah Ismail, the two men who dominated Aden politics after the fall of Qahtan. Their antagonism was probably more personal than political, although there were differences of emphasis between them. While Ismail was unswerving in his loyalty to Russia and enjoyed a power base amongst the urban proletariat, Robayya returned from a visit to China deeply impressed with their doctrine that revolution should be based on the countryside, so he maintained more links there. However in November 1972 he went to Moscow and evidently established his credentials as a good Communist, for the communiqué spoke of "an atmosphere of friendship and complete mutual understanding in which the respective positions on basic world problems was either close or identical".

Despite this Robayya had not fought to exchange domination by Britain for total subjection to Russia, and he started to look for additional friends. He was helped in this by a series of economic crises which enabled him to convince a majority of his colleagues that financial aid had to be obtained from the rich Arab states, and to pay the necessary political price. He managed, too, to secure some relaxation of the total grip of the authorities on internal economic life in the interests of efficiency.

Ismail was prepared to bide his time and to devote all his efforts to securing control of the party machinery – the classic way to rule a Communist country. In January 1975 he strengthened his position by the formal absorption of the technically illegal but tolerated Communist group, the People's Democratic Union, and the few Baathists comprising the People's Vanguard into the National Front. This was rechristened the United National Front Political Organisation (UNFPO) which was to be "guided in theory and practice by the principles of scientific socialism" – a phrase that the NF had used from the beginning for it sounded less alarming than Marxism from which it was in fact indistinguishable. The "National Democratic Phase" of the Revolution was declared to have begun.

Ismail secured further appointments of friends to key positions in a Cabinet reshuffle in December which brought back Ali Salim al-Baydh to the newly created Ministry of Local Administration. The Communist Abdullah Badeeb and the Baathist Anis Hassan Yahya who had been pushed into Haytham's Cabinet six years before were moved across into organisational posts within the party structure, but their interests were safeguarded by the giving of Departments to Badeeb's brother Ali and the Baathist Nasr Nasser. Nevertheless, Robayya was able to bring about the establishment of relations with Saudi

Arabia in March 1976 and during that summer there was a considerable thaw in relations with the West.

In the same summer the situation in the Horn of Africa started to become critical and the Russians felt unable to risk the chance that Robayya might be swayed by his new-found friends. Ismail went to Moscow and subsequently met the East German leader Willi Stoph on 29 September, and it was probably as a result of these meetings that he had apparently contrived to win the support of the police and army chiefs away from Robayya. A few days later at the fourth session of the Central Committee of UNFPO he won a clear majority and Robayya was forced to ratify a series of political and economic agreements with Russia that he had held up in some cases for years.

By the end of December, however, it seemed as if the balance had swung back in favour of the President, who contrived to exploit the fact that he was less distrusted than his rival in the rural areas. The Central Committee announced that as the establishment of Local People's Councils in the Fifth Governorate had proved a success, the experiment would be extended to other areas. Arrangements were made in June for elections at Governorate, Province and District levels. These were held in the following November, when it was said that 93 per cent of those qualified voted. Twenty-one women were among the 204 successful candidates.

The struggle continued and was reflected in the seesaws of the Republic's foreign policy. Within the two months from mid-February to mid-April 1976 Aden received visits from President Castro, a Russian Deputy Minister of Defence, the Czechoslovakian Foreign Minister, Shaykh Zaid of Abu Dhabi and the Foreign Minister of Saudi Arabia, all cajoling and competing to offer favours. At the end of July while the President was in Saudi Arabia, the Prime Minister was in Moscow.

In October the President was greatly weakened in a Cabinet reshuffle for the Prime Minister, Hassani, who tended to share his views on the advantages of keeping lines open to the Saudis and the West, was forced to divest himself of the Ministry of Defence which was given to a supporter of Ismail, Ali Ahmad Nasser Antar. Antar was able to neutralise Robayya's role as

Commander-in-Chief and to canvass backing in the army. We can now see that this marked the beginning of the end for Robayya: not long afterwards he seems to have lost the allegiance of Hassani, who presumably wished to adhere to the winning side while there was still time.

Ismail now initiated a series of purges intended as Hassani said, "to screen out those elements who cannot belong to the membership of the vanguard party" and to form a "new-style, leading political party which is based on scientific socialism and proletarian internationalism". Robayya was clearly unenthusiastic about such a formal commitment to the Russians and the inevitability of its souring relations with the Saudis, and he fought a dour but losing rearguard action. In his speech on May Day 1977 Ismail referred to the need for "cleansing old suspect elements by the masses of the people" and for "a transfusion of new blood from among the most active of the workers and peasants". He even canvassed support amongst "men of religion, Imams and preachers" by stressing that "we are proceeding essentially along the right path which Islam laid down". Meanwhile Ali Antar systematically removed officers loyal to Robayya and early in June he went to Moscow, where he presumably received assurances that Russia would approve the removal of the President. Everything was now ready for Ismail to take formal power.

The Presidency of Hamdi

Hamdi abolished the Presidency Council and did not formally assume the title himself, although it will be convenient to use it in these pages. He exercised power as Chairman of the Military Command Council (MCC) which included the Chief of Staff, Colonel Ahmad Hussein Ghashmi, a leading member of the Hashid tribe, two sons of the Bakil chief Abu Luhum who were related by marriage to Muhsin al-Ayni and a left-leaning Shafai officer, Major Abdullah Abd al-Alim, who commanded the Parachute Brigade. The latter, together with Hamdi's own brother who commanded the largest and best equipped Brigade in the army, were the new leader's closest associates. He consolidated his grip by assuming the post of Commander-in-Chief and by removing the two most senior officers, the former Commander-in-Chief who was a relative of Iryani and the Chief of Staff Colonel Maswari. They were both sent abroad as ambassadors.

Hamdi determined to make a clean sweep and at once he suspended the Constitution and the Consultative Council, referring to its "exhaustive feuds" with Iryani. The Council had been the mouthpiece of the tribal chiefs but their loyalty to the new regime seemed assured by the appointments to the MCC and their previous demand for the removal of Iryani. In a series of meetings, one of which took place on 22 June chaired by al-Ahmar, they expressed their satisfaction.

Hamdi at first asked Hassan Makki to remain as Prime Minister but after a few days he made his own choice by appointing Muhsin al-Ayni. Al-Ayni was always said by journalists to be a Baathist, although they never explained what precisely this meant in the context of Sanaa politics. The selection of a Baathist as Prime Minister would have been strange, as an alleged Baathist plot had sparked off the military takeover. However, al-Ayni's appointment was a shrewd move: he was definitely no reactionary and his presence reassured the supporters of Iryani and moreover showed Aden that no reversal of the policy on union was intended. Al-Ayni had strong tribal connections and furthermore was one of the most competent administrators in the country. Hamdi's invitation asked him to clear up the "administrative and financial chaos and indiscipline prevailing in departments and establishments to the extent of making many despair of reform or of restoring a normal atmosphere". There had been, he continued, "a political collapse which came as a surprise to the armed forces which had to assume full responsibility". In accepting, al-Ayni stressed the importance which he attached to good relations with Saudi Arabia and although he assumed the Foreign Ministry himself, he reassured Riyadh by giving a Cabinet post to Asnag. He promised also to "fight the high cost of living and to continue with the economic projects and their expansion" and to ensure this he made his predecessor Hassan Makki Deputy Premier for Economic and Financial Affairs.

One may wonder if the take-over by the army was really as unplanned as Hamdi liked to say. Within a week a provisional constitution was promulgated by the MCC which declared Yemen indivisible and the Shariah the source of all laws.

Sovereignty was vested in the Chairman of the MCC which assumed the functions of both legislature and executive with the government as its administrative instrument. Action was pledged "to restore constitutional and democratic life on a sound basis in view of the need to provide the Yemeni people with a dignified life and a bright future".

Hamdi and al-Ayni started working together to improve the administration and within two months the President could claim that large sums had been saved by checking "favours, cheating and amusement". He threatened to "chop off every hand extended for bribery" and "to investigate every person whose conduct is not that of a good citizen. Then we can put whoever deserves the gallows on the gallows." In fact his measures were far less drastic and eighteen months later he admitted that there was still very much to do. He pressed for economic development, saying that he wished local capitalists to start industries and to increase opportunities for employment.

Muhsin al-Ayni asserted that the regime was serious in trying to return to Parliamentary life, but in the meanwhile it was decided to persevere with the Consultative Council which had been suspended at the time of the take-over "until normal conditions are restored". In November 1974 it met again, praised by Hamdi as "embodying the people's hopes and aspirations" and instructed by him to try to devise a procedure for elections. The problem of how to create an Assembly which would not be dominated by the tribal leaders, and yet not alienate them and also to give fairer representation to the Shafais and the town-dwellers was indeed formidable.

By mid-January 1975 it was clear that al-Ayni could not solve it and he was dismissed, allegedly for his failure to present any programme to the legislature but in fact because he had upset al-Ahmar and worried the Saudis by being conciliatory towards the South. He was replaced by a highly efficient non-political technocrat, Abd al-Aziz Abd al-Ghani, Governor of the Central Bank, who brought many new faces into the Cabinet but massaged Saudi susceptibilities by appointing Asnag to his old office of Foreign Affairs. Hamdi instructed the new government "to establish a modern civilised state and pay particular attention to financial and administrative reform".

Hamdi came to realise that his dream of a "modern civilised state" was impossible while much of the country was dominated by implacably conservative shaykhs supported by masses of armed followers, and gradually he moved into confrontation with them. During the summer of 1975 he dismissed the tribal representatives from the MCC and in October he prorogued the Consultative Council. He abolished the use of titles and banned the carrying of weapons in towns and he tried to weaken the chiefs financially. In a budget debate in 1973 al-Ahmar had denied that tribal subsidies absorbed 20 per cent of the state's expenditure and claimed that it was only 2 per cent, but whichever figure was right, they received large sums as payment for tribal levies which often existed only on paper and when they were genuine had little military value. In November 1976 Hamdi established a Higher Committee for Financial and Administrative Reform which was to supervise allocations to the tribes and stamp out corruption. Al-Ahmar had already pointedly left the capital and gone to organise his men.

During 1976 Hamdi tried to arrange for a new Assembly, elected under different rules, to replace the Consultative Council. On the anniversary of his seizure of power he declared that he was preparing for "direct and free elections, free from falsification and any exploitation of influence" and this pledge was repeated in other speeches. In November he gave it more concrete form by establishing a Higher Committee under the former Prime Minister Abdullah al-Hajri to investigate the ways of ensuring "genuine representation of the people".

Relations between the President and the tribal leaders deteriorated sharply in 1977 and in January it was reported that the shaykhs had met to concert resistance and that they were seeking help from the Saudis. Hamdi, as a member of the Qadi class, had no special feelings for the Northern tribes and determined to end the semi-independent status that they had unofficially enjoyed for so long. He was feeling his way towards closer relations with Aden and to achieve that he needed to cripple their inevitable opposition. He therefore demanded that they should hand over their arms and in reply al-Ahmar mobilised his tribesmen.

Hamdi started to woo the Shafais with the help of Abd

al-Alim, and many of them were promoted to important posts. He allowed left-wing parties, some Nasserist, some Baathist and some with links with Aden, to emerge in Hujariyyah and did not discourage their coalition to form the National Democratic Front (NDF). He declared that he was neither rightist nor leftist but that tribalism had to be broken. It is possible that he even sought assurance of help from the PDRY if it were to be needed.

In the summer of 1977 there was actual fighting as Hamdi used the airforce against tribal strongholds, and it appeared that he was getting the upper hand. In the autumn there were reports of a reconciliation as a result of which the Zaydi chiefs would surrender their arms and rejoin the government. However, before this could be effected, Hamdi was murdered.

The circumstances of Hamdi's death, together with his brother and the commander of the armoured troops on the night of 11/12 October 1977, remain a mystery: an official enquiry never published its report. The YAR Delegate at the UN session which paid tribute to his memory said that he had been driving at night without an escort while a government statement some days later said that he had been killed by "criminal hands" at a rest-house where he and his brother used to go for relaxation. Spice was added to this account by the reported discovery there of the mutilated bodies of two French "models" and it was suggested that outraged fanatics had surprised the men at an orgy. Many believed that he was killed by an army officer, Major Ali Abdullah Salih, at the house of the Chief of Staff, Colonel Ahmad al-Ghashmi, and that the corpses were than moved and the evidence faked.

The motives for the murders have likewise never been explained. The President had enemies on all sides as he tried to build a modern state by maintaining a balance between contending forces at home and an independent policy abroad. It is possible that he was killed by Zaydi tribesmen in revenge for his operations against them or to forestall the visit that he was about to make to Aden, while others believed that leftists had acted to prevent the rumoured reconciliation with the Northern leaders. He might have been assassinated by either right or left to frustrate the elections that he was planning, in a palace struggle for power, or even by mistake and that his brother was the real target in a personal quarrel. Many saw in the event the hand of Saudi Arabia, alarmed at his rapprochement with the PDRY and fearful that he was trying to escape from their financial grip by wooing the Iranians, the Gulf States or even the Russians. These suspicions were so widespread and so persistent that Riyadh took the unprecedented step of issuing an official denial that it was involved.

Hamdi had proved himself the most effective ruler of the country since the Imam Ahmad and certainly the most popular. He was young, progressive, possessed of an attractive personality and able to inspire his people. He was a sincere but unbigoted Muslim who thought that religion would be strengthened by not being involved in every act of state. He reformed many abuses such as out-dated marriage laws and tried to win the loyalty of the countryside by a real effort to spread social services, and he was concerned with the largest development scheme ever projected for the area. Three years later his untimely passing was still mourned.

The Presidency of Ghashmi

Within hours of Hamdi's murder, the rump of the MCC – now consisting of Ghashmi, Abd al-Alim and the Prime Minister Abd al-Ghani – met and announced that the Chief of Staff, Ghashmi, would be its new Chairman. His first declaration was that there would be no change in policy and that he would not relinquish or bargain over the blessed march initiated by his martyred predecessor. His first action was to propitiate the army by arranging for a free daily issue of *qat*: even so there was an immediate close range attempt upon his life by an officer.

Certainly the problems with the tribal dissidents did not go away and, soon after taking over, Ghashmi said that there could be no negotiations with them until they submitted to the state. In January 1978 Asnag, retained as Foreign Minister, repeated that there could be no compromise with shaykhs who were "opposed to all development efforts. If we agreed to come to terms with them, we should be condemned by the people, and this would play into the hands of the extreme left…they constitute a state within a state whereby they undermine the effectiveness of both the government and the army.

We have no special resentment against the tribes but it is essential that this problem be resolved once and for all." He appealed to the Saudis not to support them. Ghashmi, although he himself had links with the Hashid, tried to put pressure on them by threatening negotiations with the NDF.

Ghashmi was extremely cautious about any advance towards democracy, although he declared that this was the matter closest to his heart. He announced vague plans for a National People's Conference, but, he said, only after careful preparation would this be possible. In the meanwhile, in February, he established a Constitutional Assembly of 99 members, chosen by the MCC. Those selected were mostly rich merchants from the main cities and they appointed as their Speaker not al-Ahmar who had for years presided over the previous body but a former Minister, Qadi Abd al-Karim al-Arshi. However, they showed little independence and one of their first actions was to invite Ghashmi to become President – the first to bear the title since Sallal.

The MCC was automatically dissolved and of its other members, Abd al-Ghani remained as caretaker Prime Minister while Major Abd al-Alim found himself removed from the centre of power. He decided to exploit his own and his fellow Shafais' and fellow leftists' resentment at the murder of Hamdi, upon whom they had once pinned great hopes. He went south to his native Hujariyyah to raise the standard of revolt. His rallying call accusing the Saudis of the assassination was published in a Libyan-financed newspaper in Beirut, and he probably expected substantial aid from Qadafi and from Aden. This was not forthcoming and neither did the Hujaris, enjoying an unprecedented prosperity, rally to his support. Although for a few days the country seemed on the verge of civil war and even of collapse with the North under al-Ahmar and the South under al-Alim, the government, controlling the Tihamah and the centre, rallied its forces. The insurrection collapsed after some fighting with the army and Abd al-Alim and some of his men, having killed their hostages, fled to Aden as refugees. Ghashmi had little opportunity to exploit this success – on 24 June he too was murdered.

The circumstances of Ghashmi's assassination, like that of

his predecessor, are mysterious. There is no doubt that he was killed when a bomb exploded while he was receiving a special envoy sent urgently from Aden by President Robayya, but it is not certain who plotted the deed. There were some rumours that it had been planned locally to revenge Hamdi and that a bomb had been placed in his office: a theory that is unlikely for there is no doubt that his death caused complete surprise in Sanaa and no group appeared ready to exploit it. It seems therefore as if the bomb had been brought from Aden, and forensic evidence showed that it had been contained in the briefcase of the messenger. As the messenger was himself killed instantly, it is unlikely that he knew what was about to happen, so it seems probable that his case had been switched for another. We may think that either Robayya did send the messenger but acted under duress or that someone else concocted a plot to destroy both Presidents. Robayya's career had been built upon his successes as a murderer and conspirator but even if he had any motive for assassinating Ghashmi, and none is known, it is incredible that he would have chosen a method which so crudely incriminated himself.

Sanaa Radio officially mourned the "martyr Ghashmi, the founder of our democratic life", but in fact he achieved nothing in his eight months of office. Hamdi's hopes of a united Yemen pursuing an independent policy had been decisively checked: his work for unity with Aden was allowed to go by default and Sanaa drifted into becoming a Saudi satellite. The Zaydi tribes remained unreconciled while disaffection spread to Hujariyyah where the NDF rapidly gathered strength. The army was discontented, the administration lost any impetus that it might have gained and hopes of democracy petered out in the facade of the nominated Consitutional Assembly. Ghashmi had floundered out of his depth, commanding little respect.

There was no natural successor so a makeshift Presidential Council was formed under the chairmanship of the respected, politically neutral Speaker of the Assembly, al-Arshi. The other members were the Prime Minister Abd al-Ghani who remained in office, the Chief of Staff Colonel Ali Salih al-Shayba who was appointed Commander-in-Chief and Major Ali Abdullah Salih, the reputed killer of Hamdi, who served as his deputy and succeeded him as Chief of Staff. The first act of the new regime was to accuse Aden of the murder and break off relations with it.

The Presidency of Ismail

Abd al-Fattah Ismail and his supporters were either not surprised by these events or reacted with most impressive speed. The following day he called a meeting of the Central Committee to which, according to Ismail, the President refused to come but sent instead his men to attack the party HQ and other official buildings in a "long-prepared coup which almost succeeded in drowning the country in a bath of the blood of honourable militants and innocent citizens". In fact early on the morning of 26 June 1978 it was Ismail's militia and the airforce that were attacking the Presidential Palace. The guards resisted fiercely and there were reports that Russian warships shelled the building and that Cuban troops were needed for the final assault: if this were indeed true and the President had attacked first, orders to intervene could hardly have been received from Moscow in time. According to the party communiqué, Robayya and two companions were "tried by a special court" and shot within minutes of sentence.

It was then "discovered" that Robayya had been guilty of "loathsome mistakes", of "individualistic practices and behaviour" and with his "deviate group had committed the most terrible crimes against the people and gone against the constitution and laws and the collective decisions of the Central Committee and inflicted on the revolution and the gains of the people and workers heavy losses". He had engaged in apostasy and empiricism and had "worn the veil of bogus realism as well as that of extreme leftism". He had tried to gather all powers to himself, divide the armed forces, shown hostility to the Ministry of Culture, opposed research in antiquities, tried to sabotage the economy, the plans for developing drama and the arts and the creation of a vanguard party. He had conspired with the Saudis to establish a reactionary regime and it was hinted that his messenger had gone to Sanaa to enlist Ghashmi in this plot. If he had indeed done all of this, we must admire the saint-like meekness of Ismail in waiting to take any action until Robayya physically attacked his office.

Hassani later declared that Robayya had attempted "an

opportunist leftist coup" but a more significant clue to the timing is to be found in the fact that a few days later Robayya was due to receive an envoy from the United States. This was recognised by the Cuban press which referred to his killing as a severe blow to the manoeuvres of American imperialism.

Robayya was just as convinced a Communist as Ismail and as brutal an exponent of repression, but he felt that these aims could be better achieved without constant conflict with neighbours who were in a position to give economic help. He saw no advantage in alienating them by serving as a catspaw for Russian policy in the Horn of Africa but the stakes there were too high for the Soviets to tolerate any lukewarmness.

Unlike the authorities in Sanaa, those in Aden showed no surprise or indecisiveness at the sudden disappearance of their President. Even before the people were told that Robayya had been shot it was announced that Hassani had succeeded him and an obviously well-prepared purge was started. The arrival of additional Cuban troops to bolster the new regime was also reported to have taken place within hours, while Moscow announced that it would help against any outside intervention. Places on the reformed Presidency Council were given as rewards to the Defence Minister Ali Antar and the Communist Ali Badeeb.

For a moment the PDRY tottered on the verge of civil war as violence flared in the rural areas where Ismail was particularly distrusted. Officers and men, sometimes in whole units, one of which according to Asnag was 700 strong, defected to the North or sought refuge in Oman and there was a series of clashes on the frontier. The party and the militia stood firm and by the end of July Ismail felt strong enough to announce that elections would be held in November.

In October Ismail was at last able to have his way and the new official single party, the Yemeni Socialist Party, came into being with its policies based as usual on "scientific socialism". It had a membership of 26,000 with stringent rules for admission and discipline. Ismail said that "no voice will rise above the voice of the Party" and Hassani explained that its role was to "define the general principles for the development of society and the country's home and foreign policy guidelines". In theory every issue was discussed by the Party cells and then the decisions reached as a result of "democratic centralism" were put into effect by the Political Bureau, but in practice it worked in the reverse direction. Ismail took office as Secretary General and the Central Committee contained such old allies as Ali Badeeb, Ali Salim al-Baydh and Ahmad Hassan Yahya as well as Hassani, Foreign Minister Muti and the Ministers of the Interior and State Security. In December 1977 Ismail became formal Head of State, chairing a Council which included representatives of the Women's Federation, the Trade Unions and the Peasants' Union, and in a government reshuffle all the leading Ministers kept their places. As time went on, however, there were indications that as Ismail became ever more obviously ready to sacrifice everything to ideological considerations, once again a pragmatic group was starting to form.

The Presidency of Ali Salih

In the North the Presidency Council established after the murder of Ghashmi survived for less than a month. In July 1978 a large majority of the Constituent Assembly elected Colonel Ali Abdullah Salih as President. He was young, uneducated, and little known, and apart from membership of the Hashid tribe, his main qualification was an apparent readiness to assume a post that had proved fatal for two incumbents in less than a year. The exiled Major Abd al-Alim denounced him as a stooge of the Saudis. He appointed his acting predecessor, al-Arshi, as Vice President and confirmed the Prime Minister and the Chief of Staff in their offices.

Salih's first move was to attempt to conciliate the northern tribes and al-Ahmar and other shaykhs were brought into the Assembly. Abd al-Alim was condemned to death *in absentia* and some of his supporters shot. In his speech on the anniversary of the Revolution Salih announced that as a first step towards the establishment of "real democracy", municipal councils would be elected but this did nothing to curb the growing strength of the leftist, Aden-supported National Democratic Front in the south of the country. There were frequent clashes in one of which Aden reported that more than a hundred government soldiers had been killed. The country

281

seemed near collapse and there were also reports of fighting in the regions of Sada, Jawf and Marib. Salih appeared to have little option but to try to revert to the old Imamic policy of using the Hashid and Bakil, if he could command their loyalty, to coerce the rest of the country.

Three months after becoming President, Salih narrowly escaped the fate of his predecessors when "agent and infiltrator elements" succeeded in capturing the airfield and the radio station. After heavy fighting, the revolt was put down by the airforce with the help of Hashid tribesmen, and some of its leaders escaped to Aden. It was clear that the general discontent had spread to the army for nine senior officers were amongst those executed and several others were arrested. Some of those who escaped, calling themselves the 13 June Organisation, claimed that they were acting to avenge the murder of Hamdi and early in January this group merged with the NDF under the patronage of the rulers of Aden. In a desperate attempt to establish some form of national unity, the Salih regime kept up a violent radio war against the PDRY until it eventually lurched into a shooting war that it could count itself fortunate to survive.

Relations with the Western powers

The government in Sanaa continued to develop the friendly relations with the West which had started at the beginning of the decade. British trade and aid ranged from the activities of the British Council as the main source of English Language Teaching to the mapping of the country by the RAF and contracts for irrigation in the Tihamah for which Whitehall made a loan of £1 million. Cable and Wireless provided Sanaa's link with the outside world and Costains were engaged to build an extra runway at Hodeidah. British businessmen, to their surprise, found the YAR the fastest growing market in the Middle East, with trade rising from £6 million in 1974 to nearly £50 million in the first nine months of 1979. Many Yemenis made official or private visits to London while English students could be found even in remote places like Hajjah and tourists took photographs at Marib. The activities of the British-run branch of the Save the Children Fund attracted considerable attention.

Within months of the restoration of diplomatic relations, the Americans resumed aid, giving $1.5 million for irrigation and later there were grants for mineral exploration and for a new drinking water system for Taizz. Trade increased also and in November 1975 the first American bank opened for business. The most important relationship, however, was in the provision of arms, although Washington was always haunted by the fear that owing to the instability of the regime, they might fall into the wrong hands – those of dissident tribesmen or military conspirators or even the government of Aden. However in April 1976 President Ford announced that he would provide $139 million worth of weapons, which had been paid for by Saudi Arabia, and the first consignment of artillery and vehicles arrived the following February. After the clash of February 1979 President Carter agreed to furnish a further $500 million worth despite the view of many experts that they would prove too sophisticated for Yemeni military personnel. Soon afterwards a journalist reported seeing Russian technicians training pilots on MiG 21s at one end of Sanaa airfield while at the other American instructors demonstrated the use of F5s: all the aircraft had been bought with Saudi money.

The quest for military equipment also took the Chief of Staff Colonel Ghashmi to Paris in June 1976 and he was followed a year later by President Hamdi making the first official visit by a Yemeni Head of State to a Western country. This proved highly successful and he returned with $205 million worth of aid for the development of telecommunications, airfields, education, roads, agriculture and tourism. Later the nationalised Renault company went into partnership with the Yemenis to organise a bus service.

There were similar contacts with other Western countries. The Germans gave technical and economic aid, continuing their work on the roads and airfields and at least studying the possibility of providing the ancient city of Sanaa with a modern sewage system. The German branch of Shell prospected for oil while a Swiss company investigated the feasibility of rebuilding the historic dam at Marib with money given by the Shaykh of Abu Dhabi. The Danes and the Dutch made loans and the latest statistics published by the Central Bank showed that in addition to Saudi Arabia, all the YAR's main trading partners were Western aligned countries.

Adeni relations with the West fluctuated according to the balance of power within its government. The virtual end of the insurrection in Oman in the winter of 1975/6 meant that there was no longer a cause of friction with Britain and memories of the struggle for independence became less bitter. A British firm won the contract for purchasing equipment for the national airline and Hunting Survey another for searching for minerals, while the Crown Agents were involved with roads. Businessmen spoke with approval of the efficiency and decisiveness with which they were received and compared this most favourably with much of the Peninsula, but the actual volume of trade remained small – under £20 million a year. In April 1979 an amicable agreement with BP led to the handing over of the refinery which the Company was glad to be rid of, for despite its capacity of 8.3 million tons it had been able to produce only 1.5 million in the previous year and there had always been the possibility that it would be seized without compensation. Some expatriate staff remained on contract to manage it and later Cable and Wireless were equally satisfied with the settlement that they negotiated.

During the period of Robayya's "thaw", contracts were made with Japanese, Italian and Canadian companies to search for oil and the Canadians given the right for six years to prospect on and around Socotra. In December 1976 the Foreign Minister Muti went to Paris, which he called "the window for the whole of Western Europe"; there he stressed his desire for closer relations with the Common Market and praised the French decolonisation of Djibouti. In the same year, for the first time since 1969 the West Germans provided aid, working on the water and sewage improvements needed in Aden. The swing back of power to Ismail prevented any significant follow-up of these contacts.

During most of the period, the US continued to be regarded as the principal enemy. In June 1973 Ismail accused it of planning a new war and denounced its "hostility including the unleashing of hate campaigns, the recruitment of mercenaries and the carrying out of subversive operations aimed at protecting oil interests in the Gulf in the face of popular uprisings". Great publicity was given to the arrest of some alleged spies in August 1972 and their subsequent conviction for working for the ITT and the "Zionist Agfa Company".

In November 1973 after the October War, Hassani called on all the Arabs to break with the US and nationalise all its interests. The official media constantly harped upon its links with Israel and denounced the peace-making efforts of Kissinger and Carter. They expressed apprehension, too, over American military activity in the area, called the sending of the Seventh Fleet into the Indian Ocean provocative and feared the building of a base on Masirah Island "for aggressive war purposes".

However it was clear that Robayya at least hoped for a better understanding and on his visit to the UN in October 1977, despite a public speech calling for independence for Puerto Rico "now in the grip of imperialism" and a ritual attack on American interference in the Indian Ocean, he met the Secretary of State Cyrus Vance and discussed the resumption of diplomatic relations. In the following January he took the opportunity of receiving a visiting Congressman to send his best wishes to Carter and to talk of closer ties. A State Department official was actually on his way to Aden in June 1978 when the disappearance of Robayya ended any chance of rapprochement and the media, with all its old zest, reverted to routine condemnation of American activities in the Middle East.

A continual source of irritation to the West was Aden's support for international terrorism. Ismail openly declared that the PDRY was "one with liberation movements everywhere" and "an integral part of the forces directing world revolution". In February 1974 a mixed gang of Palestinian guerrillas and Japanese Red Army extremists arrived at the airport having attempted to blow up a refinery in Singapore while their comrades had seized the Japanese Embassy in Kuwait: all were set at liberty. In March 1975 five German anarchists of the Baader-Meinhoff group flew to Aden with a politician that they had captured and the Bonn government's request for extradition was refused.

However the Aden government became worried about its reputation or more probably feared reprisals for shortly afterwards when some Somali extremists arrived with the French Ambassador whom they had captured, it released him and returned the ransom. In May 1977 it indignantly denied American charges that like Libya and Iraq it assisted international terrorism, drawing a distinction between that and liberation movements and could not forbear to add "imperialism has been and still is, a permanent source of international terrorism". Subsequently in October it refused to allow a Lufthansa aircraft hijacked by Palestinian guerrillas to remain and in February 1978 it would not accept the entry of the Palestinian murderers of an Egyptian journalist.

Relations with the Communist bloc

The intimate relations between Moscow and the South caused YAR leaders to regard Russia with a very wary eye, and to work to maintain a posture that was neither too close nor too distant. In August 1973 the Foreign Minister Muhammad Ahmad Nu'man said that non-alignment was a fiction for everyone had ultimately to take sides with one super power or the other, but his colleagues endeavoured to get as much as they could from the Western nations without alienating the Eastern bloc. This national attitude was reflected within the country where groups dependent upon Saudi Arabia had to contend with elements sympathetic to Communism which were able to call upon covert help from Aden.

The Russians, too, had to tread delicately. In November 1972 they expressed delight at the signature of the agreement on unity but three months later Iryani told a journalist that he understood that they were now against it. They had little hope that their own adherents would come to power in Sanaa in the face of tribal and military opposition. They feared that a union would submerge their small number of supporters in the South in the larger population of the North and that their greater discipline and cohesion would not be enough to prevail: a united Yemen, they considered, would most probably gravitate into the Saudi and Western camp. Their policy, therefore, was to strengthen the PDRY and to do as little as possible for the YAR without alienating it completely.

One of the key problems was the supply of arms for, as Iryani said in January 1973, "we prefer to receive arms from the Russians, as ever since our revolution was launched, our weapons have been Russian and our troops trained on the Russian pattern" but he went on to say that promises to provide them were not being kept, although they were made available in large numbers to Aden. By August 1975 the situation had become acute and Hamdi revealed that military relations with the Soviets were "frozen" and that he was seeking equipment from the Americans. There were reports that some Russian military advisers had been expelled, but in November a delegation led by Major Abdullah Abd al-Alim went to Moscow where it had "a warm and friendly" reception from the Defence Minister Marshal Grechko. This can have borne little fruit for in June 1976 the Chief of Staff, Ghashmi, seeking arms in Paris, alleged that the Russians had refused to deliver spare parts and would not supply "sophisticated or even modern" equipment. He preferred, he said, to deal with a country which would not interfere in the internal affairs of its customers, and that Yemen would shortly be dispensing with the services of its Russian military advisers. Still there was no definite breach and in January 1978 Asnag said that there were 89 military and civilian advisers in the country although he added that "they have no political influence whatsoever". Sanaa's policy was clearly to scale down the Russian presence rather than to abolish it, despite the constant fear that the military advisers might pass on information to their colleagues attached to the army of the PDRY. The mutual desire for some form of relationship evidently continued for in April 1978 the new Chief of Staff Colonel Ali Salih al-Shayba spent two weeks in the Soviet Union and contacts were never completely broken.

In the development and economic spheres the Russians gave up any attempt to compete with the West or with the Saudis. Apart from a few scholarships they gave no significant aid and neither did their satellites, although the East Germans established diplomatic relations in December 1972.

Apart from links maintained through Aden with the NDF, the Russians had little success in attempting to influence Yemeni politics by subversive means. In August 1977 the *TASS* correspondent was expelled and in October 1978 they were ordered to close their consulate in Taizz amidst hints from Asnag that it had been involved in the abortive coup a few days before.

Immediately before signing the union agreement of November 1972 Robayya went to Moscow and secured a promise that Russia would continue to supply arms; as no other power showed any indication of willingness to make them available, dependence on the Soviet Union in military matters continued throughout the decade. Its experts established control over the training of officers, attaching advisers to the army, staffing an Airforce College at Mukalla and providing a Naval College. The Sudanese and later Sadat had showed that it was possible to break such military links, but Aden felt itself much more threatened by its neighbours than ever they had done – even if the will for such a breach had existed, it is unlikely that the Kremlin would have surrendered its last strategic stronghold in the Arab world quite so tamely.

There is also no doubt that the PDRY leaders were convinced and genuine Communists, in particular Ismail who spent several periods of weeks in the Soviet Union, and that he and others were prepared to sacrifice the short-term interests of their own people to the goal of world revolution as conceived by the Kremlin. Attending the Twenty-Fifth Congress of the Russian Communist Party in March 1976 Ismail stressed the importance of "strong relations between the two Parties" and a similar point was made later in the year when the East German Stoph said that the link between the parties was "the core of the entire relationship between the two countries". Contacts were maintained with out-of-power Communist parties such as those of Britain, France, Lebanon, Cyprus and Portugal, and delegates from most Communist countries attended such functions as the first Conference of the Yemeni Union of Democratic Youth in February 1973. Ismail and those closest to him saw themselves as part of an international movement.

This was symbolised by growing intimacy with the revolutionary leadership of Cuba. Although diplomatic relations were not established until May 1972, friendship blossomed rapidly and a series of delegations to discuss medical aid, sugar, joint fishery and tobacco enterprises were in progress by that October when, during the unity negotiations, Ismail went to Havana. He was greatly impressed, signed a protocol for party co-operation and shortly afterwards declared that Aden was "the Cuba of the Arabian Peninsula": the identical views of the two countries on imperialism and Zionism formed the main part of the communiqué when the PDRY Foreign Minister Muti visited Havana the following February.

By the summer of 1973 the American press was reporting that there were a hundred Cuban instructors in Aden and there was speculation that their pilots might have been in action against the Saudis some months earlier. They were said to be teaching pilots to fly MiGs and they were certainly training the militia – at a passing out parade on 23 May Ismail expressed his gratitude for their work. There were fears that they might have come to revive the flagging insurrection in Dhofar, and their "devilish intentions" were denounced by the Shah. A Tehran newspaper even said that "professional Cuban agents, who are the mercenaries of Communist imperialism, are in control of the Aden rulers". However in January 1976 a State Department official said that reports that thousands of Cubans were in the PDRY were greatly exaggerated and that their numbers did not exceed a few hundred.

Russian economic aid was important too, but the annual subsidy gf £12 million which enabled the government of the PDRY to keep afloat could easily have been bettered elsewhere in return for changes of policy. So also could such development help as prospecting for oil, building hospitals, irrigation expertise, scholarships and power units: indeed, Western technology was more respected. The economic aid that the satellites gave – the Romanians with agriculture and a cement factory, the Czechs with a TV station, the Poles with ships, the Hungarians with prefabricated flats, the Bulgarians with a tourist hotel and a bungled development scheme in Abyan or the North Koreans with a soap factory – was likewise not irreplaceable, although it would have been difficult to find anyone else to organise a repressive security apparatus with such brutal efficiency as the East Germans. The hold that the Communist Bloc had on the PDRY was not economic but military and ideological.

Despite this, during the "thaw" the Russians seem to have been uneasy that Robayya's search for contacts with Saudi Arabia and the West could diminish their influence and there were rumours of quarrels between him and the Soviet Ambassador. In April 1976 when Abu Dhabi announced aid of $9 million, Moscow was moved to outbid them by offering to lend $12 million for irrigation, a geological Faculty for the University and a power station. However, a developing crisis in the Red Sea area meant that sterner measures were necessary.

Since its incorporation against its will into Ethiopia, the mainly Muslim population of Eritrea had carried on spasmodic guerrilla warfare demanding independence and this had received the support of the Arab states. A Marxist faction had split away from the main Eritrean Liberation Front in the winter of 1971/2 and this enjoyed the backing of Russia, Libya and Aden while the rest of the Arabs continued to recognise the original group. When Kamaran was occupied by the YAR during the fighting of the autumn of 1972, a cache of arms, made in Russia, paid for by Libya and sent there for transshipment to the Eritreans by the PDRY, was found.

In September 1974 the old Emperor Haile Selassie was overthrown by a group of officers who remained for a time preoccupied with their own internal feuds and with revenge, while tribal revolts added to the chaos. In June 1975 the reopening of the Suez Canal meant that the Red Sea again became a strategic international waterway, and Sadat's formal abrogation of the Egyptian Friendship Treaty with Russia the following March made it even more essential for Moscow to prevent Aden from falling away. This was particularly important as it was starting to look as if pro-Communist elements might prevail in Ethiopia and a base nearby was needed to succour them.

In May 1976 Russia prevailed upon the PDRY to stop any further supply of arms to the Eritrean nationalists who still, of course, enjoyed the support of most of the Arab world. Robayya told a visiting delegation that Aden would "struggle by the side of Ethiopia in the case of any threat to the Ethiopian revolution". Despite this Moscow still had reservations about the President and strengthened Ismail to sabotage any attempt by him to have an independent policy. As we have seen, this support proved decisive, and in October Robayya suffered a substantial rebuff. A few days later Moscow broadcast special congratulations to Ismail although Robayya was also tactfully included.

That autumn the pro-Russian Colonel Mengistu emerged as the strongest figure in Ethiopia and this was made evident by a formal declaration by the Derg (ruling committee) in December that its principles were Marxist-Leninist: it was now clear that the country was in the Eastern camp. It was however still struggling for its existence with rebellions in every province and utterly dependent upon outside support. A flurry of Russian officers, the First Deputy Defence Minister in February 1977, for example, visited Aden to work out the details of how this could be provided and a flow of weapons started.

The Russians hoped to shore up the Ethiopians by forming some sort of grouping for them with their other two allies in the neighbourhood, Aden and Somalia where, at Berbera, they maintained what was apart from Cuba their biggest overseas base. The envoy chosen for this was Fidel Castro. He visited all three countries in March but failed to convince the Somalis, who were becoming increasingly preoccupied by the struggle of their fellow tribesmen in the Ogaden area to achieve independence of Ethiopia. Mengistu, however, listed the exclusive club of friends of the Ethiopian revolution: its members were Russia, East Germany, Cuba and Aden.

The importance of Aden to Moscow increased dramatically with the rapid deterioration of relations between the Russians and the Somalis. In July 1977 Ethiopian positions in the Ogaden were attacked by what the Somalis claimed were freedom-seeking guerrillas but which were, according to Addis Ababa, the regular forces of the Somali Republic. Most Arab countries automatically backed their fellow member of the Arab League but the PDRY, which previously had had the most cordial relations with Mogadishu, followed the Russians in upholding Ethiopia. In November the Somalis denounced their Friendship Treaty with Moscow and expelled all Soviet technicians. The Berbera base was closed and many of its installations, including a dry dock for servicing the submarines of the Indian Ocean Fleet, were transferred to Aden. Within a few weeks the estimated number of East Bloc military experts in the PDRY rose from 1,000 to over 4,000, and it was reported that there were constant arrivals of huge Soviet transport aircraft bringing in tanks and other equipment for onward transmission. In January 1978 Robayya told a Congressman that Russia "does not and will not have a military base in Aden" but did have "facilities": the distinction was obviously a fine one.

Fighting continued as the year ended and the Somali President claimed that over 10,000 Cuban troops were engaged on the Ethiopian side, drawing their supplies through Aden. In February the Somalis admitted that their regular forces were involved and one of their Ministers stated that 2,000 Aden soldiers were ranked with the Ethiopians against them. By mid-March most of the fighting was over, the Somalis accepted defeat and retired within their old frontiers. Later Mengistu launched a campaign to crush the Eritrean separatists but he either did not need or was refused the support of troops from Aden and they were withdrawn: they had done enough to show that the sympathies of the South Yemenis were with international Communism rather than with Muslims. The same point was made a few months later in May 1978 when the PDRY was the first Arab country to applaud the Russian takeover of Afghanistan.

It would have been impossible for the Russians to have saved the friendly regime in Ethiopia without the help of the Aden "facilities", and their importance increased still further as the Kremlin's interest in Middle Eastern oil grew. In May 1978 the Commander-in-Chief of the Soviet Navy visited Aden and went especially to Mukalla where it was said that a base was under contemplation. It is also probable that the Russians gave advance blessing to the overthrow of Robayya the following month: a few days after it occurred they sent a message to Ismail hoping that relations would be yet stronger and as tension mounted on the frontier, Moscow warned the Saudis not to interfere. Ali Antar echoed that "we shall not be alone and will have allied forces" if war broke out.

In September 1978 Hassani told a Jordanian newspaper that the Russians were the "natural allies of all who wanted freedom, independence, progress and peace": he did not add that his regime could not survive without them. Amongst the ordinary people they were hated for this and for their arrogance, meanness, lack of humour and aloofness and were also accused of milking the country of its few resources, such as fish and cotton, in return for expensive weaponry. By the end of 1978, on the surface, the PDRY was a Soviet satellite, as clearly in thrall as Czechoslovakia or Bulgaria. However, its distance and the availability of support from its neighbours might enable it to break the chains if it ever wished to do so.

In the communiqué that followed his visit to Aden, Castro and his hosts "expressed their earnest striving for redoubled and fruitful efforts towards the strengthening of full comradely co-operation between themselves...and towards expanding the exchange of experience and expertise at all levels through the organisation of direct contacts between the leaders and exchanges of party, government and mass delegations". Castro proclaimed his admiration for Aden's "socialist transformations" and "its political line on Arab and international issues". Cuban presence continued to grow and to play an important part in education and the health service,and there were reports that at least in rear echelon posts they helped in the victory over the YAR forces in February 1979. In May 1978 the State Department believed that there were more than 500 of their "experts" in the country.

There is little that needs to be said about relations between Sanaa and Peking, which remained cordial throughout the decade. The Chinese continued to provide practical aid in development, there was an agreement for technical co-operation signed during a visit by Hamdi in December 1976 and in March 1978 it was announced that they would build a second textile factory, a hospital and a cotton oil-seed plant in Hodeidah.

Relations between Aden and Peking were more complicated. For some time Chinese aid continued: in July 1974 they completed work on a road into Upper Aulaqi and on a bridge in Abyan and in June 1976 they finished expanding the salt works and a metal and implements factory which was scheduled to produce 450 tons of wire and 650,000 tools a year. Politically the situation was also more complicated, as many observers tended to report the Aden scene as a conflict between the pro-Chinese Robayya and the pro-Russian Ismail. However, it has already been suggested that this was a symptom rather than the cause of their rivalry.

It became increasingly awkward to be friendly with both Communist giants. When in February 1977 Foreign Minister Muti went to the Far East he signed agreements with Vietnam and North Korea but none with China, where his reception was on a lower level than elsewhere. No further Ministerial visits took place and although early in 1978 Hassani was due to go to Peking, he called off the visit pleading ill health.

The Chinese had grave misgivings about the build-up in the Indian Ocean of Russian naval forces of which they felt they were the potential target, and they knew that this was impossible without the facilities accorded by Aden. As more Russian and Cuban military personnel arrived, it was reported that 400 Chinese instructors had been sent home. In May 1978, even before the fall of Robayya, the Chinese showed their displeasure with Aden by establishing diplomatic relations with its former enemy the Sultan of Muscat and gave a cordial reception to his Minister of State for Foreign Affairs: no other move could so publicly have signalled the deterioration of its once close friendship with Aden.

Relations with the other Arab States

We have seen that at the beginning of the decade the government of the YAR became financially dependent upon Saudi Arabia, and this relationship was to continue throughout the decade. Riyadh underwrote Sanaa's budget, providing more than a third of official expenditure with an annual contribution averaging around $80 million, while much of the development that occurred was also financed by the Kingdom. In 1977 the Deputy Chairman of the Saudi Development Fund said that North Yemen "tops the most favoured countries list" and in 1975 a joint Commission for Economic Co-operation was established, due to meet every six months in the alternate capitals with senior Ministers presiding over discussions of foreign policy, education, information and agricultural matters. The first session produced $273 million in aid, mostly for roads linking the two countries, which also of course had strategic importance. There were also electrification projects, silos, flour mills and later $180 million for a refinery. When in

1977 the YAR announced its Five Year Plan, it relied heavily upon a Saudi promise of $571 million spread over the period. There were special grants to pay teachers, build schools, provide sewerage and water, and in 1978 alone aid from the Kingdom reached more than $400 million. Unofficial receipts from Saudi Arabia easily surpassed these figures: as the Prime Minister Hassan Makki said in May 1974, nearly one million Yemeni citizens earned their livings there and their remittances provided by far the greatest part of the country's foreign exchange. In 1978 it was calculated that these emigré workers sent home more than $1,500 million.

In these circumstances, the Sanaa government had to take great care not to alienate its paymaster. In March 1973 Prime Minister Hajri visiting Riyadh felt it necessary to reaffirm his country's acceptance of the frontiers of 1934, thus formally abandoning the old claims to Asir and Najran, while his successor Makki praised the "special relationship". Hamdi went there a few days after seizing power to stress his desire for "closer relations ties with all Arab countries and particularly Saudi Arabia". In January 1975 he said that relations were "at their zenith" and he won approval by setting up an Office for Islamic Guidance with the brief of protecting the country against "imported ideologies which oppose Islamic teaching and traditions". So close were the links, indeed, that in January 1976, Ghashmi the Chief of Staff surprised journalists by saying that he expected the two countries to unite very soon and that this would begin with the integration of their armies.

The Kingdom's policy towards the YAR was dominated by the need to prevent the people from passing under Communist control. Its own enormous development projects were heavily dependent upon immigrant Yemeni labour for it was becoming difficult to find Saudi citizens who would labour on the roads and building sites. Before the act of union was even signed, Aden accused Riyadh of plotting against it and it was obvious that the Saudis would hardly welcome the emergence in the Peninsula of a new state with a population twice as numerous as its own. The Egyptian occupation showed the threat to the Kingdom's security and that of the Red Sea area as a whole if the government of Sanaa were in unfriendly hands. It had definite fears that despite the larger population of the North its ineffectual and divided rulers would not prevail over the greater dedication and dynamism of those of the South. Thus, whenever a leader seemed to be moving towards unity, Riyadh became anxious: its hand was seen in the overthrow of Iryani in 1974 (rumour had it that they provided $13,000,000 to finance the coup), the dismissal of Muhsin al-Ayni in January 1975 and even in the murder of Hamdi.

In the meanwhile Saudi Arabia financed the build-up of the North Yemeni army, providing, according to the local joke, guns that would shoot only southwards. Despite this it was never sure of the reliability of the regime and reinsured itself by keeping independent links with such tribal magnates as al-Ahmar even when they were opposed to the government: it reasoned that even if Sanaa fell to the Communists, the Zaydi tribes would still constitute a buffer. This connection became so notorious that even their friend Asnag, in January 1978 when the Hashid were making trouble, asked the Saudis to stop their assistance to them.

For two years after the agreement on union, the hostility between Riyadh and Aden continued unabated. A month after the signature, Prime Minister Hassani alleged that the Kingdom, Jordan, Iran, the UK and the US were linked in "a reactionary neo-colonialist plan" to seize the Hadhramawt and in March 1973 he sent Ministers around the Arab world to accuse "Saudi reaction" of working against the union. In the same month the Kingdom claimed that South Yemeni MiGs had attacked the frontier post at Wadiah although this was denied in Aden. Riyadh continued to finance the armed refugees from the South and its radio put out unremitting attacks on atheistic Communism and such practices as the appointment of a woman as a judge or, as Aden put it, "symbolic figures of agentry announce from the castles of their masters and the anchorage of their agenthood in Riyadh their hostility to the Revolution and the unity of the Yemeni people". However, as we have seen, Robayya was anxious to lessen his country's isolation in the Peninsula and its complete dependence upon Russia and at the Rabat Arab Summit of October 1974, he made preliminary contacts with King Faysal.

Upon his return he said "with regard to Saudi Arabia all I want is an end to the sabotage operations against our country, an end to the supply of weapons to the mercenaries, the liquidation of mercenary camps and a halt to the hostile campaign. We categorically refuse to be an aggressive state. There is not a single shred of evidence that we committed an aggression against Saudi Arabia but we have much evidence that some Saudi officials have supplied and supported our enemies." This indication that the King himself might not have been to blame for the past and the end of the call for his overthrow was indeed an olive branch, and a few days later Hamdi came to Aden and tried to help along the reconciliation. This was followed early in 1975 by a rapprochement between Aden and the Gulf States.

Disastrous floods that autumn increased Aden's need for money and the disappearance of basic goods from the shops due to the financial crisis caused bitterness that endangered the very existence of the regime. Exploiting this, Robayya was able to convince his more doctrinaire colleagues that these difficulties outweighed the commitment to spread revolution. If the PDRY dropped this, and in particular ended the aid which fuelled the insurrection in Oman, there was no obstacle to friendship with the Kingdom: indeed both countries would have welcomed the withdrawal of the Iranian troops that Sultan Qabus needed against the rebels. The Saudis now appeared to be ready to change their policy from paying people to attack the PDRY to paying its government to behave.

In February 1976 Foreign Minister Muti went secretly to Riyadh and the deal was done. On 10 March the two radio stations, long used to violent polemics, broadcast a joint statement that "proceeding from a spirit of Islamic and Arab fraternity…(the two countries) desired to create an atmosphere of mutual understanding" and would establish diplomatic relations. Both spoke of Zionist aggression, colonialist activities and "religious, historical and cultural ties and a common destiny" while Riyadh exulted that the Peninsula would now be "kept away from foreign influences". Aden, however, felt compelled to deny "the poisonous rumour" that it had received $400 million as the price of abandoning its principles and complained that "hired pens (had) portrayed the relationship as one of expediency".

Things seemed set fair and it appeared that Aden's persecution mania, resulting from being the only Communist state in the Peninsula, might have ended. Media attacks, apart from a few routine insults at Sultan Qabus, ended, the Saudis withdrew their support for the PDRY dissidents and the Adenis diminished theirs to the Omanis. In April the Saudi Airline opened an office in Aden and flights from Jeddah were resumed. In July Muti was received publicly by King Khalid "in a cordial and fraternal atmosphere".

For a year, however, the Saudis seemed to regard Aden as being "on probation" and events moved slowly. They were alarmed at the visit of Fidel Castro in March 1977 and their Foreign Minister Prince Saud al-Faysal came in person to investigate. He was apparently reassured, expressed courteous admiration for the achievements of the regime and, "in a spirit of love and brotherhood", agreed to a great extension of bilateral relations. The first Saudi Ambassador arrived and in April an agreement was signed by which the Kingdom would supply one million tons of crude oil annually to the newly nationalised Aden Refinery, for which some said it had provided the purchase money. Vast projects, including an 800-mile pipe line from the oil fields of Dhahran across the Empty Quarter to Mukalla and a railway linking Aden with Jeddah and Riyadh were discussed in a heady atmosphere, and in a more practical vein a first loan of $20 million for rural electrification was made. This was followed a few days later by another of $14 million for a housing scheme and a guarantee to cover the purchase of Boeing 707s for the Aden Airline. There was hope of an annual subsidy of $300 million (nearly four times what the YAR received) and in August Robayya was welcomed in Riyadh by King Khalid whom he invited to return the visit.

The honeymoon was soon over. As we have seen, in October Ismail prevailed over Robayya and relations rapidly deteriorated. Riyadh felt that Aden had failed to keep faith, particularly over Oman, the offer of loans was abruptly withdrawn and the Saudi Ambassador returned home. Radio polemics were resumed with Aden accusing Riyadh of complicity in the murder of Hamdi while Riyadh denounced the godlessness of a regime which permitted "naked women in places of debauchery like cinemas" and even women standing as candidates in elections. In January and February 1978 there were unconfirmed reports of frontier clashes in one of which Adeni MiGs were said to have shot down four Saudi Lightnings. Just before his fall in June 1978, Robayya had a brief return of influence and he tried, through the mediation of Kuwait, to patch up the quarrel. This failed, however, but in the autumn the two countries were brought together by a common hostility to the Camp David settlement. Hassani, now President, met the effective Saudi ruler Prince Fahd at the Baghdad Summit and a month later the Prince wrote to his "brother" Ismail inviting him to Riyadh. In February 1979 Ismail was about to go but the visit was hurriedly cancelled as the two Yemens moved towards war. In the fighting the Saudis as usual supported the North and even mobilised their forces in case intervention became necessary: there were also reports that they were paying Taiwanese to fly YAR aircraft. Our period ends, therefore, with relations between Aden and Riyadh just as bad as they had been at its beginning.

Sanaa cultivated its friendships with the rich Gulf States so as not to become entirely dependent upon largesse from Saudi Arabia. At least once a year a senior Minister visited the area and asked for money. In 1974 Makki returned from a trip which included Kuwait, which promised help for the University, schools and water resources, the United Arab Emirates which gave 20 elementary schools and salaries for 200 teachers and Qatar which offered help with education, health and roads. The following year Hamdi toured and came home with $20 million from Abu Dhabi for rural development, $4 million from Kuwait for schools and mosques and a sum from Qatar for health services. There were several other such grants, for example one of $31 million for a power project in Hodeidah, given in February 1977, and the many Yemeni workers in the Gulf added their share to the country's foreign exchange.

Aden for a time continued its refusal to deal with most of the Gulf States. In February 1973 Hassani repeated that "we fully support nationalist forces…It is on these grounds that we have refused to recognise the false independence of the UAE, Qatar and Bahrein." Kuwait still paid Danegeld, setting up a joint company for refuelling ships in 1973, lending £6 million for Abyan in 1974 and another $5 million early in 1975. Later there

was $15 million for roads between Mukalla and the Hadhra-
mawt and from Aden to Taizz, eight schools and four hospitals
which were opened in the autumn of 1976. In the same year
Kuwait provided the larger part of the $33.7 million needed for
developing Mukalla including a fishmeal factory and a power
station and $8.8 million for fishing. In 1978 Kuwait continued
"humanitarian aid" to the PDRY after most of the Arab countries decided to boycott it after the murder of Ghashmi. Ismail
showed little gratitude for all of this, declaring that Aden had a
right to share the prosperity of its Arab brothers.

Kuwait also gave diplomatic help after Robayya said in
December 1974 that he was prepared to have friendly relations
with the other Gulf States provided that they opposed Iranian
expansionism. In February the following year Muti toured the
area, and diplomatic links were established with the previously
scorned regimes of the UAE, Qatar and Bahrain. There was a
quick financial return as, amongst other donations, Abu Dhabi
gave $9 million for a geological survey and oil for the national-
ised refinery. In February 1977 Ministers from North and
South Yemen toured the Gulf asking for money and the following month Shaykh Zaid of Abu Dhabi, hoping to improve
relations between Aden and Oman, arrived with an offer of
aid. Apart from some embarrassing moments when the PDRY
representative in Bahrain was believed to have been involved in
the murder of a right-wing newspaper editor and its representative in the UAE was suspected of plotting, relations between Aden and the Gulf States survived the fluctuations of
those with Saudi Arabia.

Sanaa continued on friendly terms with Oman, receiving the
effective Foreign Minister and a resident Ambassador, and in
1976 Hamdi paid an official visit to Muscat. This cordiality
extended also to Oman's Persian ally which provided training
for Yemeni technicians and welcomed Makki in 1973 and
Hamdi in 1975. When in January 1977 the Iranian Foreign
Minister came to Sanaa the official communiqué reported
"identical views on all subjects discussed" and that arrangements had been made for co-operation in matters of culture,
communications and agriculture.

Relations between Aden and its eastern neighbour, on the
other hand, never improved, for the PDRY continued to serve

international Communism as a vehicle for the subversion in which Moscow did not wish to be seen to be involved. Aden Radio continually trumpeted that the "so-called Sultan of Muscat" was planning to annex the Hadhramawt and that Iranian troops were massing on its frontier as agents of American imperialism; it also broadcast anti-Shah propaganda under the pseudonym of The Voice of the Iranian Revolution. This endless and pointless hostility embarrassed the Arab League. In 1974 it formed a Committee under its Secretary General in an attempt to mediate, but the frontier incidents went on. In October 1975 there was a fierce flare-up when, claiming that at least 500 shells had been fired into his territory since January, the Sultan ordered his airforce to retaliate across the border. The Arab League Committee reconvened and Qabus told its members that the actions of the Aden government constituted "a grave and unmistakeable threat to peace" and that his patience was not inexhaustible. Although the guerrillas had been defeated, he said, there was "no disposition amongst the leaders of South Yemen to abandon their hostility to Oman".

Sanaa offered to mediate, but the rapprochement between Aden and Riyadh had more effect. Although the PDRY did not wish to be seen to be changing its position, in practice it removed most of the remaining dissidents from the frontier area: only six communiqués from them claiming victories were issued in 1976, instead of several a week.

It was probably convenient for the Aden government to have an excuse for keeping large forces in a remote area but whatever the reason, it adamantly rebutted all approaches from Oman. In August 1976 it broke Arab ranks and annoyed the Saudis by accusing Sultan Qabus of "imposing foreign troops on the necks of the people" at a session of the Colombo Non-Aligned Summit. In October, the Arab leaders' meeting in Cairo to discuss the crisis in the Lebanon found time to try to damp down the dispute, but Ismail said that his country had good relations with all its neighbours except for "stooge Oman". Nevertheless the PDRY did agree to close down the insurgents' radio "for technical reasons".

Tension flared up again the following month for while the Foreign Ministers of all the Gulf States, including Iran and Iraq, were meeting in Muscat to discuss mutual security, Adeni anti-aircraft gunners shot down an Iranian Phantom jet which had crossed the frontier from Oman. The PDRY denounced the "flagrantly aggressive intentions" of the Iranians, who claimed in reply that it was scandalous to attack an unarmed plane on a training flight. After a month the Saudis persuaded them to return the wreckage and the surviving pilot who, according to Aden, thanked them for their good treatment, while Tehran quoted him as saying that he had been tortured.

Aden stubbornly continued to refuse any settlement and in April 1977 declared President Nimeiri of the Sudan's statement that he had managed to mediate "completely unfounded". It claimed to feel threatened by the presence of Iranian troops in Oman, but these could immediately have been withdrawn if it had ceased to support subversion. It did, however, restrain the remnant of the guerrillas and no victory claims were broadcast between June 1977 and the following March. In his last days Robayya appeared ready to accept Kuwaiti mediation, but after his disappearance his successors said that they still backed the rebels. Even after the fall of the Shah and the departure of Iranian troops, Aden refused to be reconciled with Muscat: perhaps the sight of a neighbour who was modernising his country more efficiently and without recourse to terror and repression was a standing reproach to them.

In 1972, Iraq was the only close friend of the PDRY and the relationship based on alliance with Russia, strong support for the Palestinians, fears of the "conspiratorial and subversive role of the reactionary forces led by Saudi Arabia" and "Iran's aggressive and expansionist role in implementing the aims of American imperialism" seemed strong enough to survive doctrinal differences, as the quotations above from a joint statement after a Baath delegation visited Aden in March 1974 would suggest. Iraq continued to give economic help, paying teachers and financing joint projects, but in 1976 Aden was outraged at the reconciliation between Baghdad and its own favourite enemies, Iran and Oman, to which Iraq sent an Ambassador. In a fit of ill temper, Aden accused "the fascist Baath party" of contracting a marriage with the Shah and treacherously betraying the Arabs by allying with reactionary forces; for good measure it had also "used immoral methods and financial inducements to set up groups of spies to conspire against our revolution and try to hinder the development and progress of our people". For a time there was a coolness between the two, but in 1977 common hostility to Sadat's negotiations with Israel brought them together again.

In February 1978 Prime Minister Hassani went twice in a fortnight to Baghdad in an attempt to end the split between the governments of Iraq and Syria which was weakening the anti-Egyptian alliance. All appeared well again between the two countries: Iraq refused to attend the meeting of the Arab League which condemned the PDRY for the murder of Ghashmi and during the troubles of that summer an Adeni Minister returned from Baghdad saying that he had been promised support against any outside interference. This was followed by further financial aid, but, despite general agreement on foreign policy, ideological differences grew as the Aden regime became more Communist.

Sanaa and Baghdad had little in common and little cause for dispute. The mysterious alleged attempt at a coup to overthrow Iryani was by mutual consent allowed to be forgotten. Iraq gave some aid, supplying 50 schools and a hospital in 1974 and later oil, and funding projects to deepen the port of Hodeidah and asphalt the streets of Sanaa. In 1975 Hamdi went to Baghdad and returned with $15 million, and a similar sum was given in 1976 and in February 1979 for Hodeidah airfield.

Relations between the PDRY and Egypt were never close. Cairo provided a home for many exiles who had fled from Aden, and the second attempted murder of the former Prime Minister Haytham on its streets, allegedly by Yemeni officials, caused angry recriminations. In August 1976 Sadat visited Oman where Sultan Qabus thanked him for his aid against the rebels and thus implicitly against Aden. The PDRY was among the most vociferous opponents of Sadat's visit to Jerusalem in November 1977 and relations were formally ruptured. Over a hundred students at Egyptian Universities were either recalled or expelled and returned with wild accusations that they had been tortured. Neither side made any attempt to heal the breach.

Egypt's own poverty meant that it attracted few visits from YAR leaders, except for holidays, but relations were cordial enough. In contrast with his neighbour, Ghashmi praised Sadat's "courageous initiative" in going to Jerusalem, but otherwise remained non-committal, waiting to see what line the Saudis would take. Although they paid lip service to the cause, the YAR was not much interested in the problem of the Palestinians and it was noticeable that when such leaders as Arafat, Hawatmeh or Habash went to Aden, they did not include Sanaa on their itinerary.

As with Iraq, Aden was able to maintain links with Libya based on common enmities despite the differences in ideology. Qadafi was extremely hostile to Iran, whose troops on Arab soil he regarded as a humiliation to be wiped out at any cost – this made him equally opposed to Oman and inclined to help the PDRY. He made a visit in 1975 and was apparently convinced that obstruction to the unity of the two Yemens, on which he prided himself as being the inspiration, came only from Sanaa, and he joined with the PDRY in putting the blame for this on Saudi Arabia. Aden's hostility to Sadat and its strong line on Palestine were further commendations, and the two countries followed an identical policy in supporting Russia in the Horn of Africa. In 1978 the PDRY further ingratiated itself by supporting the guerrillas in the Western Sahara in a quarrel of which they probably understood little. As a reward, Libya like Iraq refused to condemn Aden for the murder of Ghashmi.

These foreign policy moves also brought Aden material reward; for example, $41 million were given in 1975 for a fish processing plant, $20 million for electrification in the Hadhramawt, medical and agricultural faculties and laboratories for the University and many smaller projects. In January 1979 Ismail's first trip abroad as Head of State took him to Libya where he remained for a week, signing an agreement for a joint economic and technical committee to meet regularly to channel future aid.

Whereas Aden's policies won approval, Sanaa was blamed for being lukewarm about Palestine, laggard on unity and too friendly with the West, Saudi Arabia, Iran and Oman, and so North Yemen received little and grudging financial aid from Libya. In November 1974 Hamdi said that he had had "purposeful" talks in Tripoli but returned with a mere $11 million, and it was opponents of the regime who fared best. In October 1978, as the two Yemens were lurching towards war, Qadafi backed the forces that were trying to overthrow President Salih; Asnag announced that diplomatic relations were frozen after four of the conspirators confessed that their coup had been financed from Tripoli. Relations later improved again and in June 1979 Prime Minister Abd al-Ghani included Libya on his tour of Arab countries.

The government of the YAR was particularly interested in co-operation with the other countries that flanked the Red Sea, and at the end of 1976 it was concerned about violations of its airspace which it blamed upon Israel, alleging also that it had occupied some small islands. Hamdi urged that this was a matter which concerned all the Arabs and the following March acted as host to the Heads of State of the PDRY, Sudan and Somalia in Taizz: the meeting was not attended but was blessed by Egypt and Saudi Arabia. They agreed that the zone should be one of harmony and peace from which Zionism and imperialism should be excluded. They also resolved to form a technical committee to exploit the wealth of the area. Both Russia and Ethiopia were worried that an attempt was being made to turn the Sea into an Arab lake and through Aden they later managed to ensure that any efforts at co-operation were aborted. The next year Asnag called for a Summit Conference to discuss a multi-national force for the defence of the area but as the other leaders refused to meet Sadat, nothing could be done. In June Nimeiri tried to revive the idea but Aden proved so unreceptive that his visit there, scheduled to last several days, concluded after only a few hours: Ismail was determined to work with Russia and Ethiopia rather than with his Arab neighbours.

Both Yemens participated in the activities of the Arab League although only Aden sent troops, instructed by Hassani to be "faithful messengers of the revolution and the homeland", to the peace-keeping force in Lebanon in January 1977. Later in the year both expressed willingness to join the Arab Common Market but no results were apparent. In July 1978 the majority of the League accepted Sanaa's version that Aden was guilty of the murder of Ghashmi and voted to suspend political, economic and cultural relations with Aden. However, this unprecedented decision was neither unanimous nor whole-hearted and was allowed to lapse when the PDRY's opposition to Camp David secured its readmission to Arab counsels.

We have seen, therefore, that in the period between the first agreement on unity in November 1972 and the second in March 1979, only rarely did the two Yemens find that they were pursuing an identical foreign policy. Only at intervals, and then often by chance, did their attitudes to any particular country coincide. For a united Yemeni foreign policy either Aden or Sanaa would have had to prevail over the other, and one set of friends kept and the other discarded. For all the talk of unity, each was too enmeshed in alliances and commitments for this to be feasible.

Economic and social developments

Both Yemens figured in the UN list of the world's poorest countries and neither was able to balance its budget. In 1973/4 the total revenue of the PDRY was less than £30 million but its expenditure was over £40 million, of which half went on defence and security. The government did all that it could by increasing taxes and cutting costs, in particular wages, but the position continued to deteriorate. In 1976/7 revenue met only half the expenditure.

Statistically the situation in the North was hardly any better. Nearly every year expenditure exceeded revenue by at least one-third: for example, in 1971/2 there was a deficiency of £9 million in a budget of £35 million and in 1976/7 expenditure of £150 million exceeded revenue by £50 million. The Budget for 1979/80 foresaw expenditure of £400 million and anticipated revenue at £300 million. As with Aden nearly half the expenditure was on defence but unlike Aden, which had to beg around, Sanaa could expect that all its deficiencies would be met by a single donor – Saudi Arabia. Efforts made to improve tax collection were greatly hampered by the lack of trained staff, and when the tribes did consent to pay, they expected tangible benefits in return which often cost more than their contribution.

Neither Yemen was able to achieve anything like a favourable trade balance. In the North exports dwindled to a mere $5 million in 1979 with coffee exports down 80 per cent since 1974: there was fierce competition in the world market and cultivation decreased as much of its old area was given over to *qat*. Increased consumption at home, poverty and then restrictions in Aden meant that less of this, too, was exported. The YAR had little else to offer except a few biscuits and salt, and even this ran into difficulties when its main customer, Japan, suddenly stopped buying. It is not clear whether a proposal by the YAR Delegate at the United Nations to boost the export of monkeys was put into effect, but even if it were, its impact on the trade statistics was minimal.

This failure to export did not matter while hard currency continued to flow into the country from emigrant workers elsewhere in the Peninsula. Imports rose 700 per cent between 1970 and 1975, increased from $218 million in 1974/5 to $675 million in 1976/7 and the total of imported goods and services reached $1,150 million in 1978. At times ships waited over a hundred days to discharge at Hodeidah and the *suqs* stood comparison with any in the Peninsula. Already in 1973 the official newspaper said that prices were higher than in the US and inflation ran at 40 per cent a year. Local crafts such as leather work and carpet making started to die in the face of foreign competition and a Sanaani businessman told this writer that building land in the capital was more expensive than in Central London. Investors from the Gulf competed to build hotels as they had once done in Beirut: Sanaa received the cachet of a Hilton. The well-to-do in the cities enjoyed the standard of living of an oil state but the benefits were not spread evenly throughout the country, although nearly all benefited to some extent.

In the South the picture was very different. Exports in 1977 were worth about £30 million of which one-third were products of the refinery and another third fish. However, despite the most stringent controls, imports cost about £200 million, of which one-fifth was crude oil. Aden was particularly hard hit by the increases which followed the war of October 1973, and the price of petrol was raised three times within six months. Great hopes pinned to the re-opening of the Suez Canal were doomed to disappointment, and although $18 million were spent in improving the harbour, the number of ships that called in 1978 was only a third of that of 1966.

Consumer goods became very scarce and meat was rarely available in the *suq*, while price controls meant that other articles disappeared under the counter. Wheat and sugar were rationed, their distribution being controlled by Popular Defence Committees. Intense efforts were made to increase local production, partly by such exhortations as "Eight hours of work, not eight hours at work" and partly by official action – it became necessary to depart from pure Marxism and introduce incentive bonuses of up to four months' pay for meeting targets. In December 1976 the government risked unpopularity by restricting *qat*, the chewing of which caused great loss of working hours to Thursdays, Fridays and holidays: a Special People's Court enforced Draconian penalties of fines up to £500 and three years imprisonment for breaches of this law.

Much of the development that took place in the two Yemens was financed either by brother Arab countries or by one of the power blocs and has already been described in the appropriate sections. The International Agencies continued to help with, for example, $11 million for irrigation in the Tihamah in 1973, $10 million for agriculture in the provinces of Ibb and Taizz, $7 million for a textile mill in June 1978 and $10 million for electrification the following month. The PDRY received $7 million from the FAO between 1970 and 1974 and the World Bank provided $15 million in 1975 for improving the road from Mukalla to the Hadhramawt and $5 million for rural electrification in June 1978.

The political stance of the PDRY – for example, the statement in April 1974 by Foreign Minister Muti that developing nations should take full control of their raw materials – tended to discourage investment by international capitalism. Sanaa, on the other hand, tried to attract foreign money, and in December 1973 Iryani said that there were no plans to nationalise industries or businesses. In July 1975 foreign firms involved in development were given certain exemptions from income tax and customs dues. In October 1976 Shell started to drill for oil but their hopes and those of other companies have so far been disappointed, despite occasional rumours of success. There have also been reports that rich deposits of copper and other minerals have been discovered but their exploitation has been held up by lack of infrastructure and the shortage of skilled labour. With so many men working abroad, this was a particular problem and was so acute that the textile mill and some other industries were working at only a third of their capacity.

It was also difficult to attract local capital. In the South there was little capital available, although in November 1975 a National Aluminium Industries Company was formed with 15 per cent private participation. In the North people preferred to put their money into buying or improving land rather than into banks where it could be used to finance industrialisation. However, some small factories were started, and in the mid-seventies it was calculated that about 50 of them employed a total of 1,400 workers.

In these circumstances it was clearly necessary for the state to take the lead in promoting development. We have seen in the previous chapter that the PDRY had drawn up a Plan covering the years 1972/4, but this was only 77 per cent fulfilled, partly because some promised foreign aid did not materialise. There were also administrative difficulties and the State Economic Corporation was disbanded.

At an extraordinary session of the Supreme People's Assembly in March 1974, Ismail said that a further Five Year Plan would continue the struggle for economic liberation: "We should link industrialisation to the circumstances of our country, our conditions and raw materials...The exploration of our oil and mineral resources would bring orderly and rapid progress to our economy." The Plan called for an investment of Dinars 144 million, most of which would have to come from abroad, aimed at self-sufficiency in food and a rise of 164 per cent in industrial production. There were to be 14 new factories, producing cotton goods, shoes, plastic bags, tins for fruit and fish and cigarettes, and, in addition, there were to be 1,400 km of new roads, 22 new rural post offices, cultural centres and increased electrification. It was later realised that this Plan was too ambitious and it was scaled to Dinars 92 million with the highest priorities given to minerals and fish.

In the YAR a Central Planning Organisation was set up in January 1972 and spent a year in preparing a comprehensive strategy for development in the years 1973/6. It called for an investment of $208 million of which 31 per cent was to be spent on communications, 21 per cent on education, and 10 per cent each on industry, water and sewerage. It aimed, as Aden did, at self-sufficiency in agriculture with 15 per cent for irrigation in the Tihamah, a research farm in Taizz, improving seed, etc. One hundred local Development Councils were set up to plan local advances in farming.

In June 1977 a second Plan was announced to cover the years from June 1977 to June 1982 and was described by the Prime Minister Abd al-Ghani as "midway between realism and ambition". It aimed for an investment of $3,360 million, which should increase the gross domestic product by 8 per cent a year. Nearly one quarter was to be spent on transport and communications, roads were to be increased by 75 per cent and the capacity of Hodeidah port by 200 per cent, for this was the bottle-neck which held up progress. Not far behind came industry with new factories including textile mills in Hodeidah and Dhamar, cement works in Bajil and Amran, and paper and fertiliser factories. Some way behind came electrification, which was to be increased by 240 per cent, and water. Proposals also included schools, a Hamdi Housing City and a Sports City in Sanaa. The private sector was to provide over a quarter of the money and 40 per cent was to come from abroad, of which Saudi Arabia promised $570 million. After the murder of Hamdi, some 300 delegates, including international financiers, attended a four-day conference in Sanaa to discuss the proposals and some modifications were made.

In both Yemens there was considerable progress in spreading education. Sanaa University continued to expand and one opened in Aden in September 1975 with faculties of education, agriculture, economics, commerce and medicine. The Higher School for Socialist Sciences provided ideology courses for teachers and the government expected that there would be 342,000 children attending school by 1978. Special efforts were made to reach Beduin boys, and even some girls from these tribes were brought in. In the North the advance was less marked, hampered by the difficulty that fewer than half the teachers had themselves completed a secondary education. The Saudis paid for Egyptian staff, but even so it was an enormous task in a country where 47 per cent of the population was of school age.

Hamdi took a particular interest in rural health. Once again there was an immense amount to do, as the average expectation of life was only 36 years. In February 1976 he appealed to the Arab countries to provide $790 million to help overcome malnutrition and endemic diseases such as malaria and tuberculosis. Medical training was hurried along, and there were over 130 Yemeni doctors by the time Hamdi died. Attempts were also made to improve urban amenities, but in Sanaa less than half of the population had access to piped water.

Medical care in the South was more advanced and several more hospitals were opened in the hinterland. The second Plan hoped for 310 doctors by 1979 when all but the most remote mountain villages would be receiving some attention. Another advance in the PDRY was the introduction in March 1975 of a pensions scheme which provided for retirement for men at 60 and women at 55, and was financed by public funds and deductions from pay.

As we have seen, improvement of communications was an important feature of all government plans. Metalled roads now connected major towns, and the overland journey from Aden to Mukalla now took a day instead of up to a week if the tides had made the beach difficult. Television spread beyond the main cities and proved a useful instrument in the hands of the authorities. Telephones became less chaotic and Sanaa acquired its own telecommunications satellite. The Yemens could not move very quickly but they were definitely moving forward.

The social developments that we observed in the previous chapter continued along the same lines. In the South persecution or flight removed any elements that attempted to raise their heads above the general level while the elite of the party and the government improved their position. The bureaucracy expanded rapidly from 19,000 in 1973 to 31,000 in 1977 – they and the party elite constituted the sole privileged class, while the mass of the people had only to work and applaud their masters. The influence of the religious leaders continued to diminish.

In the North the Sayyids went on losing ground; few

attained important political office, although their influence remained great in social and religious matters. The Qadi class, on the other hand, was very well represented in the highest reaches of power. We have often had occasion to notice the doings of great tribal magnates like al-Ahmar, but lesser shaykhs also had an increasing role. As the government extended even rudimentary social services into their areas, the importance of their dual role of representing the administration to the tribe and the tribe to the administration was accentuated. In the towns refugees from Aden, often abandoning hope of returning home, put down firmer roots and augmented the small indigenous bourgeoisie. In this society government officials, estimated at 31,000 in 1976, of whom perhaps 4,500 were illiterate, did not enjoy the lofty preeminence of their counterparts in the South.

In the North women made steady advances towards emancipation, with more than 300 at the University by 1976. There and in the factories they were often veiled, as they were when they worked as typists or nurses. More and more Yemeni ladies attended social functions where they met Western visitors, but none played any significant public role.

In the South women, as well as men, were expected to intensify their political and class awareness. Women were employed in a wide variety of spheres: they bore arms in the forces, they worked as barmaids and in factories. Women were also appointed as judges, and in December 1978 a woman was made a member of the Presidential Council. Numerous photographs showed unveiled women factory workers, whose part was vital as so many men had escaped abroad.

Women's emancipation was given legal form in the Family Law of 1974 which was claimed to be the most advanced in the Muslim world. A man was not allowed to take more than one wife without the permission of a court and then only in extreme cases: the first wife was then given the right to ask for divorce. All petitions for divorce by a husband had to be referred to a Social Committee of the Women's Union, which was also involved if there were an age difference of more than twenty years between prospective marriage partners. A Court clerk had to be assured of the consent of the bride and the marriage of girls under the age of fifteen was forbidden. The period of pregnancy was officially pronounced to be not less than 180 days or more than 360.

In both Yemens a significant proportion of citizens lived or worked abroad. In November 1976, Robayya gave the figure of one million from the South and while this is hardly credible, it does indicate the size of the problem. Leaving without permission was a criminal offence and those going legally had often to deposit up to £10,000 as a guarantee of their return. The members of their families who remained were often under surveillance or worse, making it difficult for emigrants to send home much money. Thus, the South did not reap the same benefits from this source of income as did the North.

The census of 1975 in the North indicated that there were about 600,000 citizens earning their living abroad: this represented about half of the national labour force. The oil boom after 1973 meant that they no longer had to go as far as Cardiff or Detroit but could find employment within the Arabian Peninsula and so remain in closer touch with their families. In the YAR the annual average income was $400 per head but in Saudi a worker could easily earn $28 a day and as we have seen, their remittances were vital to the national economy. They were important, too, at local level, for one emigrant worker could support an entire village which his money might help to transform by improving its agricultural potential. The price of land soared, it became more expensive to dig a well in Yemen than it was in Abu Dhabi. Despite often unsuitable terrain, tractors made their appearance. As 72 per cent of the population, according to the census, was working on the land, the benefits were widespread and North Yemen slowly started to become a country of increasingly prosperous peasant proprietors.

In the South land continued to be distributed for use rather than for ownership so more and more country folk were grouped into the 41 state farms and 39 co-operative agricultural enterprises which were dependent upon the state for the sale of their produce. The workers were organised in October 1976 into the Union of Democratic Yemeni Peasants, but many of them were not proprietors.

When the two Republics came into being, there were no substantial differences in their social systems and way of life,

313

but as time went on both were transformed by government action. The North retained much of what was best in Arabian tradition, while the South degenerated into a depressed reflection of an East European satellite state.

Relations between the two Yemens

A ceasefire signed on 17 October 1972 ended the main fighting between the two Yemens and arranged that forces should be moved back from the frontier, refugees allowed to return and training camps controlled. A special representative of each President and personnel from the Arab League were appointed to supervise the implementation of the ceasefire. Even so there were a few more clashes, for as Prime Minister Muhsin al-Ayni said "Aden has created a force dedicated to its own overthrow", which was not easy to subdue once it had arisen.

Ten days later the two Prime Ministers met in Cairo and agreed that they should unite to form a single unified democratic republic with one flag, capital, leadership, executive and legislature. They created eight committees to deal with the details of constitutional affairs, economic and financial matters, legislative and judicial, educational, cultural and information, military, health, and administrative and public service problems: work was to be completed within a year, during which time a constitution would be drawn up and put to a referendum supervised by the Arab League.

At the beginning of November the two Prime Ministers talked with President Boumedienne in Algiers and at the end of the month, after a five-day visit to Moscow, President Robayya met President Iryani in Tripoli for the formal signature of the act of union. They agreed that the new state should be Arab, Islamic, national and democratic with its capital at Sanaa and its flag red, white and black. Qadafi stole the limelight and preened himself as Iryani saluted him as "the Father of Arab Unity". A Lebanese newspaper subsidised by him claimed that he had threatened to imprison his guests until they signed and had then promised to make $46 million a year available to them.

The union was publicly welcomed in both countries and by the Arab world in general. Saudi Arabia and the Soviet Union also expressed their pleasure but in reality each feared that its own protégé would be the weaker partner and be dominated by the other. Before the papers were even signed, Hassani said that the Saudis were trying to undermine the union and in January 1973 Iryani said that the Russians were doing the same. The exiled Makkawi told a press conference that it was bound to fail, for Aden was merely aiming to buy time to rearm for another war with Russian aid.

As we have seen Iryani was genuinely in favour of union, but there were strong elements in Sanaa which were not. Their fears were heightened by the first meetings of the constitutional committee which showed that Aden had no intention of changing its internal policies, and the conservative Zaydis had no wish to be embraced by Communists or Shafais. When al-Ayni resigned at the end of December 1972, Iryani was compelled to appoint the pious royalist Abdullah al-Hajri, who paid lip-service to the idea of unity but had no intention of hastening it.

Nevertheless the committees still met, and in February 1973 Iryani said that their work was ahead of schedule. The representatives of the Arab League and the personal envoy of Qadafi attended their sessions. One of the first practical projects was one to amalgamate the two foreign services. This was, however, checked by the air crash which wiped out many of the leading Southern diplomats: Sanaa joined in the official mourning.

It was not long before the prospect of union received a severe set-back. On 30 May Shaykh Muhammad Ali Uthman, a colleague of Iryani on the Presidential Council and a known opponent of any merger, was murdered and the authorities in Sanaa had little doubt that those in Aden were responsible. Although the PDRY declared official mourning, it was asked not to send representatives to the state funeral. There was a further sign of deteriorating relations the following month when Sanaa accorded a state funeral to the anti-Communist writer Muhammad Ali Shuaibi whose killing in Beirut was attributed to agents of the Aden government.

Early in July, Iryani had to admit that the work of the

committees had fallen behind schedule and that it might not be possible to complete it within a year as agreed. Only the educational committee seemed to be making any progress. At the end of the month Robayya disclosed that they had not been able to settle even such comparatively simple matters as customs fees and communications. In September the two Presidents met at the non-aligned nations summit in Algiers and promised to spare no effort to make the union a reality, but when Robayya visited the North in November, they had to agree to extend the deadline.

At the beginning of 1974 the committees took some practical decisions to increase trade and to reduce duplication in development schemes, and the dismissal of Hajri in March removed an obstruction. The appointment of Asnag, however, to the key position of Foreign Minister and that of another Adeni exile Muhammad Salih Bassendwa to the Cabinet was hardly likely to help things forward. Nevertheless a visit from Hassani in May produced an agreement to set up a permanent committee consisting of himself and the two northern military leaders, Colonel Iryani and Colonel Hamdi.

The seizure of power by Hamdi caused some apprehension in the South as he was believed to be a firm ally of Saudi Arabia and thus more likely to take a hard line than Iryani. However his first move was to affirm his "determination to realise unity" and more practically to appoint al-Ayni as Prime Minister and shift Asnag from Foreign Affairs. The joint committees continued to meet but al-Ayni was sceptical as to their results, asking a Beirut newspaper whether it was conceivable that the northern tribes would accept a Communist regime or that the southern leaders would submit to being absorbed in the larger population and liberal policies of the YAR.

There were signs that the two countries were co-operating, however, for in November 1974 they presented a joint memorandum to the Arab summit in Rabat outlining the difficulties that they suffered from the rise in oil prices and, the following month Hamdi went to Aden where it is probable that he agreed to try to help Robayya to improve relations with the more conservative states of the Peninsula. The return of Asnag to the Foreign Ministry did not prove a real setback: in February 1975 a series of detailed agreements were reached by the financial and economic committee, and during the summer another committee settled some minor border disputes.

This unambitious approach to gradual unity through economic co-operation was obviously sensible, although there were difficulties caused by the fact that the YAR and its development was so dependent upon Saudi money. However in April 1976 the Deputy Foreign Minister of the North, Hussayn al-Amri, said that there was "nothing to stand in the way of economic complementarity" with the South and suggested that co-operation might start with cement and fish-canning factories and possibly a joint airline. Unity, he thought, might first be achieved in such fields as information and culture as well as the economy, leading eventually to political merger but "neither side was in too much of a hurry".

During 1976 all political leaders stressed their commitment to unity in nearly every speech but the two Presidents in particular came to see in it political advantages for themselves. Robayya was struggling to hold off the challenge of Ismail and to strengthen relations with the Saudis and the Gulf States while Hamdi wanted support against the northern tribes. In February 1977 they met in a border town and, to put new life into the negotiations, constituted a council of themselves and their senior Ministers which would meet every six months in the alternate capitals.

This was followed by new evidence of co-operation. A joint delegation headed by a Minister from each country toured the Gulf, reiterating their difficulties over oil prices and asking for aid. In March they collaborated in the attempt to turn the Red Sea into a zone of peace. Hamdi stressed that he and Robayya were sincerely working together to overcome the obstructions raised by neo-colonialism and tribalism: put more bluntly, Russian activities in the South and those of al-Ahmar in the North. In August Robayya spent another two days in Sanaa and there was no doubt that the two Presidents were collaborating very closely. There was speculation that when Hamdi returned the visit in October some really significant steps towards unity would be announced. However, two days before he was due to set out, he was murdered.

Few can have mourned the killing of Hamdi more sincerely than Robayya who attended his funeral. Aden described the murder as "a criminal and despicable operation" and was not convinced by his successor's statement of his determination to bring unity about, for he was known to have close links with the northern tribes and with the Saudis. Early in 1978 Asnag reflected his government's lack of enthusiasm when he said that its achievement would take several generations and would be "merely an emotional measure" until the political and economic systems were in harmony.

Relations deteriorated quickly as Ghashmi reversed the policies of his predecessor by reaching an accommodation with the northern tribes and repressing the Shafais after the revolt of Major Abd al-Alim. There was considerable tension on the frontier, and as many of the refugees from Aden living in the North became uneasy at the hardening of Zaydi attitudes, this was exploited by the PDRY through its links with the opposition National Democratic Front.

On 24 June 1978 Ghashmi too was murdered and his successors had no hesitation in pinning the guilt upon the authorities in Aden. That evening Sanaa Radio asserted that he had died "at the hands of treachery, evil and aggression in Aden". "Great Yemeni people," it went on, "the vicious hands in Aden have today committed the meanest and most outrageous, treacherous operation against you, your sovereignty, freedom, dignity and stability." The YAR formally broke off diplomatic relations with "the gangs of crime and treason, known for their treachery to God and the Homeland".

Aden attempted to defuse the situation by putting the blame solely upon its own slaughtered President, but Sanaa was inexorable. Other Arab countries, in particular Syria and Iraq tried to calm things down but Colonel Ali Abdullah Salih, although he declared upon becoming President that he "firmly and deeply" believed in a union, was adamant that "there could be no mediation and no dialogue". Sanaa prevailed upon the majority of the Arab League to freeze relations with the PDRY and to investigate a series of frontier clashes caused, it was claimed, by southern troop concentrations.

Salih, unsure of his position, tried the traditional policy of uniting the people against a foreign foe. By September there were almost daily accounts of incidents while each government encouraged rebels against the other: Sanaa welcomed supporters of Robayya while Aden provided a home and a radio for the NDF and the followers of Abd al-Alim. Early in that month Aden accused Salih of issuing "a reckless call for war between the Yemeni people"; Asnag retorted that the PDRY had already started a sabotage plan as a prelude to invasion.

November provided fine examples of mutual abuse. The PDRY Radio denounced "the inhuman, barbarous and black reactionary Sanaa regime…(for) importing American agents to work in intelligence, torture and repression of mass movements. The people will squeeze their throats until the hired tyrants expire." President Salih replied that "the existing dispute is not only between us and the despotic, conspiratorial communist regime in the South but between the people in the whole of the Yemen and the atheist clique in power there". Aden's answer was that "the intrinsically agent and fascist regime of Sanaa" was collaborating with "the treacherous Egyptian regime" and providing the Americans with a naval base in Hodeidah.

Behind the verbiage there was obviously considerable tension in Hujariyyah, which Aden stimulated and encouraged, broadcasting a series of communiqués from the NDF claiming to have killed at least a hundred Zaydi soldiers despite "raids of extermination, killing and destruction" which had caused 8,000 to flee, killed 15 and smashed 300 houses and 30 artesian wells. There was trouble, too, in Sanaa, in which Salih was nearly killed: he blamed this plot on Aden which gave asylum to the surviving conspirators.

In February 1979 the world was preoccupied by a war between China and Vietnam and by the sudden collapse of the monarchy in Iran. This led to the withdrawal of Iranian troops from Oman, which enabled Aden to move forces from its eastern to its northern frontier. It seems as if Aden now felt that it was an opportune moment to put an end to the incurably hostile government of Salih and to knock out the weakest link of the conservative Arab states. Claiming that they had repulsed attacks on Bayhan and Mukayras, they announced that they would teach "the agent hireling group" a lesson that it would not forget. In a series of well planned attacks, the three main border towns of al-Baydha, Harib and Qataba were all captured and the Northern army appeared on the verge of collapse. It looked as if the whole Shafai area, where many of the inhabitants had welcomed the invaders, might be overrun.

The other Arab countries intervened, a ceasefire was arranged and on 30 March the two Presidents met in Kuwait and agreed to unite as the Yemeni People's Republic. A constitution was to be drafted within four months this time but otherwise the provisions were much the same as those of 1972; few observers gave them more hope of success.

Postscript: March 1979 to October 1981

The political situation in the YAR

Colonel Ali Abdullah Salih has managed to continue in office as President although his position has often seemed extremely precarious and his control, at times, has extended little beyond the boundaries of the major cities. Although largely uneducated, he has had time to develop as a leader, showing himself artful and astute. He has managed to balance deftly between contending forces, both internal and external, and his main pre-occupation has been to avoid becoming totally committed to any group or policy. He has been able to take credit for some economic development and has had three years in which to put his relatives and fellow tribesmen in places where they can support him.

Salih has kept trying to win acceptance by promises of increasing public participation in government. Some of these have been kept. In 1979 he carried out municipal elections. On 15 February 1980 he declared that there would be general elections, but he carefully abstained from mentioning any date. On 27 May, he formed a committee to prepare for a General People's Congress, but there was little apparent progress for in March 1981 he spoke of a plebiscite of 5 per cent of the population as a sort of rehearsal. He stressed in a speech in April that there was no possible alternative to democracy, and threatened to punish anyone who disputed this statement. More recently he has fostered the idea of a "National Charter" – a form of Constitution – which would be vetted by a National Assembly of 1,000 representatives, 700 of whom were chosen through the Co-operative elections of October 1981.

It would, anyway, have been difficult to organise nation-wide elections. Some form of participation in government for the leftist, pro-Aden National Democratic Front may have been part of the concessions that were necessary as the price of peace. The NDF's leader, Sultan Ahmad Omar, a graduate of the American University of Beirut and the author of a book on the Yemen, stated that he would co-operate with the government if it would announce a programme of free elections, land reform, amnesty for political prisoners, nationalisation of industry, less dependence upon Saudi Arabia and union with the PDRY. It was clear that the NDF was asking too much, and to have conceded to all their demands would have put Salih entirely in their power and alienated the Zaydi, religious and merchant elements that he needed to counter-balance them. In the spring of 1980 Omar claimed that he had reached agreement with the President and there was talk of NDF members entering the Cabinet. However, in the summer financial pressures forced Salih to improve relations with Saudi Arabia, and the conditions for aid obviously included the breach of such a deal, if indeed any had been made.

There was continuous sporadic fighting which intensified in the last months of 1980. In December the government claimed to have broken the opposition, but it is clear that a hard-core of some 500 armed men remained in the field. This force could be expanded to about 8,000 by tribal support for specific operations. In September 1981 a newspaper reported that the NDF had established its own administration in Hujariyyah setting up schools and clinics and with its tentacles stretching almost to the outskirts of Sanaa and Hodeidah. These stories, however, coincided with the struggle by the American administration to secure Congressional approval for the sale of advanced weapons to Saudi Arabia and appear to have been exaggerated for, in fact, the NDF controls little more than the area of Qataba, immediately beyond the frontier of the PDRY.

The progress made by the NDF was sufficient to alarm the northern tribes, whose natural conservatism was stimulated by the Saudis and who were, as al-Ahmar said, particularly worried by the Russo-PDRY Treaty of October 1979. Salih maintained close links with the Hashid through one of their shaykhs, an army officer who had once been a member of

Hamdi's first Military Command Council, by giving him the important post of Deputy Prime Minister for the Interior. At the same time, the Islamic Revolution of the Ayatollah Khomeini struck responsive chords in the hearts of the Shi'ite Zaydis and strengthened religious feelings against the "godless" southerners. The northern tribes formed an "Islamic Alliance" with the claim that the Faith was in danger.

In October 1980 there was a change of Prime Minister. Dr Abd al-Aziz Abd al-Ghani had held office for nearly six years, easily a record for the Yemeni Republic, and he wished to retire: Salih, however, insisted that he should remain in the government although he allowed him to have the less exacting post of Vice-President. The new incumbent was another technocrat, Dr Abd al-Karim Iryani, the holder of an American doctorate in biology who, through his interest in agricultural development, had also become an expert on finance. He had worked as senior adviser to the Kuwait Fund for Arab Economic Development and had been Principal of Sanaa University. He was a good man to prepare for a new Five-Year Plan, and his appointment removed an influential figure who could well have been dangerous in opposition. There were further changes in personnel, but the former balance of technocrats and traditional leaders was roughly maintained.

Even before the signing of the Kuwait agreement with Aden, Salih had dropped the two southerners, Asnag and Basendwa, from his Cabinet, blaming them, rather unfairly, for urging a war which had proved unsuccessful. Asnag was retained as a "special adviser" but he was regarded very much as Saudi Arabia's man in Sanaa, and he found himself a victim when relations between the two countries deteriorated. In March 1981 his parliamentary immunity was lifted and the following month a Kuwaiti newspaper went so far as to announce his execution. He was accused, it was said, of intrigue with the CIA, of passing on information about the government's increasing links with the Soviet Union and their negotiations with the NDF, and of trying to persuade "an Arab country" to reduce its aid to the regime. There was even a story that he had "bugged" the office of the President. He was brought to trial and condemned to death, but nothing further happened. He declared his repentance, and with the improvement of relations with the Saudis and the increase in their aid, the matter was left in abeyance. His political career, starting over twenty years before when he was a Trade Union leader in Aden, has probably ended, but his eventual fate remains a useful means through which Sanaa can exercise pressure on Riyadh.

The political situation in the PDRY

Although he said "we did not bring down individual leadership to replace it with a new individual leadership", Abd al-Fattah Ismail seemed very much in personal control during the months that followed the signature of the Kuwait agreement. In August there was a reshuffle of the government but its motive seems to have been to increase administrative rather than political efficiency, for former guerrillas were replaced by technocrats at the Ministries of Finance and Planning while the Ministers removed, such as Muti, were found places in the party organisation. More significant was the creation of a Committee of State Security under the chairmanship of Hassani, the Prime Minister. In a later move, a woman was brought into the government as Deputy Minister for Culture and Tourism.

In March 1980 Ismail denied in an interview that there were any splits in the leadership, but for months exiles had been saying that once again the fanatical dogmatism of the President was alienating those of his comrades who wished to deal in a pragmatic way with the difficulties confronting them. Hassani and Ali Antar, the Defence Minister, were believed to aim for improved relations with Saudi Arabia and to end the total reliance upon Russia by buying some arms from the West. Ali Antar, who had played such an important role in the overthrow of Robayya by removing officers loyal to the then President, started the same process directed now against Ismail. The President struggled to enlarge his power base by wooing the tribes to add to his existing support amongst the urban workers: as a gesture he resurrected the old provincial names, and Bayhan, Abyan and Hadhramawt reappeared on the maps in place of the soulless and artificial governorates.

There was, however, general surprise when on 20 April 1980 it was announced that Ismail had resigned on account of ill health. Some said that even Brezhnev had found him too extreme, while others alleged that while in Moscow he had made concessions to the Russians beyond those agreed by the party leadership. If he were indeed pushed out, the matter was handled in a far more gentlemanly way than he had treated his predecessor: he was given a medal and the honorary post of President of the Party. Hassani retained the office of Prime Minister, added the key position of Secretary General of the Party, and assumed that of Head of State. He immediately announced that there would be no changes in policy.

Power now seemed definitely shared between Hassani and Ali Antar but soon there were rumours that they, too, were quarrelling, with the Defence Minister resenting the other's control over internal security. Muscat Radio reported that on 15 January 1981 Hassani ordered a special alert to forestall a possible coup by Antar, and there were even rumours that the latter had fled the country but was induced to return. Such stories were of course denied, but on 4 May Antar was moved to the much less influential post of Minister for Local Government. Hassani claimed that there had been no conflict between the two, that Antar had changed offices of his own free will and that he remained a member of the Politburo and was still First Deputy Prime Minister. The subsequent dispatch of a token military force to Syria was seen as a means of getting out of the country officers loyal to their former chief. Another possible rival to Hassani had already disappeared: in March Muti was shot "trying to escape" and he was posthumously accused of accepting money from Saudi Arabia.

The quarrels of the PDRY with other Arab countries meant increasing support for Adeni politicians in exile. In March 1980 a meeting of the "National Grouping of Patriotic Forces in Southern Yemen" was held under the chairmanship of Makkawi in Baghdad and was assured of "the love, respect and appreciation" of the Iraqi leader, Sadam Hussein. Another group, calling itself the "Twenty-sixth of June Movement", vowed to avenge Robayya and announced that it was fighting the Aden authorities. Opposition leaders, including Shaykan al-Habshi of the old South Arabian League and Muhammad

Ali Haytham, the former Prime Minister ousted by Robayya and Ismail, met in Muscat in December 1980 to hear Makkawi declare that their homeland was infinitely worse off under Russian colonialism than ever it had been under the British. He addressed supporters, too, in Cairo saying that mosques were being turned into militia halls and that Aden was now a springboard for Soviet expansion throughout the Peninsula. In February 1981 Makkawi announced that military operations were about to start, but the only sign of activity so far has been an attack on the PDRY Embassy in Paris.

Under both Ismail and Hassani, the government continued to demand vigilance against external and internal foes and intensification of political awareness. In January 1981 the Central Committee of the Yemeni Socialist Party stressed the need to "expose all forms of political, economic and ideological sabotage and to struggle against a negative attitude to work and those who put their own interests above those of the toiling masses". In April, a Supreme Public Watch Committee was created and later in the summer the Prosecutor General's office received more staff. Conscription served to bring more young men into contact with the Commissars but Hassani complained that the young were not interested in politics and more must be done to coax them into the YSP. The Yemeni Vanguard Organisation was created with this objective and attempts were made to attract participation at local level. In June 1981 local elections were held in which it was claimed that 94.6 per cent had supported the approved candidates.

Life meanwhile became even harsher with the banning of *qat* under savage penalties. The introduction of coloured television may have provided slight relief, but it is doubtful that the first programme, covering a meeting of "The Women's Extraordinary Congress" was everyone's idea of entertainment.

Finally it is worth mentioning that three names from the past were heard again in the summer and autumn of 1981. In July Aden announced "with profound regret" the death at the age of sixty of its first President, Qahtan al-Shaabi. He was given a state funeral with religious rites. In the North, during his speech on Revolution Day, Salih invited back the two former Presidents, Sallal and Iryani, "to live on our pure soil under the canopy of real democracy": both accepted and returned in early October, providing a useful propaganda point for the regime.

Relations with the Western powers

There is little that needs to be added to the previous account of relations between the two Yemens and Great Britain. In the Aden press, the United Kingdom was no longer singled out as something uniquely malevolent and dangerous and fared little worse than any other anti-Communist power: indeed the two countries seem rather to have lost interest in each other, apart from maintaining commercial links. Relations between London and Sanaa continued to be very friendly and quickly recovered from an unexpected set-back in December 1979. The Prime Minister, Abd al-Ghani, paid a successful visit to London and was about to leave when he found that his aircraft had been legally detained as the result of a claim by a British commercial company against the Yemeni state airline. Many Yemenis could not understand that Whitehall was powerless to set aside the normal process of law, but an apology from Margaret Thatcher and some tactful diplomacy convinced them that the British government had intended no insult.

The PDRY, as it has done from its very foundation, continued to proclaim its hostility to the United States, and almost every day reiterated the old charges of Zionism, imperialism, racism and intrigue against Arab interests. Particular exception was taken to the increasingly warm relations between Washington and the PDRY's unfriendly neighbours, Oman and Somalia.

Relations between Washington and Sanaa definitely deteriorated. We have seen that during the fighting between North and South in February 1979 President Carter dramatically announced that he would make $500 million worth of arms available to the YAR, even though this entailed his by-passing normal constitutional procedures; few, if any, of the weapons actually arrived before the signature of the unity agreement the following month. Even when the delivery was completed in September, the Saudis struggled to retain control over their use and the military authorities in Sanaa realised that they were still weak in comparison with their southern neighbour. In consequence Salih turned to the Eastern Bloc and this definitely angered the Americans. The subsequent increase in Soviet influence led Secretary of State Vance to say in February 1980 that there was "an important and troubling situation" in the country and, as a result, while Washington actively wooed Oman and Somalia, it pointedly ignored the YAR.

Relations with the Communist powers

As in his domestic policy, Salih tried to avoid total commitment to any group, and this and his need for Russian arms, drove him closer to Moscow. Carter had shown his willingness to supply weapons, but those produced in America seemed too sophisticated for the Yemeni army which really preferred those from Russia to which they had been accustomed for over a quarter of a century. Some T55 tanks were bought from Poland and then more tanks and further military equipment arrived from Russia. Naturally there was a need for instructors, and by March 1981 there were said to be over 500 Soviet military experts in the country while Yemeni officers were receiving training in Eastern Bloc states.

Thus, while Sanaa's relations with Washington deteriorated, those with Moscow became more close. The YAR has refrained from expressing opinions that might irritate Moscow, and though they followed the general Islamic view in condemning Soviet intervention in Afghanistan, their comments were very mild. The Russians have not used their growing influence to press hard for unity of the two Yemens, fearing perhaps that the unruly Northerners might weaken their hold on the less turbulent South. They have also been unwilling to become too involved in a situation which *Pravda* described as "complicated" – the Russians are as baffled as everyone else as to what might happen next. At the end of October, for the first time, Salih went to Moscow, possibly asking the Kremlin to try to restrain the NDF as well as presumably requesting more arms.

Aden's identification with the Communist bloc became

more and more formal until it seemed to be a full member rather than a mere supporter. In the Summer of 1979 it attended a meeting of the exclusive COMECON, and plans were discussed to tie its economy more closely with that of Russia and its satellites. In October President Ismail went to Moscow where he was received with exceptional demonstrations of esteem. A treaty was signed which seemed more intimate than those which the Soviets had previously concluded with other Arab countries and, unusually, it was to last for twenty years. It provided for mutual defence, and naturally there was speculation upon what was in other clauses that remained unpublished. There was speculation that the number of Russian and Cuban troops would be increased to 15,000 and would receive still more facilities in return for a grant of $750 million.

The treaty with Moscow was followed by another with East Germany and a defence agreement with Bulgaria. In foreign policy the PDRY slavishly followed the Russian line and was the only Arab state actually to give full support for Soviet intervention in Afghanistan. It was even rumoured that it was sending troops to fight against the Islamic guerrillas. Aden was willing to fall in with Russian plans to obtain control of the Horn of Africa in order to dominate the Arabian Sea and the Kenya coast. In the autumn of 1979 Prime Minister Kosygin visited Addis Ababa and Aden, and it was a prime object of Soviet policy to effect close collaboration between these two countries.

The removal of Ismail meant no change in attitude and Hassani hurried to Moscow to reassure the Kremlin. For his declaration that the alliance was "both strategic and a matter of principle" he was rewarded with further help in exploring for oil.

Ismail, and Hassani after him, always denied that there were any Russian bases on Yemeni territory but each time the statement was greeted with greater scepticism. There were rumours of facilities for submarines being established in Aden and even that the island of Socotra was being forcibly cleared of its inhabitants so that it could be turned into the home of a joint South Yemeni–Ethiopian task-force under a Russian commander.

Relations with other Arab States

During the fighting of February 1979, while the troops of North Yemen were reeling backwards, the Saudis, despite their previous promises of support and their mobilisation, provided the North Yemenis with no effective assistance. It was left to Jordan, Syria and Iraq to save the North from utter rout by bringing pressure to bear on the South. Salih resented this lack of help on the part of the Saudis and wished to lessen his dependence upon his powerful northern neighbour by acquiring more friends. His readiness to agree to a union with the PDRY and, apparently, to take NDF members into his government alarmed Riyadh, which was further incensed by the removal from office of Asnag. This they saw as a deliberate attempt to diminish their influence and they reacted by imposing restrictions upon the American weapons for the delivery of which to the YAR they had paid. Salih retorted by approaching Moscow.

Early in 1980 Salih dismissed his chief of security, who for years had earned Saudi approval by his activities in this important post, and this seemed a further move to the left. A few months later he increased Saudi displeasure by flirting with the so-called Steadfastness Front, the grouping of Arab states that were most pro-Russian and most implacably opposed to any American activity in the Middle East. The President visited Tripoli and welcomed Colonel Qadafi to Sanaa.

In the meanwhile there were further causes of friction. The government in Sanaa had practically lost control of the tribes along the Saudi frontier which received subsidies and conducted their own private diplomacy with Riyadh. There were rumours that oil had been discovered in adjoining Saudi territory and the Yemenis suspected that their neighbours wished either to annex any part of the field that might lie on their side of the frontier or at least to prevent them from obtaining an independent source of wealth by exploiting it. In the summer of 1979 there were accounts of clashes between Saudi and Yemeni forces and in November the NDF radio reported encroachments in the neighbourhood of Sada and in the Jawf. Salih said in February that relations between the two countries were "excellent and ideal", but in March there were stories of further fighting. It was said that 200 Yemeni soldiers had been killed, and while this figure is probably a substantial exaggeration, it did show that there must have been some trouble in the area.

Relations became so frigid that the Saudis suspended the financial aid upon which the salaries of many Yemeni officials depended and as a result these remained unpaid. They complained that the presence of Russian military personnel was a threat to their own security and they sent their Minister of Defence to Sanaa to warn of the possible consequences if Salih determined to embrace the Communist bloc. Salih saw that he could not afford to push matters too far and in August he went to the Kingdom, and presumably promised to mend his ways, for financial aid was resumed. In November, unlike the Steadfastness Front, he did not boycott the Arab summit in Amman and his newly appointed Prime Minister, Iryani, was regarded as pro-Saudi.

In March 1981 there were further accounts of frontier clashes in which it was said that over a score of soldiers had been killed. The oil company with rights in the Saudi area said that none had been found and both sides denied that there had been any incidents. The Saudi Minister of the Interior said that relations were "above suspicion". In April the Saudi–Yemeni co-ordination committee resumed its meetings in a reported atmosphere of "great fraternity", denounced any interference in the affairs of the Peninsula by external forces and ended with promises of considerable Saudi aid for development schemes.

With the other states of the Peninsula, Sanaa continued to cultivate friendly links in search of financial help. The Shaykh of Kuwait visited the YAR in January 1981 and promised to provide new Faculties for the University. The YAR, however, resisted invitations to work with the new Gulf Co-operation Council, pleading that its policy was to remain apart from all blocs.

It took a considerable time for relations between Aden and Riyadh to recover from the Kingdom's overt hostility at the time of the fighting of February 1979, when it had put its forces on alert. A year later Ismail said that they had improved to a state of "coolness, not tension" but there was an obvious change upon his fall. A few weeks after taking power Hassani was received by the King, with whom he had "brotherly and frank" discussions, and seized the opportunity to parade his credentials as a good Muslim by going to Mecca where he performed *umrah*, the lesser pilgrimage. He denied, however, that he had been promised $200 million in aid. In January 1981 he attended the Islamic summit in Taif and, despite his increasing involvement with Libya, relations between Aden and Riyadh seemed better than they had been at practically any other time since the PDRY had become independent.

Hassani tacitly dropped overt attempts to export revolution to the oil states of the northern Gulf and kept on friendly terms with Kuwait. The Shaykh visited Aden in February 1981 and Hassani returned the call at the end of October. Hassani continued, however, the old feud with Oman and did his utmost to persuade the people of Dhofar that they were wrong to be satisfied with the enormous benefits that they were receiving from the rule of Sultan Qabus. More and more of the guerrillas drifted away and Aden was reduced to using its regular troops to cause incidents across the Omani border: two of them were captured in June 1981. Various efforts were made to settle this pointless quarrel, by Salih in October 1980, by the Kuwaitis in April 1981, and by the Gulf Council in the autumn; but Aden remained adamant. It denounced any co-operation of the Gulf states which involved Oman and used the increasingly warm friendship between Muscat and Washington as a pretext for keeping the quarrel alive. The Omanis retorted with reason that if their neighbour ceased its aggression, they would not need to cultivate such external links.

Outside the Arabian Peninsula, the two Yemens had very different friends. Sanaa maintained friendly links with Baghdad, received considerable aid and exchanged official visits. It gave unequivocal support to Iraq in its war with Iran.

Aden, on the other hand, had doctrinal differences with the Baath party in power in Baghdad even before an angry dispute occurred in the summer of 1979. An Iraqi communist in exile in Aden, where he was given a post at the University, was murdered, and the PDRY stated that Iraqi diplomats were to blame. PDRY officials therefore, in breach of all laws of diplomacy, stormed the Embassy and arrested those that they held responsible. The Baghdad authorities replied by recruiting a mob to attack the PDRY Embassy there. Matters cooled down for a while but flared up again in April 1980 when the South Yemenis, seeing the Iraqis thawing towards the West, said that the Baathists there were worse than Sadat. Aden claimed to have arrested some Iraqi spies and the Iraqis retaliated by expelling South Yemeni students. Hassani, on coming to power, said that relations were "tense", and a year later he claimed that the fact that they had not improved was not his fault. When Iran and Iraq went to war in September 1980, the PDRY went against the general Arab consensus and supported the Iranians, and the following year they opened an Embassy in Tehran. However, they did join the general expression of Arab outrage when in June 1981 the Israelis bombed the nuclear reactor outside Baghdad.

Aden continued its shrill attacks upon President Sadat and rejoiced at his murder. When President Nimeiri restored links with Egypt, the PDRY demanded that the rest of the Arab world should punish the Sudan. The YAR remained largely aloof from these events.

The most important development of Adeni foreign policy in the two and a half years that have followed the unity agreement of March 1979 has been an increasingly intimate friendship with the two states that were most staunchly anti-Western and pro-Soviet – Libya and Ethiopia. In July 1979 Qadafi visited both Aden and Sanaa to urge progress in the unification talks; some months later he was followed by his deputy, Major Jalloud. In January 1980 Ali Antar went to Addis Ababa and signed a defence agreement with Colonel Mengistu: it was said that one provision was that Aden should send some troops to provide the Ethiopian ruler with a reliable bodyguard. Mengistu went to Aden in November and further co-ordination of policies was arranged.

Libya agreed to supply all Aden's oil needs for the years 1980 and 1981 and this economic link was strengthened by political means. In September 1980, after Libya and Syria declared themselves a single state, Hassani went to Tripoli and Damascus and went back again in February and July 1981. These diplomatic activities reached a climax in August when both Qadafi and Mengistu were received in Aden "in a spirit of solemn and militant enthusiasm". In the middle of their deliberations, two Libyan aircraft were shot down by the US Navy in disputed waters and Qadafi demanded that "the whole world should hear the voice of the Yemeni people challenging America". The official communiqué gave lavish praise for each revolution in turn and each espoused causes dear to the others: Aden and Ethiopia expressed support for Libya's activities in Chad and found time to congratulate the revolutionaries of Grenada.

When the text of the Treaty between PDRY, Libya and Ethiopia was officially published, it was shown to provide for a Supreme Council of Heads of State to meet annually and for political and economic committees of Ministers to assemble more frequently. It laid down mutual co-operation against aggression, but obviously there was much more to it than was admitted. Qadafi, in the middle of one of his most acrimonious disputes – this time with Saudi Arabia – said that the pact would lead to the "liberation of the Arabian Peninsula", while for Cairo it represented "a new Soviet move, carefully planned by Moscow, to intimidate the Arabs, encircle Egypt and the Sudan and infiltrate Africa". Muscat went even further, alleging that a Russian representative had taken the chair at the most important sessions "working out ways of opening new doors to Soviet expansionism". The Russians planned, said Muscat, to destabilise the Gulf and – by supporting the NDF – North Yemen, while joint manoeuvres of troops of the three countries were to take place under Russian command to counter those planned by the US, Egypt, Oman and Somalia. These events may lie in the future but the first actual step was a meeting of the economic committee in Tripoli in October.

The YAR took no part in these events, although, if this Tripartite Treaty survives it will vitally affect the whole question of the unity of the two Yemens. A Minister, visiting Bahrain, did say, however, that his country was not in favour of "the formation of alliances or regional blocs".

Relations between the two Yemens

It seemed possible that the signature of the unity agreement in March 1979, in the presence of the Shaykh of Kuwait, might have been a mere tactical move by Salih to save his forces from destruction despite his dropping of the Southerners from his Cabinet and his flirtation with the NDF. The actual terms differed little from those negotiated in Tripoli in 1972 but the political situation had changed somewhat. Then, both the Saudis and the Russians had intrigued to prevent a union, fearing that its ally was the weaker party and would be absorbed into a potentially hostile state. Now the Russians, while not actively pushing for unity, were no longer absolutely obstructive. Ismail, himself a Hujari, saw "reunification" as natural, while the NDF, strong in the frontier area pressed for action. The Saudis, supported by the Americans, tried to hold back the North, while the Zaydis remained adamantly opposed to their becoming a minority in a Shafai state. Salih could not afford to be seen hindering unity and felt that southern support would be useful to him internally, but could not do anything positive for fear of driving the Zaydis into revolt: he therefore relied upon his usual policy of balancing between contending forces, and did as little as possible.

Progress was slow despite a chivying visit by Qadafi to both capitals, and the four months in which the constitutional committee was to have produced a document to be approved by referendum passed without much sign of movement. In October Hassani went to Sanaa to press for action, but later in the month the signature of the Russo-PDRY treaty of friendship still further increased the apprehensions of the Saudis and their Zaydi friends.

Early in the New Year there was a series of committee meetings which resulted in agreement to unify the postal and telephone systems, while the constitutional committee was said to have disposed of 134 items. Ismail stated that this committee had nearly finished its work, and Salih confirmed that substantial progress had been made. In February the judicial committee moved towards harmonisation of criminal and procedural matters, and steps were taken towards merging the armed forces. Ali Antar went to Sanaa and the YAR Prime Minister, Abd al-Ghani, to Aden, and on 31 May Salih claimed that the committees specialising in economic, trade and agricultural matters had reached the stage of implementation.

Soon after taking power Hassani went to Sanaa and concluded an agreement for free travel across the borders and for fuller co-operation in the cultural and information spheres. A month later he went again and this time there was an arrangement to set up a joint company to deal with travel and tourism. In September he went to Taizz before going to Tripoli and Damascus, and returned by way of Sanaa to ask for a fixed schedule for unity so that a single state could join the new union of Libya and Syria. He also established an office for unity affairs over which he himself presided. It was clear that the South was in earnest.

Salih, however, was forced by economic pressures to move back towards Saudi Arabia and perhaps now he feared also that things were going too fast, and could upset his balancing act. No significant moves were announced for some months until May 1981 when the joint companies came into existence and there were discussions for joint geological and water surveys. Hassani spoke of unity coming through a united economy, while in the same month the joint military committee held its first session of the year.

At the Tripartite meeting in Aden in August 1981, Qadafi took the opportunity of pressing the North, saying that the southern leaders had assured him that they were willing to give up their own posts and to accept Sanaa as the historic capital of Yemen and to fly the YAR flag. The possibility of being drawn into a group with uncertain and probably dangerous aims must have added to Salih's perplexities. He did not want to drop his policy of balance or accept restrictions limiting his freedom of action, but he could not afford not to work with the South: he had to show every sign of yearning for union while preventing it from happening. However, a month later he met Hassani and they both expressed their satisfaction at the progress made and in foreign policy at least managed to achieve a unanimous denunciation of South Africa, and of American activities in the Gulf and the Red Sea.

Convention seems to demand that a book such as this should end with prophecy. Will the two Yemens be reunited? My own guess is that this will not happen unless circumstances change dramatically. It would be possible if the people of the South, fired by the revival of Islam taking place in other parts of the Muslim world, succeeded in breaking the bonds in which they are held to the Russians and their local adherents. The Kremlin has already lost apparently unassailable positions in Egypt, Sudan and Somalia, and this could conceivably occur in South Yemen. It would not be so easy for them to intervene with force as they are doing in Afghanistan, because the other Arab states would rally to the support of their brother struggling to be free. Because of communications difficulties, the Russians could reinforce their troops in the area only by sea, and they would anyway probably find it politically unacceptable to be seen reimposing a deposed regime by fire and sword. Unless there is such a revolt, I feel that the Yemeni problem, like all others in the Middle East will never be solved as long as Super-power rivalry endures, for neither Moscow nor Washington could afford to permit a united Yemen to join a hostile bloc.

There is a possibility that some form of union might come about with North or South losing its present shape. If the YAR were to collapse, there could be a partition with the Shafais of Hujariyyah linking up with the PDRY and the Zaydis reverting to their old role as an isolated mountain state, probably protected by a Saudi umbrella. It is less likely that the PDRY might fall apart with the Hadhramawt joining Saudi Arabia or Oman and the old Western Aden Protectorate realigning with the YAR. Perhaps a solution could be found in some sort of Federation of the Arabian Peninsula, growing out of the new Gulf Council with its intimate link with Saudi Arabia. This would consist of internally self-governing states with a single foreign and defence policy.

However, as G. K. Chesterton remarked, the favourite game of mankind is "cheat the prophets" and one remembers how many times in the last thirty years one has been told that King Hussein could not possibly survive for another six months. It is, after all, only ten years since all kinds of upheaval were forecast for Saudi Arabia when King Faysal should leave the stage, and less than three years since the CIA forecast that the Shah would overcome all his enemies. I shall, therefore, not be surprised if some outcome that I have not even considered has happened before this book appears in print.

Bibliography

In a book designed for the general reader, I have not thought it necessary to give an exhaustive bibliography. I have therefore not listed articles in scholarly journals as professional academics will be able to find them easily enough through Professor J. D. Pearson's *Index Islamicus* or through the bibliographies of the major works that appear on my list and I do not think that others will bother to look for them. I have also not listed sources in Arabic as they will not be accessible to the general reader. Similarly I have not given the details of files in the India Office Library or the Public Record Office as experienced research workers will have no difficulty in using the catalogues.

I have listed separately for each chapter books that may be consulted for additional information. The best bibliography though naturally now outdated is

MACRO, Eric   *Bibliography on Yemen and Notes on Mokha*, Coral Springs, 1960. I found two more recent bibliographies rather more hindrance than help.

The following books may be consulted for information about longer periods than those covered in any individual chapter:

BIDWELL, Robin   *Travellers in Arabia*, London, 1976

GAVIN, R. J.   *Aden under British Rule 1839–1967*, London, 1975

INGRAMS, Harold   *The Yemen*, London, 1963

MACRO, Eric   *Yemen and the Western World since 1571*, London, 1968

PLAYFAIR, Robert L.   *A History of Arabia Felix or Yemen*, Bombay, 1859, reprinted Amsterdam, 1970

SERJEANT, R. B. *and* LEWCOCK, Ronald (*eds*)   *Ṣanʿāʾ An Arabian Arab City*, London, forthcoming in 1982

STOOKEY, Robert W.   *Yemen*, Boulder, 1978

For the period since about 1950 the following sources have been extensively used (and indeed for the final chapter there are few others):

The Summary of World Broadcasts
Arab Report and Record, 1967–1979
Reports of the Economist Intelligence Unit
Middle East Annual Review
Official hand-outs
UN and locally published statistics

The reports of leading journalists such as Peter Mansfield and the much-lamented David Holden of *The Sunday Times*, Patrick Seale and Robert Stephens of *The Observer* and various correspondents of *The Times, The Guardian* and *The Daily Telegraph*

Private information from Arab and British friends.

Chapter I
(a) *Pre-Islamic period*
   Most information about this period is to be found in articles in scholarly journals by such authorities as Professor A. F. L. Beeston of Oxford and Professor Jacques Ryckmans of Louvain. A recent book is

DOE, D. B.   *Southern Arabia*, London, 1971.
(b) *Mediaeval Islamic period*
KAY, H. C.   *Yaman, its early mediaeval history by Najm al-Din 'Omārah al-Ḥakami,* London, 1892

al-KHAZRAJI,
   Ali b. al-Hassan   *The Pearl Strings: a history of the Rasuli Dynasty of Yemen,* translated by Sir J. W. Redhouse, London, 1906 and 1907

RYCKMANS, Jacques   Translation into French of Arendonk's *De opkomst van het Zaidietische Imamaat in Yemen,* Leiden, 1978

SCHUMAN, L. O   *Political History of the Yemen at the beginning of the sixteenth century,* Amsterdam, 1961

SMITH, G. R.   *The Ayyubids and early Rasulids in the Yemen,* London, 1978.

Chapter II

D'ALBUQUERQUE, Alfonso   *Commentaries*, vol. iv, London, 1884
DE LA ROQUE   *A voyage to Arabia the Happy*, London, 1726
DI VARTHEMA, Lodovico   *A history of travayle* . . ., London, 1577
HAMILTON, A.   *A new account of the East Indies*, Edinburgh, 1727
HANSEN, Thorkild   *Arabia Felix*, London, 1964
HOSKINS, H. L.   *British Routes to India*, London, 1961
JOURDAIN, John   *Journals*, London, 1905
NIEBUHR, Carsten   *Travels through Arabia*, Edinburgh 1792, reprinted Beirut, 1968
TRITTON, A. S.   *The Rise of the Imams of Sanaa*, London, 1925
VALENTIA, Viscount   *Voyages and Travels*, London, 1809

Chapter III

"ABDULLAH MANSUR"   *The Land of Uz*, London, 1911
(G. Wyman Bury)
BENT, J. T.   *Southern Arabia*, London, 1900
HARRIS, Walter B.   *A journey through the Yemen*, Edinburgh, 1893
HUNTER, F. M.   *An account of the British settlement of Aden*, 1877, reprinted London, 1968
JACOB, Harold F.   *Kings of Arabia*, London, 1923
MARSTON, Thomas   *Britain's Imperial Role in the Red Sea Area 1800–1878*, Hamden, Conn., 1961
WATERFIELD, Gordon   *Sultans of Aden*, London, 1968
WYMAN BURY, G.   *Arabia Infelix or the Turks in Yemen*, London, 1915

Chapter IV

BELHAVEN, Lord   *Kingdom of Melchior*, London, 1949 and other books.
COLONIAL OFFICE   Annual Reports
HICKINBOTHAM, Sir Tom   *Aden*, London, 1958
INGRAMS, Harold   *Arabia and the Isles*, London, 1952
SINCLAIR, Reginald W.   *Documents on the history of South West Arabia*, Salisbury, N.C., 1976
STARK, Freya   *The Southern Gates of Arabia*, London, 1936 and other books
TREVASKIS, Sir G. K. N.   *Shades of Amber*, London, 1968
van der MEULEN, D.   *Aden to the Hadhramaut*, London, 1947 and other books

Chapter V

FAYEIN, Claudie	*A French Doctor in the Yemen*, London, 1957
RIHANI, Amin	*Arabian Peak and Desert*, London, 1930
SCOTT, Hugh	*In the High Yemen*, London, 1942
WENNER, Manfred	*Modern Yemen, 1918–1966*, Baltimore, 1967

Chapter VI

CROSSMAN, Richard	*Diaries of a Cabinet Minister*, London 1975–7
DARBY, Phillip	*British Defence Policy East of Suez 1947–1968*, London, 1973
EL-HABASHI, M. O.	*Aden*, Algiers, 1966
HALLIDAY, Fred	*Arabia without Sultans*, Harmondsworth, 1974
HARPER, Stephen	*Last Sunset*, London, 1978
HOLDEN, David	*Farewell to Arabia*, London, 1961
JOHNSTON, Sir Charles	*The view from Steamer Point*, London, 1964
KIRKMAN, S. P.	*Unscrambling an Empire*, London, 1961
LITTLE, Tom	*South Arabia*, London, 1968
MACMILLAN, Harold	*At the end of the day*, London, 1973
MITCHELL, Colin	*Having been a soldier*, London, 1969
PAGET, Julian	*Last Post Aden, 1964–1967*, London, 1969
TREVASKIS, Sir G. K. N.	*op. cit.*
TREVELYAN, Humphrey	*The Middle East in Revolt*, London, 1970
WILSON, Harold	*The Labour Government 1964–1970*, London, 1971

Chapter VII

BADEAU, John S.	*The American Approach to the Arab World*, N.Y., 1968
DEFARGE, Claude *and* TROELLER, Gordian	*Yemen 1962–1969*, Paris, 1969
HADDAD, George	*Revolution and Military Rule*, N.Y., 1973
HORN, Carl von	*Soldiering for Peace*, London, 1966
O'BALLANCE, Edgar	*The War in the Yemen*, London, 1971

341

SCHMIDT, Dana Adams *Yemen: the unknown war*, London, 1969
STOOKEY, Robert W. *America and the Arab States*, N.Y., 1978

Chapter VIII
ABIR, Mordecai *Oil, Power and Politics*, London, 1974
LUQMAN, Farouk *Democratic Yemen Today*, Aden, n.d.
LUQMAN, Farouk *Yemen 1970*, Aden, n.d.
PETERSON, J. E. *Yemen*, London, 1982, which would have been of much help, appeared while this book was already at proof stage and so was not actually used.

Index

Controlling the entrance to the Red Sea, South West Arabia is of great strategic importance. It is also an area of scenic beauty with green fields and mountains, and the unique architecture of Sanaa and Shibam.

Historically, the land has had a long and often bloody past. Trade routes from the Mediterranean, East Africa and the Far East converged here and incense, myrrh and alabaster were exported. Under the early dynasties a civilisation grew of which many of the elements persisted, little changed, until the 1960s.

Until the mid-nineteenth century Yemen developed as a single unit and the people as a single people. Then came the British, and later the Ottoman Turks, who instituted a frontier dividing North from South. Thenceforward the countries which were to become the Yemen Arab Republic and the People's Democratic Republic of South Yemen developed independently under different systems of government.

1967 saw the withdrawal of the British and the rise to power in North and South of regimes which claimed a United Yemen as their dearest wish. Twice since then agreements to bring this about have been signed, but have not taken effect.

This book spans two thousand years, telling the story of the Yemeni people and featuring them as a single entity: it is probably the first book to do so for over a century. Doctor Bidwell's account is unique in that the author has known personally some of the most important figures in the history of the last twenty-five years and has had access to fascinating information which has never before been published.